THE OTHER GERMANY

Also by John Dornberg

SCHIZOPHRENIC GERMANY (1961)

THE OTHER GERMANY

JOHN DORNBERG

DOUBLEDAY & COMPANY, INC., GARDEN CITY, NEW YORK

Library of Congress Catalog Card Number 68–11763
Copyright © 1968 by John Dornberg
All Rights Reserved
Printed in the United States of America

Preface

Most books about postwar Germany concern themselves with its
Western part, the 96,000-square-mile area known officially as the
Federal Republic of Germany. This is the Germany of daily headlines, tourist folders, beetle-shaped automobiles, war crimes trials,
beer, sausages and *Gemuetlichkeit*, of economic and *Fraeulein*
miracles, of castles on the Rhine, *Lederhosen* in Bavaria and
cuckoo clocks in the Black Forest. It is the Germany of Konrad
Adenauer, Ludwig Erhard, and Kurt Georg Kiesinger, the Germany famed for its spectacular rise from the debris of war and
dictatorship, the Germany linked closely by political, military,
and commercial ties to NATO, the Common Market and the
Western world. A land of 58,000,000, it is the Germany which
claims for itself—and is generally ceded—the legacy of the old
Reich: its privileges and responsibilities, its rights and obligations,
its possessions and its debts, its fame and infamy.

But beside it there is another Germany—less than half as large
and with not even one-third as many inhabitants. Though it is
the Germany of Martin Luther, of Johann Sebastian Bach, of
Humboldt and Bismarck, the Germany which is governed not
from Bonn but the traditional capital, Berlin, it is a Germany
about which the Western world knows almost as little (perhaps
even less) as China. Yet, it is extremely important, for it is the
Germany which is pivotal to the future security of Europe. This
is Communist, or East Germany: a somber, irascible little state
which defiantly and adamantly insists on being called the German
Democratic Republic or "GDR." It is the home of the Saxons and
the Prussians, a land of 17,000,000 living on 41,000 square miles
bordered on the east by Pomerania and Silesia (a region Poland
now claims as its own); on the south by Czechoslovakia; on the
west by the Federal Republic; on the north by the Baltic Sea.

Among the world's civilized nations, it is unique for having walled its people in and the principal subject of this book is what has transpired behind that wall since it was built on August 13, 1961.

For me this other Germany has had a special fascination. It derives in part from the fact that I was born there—though I left it as a child for the United States in 1939, at a time, in other words, when there was but one Germany. In part it is due to the fact that my wife was also born there—though she left it as a teenager for West Germany in 1949—at a time when there were already two Germanys. Aside from these personal reasons, East Germany presents one of postwar Europe's greatest enigmas. Nowhere has the confrontation between Communism and capitalism been more direct, nowhere has it been possible to study and observe the Communist revolution at closer hand. If Germany's pre-Hitler Communists could regard any region as their stronghold then it was Saxony, the heartland of the GDR. Yet it was also an area incredibly ill-suited for such experiment, for the aftermath of war under the Soviet occupation, coupled with East Germany's natural paucity of raw materials, made it an economic and spiritual wasteland. Consequently, nowhere did the Communist revolution flounder as chaotically in the early years as in the GDR. Yet eventually—in very recent times—that experiment has shown signs of remarkable success.

The first opportunity to satisfy my curiosity over these developments came in 1960 when, as an American newspaperman, I made my initial trip to East Germany and East Berlin. Since then I have traveled in and reported on the GDR repeatedly. I have been in all of its major cities, many of the smaller ones and in countless villages—both on assignment as a reporter and while visiting friends and relatives. I have made a dozen trips to and through East Germany—most of them without a guide or the official "companion" which East German authorities usually assign to Western correspondents.

I have driven the length and breadth of the GDR in my own car—from Rostock on the Baltic Sea to Zwickau at the foot of the Erz Mountains, from Marienborn in the west to Frankfort on the Oder in the east. I have talked to hundreds of East Germans in all walks of life and of all political and ideological persuasions: factory workers, unskilled laborers, housewives, farmers, executives, economists, journalists, students, engineers, scientists, physicians, cab drivers, truckers, policemen, soldiers, waiters, shop clerks, state officials, Communists, anti-Communists, Catholics, Protestants, and Jews. Moreover, I have kept—and continue to keep—abreast of developments by corresponding with numerous East Germans, discussing GDR affairs with expert analysts in West Germany and reading daily the East German press.

I have collected countless interviews on tape—all of them obtained without the presence or surveillance of either a guide or a Communist official. I have engaged in such unorthodox practices (for reporting in Communist countries) as entering apartment houses, ringing doorbells indiscriminately, and talking my way into the living rooms of ordinary people. I have stopped passersby at random and interviewed collective farmers in the fields. I have called on industrial executives directly without obtaining permission via complicated bureaucratic channels from the appropriate government agencies. Wherever I went and with whomever I spoke, I was invariably received warmly, openly, and courteously. The number of people who either refused to see me or answer my questions can be counted on one hand. At no time was I restricted or hampered in the gathering of information.

In the course of my travels I have found the GDR to be a far more open and frank society than its reputation as an authoritarian state would have led one to expect. Outspoken critics of the regime were as willing to go on record with their views as Walter Ulbricht's most enthusiastic supporters.

By visiting the GDR repeatedly since 1960 I have been able to observe its transformation from the grim last bastion of Stalinism to a country burgeoning with confidence and nascent nationalism. I have seen East Europe's most bitter and disillusioned people turn into a nation of 17,000,000, defiantly and defensively proud of their accomplishments. I have observed the development of Communism's most chaotic and hopeless economy into the Soviet bloc's second largest, the world's eighth greatest industrial power.

As a result of these changes there are today, in fact and not just by Soviet decree, two Germanys and the one to which this book devotes itself has become a political and economic factor which can no longer be ignored.

In writing this book I have drawn frequently on the works of several authors who have concerned themselves extensively with the GDR: notably Carola Stern, in her excellent biography of Ulbricht; Professor Hans Apel who has devoted himself to a painstaking study of the East German economy, and Professor Ernst Richert whose analyses of the GDR's power structure are indispensable to an understanding of the country.

I am grateful to my American and German newspaper colleagues as well as my German friends and acquaintances with whom I have discussed developments in the GDR at length and who have provided me with helpful suggestions, background information and research material.

My most heartfelt appreciation goes to my wife who took the time to read and make improvements on the manuscript.

J.D.

Vienna, Austria

Contents

PART ONE

THE
AFFLUENT
OUTCAST

CHAPTER I

After the Wall

It was 1:11 A.M., Sunday, August 13, 1961, when the clank of steel on cobblestones, the staccato chatter of motorcycles and the deep rumble of truck engines echoed down dark and empty streets to startle East Berliners out of their sleep. Frightened by the nocturnal cacophony, they peeked from behind their curtains to see military convoys stretching for blocks. First came the outriders, then armored scout cars, followed by trucks and buses crammed with grim-faced People's Policemen and steel-helmeted troops of the National People's Army. Droning ominously in their wake were two hundred Russian-built tanks. At each strategic intersection a squad of soldiers stayed behind and took up position with machine guns. The rest thundered on toward the sector border—that 28-mile-long frontier which rips through the heart of Berlin like a ragged wound.

As the *Vopos* and *Volksarmisten* arrived at nearly eighty crossover points between the city's two halves, rolls of concertina wire, concrete and steel posts, wooden horses, picks, shovels and jackhammers were already being dumped from trucks. For hours through the night, into the bright, warm light of that summer morning, jackbooted soldiers and policemen built barricades, rolled out barbed wire entanglements, erected fences and gouged up streets and sidewalks to improvise trenches and car traps.

All the while other squads raced to lock the gates of the elevated and subway stations that serviced trains to West Berlin. Telephone connections between the Soviet and Western sectors of the city were severed. Within East Germany itself, rail traffic jerked to a halt as thousands of travelers were hauled off trains entering East Berlin and ordered back to their homes.

By noon, Berlin bristled like a fortress. Machine-gun, rifle- and bayonet-brandishing *Vopos*, soldiers, coveralled members of factory battle groups, reinforced by armored trucks and motorized high-pressure water cannons stood a grim watch over the barriers that sealed off the Russian half of the city.

On Tuesday, two days later, police and army engineers began replacing the barbed-wire obstacles with slabs of concrete to form a wall. East Berlin and East Germany were bolted shut in the manner of a huge ghetto. The escape hatch, through which 160,000 of Walter Ulbricht's subjects had fled during the preceding seven months, was shut.

While the Western world looked on paralyzed with disbelief, Ulbricht, East Germany's spade-bearded, bespectacled Communist ruler, unctuously justified his "anti-fascist protective wall." He called it an ineluctable measure to thwart "a planned, revanchist West German attack" and to repulse "Western agitators, provocateurs and kidnappers."

It was not the first time in history that a powerful ruler had walled in his domain. But Berlin's Wall is unique as the first designed solely to keep a nation's subjects in, not its enemies out. And for all of Herr Ulbricht's imputations to the contrary, there was no sane observer anywhere who would doubt that the wall had but one purpose: to interdict once and for all the gushing hemorrhage that in sixteen years had deprived the country of its lifeblood—the mass exodus of 3,500,000 workers, farmers, merchants, physicians, engineers, intellectuals, housewives, and children.

For five years, from mid-1956 until August 1961, that exodus had funneled through the last safe escape route from East Germany—Berlin—where often the price of moving from autocracy to freedom, from economic depravity to dazzling, alluring affluence, was no higher than the cost of a subway ticket. Soviet Premier Nikita Khrushchev, in his effort to internationalize and isolate the city, had called Berlin a "bone stuck in our throat." Indeed it was: a bone of millions of people who had used its open sector borders to turn their backs on Communism.

The Berlin Wall blocked off that escape route and most Western observers expected it to act like the stopped-up valve on a pressure cooker. They predicted an explosion, a revolution or rebellion of the type that, on June 17, 1953, had sent thousands of seething East Germans into the streets of Berlin, Halle, Magdeburg, and Dresden to throw rocks at heavily armed Soviet tanks. To his Communist cronies and Russian benefactors, however, Walter Ulbricht prophesied, that plugging the refugee leak which had undermined his frail economy for sixteen years would provide the stability he needed.

At first neither happened. Instead, the Wall affected East Germany like a closed oven flue. It choked. The sparks and occasional licks of flame which had brightened it since 1945, flickered to a weak glow of morbid resignation, indifference, and stagnation. The economic growth rate declined by half. The rump country, which most West Germans still call the Soviet Occupied Zone and which advertises itself as "Germany's First Workers' and Peasants' Power," stood in danger, not of exploding, but of plodding to a halt.

Then an unanticipated transformation took place to prove Ulbricht right. After a two-year period of torpidity, the Wall began to accomplish what Ulbricht had intended. Resigned to the knowledge that there was practically no escape—except at the high risk of life, limb, and prison—East Germans started to make the best of their predicament. Apathy and lethargy succumbed to a determination to make do.

Behind that wall, which the West continues to scorn as the ugly symbol of a tyrannical regime's moral bankruptcy, a revolution is indeed in progress. But a kind of revolution which no one had foreseen. While the West has isolated and shunned it as a pariah, East Germany has silently been flexing its muscles until today it is an economic, political, and military force which no one can afford to ignore. Behind the Wall in this little-known rarely traveled and largely dismissed half country which is both Communism's westernmost bastion and the fulcrum of the East-West confrontation, a second German "economic miracle" is being performed. And though it may seem belated, it is no less spectacular than West Germany's erstwhile *Wirtschaftswunder*.

As the Communist bloc's second, Europe's sixth and the world's eighth largest industrial power, the German Democratic Republic (GDR) is no longer a Soviet satrapy which could be "repatriated" to West Germany whenever the Kremlin feels generous, but a nation in its own right. It burgeons with a sense of self-confidence, resentment at diplomatic isolation and a nascent spirit of nationalism to which, sooner than later, the rest of Europe will have to become reconciled.

East Germany today produces more electricity than Norway, Sweden, Switzerland, Australia, or India. It is the world's largest producer of soft coal and lignite and its output exceeds that of the United States, Soviet Union and Federal Republic combined. It is one of the world's principal manufacturers of calcinated soda, caustic soda, and potassium fertilizer. It is the world's seventh largest producer of plastics and the fourth largest of artificial rubber. In Wolfen, a grimy town near Halle, the Orwo film works—state-owned like 90 percent of East German industry—now export a complete line of high-grade still, movie and X-ray films to sixty countries. East German cameras and optical goods are available in every nation in the world, including the United States. East German television sets, radios, record players, household appliances—from hair dryers to dishwashers—are in demand all over Asia, Africa, and Europe: even in West Germany where they are sold by the largest mail-order firms with a variety of brand names. At Rostock's sprawling Warnow Yards, literally gouged out of a fallow meadow after the war, East Germany has created the world's ninth biggest shipbuilding industry which in 1966 turned out freighters and passenger liners totaling more than 325,000 gross tons. The GDR's state-owned merchant fleet, with 162 ships totaling a gross tonnage of 1,000,000, is one of the fastest growing in Europe. Fourteen years ago the line consisted of one rusty, leaky freighter with a displacement of 917 tons.

The same dramatic renaissance has transformed the surface—and in many instances the substance—of East German life. Cities which in 1961 and 1962 were largely desolate wastelands of ruin, rubble, and wistful rumination, now sparkle ostentatiously with steel and glass. In Dresden, the German Hiroshima, once famed

as the Florence of the Elbe, the magnificent eighteenth-century
Zwinger and the graceful old Gewandhaus have been completely
restored, stone by stone. A new city, reminiscent of the old splendor is rising from the debris. In Leipzig, the trade-fair city which is
Communist industry's showy gateway to capitalist markets, new
apartment houses are mushrooming into the sooty, smoggy, chemical air that blackens what remains of its street upon street of
turn-of-the-century façades. In Rostock architects have even tried
to restore the red brick and spired style common to all the towns
of the once powerful old Hanseatic League. Even Berlin's Unter
den Linden—scene of some of the 1953 uprising's bloodiest and
most tumultuous encounters—now dazzles with new commercial
splendor and the memorabilia of Prussia's glory. It boasts not
only the rebuilt opera, national library, Humboldt University,
and a congeries of neoclassical statuary but automobile show-
rooms, expensive shops, a luxury hotel, and sidewalk cafés. In its
restaurants waiters in tails rush to serve the upper classes such
delicacies as Andalusian egg salad with toast, Hungarian shep-
herd's soup, filet steak Colbert, or Bulgarian Kawarma and
chocolate Neapolitan—all for $3.90. In spring and summer the lin-
den trees, planted as saplings by the Communist administration
in 1950, bloom once more and Berliners (East) think nothing
of spending Sunday hours just relaxing on one of the white
benches or patio chairs set out at random on the corso that divides
what the Communist functionaries hope will again become one
of Europe's most elegant avenues. *"Jetzt,"* a diva from the nearby
Comic Opera said in a degenerate-revisionist tone, *"können wir
wieder leben."* ("Now we can live again.")

And life, by East German standards, is good.

Dumpy housewives, wearing the same inverted flower-pot hats
so popular in Frankfurt, Munich, Cologne and Hamburg, now
spend the afternoons sipping coffee and gulping down huge portions of *Kuchen und Schlagsahne* (cake and whipped cream) in
Dresden's Café Prague, Berlin's Moscow Restaurant, Erfurt's
Mocca Stube, or Rostock's Café-am-Hochhaus. To suggest that
East Germans are starving, as has been the wont of Bonn propagandists, is ridiculous. Admittedly, luxury foods and delicacies,

because they cost too much in foreign exchange, remain scarce. Indeed, butter is rationed to one pound per person every ten days. But East German butter consumption, despite this restriction, exceeds West Germany's by 50 percent and any attempt to tell an East German that too much butter may be harmful to his health meets with the immediate response: "That's nothing but propaganda because the regime can't provide us with enough." True, spices and citrus fruits, because they must be imported, are rare. But it is ludicrous to suggest that East Germans are ready to rebel because of that shortage. "People in the West just don't understand us," a young Rostock executive explained to me. "I have a friend who fled to West Germany many years ago and recently I thought I'd do him a favor by sending him a photo album of the city as it looks now. I hinted discreetly that if he wanted to reciprocate, he could send me a copy of Boris Pasternak's *Doctor Zhivago* which we cannot buy here. You know what he sent me instead? Five pounds of oranges and a used dress for my little girl. Now really! As if suitable dresses were not available in the stores or our life depended on oranges." It doesn't. For those who have money, every conceivable delicacy —from French cheeses to English marmalade, from Swiss chocolate to Chinese bamboo sprouts—is available in new Delikat grocery stores, the first of which opened in mid-1966 on Berlin's Unter den Linden. The prices are inflated—an outrageous $15 for a bottle of French cognac, $20 for a fifth of brand name scotch and $2 for a pack of American cigarettes. But the customers queue to be served.

Even if they must still wait three years for a plastic-bodied, two-cycle, 24 horsepower, four-passenger Trabant sedan and pay 8000 marks for it—more than twice the price in the West—East Germans today have reached a level of affluence undreamed of five years ago. Though the price of a television set equals two to three months' pay of an average skilled industrial worker, every second family today owns one. New receivers are available not only on the installment plan but customer service, in strict imitation of the West, is so good that any appliance shop will send out a selection for approval and install a unit on the day of purchase. "I recall when I bought my first TV about ten years ago," said an editor of an East Berlin industrial trade journal. "Nearly two years passed between delivery and order. Then, when it finally arrived, they sent me a postcard from the store and told me to pick it up. I had to borrow a friend's bicycle, tie the TV on the rear fender and wheel it home—fearful every step of the way that it would crash to the sidewalk and shatter into a thousand pieces. Several months ago that set finally wore out and I decided to buy a new one. The clerk nearly stumbled over himself trying to please me, offered me terms and then asked: 'When will you be home tonight? We'll send a technician to install it any time at your convenience.' That's when I realized that, under socialism, we had made some progress."

With other consumer goods the development has been the same. More than one-third of East German families own a washing machine (though perhaps not an automatic one). In 1965 delivery quotas on refrigerators were still seven to nine months. Today stores offer them on an eight-day free trial and 40 percent of all households own one. Also every third family owns either a motorbike, motorscooter, or motorcycle, and nearly 10 percent possess an automobile.

In the winter months delivery on bikes, scooters, and cycles is immediate and the state-owned dealerships, faced with a growing trend from two wheels to four, even offer seasonal discounts to help move the merchandise. Shop windows are filled with household gadgets and appliances, most of which are styled to meet export standards. Furniture and department stores, supermarkets, toy shops, boutiques and haberdasheries no longer fill their display windows with oversized portraits of a smiling Walter Ulbricht or slogans exhorting the masses to toil for the common good, but merchandise: abundant and in ample choice of style, color and price. As recently as October 1964 it was a sensation when the management of a department store on Halle's Grosse Ullrich Strasse stocked a window with a selection of floor and table lamps and encouraged women shoppers to fill out ballots with their choice of the best designs. Three years later such direct, point-of-purchase consumer testing, with a flair of democracy un-paralleled in East German political life, is commonplace.

There is, in fact, little that even the most discriminating shop-per in East Germany will not find—provided he or she has the money. The all-night bars connected to each of the luxury-class Interhotels unblushingly serve French cognac at $1.35 per shot, Moselle wines for $5 and up per bottle. Unter den Linden's new *Form-Farbe-Raum* gift and furnishings store features the best of both German and Scandinavian craftsmanship. The adjacent fur shop—no prices in the window—looks like a transplant from the Kurfürstendamm. Every city of 100,000 or more population has at least one *Exquisite* men's and women's ready-to-wear haber-dashery or boutique where members of the highly-paid intelli-gentsia or the *nouveau riche* captains of people's owned industry can buy English suits, French dresses, Belgian shoes and Italian handbags. And for the fashion conscious *grandes dames* of Com-munist society there are even the creations of Heinz Bormann, the "Red Dior" of Magdeburg, a rising star of *haute couture* on both sides of the Berlin Wall.

East Germany's living standard today is the highest in the Soviet bloc—so high in fact that the Soviet Union has barred the distribution of East German illustrated and women's maga-zines in the USSR because they are filled with advertisements and photographs that depict a way of life which would generate un-fulfillable wishes and dreams in the average Russian.

Credit for much of this achievement goes to the new attitude that gripped East Germany once the Wall was built. But in no small measure it is also the salubrious effect of the economic de-Stalinization which Ulbricht introduced as the "New Economic System of Planning and Management" at the VIth Congress of his Socialist Unity Party (SED) in July 1963.

A radical departure from Stalinist traditions in the GDR, the program smacked loudly of old time capitalist concepts and mo-tives such as profit, profit sharing, productivity and rationalization incentives, production of consumer goods and greater reliance on the laws of supply and demand. Stripped of jargon particular to German Communists, it is nothing more than the scheme for

decentralized production originally conceived by Soviet economist Professor Yevsei G. Liberman. Nevertheless, it was East
Germany, often derided as "the last bastion of Stalinism," which
first applied it in practice.

Instead of resorting to cajolery, public embarrassment, medals,
titles, interminable propaganda harangues, bare-fisted threats and
even imprisonment, the new system relies on material incentives:
premiums for plant profit, for better quality goods, improved and
rationalized production processes. By decentralizing the top-heavy
economic structure, vesting more authority in the hands of directors of so-called Vereinigungen Volkseigener Betriebe (VVBs
—some eighty trusts or holding concerns which operate East Germany's people's owned industries) the economy has been stripped
of many of its ideological encumbrances. Although the New Economic System does not permit price setting purely on the basis
of supply and demand, it does require plant managers to work at
a profit and employ genuine cost accounting. In daily operations
this system has abolished the old tonnage ideology which induced plant managers to produce the heaviest, most cumbersome
goods in the effort to fulfill or oversubscribe a plan which apotheo-
sized quantity instead of quality, weight of merchandise instead
of practicability, production for production's sake rather than
marketability. "The only thing that distinguishes us from managers in the West," said one proud, young executive in the chemicals field, "is that the profit we make goes back to the state and
eventually the people, instead of a clique of absentee owners or a
small group of shareholders. Our goals, our methods, our worries
differ little, if at all from those of an American or West German
company official. Except, unfortunately, that we still have a little
more red tape through which to cut."

Whiffs of *ideological* liberalization have also wafted across the
Mecklenburg flatlands and the hills of Saxony and Thuringia. To
date the breezes are still faint, and often they are imperceptible.
Nevertheless there has been hope since that day in November
1963 when rotund, balding, dolefully dog-faced Professor Albert
Norden, the party's chief propagandist and agitator, cautioned the
SED's Central Committee: "We cannot expect to win the confi-

dence of the people, if all we ever offer them is promises, merely exhort them to produce more but never give them a chance to enjoy the fruits of their labor. Socialism does not just mean learning more and working harder. It also means beauty, the good life and happiness." Concomitant to such heresy, Norden, in language surprisingly clear and devoid of party gobbledegook, urged the abolition of terror and coercion as means for persuading East Germans to support the system. "We cannot simply label everyone who disagrees with us a class enemy," he said. Even daring to call the Berlin Wall a "wall" instead of a "measure to protect our territorial integrity," Norden added: "In making our policies clear, party agitators should talk in terms everyone can understand . . . Insulting and defaming people with a different viewpoint conflicts with our party's principles and aims and cannot be condoned. How can we win the trust of the *entire* populace if we do not take *all* our citizens into our confidence?"

To suggest that this East German November produced an enlightened society with a free exchange of ideas would be misleading. East Germany's liberalization is but a pale adumbration of the gale that swept Eastern Europe and even the Soviet Union after Nikita Khrushchev's denunciation of Stalin at the XXth Party Congress in 1956. *Avant-garde* art is repressed, critical writers are exprobrated and barred from publishing. One of them, Christa Wolf, author of East Germany's best-selling novel *Geteilter Himmel (Divided Sky)*, was voted out of the Central Committee in April 1967 because she dared to object to ideological restrictions publicly. The GDR is prosperous, but it is also sanctimoniously proper. Just as the USSR has banned East German magazines because of the high standard of living they portray, so the GDR has now boycotted Russia's new-wave films because their message of social criticism could have repercussions which the SED would be unable to control. The GDR is enveloped in an atmosphere of Communist puritanism, dictated by ideological moralists who drink their Marx straight and wag a warning finger at the libertines in Prague, Budapest, and Warsaw.

Though some of the fetters of regimentation which once made East Germany a propagandist's best argument against Commu-

nism have been stripped away, the party continues to campaign
ruthlessly against what it calls "decadent, imperialist Western influences." Among these are the sound of beat music and the
Liverpudlian cult of unisex. In 1965 and most of 1966 the SED
waged total war against the disciples of the Mersey rhythm whose
male exponents are easily recognizable by their long tresses. The
youths were rounded up and threatened with stiff fines or forced
labor unless they cut their hair. Now the approach is more benign:
they are ridiculed at every opportunity. But the long-maned
rebels with the bell-bottomed trousers, pointed shoes and cruci-
fixes (which have nothing to do with any religious motivations
on their part) are persistent. Every Saturday and Sunday afternoon they loll defiantly on the edge of the pool in front of East
Berlin's Linden Corso Espresso Bar. "We've learned to leave them
pretty much alone," insisted one dapper, fortyish executive and
party member, bemused by my astonishment. "Except for articles
in the papers or one or the other who may be hauled into a
company tool shed for a shearing by fellow workers, no one really
bothers them any more."

The GDR has unquestionably come a long way since the Wall.
Yet any assessment of East Germany must be qualified by one
reservation: it will not stand the test of comparison with West
Germany and, perhaps, never will. Attempts by the Communists
to make such a test are self-delusionary if not hypocritical. There
can be no comparison because, by West Germany's opulent, super-
affluent standards, East Germany is drab, dull, dark, shabby,
scruffy, somber, ragged, neglected and listless. Seen through Western glasses, a leaden, gray pallor hangs heavy over the country
and East German life—from the appearance of its cities to the
apparel of its inhabitants; from the lack of selection on the shelves,
to the dirty, sooty stucco that cascades off the façades of older
houses to which neither a painter nor a plasterer has laid brush
or trowel in twenty-one years; from the smuttiness of even the
best restaurants where, invariably, tablecloths are always stained,
to the dearth of traffic on the highways. The sights, sounds and
smells of ersatz fill the air.

Moreover, compared with the neon-lighted superabundance of

the West, East Germany appears to have stood still for thirty years. Saxons and Thuringians, Brandenburgers and Mecklenburgers seem to live, largely, in a physical world of yesteryear. Not just because the ubiquitous, omnipotent plan placed modern design on the backburner for so many years. Unlike West Germans whose society is attuned to Americanisms and whose habits and mores have been influenced viscerally by travel abroad, East Germans have preserved the customs and attributes of their provinces and prewar Germany. The Russian influence—notwithstanding countless Stalin Allees, now all renamed—is minimal because it was never welcomed. And travel to other than East European countries has been a luxury denied them both by economic circumstances and government restrictions. East Germany is somehow far more German than its Western counterpart and for the nostalgic visitor an unspoiled spot in which to relive memories of the "good old days."

Any evaluation of life and conditions in East Germany, therefore should commence with the premise that the only fair yardstick must be East German—simply because the two Germanys had such an uneven postwar beginning. It is a simple propaganda trick to write off both the GDR's economic system and regime as failures, merely by pointing to West Germany's achievements. Though frequently used and unquestionably an effective polemical technique, it ascribes all the GDR's shortcomings to the absence of free enterprise and political free choice. Rooted in the messianic politics of the cold war era when both East and West could do no more than portray each other as incarnated devils, this argument elides the most significant difference between the two Germanys: that they started the postwar era as very unequal competitors. Other than having reached a par of industrial know-how by 1936 and suffering almost equally severe destruction during the war, Germany's two halves had little in common on that May day in 1945 when Field Marshal Alfred Jodl signed the surrender documents at Reims.

As an entity, the three Western zones, had all the qualifications for again becoming an industrial might: resources, manpower, communications and a transportation network. But the

Soviet occupation zone was merely an amputated third of a nation.

Most lines of communication and transportation had run from eastern to western Germany. And by "eastern," geographers generally meant the regions of Pomerania and Silesia, as well as East Prussia, all of which were ceded to Polish or Soviet administration in 1945, hence severed probably forever, from what was once the German Reich. Thus, the Soviet Occupation Zone was cut off artificially from the Western zones and for all intents and purposes, permanently from its Eastern hinterland which has now become "friendly, socialist" but nonetheless foreign territory. All the GDR could boast in those early days was a modest section of the Elbe River; use of the Oder but not its estuary to the Baltic; a short stretch of the Mittelland Canal, until then Germany's most important artificial waterway; portions of the once great east-west railway network; a few complete, a few disrupted rail lines in the south, and a sparce webwork in the north.

Far worse, though East Germany had a strong tradition as the machine shop, chemical kitchen, textile mill and optical factory of the Reich it was critically undernourished in both raw materials and heavy industry. Since the industrial revolution, Central Germany's—that is, Saxony's, Thuringia's, and Mecklenburg's industry—had been almost wholly dependent on resources and half-finished products from Silesia and the Ruhr. Though towns such as Magdeburg, Gera, Chemnitz, Dresden, Cottbus, Halle, Weissenfels, Frankfurt on the Oder, and Erfurt were famed for their reservoir of skilled workers, craftsmen, and technicians, the territory encompassed by the Soviet Zone had produced only three percent of the prewar Reich's total iron and anthracite coal and less than six percent of its rolled mill products.

Moreover, contrary to popular belief, enthusiastically propagated by West Germany, the area which now comprises the GDR was never agriculturally self-sustaining. Though the GDR encompasses portions of Mecklenburg, Brandenburg, and even Western Pomerania, the real German bread basket lay farther east—in those regions which since the end of the war have been ceded, if not de jure then de facto, to Poland.

This placed the GDR in the gloomy dilemma of lacking the resources with which to prime its manufacturing economy, insufficient in agricultural resources to feed its workers and destitute of either agricultural or manufactured products to trade against raw materials.

This predicament was compounded by the Soviet Union's insistence on observing to the comma and the decimal point those terms of the Yalta and Potsdam agreements beneficial to the Kremlin. The Soviet Union had been promised $10,000,000,000 in reparations. What it eventually milked out of the GDR in the form of dismantled industries, deliveries of finished goods, profits from Soviet-owned industries, and extortionist trade agreements probably amounted to $20,000,000,000. To the consternation of East Berlin's young managerial types, some exploitation, albeit in far-more refined fashion, continues to this day.

Motivated by hatred, thirst for revenge, and the need to rebuild their own decimated industrial potential, the Soviets inaugurated their occupation of East Germany with the so-called Trophy Action. It was a plunder-campaign that not only robbed Germans of their art works but raw material reserves, finished goods, cattle, timber, and abandoned Wehrmacht quartermaster stocks which might have alleviated widespread suffering. Merely the agricultural pillage is valued at $250,000,000.

Spoliation was followed by the dismantling of the Soviet Zone's industrial capacity. On some sectors, such as plywood manufacturing and optical and precision instrument making, equipment removal deprived East Germany of 70 percent of its capacity. Between May 1945 and the fall of 1946 the Soviets carted off 50 percent of East Germany's most important industrial potential: machine factories, automobile works, chemical and power plants. By the time dismantling ceased, 40 percent of East Germany's 1936 industrial capacity had been spirited away into the USSR —along with its parallel track of every East German railway line.

Whatever the Russians failed to dismantle they converted into two hundred so-called Sowjetische Aktien Gesellschaften (SAGs) —Soviet stock corporations—which produced goods and profits solely for Soviet benefit at a loss of approximately $1,000,000,000 to the East German economy. The last of the enterprises was not repatriated to the GDR's control until 1955, and for their return East Germany paid the USSR approximately $750,000,000. In addition, the Soviet Zone had to pay the Russians $10,000,000,000 in direct reparations—cash, finished products, and occupation costs.

Just during the first five postwar years, according to U.S. economist Dr. Hans Apel, East Germany, with a population one-third as great as West Germany's, paid the Russians $11,000,000,000. During the same period West Germany put out less than $2,500,000,000, primarily in the form of occupation costs to Britain and France. Simultaneously the U.S. was already pumping money into West Germany and by mid-1950 had given it nearly $3,000,000,000 in Marshall Plan and other aid. Ere the assistance programs ended in 1961, the Federal Republic had received another $800,000,000.

East Germany's economic deprivation contributed to an exodus of people who had already caught the glimmer of impending affluence in the West. No exact figures on the refugee flow are available through 1948, though it is estimated that 600,000 left the Soviet Zone in those years. From January 1949 to August 1961 another 2,900,000 fled so that East Germany's total manpower loss before the Wall amounted to 3,500,000. Translated into dollars, the exodus cost the GDR billions. Apel, in a highly provocative study, in which he balanced East German manpower, material, and productive losses against West German gains and losses has concluded that from 1945 to 1961 reparations, dismantling, pillage, and the refugee flow deprived the GDR of no less than $26,750,000,000. Some West German economists, such as Professor Fritz Baade, set the amount even higher. In the summer of 1966, when Ulbricht claimed that West Germany owed him more than $17,000,000,000 as its share for reparations and manpower gains from the refugee flow, the Bonn government scoffed and termed it "outrageous propaganda" based on "milkmaid economics." But responsible West German economists did not laugh. On the contrary, they considered it a conservative estimate.

Aside from such direct losses, East Germany's economy was a

slow starter because of Moscow's ambivalence on the German question. Not until the 1955 Geneva conference, when all reunification schemes were permanently shelved, did the Soviets unbridle Ulbricht and permit him to rebuild and gear up the economy.

Of course East Germany's lag cannot be ascribed solely to these factors, but a complex multiplicity of causes must be taken into account. Not the least of these were the enormous economic blunders committed by Ulbricht and his amateur economists in the face of adversity. There is hardly an East German party functionary who would not agree—albeit in private. "We made enormous mistakes in the 1940s and 1950s," said a very young but senior official of one of the GDR's fastest growing industrial trusts, "and in part we are still paying for them today."

Motivated by the phantasmagoria of Marxist-Leninist-Stalinist ideology, Ulbricht and the apparatchiks whom he loosed upon the economy in the first fifteen postwar years could do nothing right—even when the Soviets gave them the opportunity. They embarked on a land reform that divided an innately weak and inefficient agriculture—plagued by lack of fertilizer, seed and manpower—into unprofitably minuscule parcels. No sooner had the new smallholders developed a basis that showed promise of being able to nourish part of the country's 17,000,000 inhabitants, than doctrinaire ideologues, with Ulbricht's blessings, brutally coerced them into collective farms. When collectivization was complete, in 1960, nature took revenge in the form of one of Europe's worst crops in recent history. Simultaneously the regime compounded its troubles by embarking on its own version of China's catastrophic Great Leap Forward: a futile but costly campaign to catch up with West Germany's lead-running economy. The plan was illusory and has long ago been scrapped. But until it landed in the wastepaper basket of other worn-out, useless slogans, it disrupted an economy that had begun to show signs of stability by causing inestimable confusion, generating mass public resentment and fanning the exodus.

Yet, in spite of the regime's mismanagement it is irrefutable that the brunt of responsibility for the GDR's lag behind West

Germany is to be found in the other disadvantages it faced. It only remains then to ask whether a capitalistic economic system, faced with similar or identical obstacles would have fared any better. Dozens of East Germans to whom I have posed this question replied with an emphatic "No." And many added: "On the contrary, capitalism might have done worse. It was a situation that begged for a planned, collectivized economy." This speaks for the new mood that has gripped the country since its economy has moved toward rapid growth and recuperation from the deluge of initial disadvantages and setbacks. It is a buoyant, ebullient temper shaded by rudimentary nationalism.

"We began with less than nothing," a young executive of Rostock's state-owned shipbuilding trust told me almost plaintively. "What we have today we built with the sweat on our brows and the calluses on our hands, without help from anyone. And it is pretty good. Just look around you. People live well, they're beginning to get the luxuries of life, their future is secure—which you can't say for West Germans who must now worry about a recession or economic slowdown and unemployment. Of course it's been rough. Damn rough. And we're still not over the hump. Just look at the millions we had to invest to even provide a basis for a viable, independent economy. Go out to the yard in Warnemünde and look at the ships we're building. But keep in mind that in 1945 nothing was there but grass. This part of Germany used to account for four percent of the old Reich's total shipbuilding potential, now we're among the world's top ten. And it's that way on every sector of the economy."

In Erfurt, the thirty-five-year-old development chief of the burgeoning computer and office machine trust, echoed those words. "We were a squeezed-out lemon in 1945. Now our products are sold in sixty countries, our new computers win admiration at every trade fair and even American companies are interested in working with us. If that's not an economic miracle, show me one."

"We're not stupid and we're not blind," an Eisenhüttenstadt iron worker told me with a hint of defiance. "We know what's going on in the West and that life is better there. But what we have here we built from scratch. It's good, and above all, it's all ours."

Such views help explain the most surprising transformation of East German attitudes today: a growing preference for a collectivized economic system—the very thing which most West German observers unswervingly predicted would be the Achilles heel of the Ulbricht regime. "Make no mistake about it," a young sales executive at a Leipzig trade fair exhibit said to me in 1964, "this part of the country has always been more leftist oriented than West Germany. People here appreciate the educational benefits, the social security gains won under this regime. And I do not think they would be inclined to return the factories and big stores to their original owners."

That view, articulated more eloquently, has been reiterated on dozens of occasions in the years since 1964. A correlation of the most extensive and reliable surveys of East German opinion with the hundreds of interviews I have conducted in the GDR leave me with but one conclusion. The vast majority of East Germans —I would estimate 80 percent—while not necessarily loyal or favorably disposed to the regime or its leaders, subscribe to the economic principles of the system. They do not want to return to the type of capitalism they recall—or have been told about by fathers and mothers. Nor do they yearn for the kind of capitalism practiced and propagated in the Federal Republic.

As one East Berlin editor, proudly displaying the SED party emblem on his lapel, put it: "We have been raised in this system. It is ours and we believe in it. We know that life here can only get better—a prediction one cannot make safely for West Germany."

East German views of West German life are colored and distorted by two influences: the Western TV most people watch and the incessant exaggerated propaganda of their own regime. Judging from current attitudes, Ulbricht is winning the battle for men's minds. As economic conditions improve, his victory only becomes more secure.

Though the majority of East Germans insist they still would like to see Germany reunified some day, they also qualify this hope with the adamant reservation that they would not be willing to pay the ultimate price of reunification which Bonn may demand: jettisoning Communism. Even a stanch, outspoken critic of the regime and its leadership said unequivocally: "Well, if you put it to me that way, the answer is no. Then I'd rather opt for continued division."

This metamorphosis of East German attitudes, cognizance of which is essential to Bonn's formulation of policy, has over the past years been understood by only a handful of West German politicians. Even they admitted it only privately and not for the record. Erich Mende, Bonn's former vice-chancellor and minister for "all-German affairs," whose withdrawal from the government in October 1966 precipitated the fall of Ludwig Erhard, once said: "Of course we realize we may have to temper our views. If the majority of East Germans want to continue their system of state-owned industry and collective farms, we in the West will have to accede to their wishes. If reunification would ever be possible—and it is a long time off—then we will simply have to take a vote and let the Saxons and Thuringians opt for whatever economic practices they prefer." But Mende was an outsider in this respect and certainly did not reflect the view of the Adenauer or Erhard governments. Not until the formation of the grand coalition government of Social Democrats and Christian Democrats in December 1966 did Bonn begin to think in more pragmatic terms. But by then it may have been too late. Thus far, all overtures toward co-existence by Chancellor Kurt Georg Kiesinger have been rebuffed by Ulbricht.

Nascent nationalism, and dramatically improved living conditions—not just the Berlin Wall or the barbed wire and mine fields—have also diminished the urge to flee. Though 25,000 East Germans have risked their lives to escape to the West since August 13, 1961, the exodus has dwindled to a trickle. In 1966 only 1155 fled and the dangers involved are not the primary deterrent. Or how else can one explain the 68,000 West Germans and former refugees who have moved to the GDR since the building of the Wall?

East Germans are accepting their way of life and becoming

suspicious of the West's whose remnants of Nazism and superficial values they distrust.

The initial impression on any trip to East Germany—no matter how often one has visited it—is the drabness and darkness of the cities. But after twenty-four hours the darkness and scruffiness no longer seem unusual and even the most provincial East German town looks normal. I mentioned this curious sensation to a thirty-nine-year-old East Berlin executive whom I once met on an Unter den Linden park bench. "And I find the West just too ostentatious," he replied. "The garishness, the pace, the cutthroat, winner-take-all competition and the superficiality of Western life repel me," he added, explaining that he is one of the privileged few who is permitted to travel to West Germany on business periodically. "But I would never want to stay there. I just don't like it. Now don't start raising your eyebrows. There would be nothing important to keep me here. I'm not a hundred percenter, I have enough self-confidence to believe I could make the grade in business in the West just as I've made it here. And if you want to bring up that old argument about how they'd induce me to come back with threats to my family, you have the wrong man. I have no family, my parents are dead and I'm a bachelor. I go to the Hanover industrial fair each year and return here, thankful to be in a place where life may not be quite as affluent but therefore more genuine."

A top executive in the GDR's expanding chemistry and plastics industry, touched a point that explains not only why many East Germans prefer their way but inadvertently proffered one other reason why the GDR's industry may not have progressed as fast as the planners had hoped.

"People value the security of this system," he told me with unabashed candor, "the state honors and remunerates the hard worker, but it also protects the one who cannot or does not work as hard. Western businessmen have asked me why I don't flee to the Federal Republic where I would be offered a position that pays ten to twenty times what I earn here. Frankly, I'm afraid I might not make out in the harried, hurried competitive jungle of the capitalistic business world. And if I did, at what price? Our tempo is slower, we take it easier. True, maybe this lack of competitive pressure and initiative has kept us behind, but I wouldn't want to change my job for a similar one in West Germany."

A feeling of security pervades the East German atmosphere, an attitude that the future is safe from the economic fluctuations which beleaguer a capitalistic society. Joblessness, stock market crashes, protracted family illness with skyrocketing medical bills—these are all problems with which the East German need not concern himself. And not a few mention it first when attempting to explain why, despite the West's higher standard of living, which borders on luxury, they would still prefer to remain in the GDR. "Here," said one automobile worker in Zwickau, "I know what I have, though it may not be as much. Who'll guarantee that in West Germany I wouldn't be on the streets selling apples a day after crossing the border? It happened once in Germany. What's the guarantee that it won't again?" No matter how much this notion may have been artificially cultivated by an incessant and permeating propaganda which portrays West Germany in varying hues of black, the feeling is genuine.

Moreover, most East Germans are apprehensive of and repelled by the spectre of residual, latent, and renascent Nazism which, they feel, haunts West German life. It is impossible to engage in any conversation in the GDR—formal, friendly, or familial—without being confronted by this issue. East Germans harbor a deep anxiety that nothing has changed for the better in the Federal Republic. Repeatedly both strong opponents and enthusiastic supporters of Ulbricht's regime have asked me: "How could so many high-ranking Nazis have gotten into positions of power after the war? Why is the Communist Party outlawed but not the National Democratic Party with all its neo-Nazi overtones? Why do the West Germans keep on prosecuting war criminals, then sentence them to penalties so light that they mock the victims of Nazi persecution?"

Of course East Germans see the Nazi apparition through the magnifying glass held up by their own agitprop artists who conduct daily harangues in the press, on radio and television to portray Bonn as a Nazi den of iniquity and the Federal Republic as a country where the brownshirts are marching again. East Germans have systematically transferred all responsibility to the other side of the Wall. Communist liturgy has consistently held that Hitler was not a German but a capitalistic phenomenon. Ergo, East Germans who have expurgated capitalism cannot conceivably be harboring either latent or renascent Nazi inclinations. In West Germany where capitalism reigns unbridled, they are told, the seeds of Nazism have been sown anew or carefully nurtured by powerful "revanchists, nationalists, and imperialists." Moreover, the propagandists have inculcated upon East Germans the half truth that all really important Nazis fled to West Germany in the early postwar period. In all this there is enough of a kernel of truth to make it plausible. Ex-Nazis *have* played a far too influential role in postwar West German affairs. The rise of the National Democrats *is* a disturbing development. West Germany's attempts at expiation have often been marked by hypocrisy. Objective comparison of the two halves of what remains of Hitler's Reich ineluctably leads to the conclusion that East Germany did clean out more Nazi bacteria than West Germany. At a time when Konrad Adenauer justified the large number of ex-Nazis in his foreign service, by arguing, "where else can we get capable people with whom to develop a diplomatic corps?" East Germany was being run by amateurs—men and women who from the proletarian ranks had been vaulted overnight into positions of power and responsibility. (And their performance often showed the lack of experience.)

Frequently East German propaganda intimates not only that West Germany is susceptible to a new Hitler but that the old one is entirely Bonn's affair. This is a gross self-deception, for, hard as it may be to contest the thesis that there are today two distinct German states, it is ludicrous to contend, as Ulbricht attempts, that there are also two German pasts.

Despite the GDR's ambivalence, East German fears of a West German Nazi renaissance are deeply rooted. "Our youth," said a woman executive at one of the sprawling chemical plants near Halle, herself the mother of a teenager, "seem to have a much more positive attitude toward Germany's past history. They know exactly what happened. The way textbooks and teachers in the West try to hide the truth is really a scandal, though symptomatic of everything else in the Federal Republic. You have no idea how many people here, especially young ones, are repelled by Bonn for just this reason. No one wants to see history repeated."

And the wife of an Erfurt physician, herself uncompromisingly critical of the East German regime, told me adamantly, "But the idea of living in West Germany, where so many Nazis are left or returning, is just as repugnant to me as staying here. I can't understand why this is condoned."

Nor can East Germans understand the Bonn government's intransigent claim to the borders of 1937, that is, to the territories of Silesia, Pomerania, and East Prussia which de facto have been ceded to Poland. Said one Eisenhüttenstadt worker: "I was born on the other side of the Oder, not far from here. I still consider it my home, but I would never think of it as German again. It's Polish. After all, somewhere along the line we had to pay a price for the war, and that's it. In West Germany the refugees and expellees from the 'eastern territories' keep shouting that these must be returned to us. How ridiculous. To the Poles they are the 'western territories,' and in the meantime a new generation has matured there—millions of Poles who were transplanted from somewhere else and whose children were born in Silesia and Pomerania. To them it's as much home as it was to us. The idea of going to war or resorting to threats to get back these lands, as the expellees in West Germany imply, is just anathema to us."

If pride of accomplishment, yearning for security and apprehension over West Germany's Irredentist and nationalistic tones nurture East Germany's budding nationalism and sense of independence, the natural development of two distinct societies with divergent social outlooks contributes to progressive dichotomy.

A middle-aged Dresden woman told me: "I've lost touch with most of my friends and relatives in the West. We no longer read the same authors, nor talk about the same artists. We have completely different problems here which no one in West Germany can understand, just, as I'll admit, I can't seem to get excited about their problems any more. My husband worries about whether the production plan will be fulfilled, their husbands about fluctuations on the stock market. We're developing our own mentality, have our own outlooks and viewpoints on life. The only thing that can hold Germany together is our common language."

Even the language becomes a weaker link day by day as the phenomenon of "East-speak" and "West-speak," presently being analyzed by Professor Hugo Moser of Bonn University, takes on progressively significant proportions. Just a perfunctory glance will reveal that two completely divergent socio-political systems are destined to develop their own distinct vocabularies. West German is being Americanized. And if East German is not actually being Russified, it has been "enriched" by a vocabulary of ideological mumbo-jumbo which only the initiated, certainly not a West German, can understand.

Divided by a Wall in Berlin, an 800-mile border of barbed wire, trip mines and guard towers, the two Germanys, for all the platitudinous lip service they give to reunification, are drifting apart. For the first seventeen years of this process, the East Germans were a factor which no one needed to take seriously. Since 1963, when the economy finally began to function, when attitudes began adapting to circumstances, it can no longer be ignored. It is not without reason that even opponents of Ulbricht today speak proudly of "Our Republic" when referring to what Bonn officials have for so long derisively called "the Soviet Occupation Zone." Obviously Ulbricht and his associates pine for more prestige and diplomatic recognition around the world. But when ordinary East Germans demand it, too, then the GDR stops being a Soviet puppet state which someday can be purchased from the Kremlin, providing the price and time are right.

"Just where do Bonn and the West derive the right to ignore us and say we do not exist?" asked the young, Nordic blonde wife of an East Berlin executive, her blue eyes flashing with anger. "Look at what we've accomplished here and then tell me whether we should be recognized or not."

PART TWO

FATHERS
OF THE
REVOLUTION

CHAPTER II

The Proctor's Return

At six o'clock on the morning of April 30, 1945—just hours before Adolf Hitler shot himself, his mad dreams of world conquest shattered in the rubble of Berlin—the streets of Moscow were still empty. A bus pulled up to the entrance of the Lux Hotel, off Gorky Street. Ten men, heaving suitcases and traveling bags, clambered in for the fifteen-minute ride to the airport where they boarded a DC-3 with Soviet markings. Three hours later they landed at Calau, between Küstrin and Frankfurt on the Oder. From there they rode, first in a Red Army truck, later in a caravan of limousines, to the headquarters of Soviet Marshal Georgi K. Zhukov's political staff at Bruchmühle—a small town nineteen miles east of Berlin.

After twelve years in exile Walter Ulbricht, Stalin's proctor in Germany, had returned to the land of his fathers.

His instructions at the time went no further than to "assist Soviet military commandants in taking all necessary measures for normalizing the life of the German populace as quickly as possible." But there was upon his arrival a prophetic slip of the tongue by one of the Russian officers who had come to greet Ulbricht and his retinue of aides. "It is a special pleasure to greet you," said the Russian, "because we have heard that you are the members of the new German government."

The prophecy was only partly true. Of the ten members of the Gruppe Ulbricht, all of them German Communists who had lived out the Nazi regime as émigrés in the Soviet Union, only three—including Ulbricht—are today in positions of any power. Five have either been purged by Ulbricht or are in minor posts, one went to West Germany to help reorganize the Communist

Party there. The tenth—and youngest, Wolfgang Leonhard—fled to Yugoslavia in 1949 and eventually West Germany where he wrote his classic autobiography of a young German Communist: *Child of the Revolution.*

Though two other groups of German Communists—one under Anton Ackermann, the other led by Gustav Sobottka—were sent into Germany that day, it was Ulbricht's that really mattered. Next to aging Wilhelm Pieck, the first secretary, Ulbricht was the highest ranking member of the party and its real power behind the scenes.

As Leonhard has described them, the members of the Ulbricht group were all long-time Communists and Comintern-trained agents, hand-picked by the Soviets and the German CP exile organization in Moscow for their specialties, loyalty, and willingness to obey orders. Next to Ulbricht there was Otto Winzer, then forty-three, who had joined the German Communist Youth Movement in 1919, the party in 1925. As a Moscow émigré he was an active agitator in the National Committee for a Free Germany, a popular front movement started in 1942 to brainwash captured German soldiers and officers of the Hitler ideology. Winzer, an "ice cold functionary" whose long service in the party apparatus has deprived him of any relationship to the active workers' movement or socialist ideals, is now East Germany's foreign minister.

Karl Maron was forty-two when he accompanied Ulbricht to Germany and had demonstrated his worth to the party as an all around apparatchik. From 1945 until 1948 he was a deputy mayor of East Berlin, then served a one-year stint as assistant editor-in-chief of *Neues Deutschland,* the SED's official daily. From June 1950 until 1955 he headed the Volkspolizei (People's Police). Until 1963 he was the GDR's interior minister. Now he directs the Central Committee's Institute for Opinion Research.

Hans Mahle, born in Hamburg in 1911, had joined the party's youth movement in the 1920s. In Russia he was one of the key propagandists of the National Committee for a Free Germany. His career under Ulbricht has been vicissitudinous. A 1951 purge plummeted him from the heights, as boss of all radio broadcasting in the Soviet Zone, to a role of advertising manager in a co-operative store chain. Since 1954 he has worked his way back slowly through various provincial newspapers to the editorship of *Wahrheit*, a party opinion journal in East Berlin. According to Leonhard, Mahle, despite many years in the party apparatus, was one of the few top functionaries who could still laugh, be happy and express himself in words that were not mere echoes of official jargon.

Richard Gyptner, then forty-four, joined the party as a teen-ager in Hamburg in 1919, worked his way up in the apparatus and served for a while as secretary to Comintern chief Georgi Dimitrov. After Hitler came to power, Gyptner fled Germany, arriving in the Soviet Union in 1935. A man without an iota of humor, pedantic and obeisantly adaptable to changes in the party line, he served as the GDR's ambassador to Poland from 1961 to 1963, now is retired and writes occasional articles on the history of the German labor movement.

At fifty-eight, Gustav Gundelach, also from Hamburg, was the group's oldest member. After first heading the Soviet Zone's social security administration, Gundelach went to West Germany in 1946 to help reorganize the party, and was elected to the West German Bundestag in 1949. He died in 1962.

Fritz Erpenbeck, then forty-eight, born in Mainz, had made a name after World War I, first as a reporter and editor of Communist papers, as a left-wing satirist and later as an actor and director working with Erwin Piscator. From 1959 until 1962 Erpenbeck was chief director at the East Berlin Volksbühne Theater. Since then he has worked as a free-lance writer and critic.

The youngest on the team was Leonhard, then twenty-three, who had emigrated to the USSR in 1935 with his mother, a veteran Communist. He was educated in the Soviet Union, spent nearly two years at the Comintern school in Kushnarenkovo, and since his 1949 break with Ulbricht, has become one of West Germany's leading Sovietologists.

Two days after their arrival, on May 2, the members of the Ulbricht group undertook their first joint expedition from Bruchmühle to Berlin. It was an abysmal, ravaged, and chaotic Germany that presented itself. Berlin was a wilderness of death, fires, and mountains of rubble. Thousands of hungry and ragged people, erred aimlessly like poisoned ants through the shambles of what once was a great and proud city. Disillusioned, broken, and defeated German prisoners of war lined the roadsides. Singing, carousing soldiers of the victorious Red Army roamed the streets, plundering stores, raping the women and terrorizing the battle-scarred populace. In those parts of the city where the fighting had stopped, the *Trümmerfrauen* (the rubble women) were already at work clearing the streets of the debris of war, usually under the watchful, distrustful eye of a Soviet guard. In front of the soup kitchens, Wehrmacht warehouses and public fountains, thousands of hungry, thirsty Berliners queued for hours, hoping for a morsel of food, a pailful of water. And everywhere, from the gaping, glassless windows of the battle-pocked houses, the flags flew: white ones made from bedsheets to show surrender; red ones hastily cut out of old Nazi swastika banners, to hail the Soviet occupation.

Ulbricht's mission in those early days of May: to get the local administrations in Berlin's twenty boroughs functioning as fast as possible so the Western allies would have no choice but to confirm them when they arrived. Even before the Wehrmacht's formal May 8 capitulation at Reims, Ulbricht and his team were ferreting out those Communists who had managed to last through the Hitler regime in hiding.

But the objective was not to put Communists into the forefront. On the contrary. All the representational posts—burgomasters and directors for traffic, health, church affairs, social welfare, and trade—were to be filled with non-Communists: anti-fascist democrats of every political persuasion. "It has to look democratic," Ulbricht warned, "yet the real power must remain in our hands." The motive: to avoid anything that would look like an overt Communist coup and thereby jeopardize the "anti-Hitler coalition" between Russia and the West. Ulbricht decreed that Communists in the borough administrations should fill only one-third of the posts: but the pivotal ones. Socialists, democrats, conservatives could act as mayors. But Communists were appointed as deputies—positions which by tradition included responsibility for public safety, police, education, labor, and personnel. In each borough Ulbricht's men carefully apportioned executive responsibility according to the area's traditional sociological and political structure. In bourgeois districts, such as Wilmersdorf, Steglitz, and Zehlendorf, bourgeois officials predominated. In the traditional proletarian sections of the city—Wedding, Neukoelln, Kreuzberg—Social Democrats and Communists got the key jobs. To the eye untrained in Communist strategy, it looked like the administrations had evolved organically.

On May 17, two weeks after Ulbricht's arrival and more than a month before the first Allied troops entered Berlin, General N. E. Berzarin, the Soviet commandant, announced the formation of a citywide government headed by Dr. Arthur Werner, an independent, as lord mayor. Of Werner's first sixteen-member administration only seven were Communists. The key to Communist power lay not in numbers but in positions. They controlled the departments of police, finances, communications, labor affairs, social welfare, education and personnel. This democratic masquerade which Ulbricht staged in Berlin, was emulated by Ackermann and Sobottka, his counterparts in Saxony and Mecklenburg.

Oddly enough, the Soviet military administration's original plans did not envisage an early re-establishment of the German Communist Party. On the contrary, before leaving Moscow, Ulbricht's men had been told emphatically that all political activity in the beginning would have to be conducted under the aegis of one large, non-partisan anti-fascist movement—a bloc of militant democracy. But as so often under Stalin, the line changed by 180 degrees overnight. One reason may have been the spontaneous growth of local Communist Party groups in various East German cities, many of which had started negotiations with the Social Democrats for formation of a "socialist unity party" which would settle, once and for all, the ideological dispute that had divided German Marxists since 1919. But there was no room for spontaneity in the Stalinist order which held that all activity must be centrally directed from the top.

When Wilhelm Pieck and other top leaders of the exiled party

arrived from Moscow in late May, they brought along new directives calling for speedy formation of the German Communist
Party (KPD). On June 9 the Soviet Military Administration announced that political parties would be permitted. Just two days
later the new KPD was in business.

It was hardly the kind of party envisioned by those comrades
who had spent the Nazi years in Hitler's concentration camps.
Of the sixteen men and women who called themselves its central
committee, thirteen had returned to Germany from the Soviet
Union. Only three—Franz Dahlem, Ottomar Geschke, and Hans
Jendretzky—were real anti-Nazi resistance fighters who had endured the Third Reich behind barbed wire. It was a central
committee, or Politburo, tailored to the times. All but a handful
of its members had climbed the hierarchical ladder under Stalinist tutelage and experienced his purges in Russia from 1936 to
1938.

Like all parties in all four occupation zones, it required the in-
dulgences of the military government administration. But the
KPD was doubly dependent. It was a conveyor belt for Stalin's
policies. The thirteen who had come from Russia were reliably
attuned to every change in the wind from Moscow. Though this
sensitivity caused bitter feuds in the party's ranks, it assured the
Russian trained leaders of full support from the Soviet Military
Administration—not to mention generous privileges such as
limousines, comfortable villas, and countless luxuries which set
them off sharply from the spartan routine of postwar German life.
It was a leadership long trained in the art of smothering flickers
of individualism among the rank and file, a team both assiduous
and obsequious in responding to orders from the top. In short,
here was a party eminently qualified for implementing the Soviet
occupation concept.

That each of the four victorious powers would attempt to re-
create a Germany in its own image was only logical. Re-education
was predestined to be a process of fashioning in each of the four
occupation zones, a Germany which reflected the social, political,
and economic attitudes of each of the four conquerors. Long after
the end of the occupation era in the West, cultural, political, and

economic differences continued to characterize the French, American, and British zones. Not until the start of the present decade did those distinctions sublimate into the synthesis of what has become postwar Germany's way of life. Proselytism was a natural consequence of messianic victory over a megalomaniac aggressor nation which had attempted to remake the whole world. Just as the U.S., Britain, or France would never have communized West Germany, so Stalin could not have been expected to install a system in East Germany which differed substantially from the one he had created in the Soviet Union. Re-education and occupation in the three western zones reflected the bourgeois, capitalistic traditions familiar to most Germans. In the east, the Soviet administration was oriented toward norms of Bolshevist revolution and collectivism.

Joseph Goebbels' propaganda tirades had not conditioned the Germans to welcome *either* conqueror with shouts of adulation, but Nazism's innate anti-Bolshevism had prepared those Germans who lived in the Russian zone to portend calamity. Said one woman in a Saxonian town first captured by Americans: "When the Amis came we thought it would be the end of the world. Then, in July, the zonal borders were drawn, the Americans withdrew and the Russians arrived. We were sure it meant the end of the universe."

For many Germans it was. In stark contrast to the Americans who had tried to stamp out Nazism by smothering "their" Germans with chewing gum, candy and kindness, the Russians mixed intensive indoctrination with plunder, rape, ruthless justice and often the crudest brutality. For Walter Ulbricht and the renascent German Communist Party, it was a hopelessly schizophrenic situation. While the KPD functionaries were extolling the virtues of German-Soviet friendship, Red Army soldiers were still ravaging German womanhood, plundering German homes and dismantling wholesale what remained of East Germany's bomb and war-scarred industrial potential. The result was a credibility gap between Ulbricht and East Germans which the regime has not bridged completely to this day.

Aside from a general theory, Stalin at that time did not have clearly defined concepts of what to do with "his" Germany. Even before the end of the war, he had gone on record against permanent division. And in 1945 the Soviets still counted on a relatively short period of occupation from which would emerge a thoroughly de-Nazified, militarily castrated and economically dependent but politically unified state. If Stalin ever aspired to create a unified *Communist* Germany, it is reasonably safe to assume that he abandoned those plans about the time Josip Broz Tito first started flexing the muscles of "independent" Communism in Yugoslavia. If anything was inimical to Stalin's concept of world Communism, it was ideological separatism. The Soviet dictator was shrewd enough to realize that a unified, Communist Germany, with its tradition as the ideological cradle of Marxism-Leninism, might some day pose a greater threat to Moscow's hegemony over the movement than a neutral, capitalistic Germany.

Just when Stalin conceived of a policy of a divided Germany is as difficult to determine as when progressive division became irreversible. Only one thing seems certain: Germany's division was not, as many West German politicians contend today, the cause of the Cold War, but rather the *result* of the widening chasm between East and West.

Without a doubt, the divisive process in Germany began on September 6, 1946, when U. S. Secretary of State James F. Byrnes, speaking in Stuttgart, announced the creation of Bizonia—an economic fusion of the British and American zones. Though this move was itself no more than a reflection of the mounting tension between the Soviet Union and its wartime allies, it initiated the process which has led to the creation of two Germanys.

Much of Anglo-American policy was motivated by an erroneous assumption that the Soviets intended to communize all of Germany—a Western fear that heightened when the Communists seized power, by coup d'etat, in Czechoslovakia in February 1948. What followed was pell-mell deterioration of the last vestiges of German unity and a headlong plunge toward division. Erich W. Gniffke, a Social Democrat who helped found the East German Socialist Unity Party (SED), and later fled to the West, wrote in 1958: "Ulbricht's present power in both the party and state are due less to any help from the East than the West. Stalin and the Moscow Politburo were committed to basic adherence to the terms of the Potsdam agreement and prepared to make concessions in the German question as late as the end of 1947. Until the spring of 1948, Ulbricht was isolated. Only when the West coupled the Marshall Plan with its Policy of Strength did the Soviets change their course in the German question as well. Even then they tried to keep the door open for negotiations. Not until mid-1948 did Moscow give the signal for the Soviet Zone's development along the lines of a people's democracy under Ulbricht's leadership."

Regardless of his original intentions, by early 1948, Stalin probably realized that German division was inevitable. As he told Yugoslavia's then vice-president Milovan Djilas in a dinner conversation: "The West will make West Germany its own and we shall make our own state of East Germany."

The making of two Germanys began in earnest with the Western currency reform on June 20, 1948, to which the Soviets responded by blockading Berlin four days later. On June 26 the Berlin airlift was under way. On July 1 the three Western military governors commissioned the minister-presidents of the West German states to form a constitutional convention and draft a basic law for the formation of a separate state. The convention met in Bonn on September 1, 1948.

Eight weeks after that, East Germany's so-called People's Council started drafting an East German constitution. West Germany's was adopted on May 8, East Germany's on May 30, 1949. On September 15, Dr. Konrad Adenauer was elected chancellor in the new Bundestag and one week later rule by military government of West Germany ended formally. The Federal Republic was a fait accompli. Within two weeks, East Germany's Volksrat voted with a unanimous "Ja" to transform itself into the Volkskammer. On October 7 the German Democratic Republic was born.

Otto Grotewohl, a former Social Democrat, was named its first premier; Ulbricht, one of his deputies; Wilhelm Pieck its first president. When Pieck, seventy-three, jovial, snow-haired and beaming took the accolades in public on October 11, war-ravaged Unter den Linden sparkled with fireworks, searchlights, and blazing torches such as Berlin had not seen since the heydays of the Nazis. From its ruined public buildings fluttered the red, black, and gold banners of the GDR—the same colors as those of the old Weimar and new Bonn republics. Marx-Engels Platz thronged with a quarter million flag-waving Germans. An open black Mercedes rolled into the square and from its rear seat rose rotund Pieck, his clenched fist raised in Communist salute to the crowd. On the reviewing stand, overshadowed by his own and Stalin's ten-foot portraits, Pieck beamed as blaring brass bands and blue-shirted members of the Free German Youth (FDJ) paraded by. They bore painted likenesses of Stalin, Lenin, Mao Tse-tung and Pieck and huge red banners reading "Long Live the National Front of Democratic Germany."

Although Germany's course was now irreversible, Soviet policy was still not clearly defined, a fact reflected in the hesitant and uncertain fashion in which the Communists launched East Germany's transformation into a people's democracy.

Indeed, the definite decision to develop the GDR into a separate state was not reached until three years later—in 1952—after a quite serious proposal by Stalin for German reunification under terms of strict political and military neutrality was rebuffed by both Washington and Bonn. That was the pivot on which Soviet policy changed course radically. All reparations payments were suddenly suspended and the Russians began repatriating the industrial plants they had converted into Soviet stock companies— a process that was not completed until 1955.

If Soviet indecision hampered East Germany's economic development, it nearly destroyed postwar chances for the organic growth of a genuine, unified popular socialist movement. Yet, if ever there was an area of Germany where such a movement stood chances of growing grass roots, it was in the Russian Zone. Until 1930 this region of Germany had voted 50 percent socialist and was, even at the time of Hitler's rise to power, the last solid Marxist stronghold in the country. Though most of the labor vote had gone to the Social Democratic party, the Communists generally ran a respectable ten to fifteen percent and could claim that nearly one-fifth of all their Reichstag deputies were from Saxony.

Thus, it was no surprise that in 1945 both the Communist and Social Democratic parties' rank and file overwhelmingly supported a land reform plan which gave 500,000 farm laborers and small-holders nearly 6,000,000 acres confiscated from 14,000 junkers, rich farmers, and former Nazis. And in March 1946, when the Communist Party in Saxony sponsored a referendum calling for expropriation and nationalization of 4800 large and medium-sized business and industrial enterprises owned by high-ranking Nazis, war criminals and profiteers, 77.6 percent of the eligible 3,400,000 voters registered approval, only 16.5 percent voted no.

To say today as the West German government does, that a socialist society was imposed on the East Germans against their will is stretching the truth. The soil and sympathy for socialism were extant in Saxony and Thuringia long before the Soviets arrived. Even the new Christian Democratic Party said in its platform, drafted on June 26, 1945: "Ownership of natural resources, the mining industry and other key, monopolistic enterprises should be subjected to state rule." Nearly a year later Jakob Kaiser, the CDU's leader, who subsequently fled to West Germany and served in Adenauer's first cabinet, said: "Private ownership becomes a menace when it gives individuals the power to rule over others, to exploit the treasures of nature. We advocate public ownership of all natural resources and strict control of all private land holdings. As Christians and as democrats we demand a healthy socialist order. Democracy means more than the formal right to vote. Every citizen must have an equal chance to participate in the formation of policy. This, however, can never be achieved as long as a few individuals in society can exercise unrestricted power derived from economic preeminence and ownership of property."

Throughout this early period, the Communist Party, taking orders directly from an ambivalent Kremlin, acted as the brakeman on the mechanism. It is ironic but true that through most of 1945 and the early months of 1946 the Social Democrats were clamoring for socialization of all basic industries while Ulbricht and the KPD advocated "completely unrestrained development of free commerce and enterprise on a basis of private ownership."

Even more ironic: the Social Democrats were the first to propose formation of a socialist unity party while the Communists rejected this scheme as late as November 1945, only to become its stanchest champions by January 1946. Even before the Nazi guns had stopped firing, Socialists and Communists were discussing the possibility of a unified party and, in a few small towns, actually formed local chapters, only to see them suppressed by the Russians, skeptical of any grass roots democratic development over which they had no control. On June 15, 1945, four days after the establishment of the KPD, the Soviet Zone SPD was founded: Its platform was a singular appeal for fusion. "We want to conduct the battles of the future on a basis of organizational unity of the German working class," said the Social Democrats. "We see in this a moral reparation of the political mistakes of the past . . . the banner of unity must become the glowing symbol of political action by the working class."

The common battle against the Nazis, the mutually endured suffering in Gestapo jails and concentration camps, had glossed over the cracks of disagreement between most Socialists and Communists. It was the consensus among those who had stayed behind to battle fascism at home, instead of from exile, that the German working class movement had failed in 1933, due largely to the schism between Socialism and Communism which began in 1919.

That view, however, was not shared by the KPD's leadership, comprised primarily of men who had spent the Hitler era in reasonable comfort in Moscow. There they had dissociated from the party's rank and file and degenerated into an isolated, hard core of revolutionary theorists whose primary goal was to keep one step ahead of changes in the Kremlin line and the Stalinist secret police. Numerous times in May and early June of 1945, Otto Grotewohl and Max Fechner, the leaders of the East Zone SPD, met with Ulbricht and urged him to join in forming a socialist unity party. Ulbricht, as de facto, if not the nominal, chief of the KPD, rejected the proposal. "The time is not ripe," he insisted, "and premature unification would only carry within it the seed for future disharmony. A long period of informal cooperation between the two parties will have to precede organizational union."

Ulbricht's real reason was his aversion to spontaneity as a political factor and his fear that the Communists might not be able to dominate a unified socialist party which they had not created in their own image. Moreover, Ulbricht needed time to consolidate his own control of the KPD. He had to bring its rank and file, and those of its leaders who had remained in Germany during the Third Reich, in line with his policy of unconditional support of the Soviet occupation authorities and unequivocal acceptance of Stalinist programs. Like the anti-fascist committees which had mushroomed in the wake of the Red Army's tanks, only to be suppressed after a few weeks by Ulbricht and the Soviet Military Administration, the Social Democratic clamor for fusion had not been preordained by Moscow. Hence it could not be condoned by the Kremlin's vicars in East Germany. It was Ulbricht's hope that the SPD could, at some future time, be forced to petition for unity from a position of weakness, not strength. With that end in view, the Soviets threw all their prestigious as well as material weight behind the KPD.

But Ulbricht was to change his mind with alacrity when he saw the SPD gaining strength on its own, independent of the KPD and in spite of the favoritism being practiced by the Soviet Military Administration.

In November after hearing a speech during which Grotewohl deviated substantially from the KPD's line and called for an end to the Soviet dismantling and reparations policy, Ulbricht became alarmed. The address reflected many of the views of Dr. Kurt Schumacher, the leader of the SPD in the western occupation zones, an unswervable opponent of fusion. Moreover, during that same month, the Austrian Communist Party suffered a scathing defeat in the first postwar elections, winning only four seats in parliament compared to 85 for the conservatives and 76 for the Austrian Social Democrats. Ulbricht took it as a warning and suddenly began urging amalgamation. Action committees for SPD-KPD unity, often created under constraint from the Soviet occupation authorities, sprouted virtually overnight in dozens of East German cities and began pressuring Grotewohl and the SPD's central committee from below.

In December 1945, the leaders of the SPD and KPD met for a formal conference on amalgamation during which Grotewohl wrung several important concessions from Ulbricht and Pieck, who were playing for time. The meeting ended with a harmonious communiqué which called for closer cooperation between the two parties and eventual fusion.

In the succeeding weeks the Communists played their hand skillfully. They geared up their campaign at the local level and wherever resistance mounted in SPD chapters, the Soviets were called in to intimidate Social Democratic leaders with arrests and censorship. Vague allusions to a "special (or third) German road to Socialism" lured many Social Democrats who objected to the Communists' revolutionary philosophy.

Spontaneous amalgamation on the local and state level gained momentum—often under the bumbling pressure of Soviet military government chiefs. Wolfgang Leonhard told the amusing story of the KPD and SPD county chairmen, somewhere in Mecklenburg, who were called to the Soviet commandant's residence one evening at seven o'clock. The commandant greeted them jovially, led them into the dining room where the table was creaking under a mountain of delicacies. "Please eat," the Russian said, and the Communist and the Socialist ate. "Please drink," he exhorted them, and they drank. And as the repast neared completion, the Russian poured one last big glass of vodka for each man and insisted they drink that. "Now," he said, "shake hands." They did and the Russian called out ecstatically, "Very good, now I can report unity in our county."

The handshaking ceremony, in fact, became a crucial element in the consolidation of the SPD and KPD. In March, several weeks before the SED became a fait accompli, KPD functionaries at their headquarters on East Berlin's Wall Strasse were already preoccupied with selecting a party emblem from a variety of designs. They finally chose—and still use today—an oval with a red flag on a white background. Superimposed on the flag, two clasped hands in gold. On a blue border around the white field are the words: *Sozialistische Einheitspartei Deutschlands.*

While the Social Democratic central committee continued to debate—with itself and the party's Western Zone leadership—local and state organizations in eastern Germany moved ahead on their own. In Saxony, Thuringia, and Mecklenburg the SPD and KPD had amalgamated by early April and soon the Communists and Socialists in East Berlin followed suit. The joint party convention held in East Berlin's Admirals Palast Theater on April 21 was but a formality to solemnize the decision. Otto Grotewohl and Wilhelm Pieck approached each other from opposing wings on the stage, met in the center and—just the way the new emblem depicted it—shook hands. Said Grotewohl, barely audible over the crescendo of exuberant applause: "The symbolic meaning of the act became clear to me as we met on stage. Wilhelm Pieck came from the left, I came from the right. But we both came to meet in the middle."

Grotewohl was soon to learn, bitterly, that Pieck had not met him halfway and that he had become junior partner in a party rushing headlong on the Stalinist path. But in that euphoric moment it looked, indeed, as if a shining new era in the German workers' movement had dawned. While consolidation of the parties was by no means as voluntary as its leaders attempted to portray it, it is ludicrous to contend, as does the SPD in West Germany today, that the fusion of the two parties in East Germany was a marriage contracted under the threat of a Soviet shotgun. It was, moreover, born in a soil of ideological *Heimweh*, the consequence of a Social Democratic leadership culpably shy of perspicacity and prudence. Today the West German SPD contends that in West Berlin, for example, where Social Democrats were allowed to vote freely on amalgamation in March 1946, the overwhelming majority of party members rejected the proposal. That is only half true. Though 19,526 of 23,755 SPD members voted against and only 2937 in favor of immediate integration with the KPD, the majority, 14,883, in a second roll call, opted for very close cooperation with the Communists on a program dedicated to common purposes.

In essence, Otto Grotewohl, Max Fechner, and Erich W. Gniffke were no better or worse than their compatriots in Germany's western occupation zones. The party's leadership had been decimated by Nazi prosecution. Those who remained, with few exceptions, were not profiles in courage. But they were motivated by the honest desire to amend what they considered— wrongly or rightly—the principal cause of democracy's decline during the Weimar Republic: the schism in German socialism. It is no challenge to their integrity but to their sagacity and percipience that they failed to recognize Ulbricht and his coterie for what they were: apparatchiks whose years in Moscow exile had made of them malleable hacks, responsive and loyal even after the most bizarre Stalinist tergiversations.

What originated as a brotherhood of equals soon became an instrument of Soviet policy in which many loyal Communists had little, the Socialists far less to say. Of the fourteen men and women who comprised the SED's first central secretariat, later called the Politburo, only two remain in power today: Ulbricht and Hermann Matern, both seventy-four. Wilhelm Pieck, who became East Germany's president in 1949, died in 1960 at age eighty-four. Grotewohl, the GDR's first premier, died broken and disillusioned, in 1964 at seventy. The other ten, Communists and Socialists alike, either fled to the West or were purged and demoted by the end of 1953.

The Social Democrats who had come half way to build a Socialist Unity Party with the Communists, were suppressed, silenced, sidelined, and subjugated until all that remained of social democracy in East Germany were the raiments of memory. Behind the façade, a Stalinist machine was actually in control.

The other parties originally allowed to form in the Soviet Zone in 1945, though still extant in name, fared no better. It is one of the ironies of East German history that they were cowed into submission and reduced to political satraps despite the fact that neither the Christian Democratic Union (CDU) nor the Liberal Democrats (LDPD) posed any real ballot box threat to SED suzerainty.

As a matter of fact, in the last few honest elections in East Germany, the SED did well. It won 53 percent of the total vote in Saxony's September 1946 municipal and county elections, 60 and 69 percent respectively in those held in Brandenburg and Mecklenburg.

One month later, during the state elections in Saxony, Saxony-Anhalt, Thuringia, Mecklenburg, and Brandenburg, the SED emerged as the strongest, though not the majority party everywhere, winning 44 to 49.5 percent of the total vote in each of the five states. Only in Berlin, where it had been forced to compete not only in the city's Western sectors but against the West German SPD as well, did the SED suffer a major defeat. It ran a poor third, lagging with 20 percent behind both the SPD and the CDU. Even in traditionally "Red" Wedding, a Berlin borough where the Communists had scored a 60 percent triumph in 1932, the SED won only 29 percent.

Disappointed in this showing, Ulbricht and the Russians began the systematic liquidation of democracy and subjugation of the other political parties to SED hegemony. Soviet commandants caused the non-Communist parties as much trouble as possible. Russian officers attended all party meetings, demanded to see all documents and minutes. The CDU and LDPD press was kept on the tightest paper ration. Party leaders were bribed and corrupted to make them economically dependent and, when that failed at the desired effect, blackmailed or arrested to create an atmosphere of terror. Members of the CDU and LDPD were barred or hindered from civil service jobs, influential or responsible positions and frequently from attending college or university. When those draconian measures failed to produce compliance from the leaders, they were pre-emptorily expelled from office. That is what happened in 1946 to Dr. Andreas Hermes, a member of the CDU's executive committee, for opposing the land reform, and in December 1947 to Jakob Kaiser and Ernst Lemmer, the co-chairmen of the CDU, for playing their opposition role too hard.

Kaiser and Lemmer fled to the West where, like other Christian Democratic politicians who had left East Germany, they soon became influential in Adenauer's CDU. Their defection, no matter how humanly comprehensible, left a vacuum which the Soviets promptly filled with their own, obeisant, hand-picked sycophants: among them Otto Nuschke and Georg Dertinger. Nuschke, who died in 1957 at seventy-four, was named party chairman to succeed Lemmer and Kaiser in 1948 and a deputy premier of the GDR in 1949. Dertinger, sixty-four, was appointed secretary-general of the CDU and became instrumental in reducing it to a pliable tool of the SED. He was rewarded first with an appointment as East German foreign minister, then in 1954 with a fifteen-year prison sentence for "treason." He served ten years and was pardoned in 1964.

Until 1949, the Liberal Party's chairman, Dr. Wilhelm Külz, fought a valiant but futile battle to maintain the LDPD's independence and identity. When Külz died in the spring of that year, the Soviets maneuvered two dependable toadies into the party leadership, one of whom, Johannes Dieckmann, is now president (speaker) of the Volkskammer.

In 1948 the Soviets created two additional political groups: the National Democrats (NDP—and not to be confused with the new rightist West German party of the same name but reversed initials—NPD) and the Democratic Farmers' Party (DBD). Their purpose: to give East Germany a semblance of democracy and popular will. Both were artificial satellites of the SED. The NDP was created to provide East Germany's two million, politically ostracized and homeless ex-Nazis with a party they could call their own. Most of its members are former Wehrmacht officers, rank and file ex-Nazis and civil servants. Named as its leader, however, was Dr. Lothar Bolz, a veteran Communist who had been in Moscow with Ulbricht and Pieck. The DBD is no less a front. Created to reconcile East Germany's dissident farmers with the regime, its Soviet-appointed leader, Ernst Goldenbaum, was also an old-line Communist.

All four of these "bourgeois" parties—the CDU, LDPD, NDP, and DBD—together with the SED and several "mass organizations" such as the Free German Youth (FDJ), the Free German Federation of Trade Unions (FDGB), the Federation of Democratic German Women (DFD) and the Cultural League (KB) —comprise the National (or popular) Front. They are represented in the Volkskammer, on the Council of State and the Council of Ministers. To call them democratic or equate them with political parties in the Western tradition, however, is delusory. They are merely simulacrums of opposition in a system where all candidates for public office are chosen from "unity" lists and competition between parties is scorned officially as just another opiate of the people. Streams of real opposition run stronger among the SED's 1,700,000 members than any of the dues-paying, card-holding 300,000 who belong to the non-Communist parties. At least the SED, despite its monolithic structure and doctrinaire history, is a party alive with currents of variegated opinion and many nuances of ideology. The other parties are a sham of opposition and a conversation with one of their functionaries invariably degenerates into a liturgical monologue.

"Of course we're a liberal party," Klaus Puschke, the LDPD's press spokesman once told me during a three-hour lunch conversation in East Berlin. "Nevertheless we also believe in socialism. That may sound strange to you (as it did, in view of German liberalism's affinity for Adam Smithian economics) but it works. There are many small entrepreneurs, farmers, academics and the like who, while they approve of socialism, cannot reconcile themselves to joining the SED. We represent their interests." How the LDPD does this remained a mystery to me despite Puschke's protracted effort to explain it between soup, steak and chocolate sundae. The concept of free political parties representing certain points of view and competing with one another for power was completely foreign to him. "Once the class struggle has ended," Puschke insisted, "there is no reason for disagreement or political competition between parties. What should we disagree on? Why develop a political program of our own when we endorse this one?" Under the circumstances, I asked in response, "Why have different parties?" "Oh," said Puschke with audible resignation, "you just don't understand." Obviously I didn't. But I knew one thing. He sounded more like a carefully schooled SED hack than a representative of the party long considered East Germany's sole hope of opposition.

"Over the years they have just been worn down by pressure, blackmail and the lures of privilege," said Puschke's West German counterpart, Wolfgang Schollwer, press spokesman of the Free Democratic Party in Bonn, himself a refugee from the GDR and one of the LDPD's early organizers. "The Communists would stop at nothing to press the Liberals into conformity: threat, arrest, extortion, and bribery. In the beginning, men such as Manfred Gerlach, the LDPD's chairman, tried inner immigration. Today, like most other leaders of the party, he is a Communist. They all made their peace with Ulbricht and began to identify with the privileges they enjoyed. The longer they remained in East Germany the more reluctant they became to leave. With a calculating eye they weighed the disadvantages of an uncertain political future with the FDP in the West against the advantages of prestige and the raiments of power as members of East Germany's élite. Of course many did flee. Some 45,000 LDPD members escaped to the West between 1949 and 1961 and that's almost half the FDP's membership today. Those who remained behind, however, sold out. Proportionately you will find more genuine individualists, liberals, and humanists in the SED than in the LDPD or any of the other parties."

The careers of non-Communist East German politicians have been likened to those of girls of easy virtue. First they did it for their own enjoyment, then for the enjoyment of others, finally for the money.

Today each of the GDR's four non-Communist parties is represented in the 434-member Volkskammer with forty-five deputies. Until July 1967, when for the first time in a national election the number of candidates exceeded the number of vacancies, deputies were elected from unity lists in an "ivory pure" sham of democracy. Voters had essentially five choices: to approve the whole slate; to reject it; to fill out their ballot in public view; to take it, under hostile disapproving glances of election officials, to a polling booth clear across the room for a secret vote, or, to boycott the election.

The result invariably was the same: acclamatory unanimity. After months of propagandistic preparation intended to whip up enthusiasm, the participation rarely dropped below 98.8 percent of the eligible voters, 99.9 percent of whom indicated approval of Ulbricht's united front ticket. It was an electoral system endemic to all Communist countries ruled by a zealotic clique of ideologues who are convinced they alone possess the key to utopia. They impose their will on the reluctant masses until public skepticism —eradicated either through incessant propaganda or by palpable achievements—yields to assent.

For nearly two decades since last risking the test of public approval in October 1946, East Germany's rulers refused to deviate from this rite. Then, in the October 1965 municipal and district elections, voters, while not accorded a choice, were given more than just the right to echo. Following a pattern established earlier that year in Poland, the number of candidates exceeded vacancies by 20 percent. Though there was still no choice of parties but a unity slate proposed by the National Front, 250,000 names were proposed for the 204,407 village, city, county and district posts to be filled. However, the regime built enough safeguards into the system to insure that its favored candidates would be chosen. Victory did not go automatically to those winning the largest number of votes. Instead, it worked this way. If twenty city council seats had to be filled, the ballot would list twenty-four names —those preferred by the SED and the National Front at the top. Even if one of the four candidates at the bottom of the list won more votes than any of the top twenty, he would not be elected. Only if one of the privileged twenty received less than 50 percent of the total vote, would the reserve candidate move up a notch and into office.

Not an election, but a selection process, it served, in theory at least to eliminate the most unpopular officials. In practice it proved meaningless as only two of the 204,407 "preferred" candidates failed to attain the minimum 50 percent. A similar system was introduced for the 1967 Volkskammer election when 581 candidates campaigned for 434 seats.

Regardless of liberalization schemes, however, an East German election is largely (albeit not entirely) eyewash and a travesty on democratic procedure. The regime measures its popularity not by the number of votes it receives but by the percentage of the turnout, and officials cajole even the lame, the blind, and the infirm to the polls.

The obligation to vote is propagated as assiduously as the duty to produce, and usually the propaganda exhorting East Germans to do one or the other is inseparable. Signs on factory buildings will proclaim: "Our Contribution to the Election: Competition for higher efficiency!" For years, in fact, East German elections have been used as a whip to step up production and it was not unusual to see collective farm placards pledging the peasants to breed more pigs "in honor of the people's election."

If Ulbricht has turned election campaigns into levers for increasing production he has also found them convenient pretexts for turning yet more trained agitators loose on the public. Rally upon rally, discussion after discussion usually precede each election and attendance becomes virtually compulsory. But East Germany's rulers have also learned from the West how to make the business of politics more palatable to the disinterested myriads. Folk festivals, rivers of free beer, and chains of sausages, music, and visiting dignitaries usually accompany every rally. A Soviet cosmonaut is as indispensable as an oompah-pah band. In October 1965, for example, Aleksei Leonov, the first man to walk in space, brought his instant grin and public relations charm back to earth in East Berlin's Marx-Engels Platz. And with fellow Cosmonaut Pavel Belyayev, he soared through factories and schools, collective farms and shopping centers to whoop up enthusiasm. The space twins waltzed with wives of provincial leaders at dozens of "Cosmos Election Balls" and paraded through countless East German towns in motorcades. To make sure no one missed the commercial, Belyayev, in heavily accented German, would repeatedly proclaim: "And when you go to vote in a few days, remember to make your mark for peace and co-existence."

Yet, for all the spuriousness of the electoral system, most East Germans will deny energetically that they have been disenfranchised. "We exercise far more influence over our candidates and representatives than is generally believed in the West," an Eisenhüttenstadt foundry worker once told me emphatically. "We may not have a choice of parties but we know who the candidates are and they get a careful screening from everyone before they are finally selected. They have to answer questions, outline their views, explain their positions and tell about their past in countless meetings before they are confirmed on the ticket.

"In the Western democracies," he added, "what choice does the voter really have? He can pick between parties but does he have any influence on the candidates they have proposed to represent him? These are nominated by a party machine over which the members, not to mention the vast majority of voters, have no control. Ninety-nine times out of a hundred the voter won't know anything about the candidates when it is time to vote. The West jokes about our unity lists and national front. But believe me, plenty of people here prefer knowing all about the candidates before the election than having to choose between names which mean nothing and being represented by men and women over whom they have absolutely no leverage."

At the nomination level, choice plays a more influential role than is widely assumed. Candidates are nominated, by their parties and the various mass organizations, to the secretariat of the National Front whose election commission compiles the ticket. The parties and mass organizations enjoy considerable autonomy in drawing up their lists of nominees. In recent years, on both the local and national level, candidates who are likely to be popular and known in their respective areas have been chosen. Theoretically every East German citizen has the constitutional right to challenge each nominee, though in practice this prerogative has been used so rarely that there is no statistical evidence of it.

Following nomination by the National Front's election commission, candidates must meet the voters during hundreds of election rallies. The procedure is relatively democratic. Office seekers introduce themselves, present a brief declamation of principles, then face questions—often tricky and embarrassing. These assemblies have become genuine discussion forums where participants vent their complaints and pent-up emotions. For the regime they are a fairly reliable sounding board of sentiment. Invariably someone will ask why only old-age pensioners are permitted to travel to West Germany and just as invariably candidates and party officials will fire back with the old shibboleths about Bonn's revanchism. The preliminaries over, candidates will be asked about inadequate hygienic conditions in plants, local factories which have not fulfilled their plans, lack of safety precautions at work and shortages of consumer goods.

The younger the participants the more polemical the meeting is likely to get. East Germany's new generation, raised and attuned to the incessant din of the regime's upbeat propaganda, is imbued with a sense of self-confidence and hedges no criticism when it detects a hiatus between promise and fulfillment. Young voters objurgate local officials for not providing enough building materials to construct weekend cottages and fulminate against the authorities for lack of kindergartens and nurseries that enable wives to work and help pay for television sets, refrigerators, motorcycles, cars, and the other symbols of affluence for which East Germans yearn.

Even if the new election system has had little practical effect in giving East German voters a greater choice, it did induce candidates to try harder. In one Thuringian precinct for example, a candidate intended for the top slot on the list dropped to a reserve position because he had failed to attend a rally. In the same precinct, another man moved up several rungs because of the good speeches he gave.

Ulbricht's changes in the election procedure are significant—if more to the party than to the outside world. They have enabled the SED to rejuvenate the apparatus and provided the party with some reading of its popularity or lack of it. Election results indicated which candidates were especially disliked, and a vote below the upper nineties undoubtedly spelled a cloud in some-body's political future.

To provide for greater turnover in public office, a recently instituted ground rule requires that no more than two-thirds of the Volkskammer candidates may be incumbents. The regulation, however, is double-edged. Though it provides for more fluctuation and enables the SED to weed out political deadwood, it also enables the party to sidetrack those who are not fully tuned in on the hierarchy's wave length.

Even if the new electoral system is but a hesitant step toward real democracy, its significance should not be underestimated. With it the SED has finally ventured onto a patch of thin ice that previously was strictly tabu for Germany's Communists. The new electoral system originated in Poland: proof that the winds of change sweeping Eastern Europe cannot fail to influence the GDR eventually. Though for the time being, the Ulbricht regime will continue to refuse a democratic test of its legitimacy by means of real elections.

Despite electoral liberalization and irrespective of its constitution, which guarantees division of power, East Germany is today a sophisticated oligarchy in which the state plays a subordinate role to the party apparatus. In fact, the governmental machinery is circumscribed wholly by the will of the party. Government is but a transmission belt for SED policy, though the Communists have imbued it with an artificial aura of independence. Its role is mainly a technical, administrative one. Policy is determined elsewhere.

East Germany's highest organ is the Staatsrat (State Council) a twenty-six-man body created by the Volkskammer (Parliament) on September 12, 1960, just five days after the death of the GDR's first and last president, Wilhelm Pieck. Comprised of one chairman—Ulbricht—six deputy chairmen, sixteen members and one secretary it is a "collective head of state." Until its establishment, Ulbricht had been a deputy premier. Pieck's death left a representational vacuum into which Ulbricht obviously wanted to step. At the same time, he needed a tool of executive power which nominally at least, lay in the hands of Prime Minister Otto

Grotewohl. The State Council provided him with both. Its functions are not only representational, being a substitute for a national president, but political. It has the power to issue legally binding decrees, ratify all legislation passed by the Volkskammer and when that body is not in session, which is most of the time, the Staatsrat functions as a miniature parliament with legislative authority. As a joint executive and legislative body it provides Ulbricht, its chairman, with a trinity of power and prestige unmatched by few other Communist leaders. He is simultaneously president, leader of a miniature parliament and a super prime minister from whose office all legislation emanates and across whose desk all laws must pass for final approval. Ulbricht's six deputy chairmen have little other function than to provide East Germany with a democratic fig leaf of multi-party representation. They are, Willi Stoph, the GDR's premier (SED); Johannes Dieckmann, president (speaker) of the Volkskammer (LDPD); Manfred Gerlach, chairman of the LDPD; Gerald Götting, secretary general of the East German CDU; Heinrich Homann, deputy leader of the NDP; Hans Rietz, deputy chairman of the peasants' party (DBD).

The Ministerrat (Council of Ministers), despite its name, is not the equivalent of a cabinet. Its chairman, Stoph, is East Germany's head of government though his role is not comparable to that of a prime minister or the traditional German chancellor. Besides the chairman, the council consists of twelve deputy chairmen (seven of whom represent the SED, five the other parties) and twenty-six members among whom are such classical ministers as defense, interior, justice, and foreign affairs, as well as the heads of such varied departments as the Ministry for Electrotechnics and Electronics or the Workers Inspection Committee.

Both by makeup and function, the Council of Ministers is largely an executive body which operates not only such traditional government activities as defense, foreign affairs, education, justice, and public order, but the entire economy. A dozen of the council members are concerned exclusively with East Germany's diversified productive and economic processes so that actual government responsibilities, insofar as they have not been usurped by the party apparatus or the Council of State, are carried out by Stoph and his twelve deputies who form a presidium and meet, like any Western cabinet, at least once a week. The entire council usually convenes bimonthly.

Neither the council, nor its presidium determines government policy except in the practical economic sphere. With the exception of Stoph, who at fifty-four is the most popular of the GDR's top leaders, East Germany's "cabinet members" enjoy the trappings of power. But they are merely field-grade officers in a complicated chain of command where the real orders emanate somewhere else: in the Politburo chamber of SED party headquarters.

The "Political Bureau of the Central Committee of the Socialist Unity Party" is a camarilla of fifteen members and six candidates who are the arbiters of East German life. Though their word is law, they concern themselves more with the general course which East German life will take than with day to day decisions of a practical nature. They determine East Germany's foreign policy and decide on questions dealing with German reunification. They set the ideological course, an area that includes literature, the arts and education. The Politburo exercises complete control over all those organs which secure its own power: the National People's Army (NVA), the People's Police (*Volkspolizei—Vopo*) and the State Security Service (SSD—*Staatssicherheitsdienst*). Finally, the Politburo regulates the pace of East German socialization.

Formally its members are equals, but some are more equal than others. Premier Willi Stoph, for example, has more influence than either Erich Mückenberger, fifty-seven, party chief for Frankfurt on the Oder district; Paul Fröhlich, fifty-four, SED boss of the Leipzig district; Horst Sindermann, fifty-two, the first secretary of the SED in Halle, or Friedrich Ebert, seventy-three, the fleshy, intemperately indolent son of Weimar Germany's first president, who, until he retired in July 1967, reigned in Wilhelminian splendor as mayor of East Berlin. The word of Kurt Hager, fifty-five, the party's chief ideologist, carries more weight than that of Herbert Warnke, sixty-five, head of East Germany's

trade unions (FDGB) which in twenty-two years have never
called a strike and never attempted to win their members a raise.
Vitriolic but brilliant Albert Norden, sixty-three, a Silesian
rabbi's son and the GDR's chief propagandist, is more intelligent
than seventy-four-year-old Hermann Matern, the only member to
have survived Ulbricht's purges and apostasies in the party line,
or Paul Verner, fifty-six, the colorless SED pro-consul of East
Berlin. Clearly, the two newest and youngest members—industrial expert Günter Mittag, forty-one, and Gerhard Grueneberg,
forty-six, the agricultural czar—know a lot more about economics
than hapless Alfred Neumann, a fifty-eight-year-old carpenter who
has rotated in and out of the chairmanship of the State Planning
Commission as if he were stuck in the wings of a revolving door.
Over them all are Ulbricht, the first secretary of the SED's
Central Committee and his heir apparent, fifty-five-year-old Erich
Honecker who, without a position in either state or government,
is unquestionably East Germany's second most powerful man
today.

Once a week, at 11 A.M. each Tuesday, a fleet of black, ostentatiously chromed Tchaika and Tatra limousines brings these men
to SED party headquarters on the Werderscher Markt—a bom-
bastic, thirty-year-old gray building, once the seat of the German
Reichsbank. There they map out the road East Germany will take.

They reach their decisions in much the way a jury arrives at a
verdict. Discussion lasts until unanimity has been achieved. In
view of Ulbricht's reputation for breaking dialectical endurance
records, more often than not the final concord reflects his preconceived notions.

Promulgating and translating the Politburo's resolutions into
action and law is the duty of the government and the ten secre-
taries of the SED Central Committee, all but one of whom are
in turn full or candidate members of the Politburo. The secretariat
is the party's executive arm. Headed by Ulbricht, the first secretary, it is the party's actual instrument of might. Each of the sec-
retaries is in charge of a technical or specialized department. For
example: Grueneberg, runs the Bureau of Agriculture; Hager,
the Commission for Ideology; Honecker, is the secretary for se-

curity questions; Mittag, heads the Bureau for Industry; Norden, is chief of the Commission for Agitation; Werner Jarowinsky, is Secretary of Trade and Supply, and Hermann Axen, secretary responsible for international Communist affairs.

In addition to the Politburo and Secretariat, the party has a fourteen-member Central Control Commission, headed by Matern, to counteract anti-partyism, corruption, careerism and misuse of authority.

In theory, all three—the Politburo, the Secretariat, and the Control Commission—are responsible to the Central Committee, a plenum of 131 full and 50 candidate members which meets two to three times yearly and is, nominally at least, the party's legislature and highest authority between quadriannual SED congresses. Its members, besides all of the Politburo, leading government officials, educators, artists, writers, captains of industry and agriculture, include atom spy Klaus Fuchs, who is now the father of atomic research in the GDR, and Gerhart Eisler, the chief of East German radio, who made headlines in the U.S. in 1949 when he jumped bail on a contempt of Congress charge and fled the U.S. aboard a Polish ship. In practice, the Central Committee is more an acclamatory sounding board for the line laid down by the top. The SED practices "democratic centralism." The party's leadership is elected from below but once in power it has complete authority. Their decisions and policies are in turn binding on the lower echelons and the SED's 1,700,000 members.

It is erroneous, therefore, to assume that the SED's tightly-knit collective leadership makes decisions and sets policies in an atmosphere of autarchic isolation. Some semblance of control from below and a measure of democratic influence, no matter how perfunctory it may seem, is always at work. But it is the personality and the style of the top politbureaucrats which set the criteria of East German life. These men, are, for the most part, apparatchiks par excellence, formed and influenced by decades of cloistered neo-theocratic rule and ideological rumination.

CHAPTER III

Profiles in Lability

"What do you want to be when you grow up, Hans?" a teacher in a Leipzig primary school asked one of his pupils. "I want to be First Secretary of the Socialist Unity Party, Chairman of the Security Council and Chairman of the Council of State," replied the tousle-headed nine-year-old without so much as a blush. "Your plans are rather ambitious," said the teacher, gulping with astonishment. "I hope you realize that to become all that you must have a lot of capabilities. For example, you'll have to be capable . . ." "I know," the boy interrupted. "Like my daddy said, 'You have to be capable of everything.'"

And Walter Ulbricht, East Germans are convinced, is capable of just about everything and anything.

Seldom has a ruler been so powerful and at once so ridiculed by his subjects, rarely has a politician been so vilified by his detractors and so adulated by his adherents, hardly ever has a man striven so assiduously for a favorable image only to find himself interminably underrated and the brunt of ultimate derision.

Ulbricht jokes, though they abound like pebbles on a beach, are the condiments of East German life. And scarce is the conversation during which someone—looking furtively over his shoulder to spot a potential eavesdropper—does not produce a new Ulbricht *Witz* or retread version of an old one.

There's the one about the day the devil came knocking on the Pearly Gates. "What do *you* want here?" St. Peter asked, "Ulbricht," said Satan, "has just arrived in hell and I'm the first refugee." Or there's the perennial story of Ulbricht, the obsequious lackey of the Kremlin, who has invited a comrade into his office to decorate him with a Hero of Labor medal. Honored and at the same time curious, the worker looked around, then pointed to a telephone on the SED chief's desk and asked: "What kind of a phone is that, Comrade Ulbricht? It has a receiver but no microphone." "Oh that," said Ulbricht disinterestedly, "that's the hotline to Moscow."

Thanks to Western propaganda, his own bumbling ways in public, his legendary sycophancy, his Machiavellian reputation, and the maladroitness of his own public relations, Ulbricht has been portrayed as the Devil incarnate and a bumbling fool, as a homeless, unpatriotic international bureaucrat of Communism and a cunning tyrant intent upon the enslavement of his subjects.

Avuncular-looking, paunchy, unimaginative and hyperorthodox, Walter Ulbricht is actually none of these. At worst he is a sly survivor of Stalinism with an uncanny weathervane nose for winds of change from Moscow and remarkable agility in keeping just ahead of them. At best he is a diligent, tenacious, even zealous administrator of above-average intelligence with a machine politician's aptitude for the strategy of power.

Ulbricht is as petit bourgeois as the doilies which adorn his living-room sofa. He is as uninspiring as socialist realism in art. And he is as puritanical as his ten Commandments of Socialist Morality which preach, among other things: thou shalt love thy fatherland . . . thou shalt perform good deeds for socialism . . . thou shalt protect and multiply public property . . . thou shalt help to eliminate exploitation of man by man . . . thou shalt strive to improve your efficiency, live frugally, and strengthen the discipline of socialist labor . . . and thou shalt live a clean and decent life and respect thy family.

Ulbricht is ruthless but not merciless. Though he has purged his Politburo and Central Committee of nearly all the men and women who accompanied him from exile in Moscow, not one has been physically liquidated, only a handful were jailed and the majority were quietly and unceremoniously shunted to lesser posts where they lead unmolested but unglamorous lives.

He is tough and obstinate, preferring, whenever possible, to outtalk and outmaneuver rather than outrank his dissenters and recusants. But he totally lacks imagination and distrusts intellect as much as he abhors innovation.

He is no rabble-rouser and totally ineffectual as a demagogue. On a public platform, on radio or television his high-pitched eunuch-like voice, mixed with the flat, dissonant dialect of Leipzig, instead of exaltation, evokes only revulsion and snickers. During World War II, as a Communist radio propagandist charged with inducing Wehrmacht soldiers to surrender and defect, Ulbricht was so ineffectual that the comrades induced him to leave the front lines and return to Moscow for the work he knew best: administration and manipulation. Ulbricht's voice and burlesque accent have given rise to what East Germans facetiously call a new unit of time: the ulb. It measures how long it takes for a hand to reach out and switch off the set after the first sound of his voice on radio or television. This probably makes Ulbricht the longest-least-listened-to speaker in the world. An Ulbricht dissertation is likely to last five to eight hours—so no wonder he is hoarse.

Physically, Ulbricht is a cartoonist's delight. With his balding head, gray mustache and goatee, his rimless glasses perched schoolmasterly on his nose, his tightly buttoned suit jackets, slipped chest and stiff-necked propriety, he looks like anyone's grandfather and his own best caricature. Yet, there is in his narrow, humorless pale blue eyes a glint which once prompted Clara Zetkin, the *grande dame* of German Communism, to say of Ulbricht, her desk neighbor during one session of the Reichstag: "May fate prevent him from ever rising to the top of the party. Look into his eyes and see how conniving and dishonest he is." His Leninist beard is the brunt of even more jokes than his voice. East Germans, who derisively call him the *"Spitzbart,"* delight in telling the one when Ulbricht went for a haircut, fell asleep in the chair and awoke startled to discover that the barber had also shaved off his beard. "Man, you're crazy," Ulbricht screamed. "That beard was the last remnant of Leninism in the party."

For all the malevolent ribbing it causes him, Ulbricht is neither embarrassed by nor reluctant to talk about his goatee. "This beard," he once told an interviewer of *Junge Welt,* the official organ of the FDJ, the Free German Youth organization, "was grown in the battle against fascism. Back in 1933 when the Nazis took power and we Communists went underground, I had to have a disguise to escape the Gestapo. I am proud of it. Konrad Adenauer never grew a beard, probably because he didn't have to. He was not a threat to the Nazis. Now, if you want to know more about the beard, let me tell you that I intend to shave it off on the day peace and the will of the people triumph in West Germany as well, the day a really democratic, nonaggressive unified Germany has been forged." Good as the story sounds, it is not true. If Ulbricht had a beard in the early 1930s, he subsequently shaved it off and did not grow it again until 1944—when in Moscow.

For propagandists Ulbricht is a barn-side target. He has been equated with Hitler and accused of having been a pimp and brothel keeper—the one a malicious distortion, the other a spiteful lie which emanates from his having been raised in Leipzig's red-light district. But for all his obvious failings—his craftily eel-like rise to power, his cunning navigation through the reefs of Stalinism, his autarchic control of people, party and state—Ulbricht is no mere footnote to either German or Communist history. He has already been in power longer than either Adolf Hitler or Konrad Adenauer, his regime has endured longer than the entire Weimar Republic or Third Reich, and soon, if fate is kind to him, he will have ruled as many years as Bismarck. In the precarious world of Communism, Ulbricht is one of those rare anomalies—a leader who has been in uninterrupted power since the days of Stalin. A Red elder-statesman, he has outlasted all but Tito, Albania's Enver Hoxa, Ho Chi-minh, and Mao Tse-tung.

Walter Ulbricht was born June 30, 1893, in a bleak tenement on Leipzig's dismal Gottsched Strasse, the first of three children of Ernst Ulbricht, a hard-working but mendicant and frequently tippled tailor, and his pretty but sickly wife, Pauline.

Though his father was a craftsman, not a laborer—thus by German standards a member of the petit bourgeoisie, not the proletariat—Ulbricht's parents were usually so poor that the distinction is academic. Both were ardent, militant Socialists and virtually from birth fed him heaping spoonfuls of Marxism. Ulbricht thrived on that diet. As soon as he started school he was nick-named "Red" and spent his free time reading editorials in the daily *Leipziger Volkszeitung* plus tomes far too weighty for his age.

For his future career as a professional Marxist, Ulbricht could not have been born in a more suitable town. Leipzig was the cradle of the German workers' movement. There in 1863 Ferdinand Lassalle and his apostles founded the Allgemeiner Deutscher Arbeiterverein—the German Working Men's Associa-tion. Two years later August Bebel and Wilhelm Liebknecht or-ganized the Social Democratic Party there and Rosa Luxemburg learned the rudiments of propaganda, as an editor on the *Volks-zeitung*.

Like most German children of his class, Ulbricht left school at 14 to learn a trade: cabinetmaking. Though he was shy and unpolished, Ulbricht was neither weak nor stupid. When he be-gan his apprenticeship he joined the Young Workingmen's Edu-cational Association as well as an Arbeiter Turnverein (a working men's gymnastic club).

Ulbricht has remained an addict of learning and sports to this day. He is forever exhorting his subjects to improve themselves. East Germany's model educational system as well as the quest for knowledge which has convulsed the country like a brush fire, are largely the result of his efforts. Ulbricht does calisthenics every morning, he is an avid swimmer and a passable skier, he took up tennis at the age of fifty-seven, and he and his wife Lotte boast of their prowess at ping-pong. Of all the GDR's achievements, Ulbricht is proudest of its pre-eminence in the world of sports. East Germany won 53 medals in the last three Olympic Games and holds 145 world and 47 European championships. Easy as it may be to discount these achievements as typical of autocratic regimes, all of which emphasize and further sports as a means for influencing youth, I am inclined to believe the GDR's particu-lar passion for *Turnen* and athletics is at least as much a reflection of its leader's only real hobby as it is a German phenomenon. *Turnvater* Friedrich Ludwig Jahn's nineteenth-century rational

] Berlin: Brandenburg Gate and Wall from eastern side at night. (Credit: John
ornberg) [All photos are by the author, John Dornberg, unless otherwise noted.]

] Ulbricht and members of Politburo making rounds of Leipzig fair (September
'65). From l. to r. Ulbricht (with hat and coat), Alfred Neumann, Premier Willi
oph, Paul Froehlich, Guenther Mittag (behind Froehlich in 2nd row), Werner
rowinsky (behind Mittag in third row) and Erich Honecker (in front row next to
oehlich). (Credit: Zentralbild)

[3] Ulbricht receiving flowers from glee club members during celebration of twentieth anniversary of East German school reform. (Credit: Zentralbild)

[4] Top East German officials making rounds of Leipzig fair in fall of 1963. Standing with tall man on left: Alfred Neumann, Willi Stoph, former foreign trade minister Julius Balkow, and Guenther Mittag (at far right). (Credit: Zentralbild)

5] Albert Norden (second from right), party's chief agitator and propagandist, alking with workers at Jena optical plant during 1967 election campaign. (Credit: entralbild)

6] Erich Honecker (left) during FDJ (Free German Youth) congress in May 1967. Credit: Zentralbild)

[7] Ulbricht and SED ideologist Prof. Kurt Hager during discussion with directors of workers' club houses in Dresden, June 1967. Ulbricht on far right, Hager next to him. (Credit: Zentralbild)

revival movement through organized gymnastic associations has left an indelible mark on both sides of the Elbe.

Despite his radical upbringing, Ulbricht's teenage life followed stodgy Wilhelminian patterns. On completion of his apprenticeship, at seventeen, he set out to see the world as a journeyman. With walking stick, rucksack, and Tyrolean hat he and some friends tramped through Italy, Switzerland, and Austria, taking work where they could get it.

For all the revolutionary thoughts that may have scurried through his head, it was a good time in Europe and radicalism was not much in demand. The Kaiser was at the pinnacle of his power, Bismarck's shrewd social legislation had taken most of the wind out of the Socialist sails. Germany was finally united and stronger than at any time in its history. Complacency was the order of the day.

By 1912, when he was nineteen and had joined the Social Democratic Party, all this had already reached the threshold of upheaval. The empires were beginning to get restless and on the distant horizon the thunderheads of war had begun to form. Ulbricht's career in the party of his father was both short and tempestuous. In 1914, when the SPD Reichstag faction, instead of practicing its sermons of international brotherhood, voted war credits to the Kaiser, Ulbricht joined the dissident, radical Liebknecht group which spawned Germany's militant Spartacus league and the Communist Party.

Ulbricht, drafted in 1915, had an undistinguished military career that included two courts-martial: one early in 1918 for deserting, a second in October for distributing Bolshevist propaganda.

His rise in the German Communist Party, whose inaugural meeting he attended in 1919, was steady though unspectacular. As Carola Stern put it in her brilliant biography of Ulbricht: "In the KPD he found an instrument for explaining the world, and once he had grasped it, never let go. Here is the reason why he abandoned Social Democracy to become a Communist. The Social Democrats would have forced him to measure his ideology against reality. The Communists permitted him, even exhorted him, to cling to dogma. It is a party which would lose its *raison d'être* once it departed from the Marxian view of the world as it presented itself in 1910." Ulbricht climbed the rungs of power through persistence, diligence and cunning, not brilliance or demagogic flair. In fact, his comrades found his platform manner so dull and dry that they nicknamed him "Blockhead." He was valued most for his talents as an organizer and his code name Genosse Zelle (Comrade Cell) derived from his expertise at underground political warfare requiring the fragmentation of larger party units into tightly knit, more easily controllable cells.

In 1924 he attended the Lenin School in Moscow, and as a Comintern agent went to Austria to work as a propagandist—a career cut short by arrest and deportation. In 1926 he entered the Saxonian state legislature and in 1928, the year his brother Erich emigrated to the United States (he lives in New York; sister Hildegard in West Germany) Ulbricht was elected to the Reichstag where he held a seat until Hitler came to power in 1933. By 1929 Ulbricht was political boss of the KPD in Berlin-Brandenburg. In 1931 Germany's highest court convicted him of treason but his parliamentary immunity saved him from having to serve the two-year term. In October 1933 Ulbricht, by then a member of the KPD's Politburo, emigrated, worked for the Comintern and the exiled German party in Czechoslovakia, France, Spain, and Sweden until he arrived in Moscow in 1938. When the Germans invaded Russia in June 1941, Ulbricht took charge of re-education of German prisoners of war, visited the front numerous times in the uniform of a Soviet colonel and was one of the key organizers of the National Committee for a Free Germany. By the time he landed at Calau with his nine loyal aides on April 30, 1945, Ulbricht had risen to the top pinnacles of power in the exiled German Communist Party. Most of his rivals had either fallen victim to Hitler's SS, Stalin's purges, or old age. Ulbricht was second only to Wilhelm Pieck, the party's nominal leader who at nearly seventy was already too old to exercise effective control.

There is no end to speculation about Ulbricht's ability to survive Stalinist excesses or about the role he played in the arrest of Ernst Thälmann, the KPD's chief, who was discovered in a hideaway by the Gestapo in March 1933, then spent eleven years in Nazi prisons and concentration camps until SS guards at Buchenwald murdered him in 1944.

Even if one dismisses as spiteful rumor the charge of some ex-Communists that Ulbricht himself tipped off the Gestapo to Thälmann's hideout, the fact remains that Ulbricht hardly waited for the cell doors to clank shut on his former boss before he began maneuvering to succeed him. Nor did he try very hard to free him when opportunity beckoned.

Three chances to spring Thälmann were scuttled by the KPD itself. Ulbricht's role, as leader of the German Communists in Paris and later in Moscow, if difficult to document, remains suspect. The first came when a Berlin lawyer, in return for a promised fee of $25,000, persuaded SS Chief Heinrich Himmler to agree to Thälmann's release on condition that he would refrain from all activity against the Hitler government and that the German Communists in Paris cease demanding a public trial of Thälmann. The Paris-based KPD turned down the offer. Thälmann was more useful as a martyr than free. On another occasion, twenty-four hours before Communist agents were to liberate Thälmann with the help of a prison guard, orders came from Paris countermanding the escape attempt. The KPD said it feared a Gestapo trap. In 1939, when German Foreign Minister Joachim von Ribbentrop flew to Moscow to sign the Hitler-Stalin pact, he was prepared to deliver Thälmann to the Russians as a goodwill gesture. Though the Russians obtained the release of a number of other Communists from the Germans, they never asked for Thälmann.

That Ulbricht survived to become the party's leader is due to luck, attrition, and his uncanny ability to outmaneuver all rivals. Of the nine men elected to the 1935 Politburo-in-exile, only one—Ulbricht—remains in power today. Besides Thälmann, who was murdered by the Nazis, three died of natural causes, three were eventually purged by Ulbricht and now live in obscurity in East Germany. The ninth, Herbert Wehner, quit Communism, and subsequently became vice-chairman of the West German Social Democratic Party and Bonn's Minister for All-German Affairs.

Rumors abound that Ulbricht himself escaped Stalinist terror by delivering his rivals into the hands of the secret police, but there is only sketchy evidence of this. More likely, he survived because he arrived in Moscow in 1938 after the *tshistka* had passed its peak and because of his ideological ambidexterity that enabled him to avoid the reefs of doctrinal controversy on which hundreds of German exiles foundered.

Certainly he avoided danger. As early as the 1920s, then during his years in Moscow, and later in his role as Stalin's proctor in occupied Germany, Ulbricht never defied the Kremlin. This hardly speaks for his intrepidity, but it is indicative of his shrewdness. Walter Ulbricht is no man's fool and it is erroneous to conclude from his ostensible behavior that he has ever intentionally subordinated German Communist interests to Moscow's. Many Germans say and have convinced themselves that in his exile Ulbricht became more Russian (he had Soviet citizenship) than German. Even when he looked and acted like the Kremlin's lackey, however, he remained Prussian at heart and many of his actions had no other purpose than to serve what he thought, rightly or wrongly, was best for Germany. He is above all an astute strategist and what may have appeared on the surface to be capitulation to Soviet power was but a ruse to enable him to fight some other day.

It was Ulbricht, for example, who first encouraged his young pragmatists to cheat the Soviets on deliveries in 1964 and 1965 so the GDR could have additional raw materials with which to expand non-Communist trade. When the Russians discovered this deception, Ulbricht reverted to character. He left his economic protégés to fend for themselves and face Soviet inquisitors in Moscow while he embarked on a triumphant goodwill tour of Siberia. Conversely, he had no compunctions about tying East German industry closer to the Soviet Union in 1966 when, as he believed, this would make Moscow dependent on East German deliveries and less inclined to sell out the GDR's interests to the West in the Soviet-American effort to relax the cold war. Soviet dependence achieved, Ulbricht did not hesitate to make another pilgrimage to Moscow in an effort to loosen the reins so his industrialists could look toward the West once more. Nor is he all as Stalinist as more perfunctory portraits indicate. Ulbricht is a Stalinist in tactics, not ideology. He himself launched East Germany's de-Stalinization—when it benefited him—all the while using Stalinist methods to pursue his aims. East Germany's economism, if not Ulbricht's invention, was inaugurated with his blessings. Odd as it may seem, the threats to his power since early 1966 have emanated from the SED's genuine Stalinists whose leader, Leipzig party boss Paul Fröhlich, is an incurable apostle of ruthless class warfare. To these men Ulbricht appears a revisionist. As yet they are no real challenge to his power and it is doubtful they ever will be. Nevertheless, to checkmate them Ulbricht has had to soft-pedal pragmatism and crank up the worn-out machine of dogmatism again.

Walter Ulbricht is a politician skilled in the use of power. He employs it as Mao Tse-tung does guerrilla warfare. He respects might and avoids conflict when confronted with it, preferring to consolidate his own forces and wait to fight on more opportune occasions. Once he knows the advantage is on his side, he strikes back fast. This has been characteristic for all his major battles.

In the party's *day-to-day* operations, however, he has proven less circumspect. At first Ulbricht will try to outtalk opposition and his reputation for this is legendary. But when he feels matters might get out of hand, he is quick to draw the line, quash all discussion and impose his will with a display of authority.

Ulbricht was always shrewd enough to make many important decisions himself, later presenting them to the Politburo as faits accomplis. He did not even inform Wilhelm Pieck, for example, that East Germany's army was being equipped with Soviet tanks —an omission that caused Hermann Matern to remark sarcastically: "Well, I just hope Walter will let us know when we are at war."

Even in private gatherings Ulbricht's authority is undisputed. His appearance at social gatherings, despite efforts to be jocular, freezes the atmosphere. One high official poignantly described the effect of Ulbricht's arrival at Erich Honecker's birthday party some years ago. "We were about ten or twelve people in Erich's very modern apartment. We had eaten well and drunk too much, were dancing and telling jokes. The spirit was almost Western. Honecker, who was pretty tight, was railing and ranting against just about everything in the SED, especially the cadre training methods. It was about 11 P.M.—we had just started playing blindman's buff—when the doorbell rang and in stepped Walter Ulbricht. The atmosphere curdled. I'll never forget how one of the FDJ leaders stood there in the middle of the room, blindfolded and dumfounded as silence settled over the group. We felt like little kids caught with their hands in the cookie jar. Ulbricht didn't feel at ease either. He tried desperately to get things started again, insisted that we keep right on dancing. The record player was turned on, Ulbricht danced with every woman. But the spirit was gone. Even when he tried to get the game going once more, it didn't help. We were almost paralyzed and I still don't know why. He is just one of those human beings whose very presence robs the atmosphere of gaiety. When he finally left, about midnight, the old spirit came back immediately."

Some Communists who know him say his aloofness is deliberate. The majority, however, are convinced that it is the result of the inferiority complexes he developed as a youth. Whatever the case, no matter how hard he tries, he can never be accepted as an equal among equals. His inability to establish rapport with other people, his reputation for autocracy, make him always—on duty and off—the feared first secretary who would brook no opposition.

In Ulbricht's quest for ultimate power, luck and fate have often been his companions. The Tito-Stalin break in 1948 gave him the first opportunity to purge the SED of its less tractable and docile elements: those Social Democrats who resented Communist hegemony and those Communists who had spent the Nazi era in concentration camps or Western exile and had refused to truckle to the Russians. Ulbricht either shelved or expelled them from the party, some fled to the West. Relatively few were jailed.

Only twice have Ulbricht's authority and control been seriously challenged. Both attempts, one in 1953, the other in 1956–58, failed.

Stalin's death in 1953 brought not only a new course to Moscow but Soviet backing for a group of Ulbricht's lieutenants intending to overthrow him. It is the greatest irony of East German history and Ulbricht's career that he was saved by a rebellion aimed at toppling him and that he defied the Russians for the first and only time by clinging to Stalinism right after Stalin died. Had East Germans known Moscow's plans for Ulbricht before they went on the streets to riot on June 17, 1953, they would probably have had a new, moderate leadership before the month was out. As it happened, Ulbricht's position was strengthened.

When Stalin died in March 1953, Georgi Malenkov and Russia's other leaders promulgated a "new course" of moderation with the emphasis on consumer goods production and a better life. They admonished the satellites to do the same and on April 15 specifically instructed Ulbricht and the SED to halt forced socialization of East Germany and reverse the hard line the GDR had pursued. Ulbricht may have been unwilling to betray Stalin's legacy. More likely, he expected the new leadership to be supplanted soon by more orthodox hard liners such as Vyacheslav M. Molotov, the long-time heir apparent. Whatever his motivations, he defied the Kremlin and turned the screws in East Germany even tighter. The country seethed with the spirit of revolt. Moscow was appalled and the SED Politburo was incensed.

Ulbricht's two chief rivals, Wilhelm Zaisser of Spanish Civil War "General Gomez" fame, then chief of the GDR's secret police, and Rudolf Herrnstadt, editor of *Neues Deutschland*, prepared to overthrow him. On June 5, Vladimir Semenov, the Soviet High Commissioner for East Germany, returned to East Berlin from Moscow with orders for Ulbricht to make an about-face in his policies. Comrade Cell proved truculent. Semenov began working with Herrnstadt and Zaisser who had the backing of Soviet Secret Police Chief Lavrenti Beria.

Zaisser and Herrnstadt drafted a political platform calling for sweeping reforms and distributed copies to those leaders from whom they expected support. The program envisaged Ulbricht's replacement by Herrnstadt as Secretary General. Zaisser was to take over the interior ministry. They proposed an extensive purge of the "degenerate SED apparatus" and hoped to make the party more palatable to the people. As Carola Stern put it: "While Ulbricht counted on such men as Molotov and Kaganovich to win the battle for Stalin's succession, Zaisser and Herrnstadt banked on Malenkov and Beria. The power struggle in Berlin was but a reflection of the battle in Moscow."

Hermann Matern, loyal to Ulbricht then and now, found out about Zaisser's and Herrnstadt's document, and demanded that it be presented to the Politburo. On June 16, while the first demonstrations against the high work norms were already taking place among the construction workers on Stalin Allee, the hierarchs, with Semenov attending, met behind closed doors. Of its fourteen full and candidate members, four were resolutely on Zaisser's and Herrnstadt's side: Anton Ackermann, once the apostle of an "independent" German road to socialism; his ex-wife Elli Schmidt; Hans Jendretzky, a veteran party member who had spent the Hitler era in concentration camps, and Heinrich Rau, the deputy premier. On Ulbricht's side were only two: Matern and Honecker. The others waited to see who would win, though the consensus of sympathy was with Zaisser and Herrnstadt. Several times messengers came in to report on mounting rebellion in the streets and about workers who wanted to speak to Ulbricht. After hours of haggling Ulbricht compromised and agreed to reduce the work norms. That evening he spoke at a hastily called meeting of party leaders in Berlin's *Friedrichstadtpalast* Theater where he identified himself with the new course. But by then it was too late. The city was seething and by the morning of June 17 the workers' demonstrations had turned into an insurrection which spread across the country. The Soviets stepped in to crush it. Ulbricht had been saved by a twist of fate. In the face of rebellion the Russians had to support him. On July 9, when Zaisser's and Herrnstadt's mentor, Beria, was arrested, their fall was imminent. They were expelled from the party and all public offices. Purged with them were a half dozen other top leaders, among them justice minister Max Fechner, Ackermann, Jendretzky, and Elli

Schmidt. Only Fechner—until 1946 a Social Democrat, not a Communist—was jailed as an "enemy of the state and the party." Amnestied in 1956, readmitted to the SED in 1958, formally rehabilitated in 1966, he is now in retirement. Zaisser died in 1958 at age sixty-five. Herrnstadt is today a researcher in the East German Archives. The others have all been rehabilitated although only Jendretzky made it back as far as the Central Committee.

For Ulbricht the Zaisser-Herrnstadt affair also provided an excellent opportunity for checkmating Franz Dahlem, his most serious rival for the party's leadership. Dahlem, eighteen months older than Ulbricht, had risen just as fast in the party but, unlike Ulbricht, he spent the Hitler era in concentration camps, not Moscow. After the war he was the only real and legitimate contender for Ulbricht's control of the KPD. To sidetrack him Ulbricht implicated Dahlem as a conspirator with Noel Field, a Quaker who was labeled a Communist agent in the U.S., an American spy behind the Iron Curtain. The charges were as phony as the whole Field case but sufficed for sidetracking Dahlem who was deposed from the Politburo in May 1953 for "political blindness in dealing with imperialistic American agents." Several months later Dahlem was also expelled from the Central Committee, but by 1956 he had been reinstated. Today his rehabilitation is complete though Dahlem's influence, as Deputy Undersecretary for Universities and Technical Schools in the ministry of education, is negligible.

Whatever the motives of the men who have tried to depose him, Ulbricht has succeeded in trumping them by consistently following the rule of divide and conquer. Whenever a new anti-Ulbricht spearhead took shape, older, defeated challengers were given a chance at rehabilitation by denouncing the new ones. In 1953, Karl Schirdewan, then forty-six, and one of the fastest-rising stars in the party, helped Ulbricht depose Dahlem. Schirdewan was rewarded with a Politburo seat. Five years later, when Schirdewan, by then Ulbricht's heir apparent, had put himself at the head of a group trying to liberalize East Germany, Ulbricht called on Dahlem who obediently condemned

Schirdewan's "factionalism" as a crime against the party. Schirdewan was deposed and Dahlem rehabilitated.

The "Schirdewan affair" was the second and last serious challenge to Ulbricht's supremacy. It began in 1956, shortly after Nikita Khrushchev criticized Stalin at the Soviet Union's XXth Communist Party congress, and lasted, like a protracted agony, until January 1958.

Khrushchev's degradation of Stalin touched off widespread intellectual unrest in East Germany just as it did elsewhere in the Soviet bloc. Party members, long resentful of Ulbricht's rigid dogmatism and chafing under his cast iron grip on the SED, clamored for de-Stalinization at home. Their restlessness was exacerbated by the spirit of liberalization spreading through neighboring Poland. As Moscow's winter thawed, opposition in East Berlin mounted: against the hard economic line and rigid centralism; against the irrefutability of codified ideology and the suppression of empiricism; against the propagation of the class struggle and last not least, against the implacability of the leadership itself.

Intellectuals and writers, students and professors, journalists and book publishers, Politburo liberals and the economic pragmatists—Communists all—flickered hopefully around these rays of a brighter socialist tomorrow. But in vain. Again fate—the Hungarian Revolution—interceded on Ulbricht's behalf.

For Ulbricht the spontaneity of these currents of liberalization was more dangerous than the ideas themselves, for his personal power depends on his ability to keep the party under control at all times and to suppress independent thought. This may breed mediocrity but in turn Ulbricht can promise his devotees protection from upheaval. Call it a kind of Communist feudalism, but it saved him on the day the guns began firing in Budapest. "If we loosen the reins the same thing will happen here," Ulbricht warned. Even the opponents agreed. They rallied to his support.

The challenge, however, had not passed and in late November Ulbricht decided to set an example of some of the intellectuals. He ordered the arrest of Dr. Wolfgang Harich, a brilliant young Marxist philosopher and editor of the East German *Journal of*

Philosophy; Bernhard Steinberger, an essayist and economist; Walter Janka, a director of Aufbau Verlag, East Germany's principal literary book publishing house, and several other intellectuals who were charged with attempting to overthrow the constitutional order of the GDR. Harich's real crime: to draft a program of reform communism which drew heavily on liberal ideas circulating in Poland. Harich was sentenced to ten years in prison, others in his group to terms of two to four years.

Among East German intellectuals the warning was heeded. But it made little impression on Ulbricht's opponents in the Politburo who continued to press for relaxation and a softer line. Because of the intra-party struggle in Moscow where Molotov and Kaganovich had challenged Khrushchev, East Berlin's politicians proved less tractable than the intellectuals. Ulbricht had to bide his time until January 1958 when he deposed not only his "crown prince" Schirdewan, but Ernst Wollweber, who had succeeded Zaisser as chief of the State Security Service (SSD), and Fred Oelssner, the Minister for Consumer Goods Distribution, on charges of "factionalism." Their aim had been to replace Ulbricht and inaugurate a general liberalization. Gerhard Ziller, the Central Committee's Secretary for Economic Questions, and the first of the pragmatists, was posthumously identified with the Schirdewan group. He had committed suicide several weeks earlier.

Like most of Ulbricht's victims, the members of the Schirdewan group have all been rehabilitated, though none has regained a position of power or influence. Schirdewan, now sixty, a highly ambitious and far from likable man, recanted and engaged in self-criticism. Since 1959 he has been director of the State Archives in Potsdam. Wollweber died in May 1967 at sixty-nine. Oelssner, sixty-three, is director of the East German Institute for Economic Science. Wolfgang Harich was released from prison after serving eight of his ten years and is now writing occasional reviews.

There have been other purges since 1958 and Ulbricht has had his troubles with both overly liberal and Stalinist factions. But his pre-eminence has never been seriously challenged again.

Though major purges have usually been accompanied by campaigns against lower echelons of the party these also rarely resulted in imprisonment. The economic penalties imposed on a man expelled from the party were often far more severe. Nevertheless, there are still political prisoners in the GDR. The exact number has never been determined, though in April 1967 Amnesty International estimated there were 6000 to 8000.

Ulbricht's relatively benign treatment of his political opponents is but one of his many paradoxes. Another is the contradiction between his private and public life. He is as strait-laced as a Babbitt. He does not smoke and to call him an occasional drinker is stretching the point. His living room is a replica of a petit-bourgeois parlor. He prefers simple, solid German food. His wife Lotte, a woman of humdrum taste and mean intelligence, is the incarnation of a German *Hausfrau*. To the surprise of fellow Communists, Ulbricht is not above meeting visitors at home in slippers and wool lounge jacket—the uniform of German *Kleinbürgertum*.

Until 1960 he and the party's top leaders lived on Majakowski Ring in the Berlin borough of Niederschönhausen. His was an austere, unpretentious one-family house, recognizable only by the candy-striped sentry hut adjacent to the garden gate. For reasons of security and prestige the East German hierarchs were resettled to Wandlitz, ten miles north of Berlin where a compound of twenty villas, stores, and recreational facilities had been built for them. The preserve, guarded by an electrified fence and a platoon of sentries and security agents, includes a swimming pool, restaurant, cinema, library, supermarket, and beauty parlor.

Legends about its opulence and grandeur, though titillating are vastly exaggerated. It is probably true that an entire railroad car full of Carrara marble was brought from Italy for bathrooms and flooring, and that Grotewohl's house was furnished with $300,000 worth of imported antiques. But Grotewohl, after all, was the premier of East Germany. Ulbricht, on the other hand, had but one special request for his twelve-room villa: Chinese silk wallpaper in the living room.

For all his Philistine ways, Ulbricht is not averse to luxury or privileges when offered. In 1961 he ordered construction of a country estate that serves him and Lotte as a vacation retreat, when it is not used as a secret conference site or for official state receptions. The two-story, 25-room château with landscaped gardens, a rifle range, volleyball court, gymnasium, and boat landing on the shores of a lake north of Berlin, is within shouting distance of what was once Hermann Göring's presumptuous residence: Karinhall. The house features such non-proletarian status symbols as heated marble flooring, bulletproof windows, and an auditorium-sized ballroom whose crystal chandeliers—made in the GDR—cost $250,000.

Despite two marriages and one affair, his relations with women border on the incidental. His first wife was Martha Hauk, a young Communist. A year after their 1920 marriage, when Ulbricht became increasingly active in KPD politics, they hardly saw each other. In 1933, when he fled, he stopped only briefly in their 3½-room apartment on Leipzig's Geisslerstrasse, then disappeared. To Dennis Newson, Bonn correspondent for the *London Daily Sun*, who interviewed her in 1962, she admitted that she never expected to see him again and was shocked when he showed up after the war. Martha Hauk's and Ulbricht's only child, a daughter, Dorle, lives in West Germany, is married and the mother of two sons.

Divorced since 1951, the first Frau Ulbricht continues to live in the same apartment into which the couple moved after their wedding. She has a small pension and income from a boarder and seems resigned to the strange turn her life has taken. Occasionally she watches Ulbricht on TV. As she told Newson: "I don't like his beard. If we were still married I am sure I would have made him shave it off." Politics is the thing she is least interested in and most reluctant to talk about.

For all his finger-wagging morality, Ulbricht never took the vows of marriage too seriously. In the late 1920s he started an affair with Rose Michel, a young French Communist living in Germany. The romance soured by 1934 but the two remained on friendly terms—even in Moscow, at the Hotel Lux where Ulbricht roomed out of wedlock with his present wife, Lotte

Kuehn, herself married to a Communist official who had been shipped to Siberia as a victim of the Stalin purges. Rose Michel had a room right above Ulbricht's.

Veteran Communists claim that Lotte Ulbricht, ten years her husband's junior, had been making eyes at him in the early 1930s while employed as a secretary in a Berlin Communist Party office.

Just when the spark of love first flickered between Lotte and Walter no one seems to know. But in 1938, on his arrival in Moscow, Ulbricht moved right in with her. It was a curious arrangement. Ulbricht's own wife was in Leipzig, Lotte's husband in Siberia and Ulbricht's ex-girl friend Rose lived in a room one floor above. They married after his divorce in 1951, and while they may not necessarily be made for each other, some people quip they deserve each other. Intellectually they are no match. Frau Ulbricht's horizons are limited, but she loves, honors and obeys him, which is a good basis for any German marriage. Even Ulbricht's.

In recent years she has played to the hilt her role as the GDR's first lady—just as Ulbricht has taken to altering his image from feared party boss to patriarchal founder of his country. It is a role in which he is still not quite comfortable, although today, in his exalted position as chairman of the Staatsrat, a job created for him, Ulbricht seems considerably mellowed. He no longer works twelve to fourteen hours a day and spends considerable time traveling the country, visiting the hundreds of schools, plants, collective farms, fertilizer factories, housing projects, and recreation centers named after him. He listens to the workers' acclamatory plaudits, inspects their products with a benevolent but knowing eye, and attempts to project an image of a spade-bearded, bespectacled Santa Claus walking through his creation and seeing that it is good.

Now that he has power, Ulbricht yearns for love and respect. His lackeys spare no effort providing it. Ulbricht's portrait hangs in every schoolroom, hotel lobby, and factory. Production quotas are subscribed and oversubscribed in his honor. And he is extolled by more mediocre poets and lyricists than any other Com-

munist ruler save Mao. Or how else could one describe such verses
as "Our Chairman" by Otto Gotschc, Ulbricht's poet-secretary,
which reads:

> The program of our future he proclaimed,
> The unity of our class he ordained,
> The foundation of our state he has wrought,
> The ethics of "we" not "I" he has taught,
> This man who for us has fought.
> This man like a rock, a man bold and free,
> Son of his class is he.

The charade of patriarchal statesmanship in which Ulbricht
engages today may hide the monocratic cunning for which he has
become infamous. But it cannot daub over that decisive characteristic which Ernst Thälmann discovered in him nearly forty
years ago. "Ulbricht," said the onetime chief of the KPD, "is
and always will be a bureaucrat."

It seems only logical that Ulbricht would turn to a man of
similar character as his successor. None fits the description more
closely than wiry, steel-eyed, graying Erich Honecker, fifty-five,
the heir apparent. No less bureaucratic, though only half as wiley,
Honecker is a Politburo member and Central Committee Secretary for Security Matters, a job that places him in undisputed
control of all East Germany's military and internal security affairs. No bank of switches could be closer to ultimate power.

Born August 25, 1912, in Neunkirchen in the Saar, as the third
of a militantly Communist coal miner's six children, Honecker
has used that power toward only one purpose: to be Ulbricht's
loyal, deferential servant. He heeds obediently his master's voice
and responds enthusiastically to his every command—qualities
for which Ulbricht has recompensed him with the mantle of
promised succession. Though he holds no public office other than
a seat in the Volkskammer, Honecker has been the GDR's and
the SED's uncontested Number Two since 1963. In December
1965 and early 1966 when Ulbricht suddenly disappeared because
of an illness which some observers believe was a mild heart attack,

Honecker ran the party. And in April 1967, at the SED's VIIth Congress, he delivered the main ideological lecture.

In spite of his meticulously trimmed hair, horn-rimmed glasses, tailor-made suits, penchant for Western shirts and Windsor knots, (because they are orderly and symmetrical), Erich Honecker appears to be a drab junior Ulbricht, so austere and pedestrian that East Germans don't even joke about him. He abhors intellectuals, speaks fluent party gobbledegook and, until Khrushchev banned it, thought Stalin's *History of the Communist Party of the Soviet Union (B)* was the only book worth reading.

During the repression of East German artists and literati which he spearheaded at the 11th Central Committee plenum in December 1965, Honecker unabashedly fulminated against original thought and equated intellectual liberalization with the "effort to debilitate the GDR from within."

Honecker was raised in a Marxist environment even more bellicose than Ulbricht's. His father, who at eighty-six remains full of Communist brine and fury, represented the KPD in the Neunkirchen town council, the Saarland coal town where he still lives. At age ten Honecker joined the Communist Children's League and, according to his father, wasted no time working his way to the top. He joined the Communist Youth League at fourteen in 1926, and became a full member of the party four years later. By 1934 he was a member of the central committee of the underground Communist Youth of Germany. Honecker is no coward and when the exile party ordered him to Berlin in 1935 to organize anti-Hitler resistance groups, he went quickly—only to be arrested by the Gestapo in February 1936. The Nazi People's Court convicted him of attempted treason and sentenced him to ten years in Brandenburg Penitentiary from where he was liberated by Red Army troops in 1945.

He set out immediately organizing the Free German Youth movement (FDJ) which he ran until 1955 when, at forty-three, he no longer qualified as youthful by any standard.

His career in the hierarchy has been a steadily scandent one based on unqualified loyalty to Ulbricht. After he gave up the leadership of the FDJ, Honecker was sent to the Soviet Union for training—a prerequisite for success as a functionary. On his return in 1957 he took charge of military, security, and counterintelligence affairs in the Politburo—the same decisive and puissant position he holds today. In 1958, he ingratiated himself to Ulbricht by delivering the accusatory speech against Schirdewan, Wollweber, and Oelssner. Ulbricht's reward: full membership in the Politburo.

Honecker has reinforced his crucial position with systematic diligence. Aides and informers supply him with the latest party gossip and details on intrigues which he uses to play one satrap off against the other. His meticulous attention to the weaknesses of SED hierarchs—which he keeps noted in a card file—provides him with inestimable leverage and might.

Honecker has been a zealous student of Ulbrichtian tactics and learned his lessons well. Even in his private life he seems to have been bent on emulating the master. At least, his relationship with women, if not quite as incidental, has certainly been as ambivalent. In 1946, the year he became head of the FDJ, he married his deputy, Edith Baumann. Their daughter Erika was born in 1948. One year later, blonde, shapely and attractive Margot Feist, fifteen years his junior, joined the staff as leader of the Young Pioneer organization. In 1951 Margot bore Honecker a daughter, Sonja. In 1952 he divorced Edith and finally married Margot who today is East Germany's Minister for Public Education.

Like Ulbricht's, all of Honecker's relatives live in the West. Honecker's, however, continue to visit him and are not ashamed about the identification. Honecker's father travels to East Berlin at least once a year. He used to stay for as long as two and three months, but in recent years has pared his calls to only a few weeks duration. As the old man put it: "They have so little time for me these days. I feel in the way." Honecker's sisters (two brothers were killed in the war) are proud of him and one said: "He has remained a nice human being. Why even his household employees sit at the dining-room table with him and call him by his first name." To the charge that he is regarded an arch Stalinist, she replies: "Listen, our parents taught us to be consistent, whatever we do. And Erich is consistent."

Just when Honecker will move to the top of the party—and how long he will remain there—defies prediction. Ulbricht's health, for all the persistent rumors, appears unimpaired and it is incredible that he would abdicate voluntarily in anyone's favor. Speculation is rife that he might relinquish the first secretaryship but retain the chairmanship of the Council of State when he turns seventy-five in June 1968, but the only basis for this is conjecture. Rumors in May 1966 that Honecker attempted to usurp power prematurely had as little foundation as the widely circulated story that Ulbricht suffered from throat cancer. Besides, for Honecker to stage an intra-party coup would be both out of character and self-defeating. His position today is predicated on the consistency of his loyalty. As the heir presumptive, the throne, because of Ulbricht's age, is already palpably near. He can afford to bide his time.

Honecker can be as certain today of the succession as we can be that once he is coronated there will be no significant immediate liberalization of policy. Honecker empathizes with the old orthodox clique of German Communists who learned the catechisms of their creed during exile in Moscow. He is as skeptical of the new breed of pragmatists in party and industry as he abhors intellectuals, and said as much at the VIIth Party Congress in April 1967. He will shun the path of an independent road to Communism. And he is no more likely to defy the Kremlin than he is inclined today to mutiny against Ulbricht.

Predictions on the durability of his rule, however, can be made with far less certainty. If the pattern of Communist power struggles has taught anything since Stalin's death, it is that heirs presumptive are rarely blessed with political longevity. Not only are they surrounded by rival paladins but their ascendency to power usually unleashes long throttled younger forces thrusting for might. The situation in the German Democratic Republic is not different.

Though the other members of the Politburo are mostly profiles in lability, their pusillanimity is the product of two decades of virtually unchallenged rule by Ulbricht. Once he is gone it is not inconceivable that one or the other might reach for ultimate power himself. Moreover, they could count on the bright young pragmatists and technocrats in industry and the party's second echelon—all of whom now groan bitterly under the doctrinal yoke of ideology imposed upon them by the old guard.

Of the other thirteen Politburo members and its six candidates, only a few merit a closer look—either because they could threaten orderly transfer of power to Honecker or because they have unusual talents.

By virtue of protocol, Premier Willi Stoph is the second most important man in the East German state, by dint of political power, he ranks third in the party. He is the only one of East Germany's leaders who—since the death of Otto Grotewohl—enjoys genuine popularity. Personable, mild-mannered, polished, and handsome with gray hair turning white, heavy dark eyebrows and a ready smile, Stoph is an anomaly among the clique of Moscow émigrés and concentration camp inmates at the top. He served in the Wehrmacht both before and during the war.

Born as a laborer's son in Berlin, on July 9, 1914, he is a mason by training and has been a Communist since his teens. From 1935 to 1937 he was a draftee in Hitler's peacetime army, then worked as a bricklayer and construction foreman until the outbreak of World War II when he was drafted again. He saw action on all the European fronts as an artilleryman and a regimental commander's driver.

Soviet military administrators discovered his managerial and executive talents and put him in charge of construction and resources procurement. By 1948, he was head of the SED Central Committee's department for economic policy. In 1952, when only thirty-eight years old, he was named minister of interior—a position that put him in charge of the People's Police (Volkspolizei) and for a while the State Security Service. He has been a member of the Politburo since July 1953. In 1956 he was named Minister of Defense and given the rank of general—the fastest and biggest promotion any former lance corporal ever had. Stoph took it in stride, ran the National People's Army (NVA) for five years. In 1962, when Premier Otto Grotewohl became ill, Stoph was named acting chairman of the Council of Ministers, and inherited the post when Grotewohl died in 1964.

Willi Stoph is not a man of either great élan, eloquence or brilliance, but he is an official of proven diligence and organizational ability. Moreover, he has demonstrated reasonable ideological reliability and loyalty. He suffers from none of that cramped introversion so typical of most of the GDR's leaders and enjoys a reputation for candid sincerity and affable simplicity. He has never masked his personal dislike of Honecker or his disdain for Erich Mielke, the Minister for State Security. Stoph is one of the few East German oligarchs who could win a free election or personality contest.

It is unlikely, however, that he'll get the chance to prove it. For many years he enjoyed the special protection of Walter Ulbricht. Stoph was usually referred to as the heir presumptive and that prospect never failed to elicit a warm glow of relief in the hearts of his countrymen. Just when and why he slipped from favor has never been determined. Suffice it to say that today he is but an also-ran in the race for the sweepstakes. At the December 1965 meeting of the Central Committee, Stoph went out of his way to underscore complete loyalty to Ulbricht and to thank him for "his great and rich contribution." It sounded like a mild case of self-criticism.

Owl-eyed Professor Albert Norden, head of the Politburo's commission for agitation and East Germany's chief propagandist, is a party official of a completely different breed. Intellectual, perspicacious, moved by a high degree of sensibility and possessed of a profound knowledge of life under capitalism, he has a gift for turning even the most untranslatable party Chinese into effective propaganda. This son of a Silesian rabbi is by far the brainiest and sharpest, albeit the most vitriolic member of the Politburo.

Norden is the inventive alchemist of the poisonous torrent of invective which the GDR's press and radio spew out daily at West Germany, the imaginative architect of the elaborate machinery for agitation and propaganda which the SED has beamed at domestic consumers. It is Norden who engineers all the campaigns against West Germany and who exposes ex-Nazis in Bonn's government.

Born in Mysluwitz, Silesia, in what he says is now Poland, but West Germans insist is still Germany, Norden joined the Communist Youth Organization when he was fifteen years old, the party one year later. From 1923 until Hitler came to power and he was forced to flee, Norden was an editor on a variety of Communist papers and magazines and served for a while as press spokesman of the Communist parliamentary group in the Reichstag.

His flight from Germany followed the well-trodden path of exile: Prague, Paris, and eventually New York. But he was a busy young man before he reached American shores. In France he came under the tutelage of Willi Münzenberg, the maestro of agitprop who was subsequently purged by Stalin and murdered in 1940 in southern France. Under Münzenberg, who had been in charge of all Communist propaganda in Germany, Norden helped prepare the 1933 *Brown Book*, the first dossier on Nazi crimes.

In September 1933 Münzenberg and Norden played an influential role in organizing the famous London "counter trial" to prove that the Nazis themselves, not the Communists or hapless Marinus van der Lubbe, had set fire to the Reichstag. The "court" consisted of an international jury of respected lawyers, among them American attorney Arthur Garfield Hays, and Britain's Sir Stafford Cripps. The truth about the Reichstag fire is still not known, though the most plausible theory today is that Van der Lubbe, a dissident Dutch Communist, set it all by himself—as he maintained throughout his trial in Leipzig. What is known is that the London counter trial was a farce and that Norden played a key role in making it one. At one point during the proceedings, Norden wearing a hood "to protect him against reprisals" marched into the august chambers of the London Law Society and identified himself as a defected Nazi storm trooper. He told a wild tale, still generally believed, of how the brown-shirts had used an underground passageway into the Reichstag building and set it aflame.

When the Nazis invaded France in 1940, Norden fled first to London, then to the United States where he became a member of the "Council for a Democratic Germany" and publisher of the bulletin *Germany Today*.

In 1947 he returned to Germany to edit an East Berlin journal called *Deutschlands Stimme* and by 1949 he was press spokesman for the East German government. Since 1955 he has been in effective control of all propaganda and agitation work in the GDR. He has been a full member of the Politburo since 1958.

Norden's most recent propaganda stunt: a second *Brown Book*, this one listing "war and Nazi criminals in the West German government, economy, administration, army, judiciary, and schools."

For all his freewheeling ways when dealing with the West, Norden is neither a wild man nor a fanatic. In the GDR hierarchy he has a reputation for being the voice of moderation and compromise. He has the respect of the Soviets and on more than a few occasions has interceded on East Germany's behalf when a conflict of interests arose between the Russians and the GDR.

It was Norden who in November 1963 cautioned the party's agitators and cadre against overly zealous propaganda work and impropriety in trying to persuade the masses. "Our comrades," he said, "must win the confidence of the people, must help the citizens understand our policies, answer their questions and doubts honestly and assist them in eradicating improprieties which plague their daily lives. Winning the confidence of the masses takes time and patience and tact. It cannot be accomplished by overpowering them with propaganda, tirades of slogans, or political meetings that deprive them of their weekends." Norden admonished against terminology which the people cannot understand, against liturgic recitations of ideological mumbo-jumbo which has no meaning.

Albert Norden's professorship is an honorary one. Kurt Hager's is not. And in Germany it makes a difference—even in a purportedly egalitarian society. Hager, fifty-five, head of the Politburo's commission for ideology and unchallenged cultural czar of the GDR, was appointed full professor of philosophy at East

Berlin's Humboldt University in 1949. However, he has not taught since 1952.

Hager is second only to Norden in pure intellect and unmatched in projecting an image of contradictions. He is best known as the official spokesman of dogmatism and the nemesis of liberalism in the arts. In truth, he is quite a liberal himself and his public pronouncements are intended mainly to keep a foothold on top of the Red Olympus. Kurt Hager is far from being the implacable ideologue some of his actions and statements would make him appear. Instead he is often the buffer between the hacks of the Central Committee and the avant-gardists of literature, film and stage. The job is neither relaxing nor rewarding.

In 1956 Hager was forced to engage in humiliating self-criticism because of association with Wolfgang Harich and the other liberals entrenched at Humboldt University. Yet, ten years later, in November 1966, at the annual East German Writers Conference, Hager admonished his colleagues: "The writer's role is that of a leader and planner of socialist consciousness of the people." It was not a case of apostasy but a demonstration of his antenna-like sensitivity for changing moods among the hierarchs. Many East German intellectuals have learned to appreciate him as a sort of early warning system.

Hager, who grew up in Bietigheim in Wuerttemberg, joined the Communist Party in 1930, was briefly arrested when Hitler came to power, then fled to France and from 1937 to 1939 fought with the International Brigades in the Spanish Civil War and directed Radio Madrid. He sat out World War II in England, returned to Germany in 1945. He was elected to the Central Committee in 1954, to the Politburo as a candidate in 1958 and a full member in 1963.

Hager's intellectual DEW line is focused primarily on Paul Fröhlich, first secretary of the SED in the Leipzig District, who is the Politburo's most contentious dogmatist. Fröhlich is the living stereotype of an apparatchik. He joined the party as a seventeen-year-old in 1930, served it underground during the Third Reich and has worked his way up methodically through the ranks since 1945, entering the Politburo as a candidate in 1958, a full member in 1963.

Fröhlich, a cook by training, hates all Western influences and suspects all intellectuals of harboring deviationist views. Whenever opportunity beckons, he embarks on crusades against them. Following the June 1953 uprising he took advantage of all his powers as a district secretary to wage total war on writers, artists, and musicians in his fief. Again in 1956, after the Hungarian revolution, Fröhlich—a stocky, square-jawed, shifty-eyed and heavy-browed man—campaigned against subversive intellectual and artistic currents seeping in from Poland and against jazz. For example, he hired gangs of muscle-bound thugs who systematically beat up all jazz and pop musicians in the Leipzig area and triggered riots in dance halls, youth centers, and cafés, giving the party a pretext for clamping down on "decadent, Western imperialist influences."

Fröhlich is a fanatic opponent of economism and thwarts, when he can, the pragmatists who have gained influence with the success of the New Economic System. He is behind the artistic and intellectual twilight the GDR has experienced since December 1965.

Among the Politburo's old guard—the men over fifty—Horst Sindermann, fifty-two, the SED boss of Halle, is the antithesis to Fröhlich. He is a gentleman in Communist gladrags. Sindermann's career is neither spectacular nor colorful. He spent eleven years in Nazi prisons and concentration camps and, like Fröhlich, worked his way up the hierarchical ladder of SED power since 1945. But he has what Ulbricht's team is desperately shy on: a bourgeois manner bordering on cosmopolitanism. It was a desperately needed quality in the Halle district where he took command in 1963 following the death of militant, ideologically intolerant old Bernard Könen, one of the Moscow émigrés. Sindermann quashed the vulgar tone that had characterized the party in this heterogeneous region where strong proletarian forces mingle with relics of the Bürgertum. His house is an intellectual salon where the professors and faculty members of Halle's Martin Luther University are frequent guests. His wife has become popular with matrons of Communist society for that most degenerate of capitalist institutions: afternoon teas. The Sindermann home is said to be a refuge for free discussion and in Halle the couple enjoys what is rare for Communist oligarchs: popularity.

With but few exceptions the older apparatchiks who have clambered to the pinnacles of state and party power are studies in mediocrity. Men and women who sailed skillfully through the rapids of Nazi terror, Stalinist purges and Ulbrichtian dogmatism, they have learned only one thing well: to veer off any course that leads to independent thought. Their minds and personalities have been forged and hog-tied into compliant shape by the authoritarian orthodoxy of Ulbricht's rule. Even if Ulbricht were to die tomorrow it is inconceivable that they could break the shackles and tear the fetters of intellectual conformity which will remain his legacy. That they have made their contribution to East German progress, sometimes in spite of themselves, is their due. As physicist Manfred von Ardenne, the brilliant Dresden autodidact, once told me: "The fact that this state is the empirical achievement of a handful of carpenters, masons and laborers who knew nothing about government, economics or administration when they started is worth admiring in itself. They have nothing to be ashamed of." Perhaps not. But their days are numbered and waiting in the anteroom of power to take their places are a new breed of East German Communists: the generation of pragmatists and technocrats, uninhibited and unencumbered by the congeries of German guilt, Marxist canons and Stalinist trepidation.

It was Ulbricht himself who conjured the genie of pragmatism when he ushered in the New Economic System. In doing so he promised not only to pull the economy out of its morass but correct the mistakes of the past—mistakes, he said during a six-hour speech, which were primarily Joseph Stalin's fault.

"Stalin," said Ulbricht, "tossed Lenin's advice about the economic criteria of socialism to the winds. In their place he instituted an administrative system that became increasingly bureaucratic—despite Lenin's bitter opposition to bureaucracy. In the last years of his reign, Stalin relied heavily on the instrument of bureaucracy because he had lost confidence in the masses and his cadre. Stalin's distrust evolved from a lack of faith in the persuasive power of Communist ideas. The result was over-centralization. He considered all others incapable and had no choice but to make the decisions himself, then employ bureaucrats to implement them. No one will deny," Ulbricht concluded, "that Stalin's theories and practices had a negative effect on *our* economy as well."

Indeed, no one could deny it. But how to remedy the effect, that was the question. Ulbricht as usual had the answer: the New Economic System. To implement it he began replacing some of his trusted lieutenants with new blood. Such relative unknowns as Dr. Erich Apel, Dr. Günter Mittag, and Dr. Werner Jarowinsky, the real architects of the New Economic System, entered the inner sanctum of power. Their goal was to make socialism competitive with capitalism regardless of the ideological ballast they would have to jettison. Apel's hour was shiny but brief. In the thirty-five months that he headed the State Planning Commission—from January 1963 until December 3, 1965 when he committed suicide—he revolutionized East German economic thinking with relentless heresy. The economic miracle which the GDR has witnessed and performed since 1963 is largely his doing. He shot himself in December 1965 rather than be party to a trade pact with the Soviets which he felt would rob East Germany of its new advantages and economic momentum. Apel is gone but his brightest disciple, Mittag, survived to become the vanguard of an entirely new breed of Communists.

Mittag, the youthful, energetic head of the SED's bureau of industry, is already in the sanctum of power—the Politburo. Four other men in their thirties and forties are in the vestibule as Politburo candidates: Georg Ewald, the chairman of the all-important Agricultural Council; Jarowinsky, SED Secretary for Trade and Supply; Walter Halbritter, director of the Government Price Office, and Günther Kleiber, State Secretary in the Council of Ministers for the coordination of electronic data processing.

Of the 131 members of the Central Committee elected at the April 1967 party congress, twenty-three are thirty-nine years of age or younger. On the Council of Ministers, fifteen of the thirty-nine members are under thirty nine and the average age is only forty-six. Half of the GDR's first echelon managers and executives are in their mid-thirties to early forties.

Disparate as their backgrounds, competence, and temperament may be, all have a variety of things in common. They are Communists to the marrow and have known no other system, no other way of life since their late teens or earliest twenties. No masons, carpenters, or laborers these, nearly all have solid educations, albeit heavy on technology, science, management, and economics. They are the GDR's new elite and know they owe their education, their power, their privileges, their prestige, and their future to the system on which they were nursed. Hence, they are intrinsically loyal and harbor no secret yens for rebellion or a capitalist revival. But they are haughtily scornful of the calcified doctrinal shibboleths which they regard as the impediments to progress. They are the iconoclasts of the proletarian revolution, ready to cleanse the Marxist-Leninist temple of its cobwebbed idols, its useless ritualism and its false prophets. Their new faith is profit, their altar the data computer and their new paradise is named success.

The ossified dogmatists in the party hierarchy sense both the personal and intellectual threat of the young Turks and react accordingly. Especially when a heretic exceeds the bounds of propriety. Such was the sad case of Dr. Siegbert Löschau, the young, brilliant, and popular director of Leuna Chemical Works, East Germany's largest single industrial enterprise, who in December 1965 was appointed Minister of Chemical Industries. Five months later, this most promising of the young pragmatists, widely known as Ulbricht's wonder boy, was already out of office, publicly discredited, sidelined to a secondary research job at a provincial chemical factory and expelled from the Central Committee. What had happened?

The most likely theory was advanced to me by some of Löschau's acquaintances and associates who said he violated the strict ethical code of the party by demanding as much pay in the government as he had received while head of the Leuna works.

Moreover, he had stormed the citadel of ideology like a kamikaze on a white steed and won the lasting enmity of the GDR's old guard by preaching against the inflexibility and pusillanimity of its economic czars. He obviously went too far when, during one interview in *Freiheit*, the SED daily for Halle, he said: "Official ways and channels are usually a hindrance to reaching our economic goals because they require nervous stamina and considerable time and energy which we could use more profitably for other purposes."

Löschau's fate may have been intended as a warning to the others of his generation who are charging enthusiastically at the preserves of power. It may mute them for a while, but not for long. Time and might are always on the side of youth. One can only hope that in the GDR the wait will not be so long that the pragmatic young Turks lose their élan and become high priests of inflexible doctrine themselves.

Günter Mittag, still in his early forties, is the actual chief of all East German industry. His career has been meteoric, his competence never disputed and his capacity for hard work has become legendary. Stocky and corpulent with a double chin that borders on pudginess, blue-eyed and with blond hair on which he tends to use too much brilliantine, Dr. Mittag looks like any successful West German politician or industrialist.

Mittag's mind works with computer-like precision. It is at its best when dealing with economic problems, though Mittag is no duffer when it comes to grappling with more general matters. In September 1966, during his maiden speech as a full member of the Politburo, Mittag demonstrated that he can talk almost as long as Ulbricht—more than three hours—and has a total grasp of subjects ranging from the price of potatoes to Chinese dogmatism, from the role of computers in modern industry to foreign affairs.

Following the suicide of Erich Apel, which forebode an economic counterreformation, there were doubts whether Mittag would survive. Judging from his September 1966 speech, he not only prevailed but is in full command. "Building Socialism," he said, "is a threefold task. It means attaining the highest scientific and technical level in production with top quality products. It means cost reduction of all goods and services. And it means the steady improvement of the standard of living for our people . . . Raising the national product and income is our primary class mission." Marx wouldn't even understand it and Stalin would be shocked.

No less anti-Scriptural is Werner Jarowinsky who was born in 1927 of German parents living in Leningrad. Jarowinsky's career has been mostly academic and administrative. He spent a couple of years as a Vopo, obtained his high-school diploma through an adult education program, then attended Humboldt University and received his doctorate in economics. From 1959 until 1964 he was Deputy Minister of Trade and Supply, then moved exclusively into party work as a candidate member of the Politburo and Secretary for Trade and Supply. Jarowinsky, a heterodox egghead, is the apostle of a new East German creed which holds that the most important economic lever for increasing investment and capital goods production is the availability of consumer goods. Not money itself but merchandise to spend it on will induce East German workers to augment their efforts, he says.

Günter Sieber, the Supply and Trade Minister, though young and zealous, is a pragmatist of a different breed. He has built his career strictly on rungs of the party ladder. A Berliner whose father was an old-line Communist, Sieber ingratiated himself to the SED in the late 1940s when, working as a forester along the zonal border, he actively reported all escape attempts to the police. The party sent him to the SED cadre academy near East Berlin. From 1954 to 1962 he served as an official of the Central Planning Commission, then was appointed deputy chairman of the Workers and Peasant's Inspectorate. Since 1965 he has been a minister.

Tall, blond, square-jawed Wolfgang Rauchfuss was only thirty-four years old when, after having been a Deputy Minister for Foreign and Intra-German Trade for four years, he was named a Deputy Premier and Vice-chairman of the Council of Ministers. His career has been meteoric and remarkably devoid of any close association with the party. He is a manager par excellence, having worked as a sales director for precision instruments and optical goods at DIA, the East German Export-Import Agency, before entering the Foreign Trade Ministry in 1961.

Löschau's successor as Minister of Chemical Industry is thirty-eight-year-old Günter Wyschowsky, a member of the SED since he was sixteen, a trained chemist by profession. Unlike Löschau, Wyschowsky built his career among the planners and party pros on the State Planning Commission, where since 1962 he had been head of the chemical and natural resources section. To the managers of East Germany's big chemical plants this made him naturally suspect. They were leery of a man who, despite his chemistry degree, had come up through the party apparatus. The fears soon proved unfounded. Wyschowsky is a pragmatist and twice as effective as Löschau because he has mastered the intricacies of navigating through the bureaucratic maze which he knows as well as his chemical formulas.

Still another economic wonder boy is Dr. Gerhard Zimmermann, Minister of Heavy Machinery and Installation Construction. Like Wyschowsky he is also a member of the presidium of the Council of Ministers. A metal worker by training, Zimmermann climbed to the Communist top via industry. For six years, from 1957 to 1963, he was director of the Warnow shipyards, then general manager of the whole East German maritime construction trust where he was instrumental in making the GDR one of the world's leading shipbuilding countries. His organizational and executive talents are already being felt in the heavy machinery ministry.

Industry and management, however, are not the only areas where opportunity comes looking for youth and talent. Except for sixty-four-year-old Foreign Minister Otto Winzer, the East German Foreign Office is a nest of shrewd young Turks. Three of Winzer's deputy ministers are under forty-three.

And in December 1965 Ulbricht appointed a young journalist as a state secretary in charge of a department for relations with West Germany. At thirty-six Joachim Hermann counts as one of the most astute and polished officials in the East German hierarchy. His department is a counterweight to the West German

Ministry for All-German Affairs, now headed by SPD vice-chairman Herbert Wehner. A Communist to the marrow but unfettered by party jargon, Hermann once gave this prediction for the world in the year 2000: "My grandchildren will be making weekend trips to the moon with the FDJ and will be calling atomic air taxis 'old jalopies.' Above all, it will be a time when the type of people in power in Bonn today will have no influence at all."

It is this kind of confidence that East Germany's new generation of managers, economic experts, scientists, technocrats, and party functionaries thrives on. Often isolated from the West, unable to make genuine comparisons or deluded by their own propaganda, they are convinced the future is theirs alone. They are not revolutionaries and they are not rebels but reformers, though not conscious ones. They honestly believe, as one young official once put it to me: "The West tried to pick up where the Weimar Republic had left off. But we started all over again, completely anew."

It is not quite true. Until very recently the SED was the private preserve of men whose roots reached deep into the Weimar Republic, were intensely proud of it and derived the legitimacy of their claim to power from the ballot-box victories and street battles they had won in that turbulent era.

But the new men of East Germany have as little in common with the old as west has with east. They have as little patience for the petrified theologians of Marxist credenda as they have for flag waving adulation of the Joshuas of Communism's yesterday. Their heroes are not the Rosa Luxemburgs, Karl Liebknechts, and Ernst Thälmanns who fought the bloody battles of the Red crusades and wars of the classes. They eulogize scientists and technologists. Theirs is a world where terms such as cybernetics, manpower management, digital feedback control and stigmatic grating spectography have replaced the old clichés of class struggle, dictatorship of the proletariat, surplus value, and the anarchy of capitalist production.

Until all the ideologues of the past are gone, this generation may suffer setbacks. But the over-all trend is irreversible. Time is on its side and victory is as certain as tomorrow. When it comes, Germany may be more divided than ever, but the wall dividing it will then come down.

CHAPTER IV

Exodus from Paradise

Walter Ulbricht, so an East German cynic has put it, is really the greatest military strategist of all time. Who else could have put 3,500,000 to flight and in a single day taken 17,000,000 captive?

It is a tribute with rancor to one of the most monstrous events of our age: the Berlin Wall which finally halted an exodus that between 1945 and August 13, 1961 bled the German Democratic Republic of one-fifth of its population.

The West German government contends that the Wall was a perfidy rivaled only by the tyranny which had driven millions of East Germans from their homeland. The explanation is not that simple. The exodus from the "workers' paradise" is a complexity of chain reactions touched off by spontaneous combustion.

Thousands fled because they were innately opposed to Communism, a system alien to everything they had known before. Others were systematically ostracized by the regime because of their backgrounds or parentage. They left because the GDR presented no opportunities. Many undoubtedly were driven off by disillusionment and frustration with the bureaucratic ways. Countless numbers departed simply because they were restricted from visiting friends and relatives in the West. Some were genuinely persecuted by Ulbricht's secret police and the Russians. The majority however, fled because of the GDR's economic deprivation which in turn was exacerbated by mass migration, for the greater the refugee flow the less chance East Germany had of pulling itself up by the bootstraps. Next to natural resources its greatest scarcity was manpower. All in all, it was a multi-rooted hemorrhage which, if left unchecked, would have bled the country dry.

For Ulbricht, the Wall was a solution to a Gordian knot of being damned if he did and deviled if he didn't. Just as the refugee question itself has been a series of paradoxes wrapped up in a quandary.

For example, whenever the East German regime attempted to halt the refugee flow by increasing restrictions, more people began to leave because of them. When the restrictions were relaxed, the flow increased because access invited flight. Attempts to mollify the GDR's industrial and intellectual elite into staying home, merely tended to disaffect the unprivileged masses. Efforts to woo the masses sent the upper classes packing.

As one East German couple once put it to George Bailey, East European correspondent of *The Reporter* magazine: "If so many people continue to leave East Germany, just think how well off we'll be. The regime will do everything to persuade us to stay." But suppose, asked Bailey, that not so many people leave and there is a definite prospect that the regime will stabilize itself? "Oh then," they replied, "we would leave."

The same illogical morality, though reversed, prevails to this day. A young East German doctor told me: "Now that the Wall has been built, I would walk across the border barefoot to get out of here." Did that mean, I asked, that he would move to the West if the Wall came down? "Of course not," he replied. "Then I would stay here."

The Bonn government's response has been equally ambivalent. From 1949 to 1961 it appealed sanctimoniously to East Germans to stay put, triumphing all the while that the exodus was proof of Ulbricht's political and economic bankruptcy. Whenever the refugee flow diminished, however, Bonn's pronouncements of relief were punctuated by an undercurrent of alarm that conditions in the GDR might be improving. Whenever the migration increased, West Germany's expressions of alarm were marked by innuendos of satisfaction that conditions were really unbearable.

East German propagandists claim the exodus was a monstrous plot by West German "head hunters" who systematically lured,

wooed, and estranged the population with false promises of prosperity. It is just slightly more preposterous than West Germany's
assertion that the refugees were predominantly political per-
secutees who escaped in fear of life and freedom. Of course Western propaganda broadcasts beamed to East Germany encouraged
flight. But they account for only a fraction of the migratory
move. Certainly some East Germans were victims of or threatened
by the excess of the Ulbricht regime, but they, too, were a minority: intellectuals and politically motivated persons who actively
opposed the regime or inadvertently got caught in its machinery.

The Bonn government contends that the principal reasons for
flight were "the lack of freedom, the lack of hope that things
might improve, the persecution of all who dared to contradict
the Communist regime."

To support this case, the Federal Republic in July 1961 published a survey intended to prove that each upsurge in refugee
figures paralleled some new or more severe policy. Ergo, 197,788
escaped in 1950, because that "was the year in which the Communists began eliminating freedom of opinion and criticism of
conditions became subject to severe penalties." Among other
causes for the vicissitudinous pattern of the refugee movement,
according to this study: actions against the churches and organized religion; arming the People's Police with Soviet weapons;
elimination of federal administration which was supplanted by
centralized government; the intrusion of ideology into the public
school system; holding military parades by the People's Army;
restrictions on travel; Khrushchev's ultimatum for making Berlin
a "free internationalized city"; the failure of the 1960 Paris sum-
mit conference.

If there is any validity to the West German analysis, then it
applies to 1953 when, as the survey put it, 331,390—the highest
number ever—"fled because of the June 17 uprising which was
followed by a wave of terror against all suspected opponents of
Communism." But even this seems a highly debatable contention in the light of statistics which reveal that the refugee flow
in 1953 was considerably higher in the months *preceding* the in-

surrection—during a period of exceptional economic hardship—than in the period following the revolt.

Whatever the role of political oppression, it pales in the face of the overriding economic motivation. East German economic figures for the years 1949 to 1961, when correlated with Bonn's refugee statistics, support this maxim eloquently for they demonstrate that the exodus flowed with every new economic catastrophe. Just as it ebbed dramatically as economic conditions improved. After 1956, for example, when reparations payments to the Soviet Union were halted and East German industry increased production of consumer goods, the refugee movement dwindled appreciably. It dropped from 279,000 in 1956 to 261,000 in 1957, to 204,000 in 1958 and 143,000 in 1959. Food shortages caused by severe drouth and forced collectivization of the peasantry brought the rate back up to 199,000 in 1960.

If an inordinately large proportion listed political or pseudo-political reasons for their flight on arrival at reception centers in the West it should be remembered that by doing so they could expect to gain a number of advantages and privileges—from preferential housing to earlier job placement.

Frequently the lines between economic and political pressures tended to blur—a natural phenomenon in a society being subjected to a Communist revolutionary upheaval. The testimonials of many refugees reveal some of this confusion.

"I had to close down my shop," said a twenty-five-year-old Erfurt upholsterer on his arrival in West Berlin in 1961. "I couldn't get any material to make chairs and couches because I refused to take the state in as a partner in my business. I went to work as a truck driver. But the same old game started: the party members got the big trips to the faraway places, I got the scraps. And then I worried because of my family. Not long ago our little boy got a rash and the doctor said it was from lack of vitamin C. My wife hunted all over for oranges or lemons. That's when we decided to leave."

Explained a thirty-year-old development engineer from a town in southern Thuringia: "My work was dissatisfying. It's no fun to be an engineer when there's so little material and when you don't know whether you can go on with your work tomorrow. I felt the time had come to start anew—in the West."

"Any mother who has eight children knows what it takes to feed them," said one tall, thin haggard woman who arrived at West Berlin's Marienfelde refugee center in late July, 1961, "But when you can't even get potatoes or fruit, not to mention butter, this becomes a vital problem. In the town where I came from, you'd suddenly see the most wonderful things in the shop windows, whenever a delegation from a foreign country paid a visit. There were bananas, oranges, lemons, ham, and bacon—all those things we never saw. But as soon as the visitors left, all the stuff disappeared."

Today, though conditions are incomparably improved, refugees still come up with economic explanations for their flight. Even the border guard members, approximately two divisions of whom have high-tailed it over the demarcation line since 1949. "You can get ahead here if you want to," said one young enlisted man who had braved the gunfire of his comrades and the treacherous minefields. "Everything looks brighter and lighter. I was in West Berlin once—eight years ago—and the lights and displays in the shop windows were something I just couldn't forget."

Certainly bright lights, oranges and meat are not the only explanation. Of the many young people who fled—until 1961 some 25 percent of all refugees were eighteen to twenty-five years of age —inability to attend college or university, for reasons ranging from refusal to join the SED to "bourgeois parentage," played a decisive role. Others, while already enjoying the fruits of the GDR's inchoate economic recovery, simply distrusted the competence and the willingness of the regime to keep on the road to progress. Often they feared that once the mass exodus forced Ulbricht to close the borders, there would be an economic relapse.

"We weren't badly off at all," said one woman interviewed at Friedland refugee camp in July 1961. "My husband is a metal grinder and until last year I worked as mechanical draftswoman. We had a washing machine, a radio and phonograph console and nice furniture. We earned a lot of money and saved a great deal.

But we worried that they might shut the borders on Berlin. Then they could have done anything they wanted."

It is well to remember, too, that one-fourth of the refugees were not native East (or as the Bonn government would say, Middle) Germans, but expellees from the Sudetenland and the territories east of the Oder-Neisse line. For them the Soviet Zone was not home. They felt no ties. Moreover, they were lured by incalculable benefits in the West. While the Bonn government spared no effort to resettle expellees by extending them vast privileges such as low-cost housing, building credits, tax exemptions and preferential job placement, the East German regime, keen on improving relations with Poland, refused to make any distinction between expellees and the indigenous population. The lure to move west was twice as great for the expellees as it was for East Germans. By comparison, the benefits which beckoned them as expellees *and* refugees made the American GI bill of rights look niggardly.

In the crux of the cold war, it was simple and convenient to argue that the East German exodus was the result of political oppression. But it is an axiom of dubious validity and serious consequences, for it leads to an erroneous assessment of conditions in the GDR as well as to grave miscalculations of East Germany's present and future challenge to both the West and the Soviet Union.

According to Professor Hans Apel, the German-American economist from Bridgeport University, "The exodus from East Germany is not akin to the typical historic episodes of politico-ideological flight into exile. Rather, it resembles the great historic migrations (to the United States, for example, during the nineteenth century) of entire nationalities in search of greater economic opportunity and a better way of life. Increasingly between 1947 and 1961, West Germany became a promised land in the eyes of East Germans whose own country had failed to fulfill their hopes of prosperity. This was especially true of those East Germans (mostly expropriated entrepreneurs, professionals, tradesmen, and moderately landed farmers) who saw in the West's material affluence the symbols of the cultural traditions they had known before the war."

Germany's west was rich in anthracite, iron ore, and other minerals, the east impoverished save for large deposits of lignite and potash. The west was the hub of the old Reich's industry, the east merely its finishing shop. While West Germany was being pump-primed with Care packets, gifts, grants, and Marshall Plan aid, East Germany was being squeezed like a lemon by the Soviets and paying—with less than one-third of the population—the war debts of Germany as a whole. Moreover, while Stalin and his successors equivocated in their German policy, keeping the SED regime in a state of limbo that lasted until at least 1952, possibly 1955, West Germany was thriving, its industry resuscitated not just by gifts but by steel and machinery orders from a United States involved in the Korean War and determined to make the Federal Republic a showpiece of capitalism.

Impoverished and handicapped from the start, it is no wonder that the Soviet Zone soon ranked high among territories most likely to be depopulated. Moreover, this dissatisfaction was compounded by disaffection from the start. Even before the first German woman was raped by a Russian, long before the first German wristwatch landed in a grinning Soviet soldier's tunic pocket, a deep rift between East Germans and their conquerors was inevitable. The legendary animosity between Teutons and Slavs, which for centuries had kept Europe on a teetertotter between war and peace, was but the least of the reasons. Hatred and fear, carefully cultivated by the propagandists and the course of history, had preordained the relationship between Soviets and Germans to one of mutual wariness and acrimonious resentment. Here, where two ideologies had battled each other to a last cataclysm of destruction, there was no soil for understanding, no climate for the hypocritical hand of friendship proffered by the Soviets. Was there a son of Mother Russia who did not see in the defeated Germans the hated conquerors who had goose-stepped, plundered, and murdered their way to the outskirts of Moscow? Was there a German who did not see in the uncouth and uneducated Soviet soldiers the very barbarian horde Joseph Goebbels had always portrayed? Worlds divided this from the American Zone where bars of chocolate and sticks of gum, the lilting beat of jazz and the easy smile had raced Eisenhower's armies to the finish line of victory.

It was inevitable that so many of the older generation, who had lost everything because of Soviet failure to differentiate between the bourgeoisie and genuine Nazis, would resent not only the conquerors but the German Communist satraps who had arrived in their wake. Ere the smoke of war had settled, they began to look with envy on what they considered more traditional developments in the western occupation zones. All the more so because the borders dividing them from East Germany were demarcation lines which separated not only a traditionally chauvinistic nation but friend from friend, brother from brother, husband from wife, mother from child.

The paucity of natural resources, the industrial indigence which the Soviet Zone had inherited, maladministration, hostility, and rancor—these were the soil in which the mood of exodus thrived. Only a skillful plowman could have cultivated it for sweeter fruit. But Ulbricht and his minions were monumentally heavy-handed.

The westward flow began in 1945 and with each person who left the prospects for amelioration worsened, just as the regime became more restrictive. It became a vicious racing circle, not halted effectively until the Berlin Wall was built.

Until 1952 many East Germans could escape to the West directly across the demarcation line. People's Police patrols were posted sparsely at the zonal boundaries, watchtowers, where they existed at all, were few and far apart. By the middle of 1952, more than 800,000 had fled—merely by walking unmolested across the fields and through the forests between Hesse and Thuringia, Mecklenburg and Schleswig-Holstein or the Saxonies.

The exodus had already caused havoc in industry and agriculture and in May of that year, East German authorities established a three-mile wide restricted area along the border. Frontier controls became more rigid, flight more difficult. But this did not stop the refugee flow. East Germans were still permitted to visit relatives in the Federal Republic and travel in West Germany on vacation—though not until they had waded through a maze of bureaucratic restrictions. The result: thousands of East Germans, instead of risking arrest by going across the borders, went to West Germany legally, then defected.

In 1956, by the time nearly another million East Germans had used this relatively convenient mode of escape, the Ulbricht regime clamped down severely. Travel authorization was denied to students and other young people as well as those East Germans whose immediate relatives had fled. As this involved nearly every second family in East Germany, "interzonal" travel dwindled.

Thus, Berlin became the needle's eye through which the refugee flow continued. Its four power status, its open sector borders, citywide subway and elevated system made flight for hundreds of thousands a mere matter of a nickel underground ride or a leisurely stroll across the street. Germans bent on escape went to East Berlin, then crossed into the city's western sectors. From there they could be flown safely to West Germany. For five years the divided city served as a massive sluice of humanity.

East German authorities imposed restrictions on travel to East Berlin and spot checked trains, removing travelers suspected of planning an escape. But it was a crippling, haphazard control system at best. East Berlin's role, as the GDR's capital and largest city, made it hard to isolate. Moreover, trains were often so crowded that Vopos would take a cursory look through the aisles, fight their ways over and around luggage and passengers, and report an all clear though they knew that perhaps half of the travelers were escape, not vacation bound.

The chaos and economic disintegration caused by this sixteen-year-long decampment of 20 percent of East Germany's population defies description. Day after day, in any village or city, the same scenes repeated themselves. A factory hand was gone. A miner failed to show up for his shift. A farmer disappeared from a collective. Shops remained shut because their owners had defected. School children came to class only to find their teacher missing and patients waited in vain for doctors who had deserted them for more lucrative practice in the West.

Multiplied a thousand times, such a situation spelled catastrophe. Between 1954 and 1961 some 20 percent of all doctors— 3000 in all—fled to West Germany, leaving entire villages and counties without qualified medical help.

Conditions were so anarchic that plant managers did not know from one day to the next how large their labor force would be, which machines would be attended, which ones not. Planning even in a capitalistic society would have been impossible. East Germany's economy was paralyzed. The regime tried everything —from massive threats to amnesty of 86,000 prison inmates in 1960—to stem the tide of mounting havoc. All to no avail. The more massive the threats and the tighter the restrictions, the greater the exodus.

Refugees arriving at Marienfelde reception center in West Berlin in those days told poignant stories of East German pandemonium. "The entire economy is falling apart," said one Thuringian cabinetmaker. "One day the buses were off schedule because four bus drivers fled. The next day the plumber left. There were no flashlights, no nails. There was no one in the shops to serve you, which was probably not important because the shops had so little to sell. We had to queue for butter, when there was butter, and when there was, it usually was inedible."

To plug one hole the regime had to make another, and calamity snowballed, depriving the interlocked production process of all labor reserves. With no reservoir to draw on, the flight of a single mechanic, machinist, construction worker, technician or engineer could touch off monumentally acute losses far in excess of the refugee's own productive contribution to the gross national product. It was a geometric progression that placed the entire East German economy at the brink of collapse.

Moreover, the refugees, as both East and West German studies reveal, were the cream of the GDR's labor reserve. The best educated, the youngest, the most capable, the most needed.

"The great number of young people, the extraordinary proportion of skilled and semi-skilled workers, technicians and professionals among the refugees multiplied the actual population loss for the GDR," Bonn's ministry for all-German affairs explains.

Between 1952 and 1961, according to one survey conducted by the ministry, 18,872 engineers, 18,661 teachers and professors, 5678 physicians, dentists, and veterinarians, 995 pharmacists, 833 lawyers and judges and 513,087 skilled and semi-skilled workers fled the GDR.

And it will be 1980 before the actual loss in population, labor force and productivity can be remedied. Then, the GDR's population will have grown by 600,000 to 17,700,000, though the labor force will have increased by only 0.1 percent over its present 7,676,000—of whom, incidentally, 47 percent are female. This is one reason why the GDR has begun importing foreign workers. The first 2500 Hungarians went to East Germany on three-year contracts in November 1967. By the end of 1968, more than 20,000 Hungarians will be working in the GDR.

Moreover, the exodus cost the GDR millions in lost educational efforts spent on professionals, technicians, engineers, and skilled workers who fled to the West as soon as they had reaped the benefits of the Ulbricht regime.

Walter Ulbricht, who blames Western recruiting and "head hunting" for the decampment, has estimated the financial loss at $7,000,000,000. Professor Apel sets it at $9,000,000,000 and West German economist Professor Fritz Baade has calculated that until 1956 the exodus profited West Germany—in terms of additional labor, trained technicians, engineers, professionals, and workers —to the extent of $5,700,000,000.

Is it any wonder then that in 1961, when the movement began to take on previously unprecedented proportions, East Germany's leaders shut down the last escape hatch of what had become the Soviet Union's disappearing satellite.

Ulbricht then had little choice. The Berlin Wall is an ugly monument. But one need not sympathize with the men who built it to understand that from their vantage point, and by virtue of the circumstances, the Wall was an inevitable step.

Fritz Selbmann, a member of the State Planning Commission, told a group of West German reporters in October 1963: "We debated the wall for a long, long time. For years we hesitated, for years we repeatedly postponed the decision. Just a few weeks before August 13 we were all against it. At that time, when Walter Ulbricht said in a press conference, 'No one has any intention of building a wall,' it was true. No one did. But then as the refugee flow became worse and worse, we were simply forced by circumstances to do something."

It is ironic and sad that the Wall was built after a period when conditions in the GDR had been improving. For years East Germany's functionaries were largely victims of economic circumstances beyond their control. The mass exodus of 1960 and 1961, however, was primarily the product of their own mistakes compounded by one of the worst drouths in recent history.

Starting in 1956, when the GDR stopped paying reparations, the Ulbricht regime suddenly found it had more money to work and play with and a greater production margin entirely for East Germany's own benefit. Consumer goods production rose by $750,000,000 annually in 1956 and 1957 and by as much as $1,250,000,000 in 1958 and 1959. Money assumed new value as consumer commodities began appearing on the market. East Germans at last had an inducement to work harder. Housewives and pensioners helped fill the gaps in the labor force by looking for jobs—now that it paid to earn. Simultaneously, housing construction took priority. Restriction on non-party members and the sons and daughters of the bourgeoisie were lifted at universities and colleges. Political indoctrination and pressure, though still intense, relaxed palpably and East Germans were even permitted to travel abroad, albeit only to the Soviet bloc countries. In May 1958 rationing was abolished. Incomes were rising at about 40 marks a month annually.

It was a surprisingly euphoric era in which Albert Norden's propagandists coined the popular slogan: "We may be temporarily poorer than West Germany but what we have is ours. We did not indenture ourselves to foreign interests." Fragile flames of incipient national consciousness flickered to such an extent that when West German soccer teams came to Leipzig and Halle to play, local fans no longer applauded them but their own.

The refugee movement reflected the mood, decreasing by 60,000 annually from 261,000 in 1957 to 143,000 in 1959.

But in May 1958, at its Vth Party Congress, the SED made its first mistake: inauguration of the "Main Economic Mission," better known as East Germany's Big Leap Forward. It called for catching up with West Germany in consumer goods *consumption* by 1961 and total per capita *production* by 1965.

This was insane. Instead of being satisfied with the already tangible progress, Ulbricht and his ideologues plunged into a race they could not possibly win. Politburo realists who were acquainted with the West's economic prowess—Heinrich Rau, the Minister of Foreign Trade, and Deputy Premier Bruno Leuschner, the "economic coordinator"—warned in vain against this mythomaniac experiment. But the Sputnik euphoria in which this wild scheme was conceived prevailed over reason. It was the mad era in which Khrushchev vowed to catch up with the United States by 1970 and Mao Tse-tung launched China on its catastrophic path of the Great Leap. Like China, East Germany is still paying for its delirium.

The East German economy went haywire. Industrial and farm wages skyrocketed while investment in socialist reconstruction dwindled. When the real requirement was to increase productivity by investment and to reduce costs through modernization, the GDR squandered its resources on wage increases which became meaningless in the face of dwindling supplies and diminished variety of consumer goods. By the end of 1960, as Leuschner reported, excess spending power equaled 1,800,000,000 marks ($450,000,000). By 1961 it had increased to 2,800,000,000 marks ($700,000,000). As wages spiraled and there was less to spend them on, the old disillusionment and dissatisfaction which had plagued the GDR from 1945 to 1956 returned. It was followed by inordinate restlessness.

On one trip to the GDR in early 1961 I was surprised to see so many new and attractive cafés, restaurants, and bars, most of which seemed to be permanently crowded. An Erfurt acquaintance explained rhetorically: "What else are people going to do?

Where else should they spend the money they have if the shelves are always empty?"

The growing gap, between excess purchasing power on the one hand and dearth of consumer goods on the other, would not in itself have triggered a new mass exodus had not two other factors contributed to East Germany's malaise. First the devastating drouth of the summer of 1959 which was compounded by forced collectivization of all agriculture in 1960. Second, the threatened cancellation by West Germany of the interzonal trade agreements for which Ulbricht attempted to compensate with a crash industrialization program designed to make the GDR independent of critical deliveries from Bonn.

The drouth which plagued Central Europe in 1959 was one of the worst of the century. It precipitated not only grain, potato, and beet shortages but a feed scarcity so severe that in the GDR nearly thousands of head of cattle and hogs had to be slaughtered. Meat was plentiful for a while, but nothing else.

In this situation, Ulbricht, goaded by some of his most radical associates, decided to rush full collectivization of the entire farming sector. Every conceivable means of pressure was employed, from the most abject cajolery to imprisonment on trumped up charges, to force farmers to join cooperatives by April 1960. The party terror then turned on small tradesmen, craftsmen, and artisans who likewise were pressured to join collectives or take up state credits and partnerships.

What ensued was a chain reaction which in sixteen months drove 350,000 to flight. Not primarily farmers, by the way, but all those who had the feeling the regime would never free itself of terrorist undercurrents. The result: nothing worked anywhere. Even those active in industry lost heart. Though the regime was still raising their wages and their spending power continued to climb they found less and less to buy.

In September 1960 the Bonn government added to the confusion by cancelling the interzonal trade agreement in retaliation for the political excesses of Ulbricht's regime against farmers and craftsmen. It was in part a short circuit reaction provoked by the rampant feeling in West Germany that the GDR was on the brink of collapse; the intent: to deliver the *coup de grâce*. Ulbricht could have forced Bonn to retreat by threatening to cut off his substantial food and machinery deliveries to West Berlin which were part of the agreement. Instead, he responded by launching the ill-fated *Störfreimachungs* campaign, a program to make the GDR independent once and for all of West German heavy machinery, chemical and metallurgical supplies. It injected a new element of irrationality and confusion into an already teetering economy. Notwithstanding the "main economic mission" whose goal was matching West German *consumer* goods consumption, Ulbricht embarked on a crash *industrialization* program. The refugee stream threatened to turn into a flood and the economy to collapse. The Wall was the only solution.

"Are we really to blame for it?" an astute, pragmatic young Rostock executive once asked me rhetorically. "Yes and no. The attitude of the people, the years of privation that forced so many to flee—those were not our fault. That we exacerbated a critical situation by engaging in economic experiments and ideological foolishness just at the moment when we were on the threshold of stability—that was our stupidity. And we pay the price several times a day: whenever a West German politician or newspaper screams anew about our inhumanity."

The screams are not without justification. Since it was built, 163 East Germans have been killed by their own police and border guards in attempts to escape: 81 of them in Berlin, 82 along the 856-mile frontier that divides the GDR from the Federal Republic. For all the benefits it may have brought the GDR—stability, economic progress, and a palpable nationalism—the Wall remains what it is: a symbol of man's cruelty to man.

To the West it presents an ugly scar of concrete slabs, bricked-up buildings, brambles of barbed wire, searchlights, watchtowers, the eerie nighttime crack of a rifle shot, the concussion of an exploding land mine, and the incessant howling and yapping of the watch dogs in the 110-yard wide *Todeszone* (death zone). Ulbricht has tried to delude his subjects that it was built, not to keep them in, but saboteurs, provocateurs, and Western agitators out. Albert Norden has concocted the wildest of tales about a NATO "Gray Plan," for invading the GDR in September of 1961. Many East Germans believe these fairy tales though they would probably be more sympathetic to the truth.

For East Germans who live far from Berlin or the West German border the fortifications are a remote annoyance—peripheral to their lives.

For East Berliners it is a different matter. The Wall is a moribund presence which no rise in the living standard, no plethora of swank cafés and luxury shops on Unter den Linden or Karl Marx Allee can eradicate easily. For them it is an ubiquitous phantom, an omnipresent admonition that they are not free. Yet, with an incongruity that only human nature can explain, they are attracted to it with a funereal, lemming-like compulsion. Every weekday a small knot of mute watchers gathers at Pariser Platz, to look silently across no-man's land to the Brandenburg Gate. On Sunday afternoons, when Germans are wont to take a *Spaziergang* before gorging themselves on *Kaffee und Kuchen*, the knot turns into a crowd. Impassively they stand there where a low stone hedge, topped by petunias has been set to designate the start of the restricted zone. Many just sit on the benches under the linden trees at this confluence of two worlds and listen: to the rumble of the subway trains which were once the subterranean lifelines of the city. The U-bahn still runs but no East Berliner can use it to ride to Kurfürstendamm, for the Wall reaches beneath the ground. Border guards patrol the last eastern station, making sure no one departs without permission. They listen to the barking of the police dogs in the death zone. And if they come at night when distant sounds are amplified, they can hear the guards talking and laughing as they patrol.

Just beyond the Brandenburg Gate—in West Berlin—a huge billboard lists the number killed at the Wall. East Berliners who peer through the colonnades of the gate can read it. "It says fifty-six," insisted one teenager whose conversation I overheard one day. "No, you fool," insisted his friend. "That's an eight, not a six. It reads fifty-eight." They peered intently for a moment, then the first admitted: "Oh well, maybe you're right. But two more or less, what's the difference anyway."

This is the saddest square in the world—here where the weeds grow in the ruins of a once arrogant empire, where Unter den Linden, dazzling in its resplendence, collides with no-man's land. This is a place where anger seethes and daring plans are made. "A helicopter is what we ought to have," said one young man who late one night had taken a seat next to me to listen to the rumble of the U-bahn below. "No," a companion corrected him. "Not just a helicopter. A rocket, a rocket is what we need."

The 26,000 East Germans who have escaped since 1961 have tried everything but helicopters and rockets. The Wall is not merely a symbol of man's cruelty but a tribute to his ingenuity. Escapees have tunneled under it, flown over it, swum around it, tightroped across it and rammed through it with armor-plated cars and trucks. But the gentleman's way is to simply outwit it: with passport flimflams of unique enterprise. They prove that Germans, though Communists, still have as healthy a respect for uniforms and an authoritative manner as they did sixty years ago when Wilhelm Voigt the shoemaker donned a Prussian uniform, commandeered a squad of passing soldiers, occupied the borough hall of Koepenick and fleeced its treasury of every pfennig.

The best East-West Koepenickade was staged by Kurt Strübind, a pudgy white-haired middle-aged Berliner who spirited 180 East Germans to the West with leather passport-like documents originally printed as membership cards in an exclusive Munich playboy club called "Confederation Diplomatique."

The cards, embossed with the initials CD, were almost indistinguishable from diplomatic passports.

One day, enroute from Munich to East Berlin to visit his aged mother, Strübind, as a joke, showed East German border guards the "CD" card instead of his real passport. "The Vopos snapped to attention, cleared me immediately and didn't even charge the Autobahn fee. That gave me the idea," he explained.

First Strübind spirited his nearly blind, seventy-seven-year-old mother to West Berlin by supplying her with one of the CD cards, dressing her in expensive clothes, and hiring an official-looking limousine. From January 1962 until November 1963, when the ploy became too risky, and Strübind had to take time out to serve a fraud sentence in a Munich jail, 386 East Germans escaped to the West: 180 using the CD club card, 206 a more sophisticated counterfeit of a United Nations passport. The price per operation: $25 for the document, $125 for clothing, limousines, and incidentals. Among his assistants, Strübind counted a professional escape ring—one of dozens operating in Berlin—and U. S. Army intelligence agents.

West Berliners still chuckle about the playboy club railway, just as they will never forget the day a Russian Army sedan took four East Germans to the West. Dressed in homemade Soviet uniforms, riding a used car that they had painted regulation olive green, they drove right through the Eastern controls at Checkpoint Charlie without arousing a ripple of suspicion.

Occasionally subterfuge—and once even murder—at the expense of the innocent has paved the way to freedom.

Clearly one of the boldest escapes was Heinz Holzapfel's high-wire act right from the roof of East Berlin's Ministries Building, a few feet from the wall. Holzapfel, a Leipzig industrial economist, his wife Jutta and their son Günter, spent the entire day in the building—once headquarter of Hermann Göring's Luftwaffe—on a pretense of official business. Toward closing time they hid in a lavatory, hanging a sign on the door: OUT OF ORDER. There they waited until everyone but a ground-floor watchman had left, then went to the roof from where they threw a nylon rope, to waiting helpers in West Berlin who attached a steel cable. Holzapfel pulled it up, fastened it to a flagpole atop the building while the other end of the cable was anchored and winched tight. Then the Holzapfel family went on a dizzying ride to freedom in hand-made harnesses attached to rollers.

Such escapes demand not only a high degree of courage but help. Deprived of mystique and propaganda, the exodus since the Wall turns out to be largely the product of organized exfiltration—an art that has become highly refined but also increasingly mercenary. For many years the center of organized escape activity was a group of altruistic theology students at West Berlin's Free University. For a moderate price, which barely covered actual expenses, and at high personal risk, they arranged escapes at the request of friends and relatives of East Germans. Ostensibly their financial support—to pay for automobiles with trick compartments, forged passports, tunnels (a reliable one can cost up to $50,000) and even miniature submarines that cruised along Berlin's rivers and canals—came from the World Federation of Lutherans and various Catholic and Protestant groups. The CIA was never far away, however. Their motives—humanity and adventure—were above reproach and they have staged hundreds of exfiltrations at an astronomical cost to their own ranks. More than thirty, including a half dozen Americans, have been arrested by East German police and State Security Service (SSD). Once caught they could count on terms of up to eight and more years imprisonment.

Far less savory are the exfiltration rings operated by gangs of West Berlin underworld characters who arrange escapes for little other motive than profit. To these must be added the networks run by some seventeen competing Allied and German intelligence organizations which bribe, cheat, blackmail and threaten with little, if any, regard for the moral or political values involved. The French are reported to be the worst in this category with one American operation a close second.

The magnitude of some of these activities was first disclosed by four escape artists and couriers who, after having been caught in East Berlin, spilled a sordid but apparently true story of corruption, manipulation and ruthless disregard for human lives by Allied intelligence agencies.

The four were drifters with a number of things in common: they were all asocial, jobless, roofless and broke. They were recruited in April 1965 in a seedy Berlin bar, outfitted with false West German passports and for $100 each, sent as couriers into East Berlin. The passports were to go to contacts in the Soviet sector who would use them to slip into West Berlin. The four couriers were to get drunk and tell border guards they had lost their identity cards. After a couple of hours of questioning, they were assured, the East German *Grepos* (*Grenzpolizei*—border police) would release them.

Instead, they were arrested and tried. For confessing, all four were put on probation and permitted to return to West Berlin where they identified a notorious Berlin underworld character and a some-time butcher with a record as long as the Kurfürstendamm as their principal contacts. The escape ring, they alleged, charged $2000 to $4000 for each job: cash in advance, no guarantee. The ring operated with obviously unworkable documents and stories so transparent that even the dumbest SSD interrogator wouldn't have believed them. Before they went on the mission, one of the four reported, each man had to sign a statement "that our motives were purely idealistic."

Their allegations challenged the sacrosanct illusion that all escape artists are either university students or theology lecturers. They are not. As Albert Schütz, forty-three-year-old boss of one of West Berlin's numerous professional rings put it: "Of course we don't do such things for free. We have freedom for sale and it has a certain value at present." According to West Berlin internal revenue authorities who slapped a lien for back taxes on him in 1966, the value in Schütz's case equals $300,000—the amount he is believed to have collected from refugees or their friends and relatives during a four-year period.

The greatest irony is that many of the escapees hardly seem worth bringing out. "In my last tunnel," said Wolfgang Fuchs, one of the brightest and most honest of the professionals, "Refugee number nine was a full professor, refugee number ten was a streetwalker." In fact, admits Fuchs, professional exfiltrators had a hand in helping most of the prostitutes of East Berlin's Friedrich Strasse to West Berlin's Augsburger Strasse, where the prices are higher. Few of the escapees are legitimate political refugees, more often they seek economic advantages. Occasionally they are drifters between the shady worlds of half legitimacy on both sides of the Wall.

In December 1966, for example, Western newspapers ballyhooed the bizarre but successful dash to freedom of a thirty-seven-year-old butcher, Hans Joachim Kläber, his wife and their three children. Amid gunfire, flares, and searchlight probes, they crawled through three barbed-wire fences. Three weeks after being hailed as a hero, Kläber was arrested by West Berlin police who discovered that he was, in fact, a fugitive from West German justice who had fled to East Germany earlier to avoid serving a jail term for assault.

Berlin is the most dramatic and most publicized escape route but by no means the one most commonly used. A considerable number of East Germans have escaped via the satellite countries by going to Rumania, Bulgaria, or Czechoslovakia on vacation where they meet contacts—friends, relatives, or professional escape artists—who smuggle them out in automobiles with fake trunks or false floors or counterfeit passports.

Some refugees have even used East Germany's two pleasure steamers—the gleaming white *Völkerfreundschaft* or the 20,000-ton *Fritz Heckert*—as vehicles for defecting in the Scandinavian and Mediterranean countries. In Trelleborg, Swedish port authorities keep out a raft for refugees who may want to jump from the East German ferry when it calls on weekend excursions.

The hardy and the daredevils are likely to go by the open sea: in dinghies, rafts and once in a while by swimming across the Baltic.

The Baltic Sea is strictly for adventurous spirits. Nevertheless, in 1966 some eighty-nine East Germans—most of them equipped with little more than a dinghy, a pair of oars, a motley assortment of personal effects and a general notion of the direction—succeeded in reaching Denmark, Sweden, or West German shores. No one knows how many failed: as victims of the elements or GDR police and navy boats that patrol far out in international waters. Some, it is known, lost their bearings and drifted right back to East Germany.

To plug this escape hatch, East German authorities have instituted strict security precautions. All pleasure boats, including larger yachts owned by party officials, must remain within territorial waters and each boat requires a special permit to leave port. Dinghies and rafts may not proceed more than 150 yards offshore. Watchtowers and carefully camouflaged police dugouts have been strung along the beaches.

Pursuit is by no means restricted to the three-mile limit and Scandinavian skippers can tell of numerous dramatic encounters with East German navy and coast guard patrols on the high seas.

In searching for a pattern of motives among the post-Wall refugees, one frequently finds some family angle. Few come from the East who do not already have relatives in the West. Sometimes it is sudden, unexpected tragedy: sickness or the death of a parent or child. Hundreds of Romeo and Juliet situations still exist and, despite the Wall, new ones are created when West Germans visit in the East. Very often a family has been split and those left behind in the East look for ways to get out—though there are also legal, albeit cumbersome ways of leaving the GDR. In fact, since the Wall was built, the Red Cross has resettled 122,000 East Germans in the Federal Republic as part of a family reunification program: almost five times as many as the 26,000 who have escaped since August 13, 1961.

Once a gush of humanity, the refugee flow has thinned to a barely perceptible trickle of only 1155 persons during all of 1966. In a few years it may stop completely. The Bonn government contends that the risks of escaping have become so great and the chances of success so small that East Germans have stopped trying. The Federal Republic argues heatedly, though not too convincingly, that there would be a new westward stampede the minute the Wall or the barbed wire along the border disappeared. Evidence for this, however, becomes progressively hard to find.

Aside from the rising standard of living and the nascent nationalism which are transforming East German attitudes, two other barometer readings of the mood in the GDR should be taken into account. Already the thrust of the current refugee movement is on teenagers and youths in their early twenties—who account for 35 percent of the escapees today. Their motives, to judge from the testimonials they give reception camp officials, are neither political nor economic but mixtures of personal grievances with a thirst for thrill and adventure. Secondly, the overwhelming majority of those East Germans who do have the chance to visit West Germany legally—old-age pensioners, business executives, writers, musicians, and artists—show little inclination to remain.

As a political factor the teenage refugees are meaningless. "I came because life is so boring over there," one seventeen-year-old explained. An eighteen-year-old youth said he fled to avoid being drafted into the army. This may make him a political opponent of the Ulbricht regime, but it is just as easy to conclude that he would have tried to beat the draft anywhere else. Every summer when school is out and young East Germans are pressured to work on collective farms, the teenage exodus increases. All of the long-haired "beatleniks" whom I have met in the GDR assured me they would "take off right now," if they had "the guts to try." But when I asked one of these youngsters why, he merely replied: "They're always bothering me here, telling me how to dress or not to dress, threatening to cut off my hair. In the West people like us can live as they please." He was visibly shaken when I told him that *Gammler* with shoulder-length hair like his were being chased off West German streets even faster than Eastern ones. It would be absurd to infer that today's refugees are not to be taken seriously. But to judge the spirit and attitude of East Germany's pent-up population by the refugees when 35 percent are teenagers, is as conclusive as assuming that Mao Tse-tung's Red Guards will determine the future political course of Red China.

A far more dependable criterion seems to me the reaction and attitude of the thousands of East German pensioners who have visited the West since November 1964—when they were again permitted to travel to the Federal Republic. Annually more than 500,000 East German men over sixty-five and women over sixty visit the Federal Republic. Only 2500—less than half a percent—elect to remain permanently, a choice tantamount to escape from the GDR.

In a country already critically overaged, desperate for every helping hand but niggardly toward every hungry mouth, the pensioners pose an additional burden to an already strained economy. The regime would have liked nothing better than to see them remain in West Germany where the Bonn government would have to pay for their support. Yet, the preponderance of these elder citizens elected to return: despite nominally higher pension payments in the West and notwithstanding the fact that most of them have children or close relatives in the Federal Republic who, one assumes, would have contributed to their support.

"Old people," West German authorities rationalized, "are more closely tied to their environment. Once people reach a certain age they are not as easily transplanted. They become reluctant to leave their possessions, their friends, their families. This is why so many of the elderly visitors from the Soviet Zone chose not to remain here."

Though this argument is valid, West Germans should realize that inducements to remain in the West are far less compelling than Bonn's propaganda suggests. As one elderly lady told me: "The pension I would get in the West would probably be higher, but only slightly. Here, however, I have an apartment that rents for only thirty-five marks per month. In West Germany I would have to pay at least three times as much. Why, I would starve on what remained unless I became a burden on my children. Now that I can go see them once a year, I am perfectly content to remain where I am. All those lovely luxury goods in West German stores are an enticement, of course. But could I afford them? And at my age, who needs them?" As one sixty-one-year-old woman from Cottbus put it bluntly in an interview with an East German paper after visiting her children in West Berlin: "I compared the living standards closely and they are way ahead of us of course. But the value of my pension mark is higher in the GDR."

One of the interesting facts of divided German life which everyone knows about but nobody talks about (because it fits into neither the West's nor the East's propaganda pattern) is the family reunification program. Even before the Wall, hundreds if not thousands of East Germans and their families were permitted to leave East Germany legally each year with all their household and personal goods.

In one such case, the husband had been barred from practicing his trade by an East German de-Nazification board because he had been a member of Hitler's Condor Legion in the Spanish Civil War. After several years he was permitted to open a small grocery store but remained under constant political and economic pressure. "They wouldn't let me work in my trade and the store didn't produce enough to support my family," the man explained. "One day I wrote a letter to Ulbricht and asked that I either be given a decent job or be allowed to emigrate to West Germany with my wife and children. The red tape was endless and my friends thought I was crazy. But finally, in the fall of 1956, after about a year of battling bureaucracy, filling out questionnaires and waiting, I was told I could leave. We took everything with us."

No doubt the strangest and least publicized phenomenon of human movements between the two Germanys is the "refugee in reverse."

Until early 1960, when New York *Herald Tribune* reporter Gaston Coblentz and New York *Times* reporter Flora Lewis first disclosed details about the mounting number of West-East refugees—which they estimated to be running at almost 50 percent of the East-West flow, Bonn officials had stanchly denied that such movement existed. Ernst Lemmer, then Minister of all-German Affairs stated flatly that the movement of Germans from West to East was "insignificant" and had at no time exceeded 10 percent of the refugee flow from East to West Germany.

West Germany's *Der Spiegel* magazine, however, reached the startling conclusion that the "reverse refugee" rate had been mounting steadily over the years. In 1959, when 143,000 East Germans had fled to the West, 63,076 residents of West Germany moved to the GDR. Nearly two-thirds, however, were "returnees"—men and women who had been disillusioned by or expected too much from the Federal Republic.

Nowadays both Germanys engage in a numerical juggling act designed to discredit the other's claims. Nevertheless, after denying for many years that there was any significant flow of humanity toward East Germany, the Federal Republic now admits officially that during the fifteen-year period from 1950 to 1964, a half million persons with West German identity papers moved to the GDR. One-third to one-half of these "West Germans," according to GDR figures, were originally East Germans who had fled and decided to return.

For the GDR, of course, these re-defectors were all "disappointed by the harshness of capitalist reality and could no longer stomach the fascist, revanchist, militarist way of life" in the Federal Republic. To read one of their testimonials—the price of readmission—is to have read them all. "Eight years ago," so said one *Neues Deutschland* article, "Ingrid Mai, a twenty-eight-year-old worker, left our Republic. Now she has returned. What induced her? Frau Mai worked in a champagne bottling plant in Offenbach. Though she toiled just as hard as her male colleagues, she earned only half as much. Such inequitable compensation is no exception (in West Germany). Here are a few examples. In the year 1961 the monopolists and captains of enterprise earned 7,837,189,560 marks ($1,959,297,340) extra profits by underpaying women." For several columns the article rambled on about the exploitation of West German women and exhorted them to free themselves of the chains of male domination. It concluded on Ingrid Mai's dark warning: "That is why I left West Germany. I paid dearly for a bitter lesson. Now I have recognized that the GDR is my real home. I am glad to be here again."

A Munich physician, moved to East Germany, as he told a *Neues Deutschland* reporter "because I could no longer let Bonn use me as a tool of its atomic rearmament policy." A worker from the Ruhr said laconically on his arrival in Eisenach: "I met the factory owners and recognized them for what they really are." One West German truck driver said, "I turned my back on Bonn because I sympathize with the North Vietnamese people." A miner from the hard-hit coal pits of the Ruhr explained that he left West Germany because, "like so many others, I experienced the harshness of the Bonn regime." And one young deserter from the Bundeswehr engaged in the epitome of name dropping when he explained, "I just got tired of sitting at the same table with War Minister Gerhard Schroeder and General Ulrich de Maizière."

Many of these migrants from prosperity are the pitiful driftwood of a country divided. Refugees once, they have simply found the ties of friendship and family more persuasive than propaganda, ideology or economic opportunity. Others are the universal failures who were cast to sea by the tough demands of life in the East, then floundered on the reefs of the West's harsh realities. They expected streets paved with gold only to discover instead that hard work is a criterion of prosperity on both sides of the Wall.

Not a few are deserters or draft dodgers who soon realize, with dismay, that East Germany also has selective service. Many are professional deadbeats who know they are safe from their creditors behind the barbed wire and mines, for East German law guarantees them immunity from collection agencies.

Yet, it would be self-deceptive to assume that all of the reverse refugees are the flotsam of social progress. Many are idealists who genuinely reject the materialism, reaction, and political restlessness which—let us be honest—makes West Germany so problematical even for its most loyal allies. Some perhaps are veteran Communists. After all, until it was outlawed and declared unconstitutional in 1956, the West German Communist Party had 70,000 members and polled 1.3 percent of the total votes in 1949. These sympathizers have not simply disappeared. What is to prevent some of them from moving East? Those who do, however, are often disillusioned by the realities of life under German Communism.

Though the GDR is gratified by the eastward movement and spares no effort to milk it for maximum propaganda effect, East German authorities do not welcome "reverse refugees" indiscriminately. They are carefully screened at two reception centers—Eisenach and Barby near Magdeburg—and subjected to several weeks of questioning and political quarantine before being provided with work and apartments. A $12.50 per person gratuity is all they receive while in the camp, though local authorities are authorized to grant "West refugees" long term, low-interest loans of up to 2000 marks ($500) to assist settlement and readjustment.

East German officials are, *a priori*, leery of all arrivals. Moreover they know that often social instability is the characteristic of returnees from the West. Interrogators attempt to weed out those who, they fear, will be a disturbing element in factory and community, the two focal points of East German life. No doubt they are guided by bad experiences and it is interesting to note that *East* German authorities have divulged the fact that criminality among returnees and resettlers is four times higher than among the indigenous East German population.

But once accepted, resettlers and returnees become East Germans like everyone else and discover—sometimes to their shock and bewilderment—that there is no return: except at great risk.

The exodus from "Germany's first workers' and peasants' state" has been effectively halted. The East German regime can now even boast that it is the beneficiary of a "reverse flow" running three to one in its favor, whatever its reasons may be. But Ulbricht's quintessential problem has not changed. The Wall which in itself has become the primary irritant and an important motivation for flight, can come down only when East Germans stop looking upon West Germany as a chrome-plated neon-lighted Shangri-la.

Two paths lead to an equalization of the disparities between East and West Germany. The GDR's oligarchs are feverishly counting on both to reach their goal. One is the hope that Shangri-la's chrome will tarnish and its lights dim as Bonn's vaunted miracle economy becomes mired in a recession. The other is melioration of the productivity and profitability of East Germany's own industrial potential so as to make the GDR a small but economically viable showcase of Communism.

Ulbricht's propagandists chortled with typical German *Schadenfreude* as the 1966 slowdown of West Germany's economy turned rapidly into the baby recession of 1967 with its half million unemployed, drastic production cutbacks, mounting stockpiles of unwanted coal, closed pits and plants and the hint of political radicalism. Even before the outlines of the slump emerged clearly, *Neues Deutschland* had brought out its biggest type to chronicle the doom of the West German boom. Ere the first layoffs and production cutbacks were announced in December 1966, East German publicists were already depicting breadlines that reached from Hamburg to Munich. In March 1967, when actual employment had reached nearly 700,000, or 2.6 percent of the West German labor force, the ideologues happily dusted off those old Marxist axioms about the seeds of self-destruction sprinkled on every capitalist's dirty dividends. The pragmatists of industry and construction predicted darkly but with audible undertones of glee that "thousands of West German workers may be coming here to look for jobs. It behooves us to make plans now to house them instead of waiting until the deluge begins."

The deluge has yet to start. But is it any wonder that East Germans say emphatically: "Go to the west? Now? I'd be crazy. At least I know what I've got here. Job security and a certain future. Our system may never glitter like theirs. But it won't produce breadlines either."

Yet, it is with the aim of producing glitter that East Germany's economists and pragmatic young managers have launched a new operation bootstrap. With profit as their god, the New Economic System of Planning and Management as their catechism, rationalization and efficiency experts as their high priests, computers as their prayer wheels, they are reaching for a new goal: competitiveness on a world standard. It is a brimstony creed of survival of the fittest which is sure to leave all the old saints of Communism from Marx to Stalin shaking their heads in disbelief. But if the enthusiasm of its faithful is any criterion of ultimate success, then the GDR appears, at last to be on a leap forward from which there will be no looking back.

PART THREE

THE
SECOND
MIRACLE

CHAPTER V

Waiting for Marx

For many years an objective evaluation of East Germany's economic system—at least its potential—became blurred by the great ideological struggle between East and West, Moscow and Washington. In both worlds, doctrine and dogma supplanted common sense and reason. We know, for example, that capitalism has little, if anything, in common with the caricatures in which Communist propagandists portray it. But in the heat of the struggle, has the West been any less guilty of distortion? Do Communist economies really make so many more mistakes than capitalist ones? Or is it, perhaps, that Eastern executives atone for their blunders with public self-criticism while Western businessmen pay for their mistakes in the bankruptcy courts?

For more than two decades the ideologies have jousted on the field where they converge: Germany. The confrontation has proven inestimably flattering to capitalism. In the West there is wealth, abundance and luxuriant comfort. In the East: a treadmill of economic experimentation, years of privation, incessant exhortation, and drabness. Yet, this tournament of the ideologies and economies is of only limited significance, for it presupposes that the two Germanys began their postwar reconstruction on an equal footing. As it was, however, their chances were hopelessly uneven.

As West Germany's *Der Spiegel* once pointed out, "The 1945 Soviet Occupation Zone's transformation into the German Democratic Republic of today is as much a miracle as the development of the three Western zones into the Federal Republic. The economic reconstruction of East Germany was thwarted by obstacles and difficulties which would have given any capitalist nightmares."

U.S. economist and *Newsweek* columnist Henry C. Wallich came even closer to the heart of the matter once when he analyzed West Germany's astounding success. "Many circumstances and developments on which Germany had no influence contributed to its economic recovery," he said. "It is hard to determine what interrelationship there was between luck and Germany's own accomplishment. In addition to German industriousness there were such factors as foreign aid, the Korea boom and others. That all these cooperated at the right time in the right spot is the real German miracle."

East Germany, on the other hand, while certainly industrious, had no luck. It was plagued from the start by a concatenation of factors, each of which acted upon the other to produce a cumulation of calamities.

Undeniably, some of the blunders committed by Ulbricht's planners and amateur economists were so monumental as to be almost ineffable. But Communist bungling is just one of many factors that contributed to East Germany's dilemma. One of the cardinal elements is the Soviet Zone's paucity of natural resources and lack of heavy industrial capacity. Another was its severance from traditional markets and sources of supply. Soviet reparations demands were another cause. So was the refugee exodus, largely exacerbated by East Germany's impoverishment. Furthermore, during the cold war years, East Germany became the victim of extensive industrial sabotage by a variety of West German intelligence agencies. Finally, the ambivalence of Russian policy delayed the GDR's postwar recovery by at least seven, possibly ten years.

All too often the Soviet Zone has been portrayed as a highly industrialized region whose productive potential was stunted by Communist mismanagement. Indeed, eastern or central Germany was industrialized. It had important centers of machine, motorcar, electrical, chemical and optical manufacturing. But the emphasis was on a light and medium industry which depended on raw materials and semi-finished goods from the west. The

Ruhr was—and remains—the true behemoth of German industry. It mined more than 90 percent of the Reich's anthracite and produced nine out of ten tons of its steel. By comparison, eastern-central Germany was an industrial dwarf. It accounted for only 24.7 percent of the Reich's machine, heavy equipment and motor vehicle production; 22.3 percent of its electrical industrial manufacturing; 13 percent of its rubber production. On the other hand, it produced more than 35 percent of the optical and precision instruments, 40 percent of the textiles, 40 percent of the cellulose and paper goods, and 30 percent of the chemicals.

Though the GDR is today one of the world's leading industrial powers, it has one of the weakest energy and resource bases. Domestic deposits of iron ore, copper and oil are insignificant. Although electric power production has quadrupled from 14,000,000,000 kilowatt hours in 1936 to more than 54,000,000,000 in 1965, only 1.4 percent of this is produced by hydroelectric stations. The GDR has virtually no water power to harness. The only anthracite coal deposits worth mentioning are in the Zwickau area of Saxony where total reserves are estimated at less than 40,000,000 tons—one-third of West Germany's *annual* anthracite production.

In fact, the GDR is rich in only one resource: brown coal, or lignite, of which it has an overabundant reserve of 40 billion tons. Hence, the GDR depends and runs on *Braunkohle* which provides nearly 90 percent of the electric power, and serves as a source for artificial high temperature coke, gas, and liquid derivatives such as phenol, tars, motor fuel, and plastics. But lignite, no matter how it is used, is unprofitable and because of its high water and sand content, wasteful.

By any standard it would have been a poor beginning for a rump state. But in addition to the penalties of nature, East Germany carried the major brunt of the Reich's defeat. Although actual destruction was higher in the western zones, East Germany's proportional losses from war damage were higher. Twenty percent of West Germany's, 40 percent of East Germany's industrial potential had been destroyed in air raids and battle. An even more crippling blow, however, was delivered by the Soviet reparations demands.

Kiel University Professor Fritz Baade says: "No one can deny that Germans as a whole owed a debt to the Soviet Union for the senseless destruction wrought there. The bill, however, has been paid by East Germany alone. On the day of reunification the eastern half of Germany will legitimately be entitled to present a demand for millions in reparations which we should have helped to pay."

Actually, Stalin first raised the issue of reparations as early as September 1941—at a time when Hitler's armies were still blitzkrieging their way toward Moscow. "What about getting the Germans to pay for the damage?" the Soviet dictator asked during a meeting with U. S. Ambassador Averell Harriman and Britain's Lord Beaverbrook. The Briton and the American evaded the question, but this early mention foreshadowed the Soviet demands that eventually proved to be the most difficult hurdle to Allied agreement on treatment of Germany.

The Russians specified their demands at the Yalta Conference in February 1945 where they proposed that Germany be required to pay reparations of $20,000,000,000, half of this to the Soviet Union. Payment was to be made in goods and property rather than cash. Half was to come from seizures, particularly of industrial property, during the first two years after the war. Industries useful solely or primarily for military purposes were to be removed entirely. Steel, electrical engineering and chemical capacity was to be reduced by 80 percent. The additional $10,000,000,000 was to be obtained in goods provided by annual deliveries over a period of ten years.

Britain and the United States responded to this proposal with cool reserve. Both sympathized with Russia's losses—which the U. S. Office of Strategic Services had estimated at $16,000,000,000 in capital and an additional $4,000,000,000 in inventories and personal property. Neither challenged the USSR's need for reparations to help postwar rehabilitation in view of the tremendous damage inflicted by the German invasion. However, Roosevelt and Churchill questioned the feasibility of extracting such huge sums without ruining the German economy and thus jeopardizing future German stability. The U.S. in particular was not interested in a reparations scheme for which it would eventually have to pay by helping to keep the Germans from starving. Though the amount of reparations was never agreed upon, the Russians took $10,000,000,000, as their share, for granted.

At the Potsdam Conference in July agreement was reached that reparations be handled on a zonal basis, each victor taking for himself what he needed and wanted. To compensate the Soviets for the lack of industrial facilities in their zone, the U.S. and U.K. agreed to turn over to the Russians ten percent of the industrial equipment confiscated in the American and British Zones. An additional 15 percent would be made available to the Soviets in exchange for an equivalent value in food and raw materials.

The plan was based on a number of assumptions which, when they turned out to be false, vitiated the whole scheme. The principal supposition was that Germany would be treated as an economic unit. Contrary to popular belief, the first obstacles in pursuing a unified economic policy were raised by the French, not the Soviets, though in the end it was Soviet refusal to provide food supplies to the western zones, coupled with the growing ideological rift between East and West, that resulted in the establishment of Bizonia in December 1946 and Germany's economic division.

Moreover, industrial dismantling—the heart of the plan—had progressed more slowly than expected—thanks in part to deliberate slowdowns by American business and military circles and objections by economists who questioned the actual monetary value of dismantling machines and industrial equipment torn out of an integrated economic structure. By the time the Marshall Plan was announced in June 1947, dismantling and reparations seemed even more pointless and for all practical purposes, the reparations program in the West came to an end. According to West German statistics it had deprived the country of no more than eight percent of its industrial capacity. The actual capital loss to West Germany has been gauged at approximately $1,100,000,000.

Compared with what the Russians took out of East Germany,

that was a pittance. The West German Soviet Zone Archive, a government agency, has valued the total cost of Russia's reparations policy—including dismantling, profits from Soviet stock corporations and deliveries of finished goods—at $23,800,000,000. Walter Ulbricht, in a speech in April 1965, spoke of $22,500,-000,000. British observers calculated the value in plant and production at $18,000,000,000 by 1953, though the Soviets continued to reap profits from their stock corporations until 1955.

In all, 1667 East German plants were entirely, 254 partly removed. More than 1600 miles of railway line were completely torn up and on an additional 7300 miles, the parallel tracks were ripped out, requiring one-way traffic. In addition, 1,200,000 wooden ties, the equipment of thirteen airports and of three radio stations wandered eastward, often to end up rusting at Brest-Litovsk where the shift from standard European to Soviet wide-gauge track caused endless traffic snarl-ups. The effect on East Germany's economy was devastating. Though rail removal provided the Russians with only 700,000 tons of steel, it crippled the Soviet Zone's transportation network for years. What the Russians did not dismantle, they confiscated and turned into two hundred Soviet Stock Corporations—SAGs.

In addition to these difficulties, East Germany was plagued by industrial and economic sabotage conducted by any of a dozen Western intelligence agencies. Though East Germans exaggerate the effect of cold war sabotage and embellish it with horror stories, there is no doubt that it had a debilitating effect on an already weakened economy.

Such activity took a variety of forms—from arson to deliberate disruption of the supply and transportation system. One of the most effective organizations was the West German Social Democratic Party's "East Bureau" whose recently retired director, Stephan Grzeskowiak Thomas, blushes modestly at mention of his various exploits to monkey wrench and destroy confidence in the GDR's economy. Thomas' most infamous stunts involved counterfeiting GDR railway shipping orders, then sluicing them into the transportation system to misdirect shipments of butter, potatoes, coal and ore in an attempt to cause shortages. In the fall of 1950, for example, Thomas' agents sent five refrigerator cars containing Polish butter, intended for Leipzig, to the Rostock freight yards where they stood on a siding long enough for the butter to turn rancid. Meanwhile railway officials searched frantically for the origin and actual destination of the cars. The following winter hundreds of freight cars containing potatoes were misdirected to dozens of sidings. Before officials could entangle this game of musical railways, the potatoes froze and rotted and East Germans went hungry.

To help compound these troubles, there was also, of course, the growing manpower exodus.

A popular pastime among economists has been to calculate what these various physical, productive and human losses, when measured against the aid received by West Germany from the U.S., actually mean to the GDR.

Probably the most accurate analysis was made by Bridgeport's Professor Apel who arrived at his conclusions with an ingenious and highly unorthodox statistical method. First he correlated all figures to correspond with the relative size of the two Germanys. Then he balanced East Germany's losses through industrial dismantling and reparations against similar West German losses as well as against Bonn's voluntary restitution payments to Israel and individual victims of Nazi persecution. He offset Marshall Plan aid for the West against Soviet loans to East Germany after 1955. Unlike East German economists, he has calculated the loss through the refugee movement on the basis of cumulative productivity, not the average 10,000 marks which Ulbricht claims was spent on the education and training of each worker who fled. Against the benefits which West Germany derived from the influx of East German labor power, Apel has deducted West Germany's expenditures for resettling the refugees, such as government-financed low-rental housing. For example, East Germany's actual productivity loss due to refugees from 1951 to 1961, according to Apel, was 36,000,000,000 marks. However, it cost West Germany 7,000,000,000 marks to house and settle these arrivals from the GDR. Ergo, the net loss in capital and substance to East Germany was only 29,000,000,000 marks. Moreover, Apel took into account that capital losses between 1945 and 1950 inflicted greater damage on East Germany's economy than the losses incurred during the following decade from 1951 to 1961.

The result of his complicated computation: East Germany's losses from 1945 to 1950 equaled 35,900,000,000 marks, from 1951 to 1961 approximately 71,000,000,000 marks—a total of 106,-900,000,000 marks or $26,725,000,000.

In this light, East Germany's economy need not shy away from comparison with the Federal Republic's. This is not to say that the GDR's planners should be absolved of all blame for what has gone and continues to go wrong. On the contrary, many of East Germany's woes result from factors inherent in a planned economy, or at least in the kind of planned economics practiced in the GDR until recently. Perhaps the costliest of all these factors was ideology which, until 1963, was the principal lubricant of East German industry. The plan was industry's highest commandment and fulfillment its ultimate aspiration.

As Ulbricht himself once remarked candidly: "Each year, just before the new plan is announced, you will find a flurry of activity in every shop or factory. Managers are busy trying to set their goals as low as possible so they can meet them without extra effort." And failing at that, they tried other ways to fulfill their plans. When a construction materials plant in Grimmau discovered it would fail in meeting its goal for producing a certain number of bricks, it simply started baking them 10 percent smaller. In Hermsdorf a factory making men's pajamas discovered in June of one year that it was running short of the plan and short of yard goods to meet it. What better solution than to cut all men's pajama pants a few inches shorter? This was the era of tonnage ideology when equipment manufacturers tried to make the heaviest machinery possible because the plan gauged success by weight not quality, practicability or salability. One result: East German diesel locomotive transmissions weighed four times as much as similar but more efficient ones built in West Germany.

This was the period when the only color to East German life came from the red propaganda banners that hung from every gray house, when even midwives and undertakers solemnly swore

Ulbricht (left) being congratulated on seventy-first birthday by Margarete
eller, candidate (and only woman) member of Politburo. Standing behind her,
m left to right: Politburo members Erich Mueckenberger, Horst Sindermann,
bert Warnke, and Werner Jarowinsky. Visible among group in background,
m left: Politburo members Gerhard Grueneberg, Paul Verner, and Hermann
tern. (Half hidden behind Verner and Matern is Erich Apel, the planning chief
committed suicide in December 1965). (Credit: Zentralbild)

[9] Honor guards in front of *Schinckels Neue Wache*, now called "Monumen Victims of Fascism and Militarism" on East Berlin's *Unter-den-Linden*.

[10] Scene of Dresden's *Zwinger* rebuilt after the war.

[11] First of new style buildings being erected on East Berlin's Alexanderpla⸱

to fulfill "the plan." These were the days when East Germans silently (and sometimes not so silently) cursed one Adolf Hennecke, the Teutonic Stachanov, who had dug 6.4 cubic meters of coal in a Zwickau mine—387 percent more than his daily norm—to become the shining but hated example of ever greater effort. It was that terrible time when, as the wits told it, two Chinese engineers visited an East German factory, and asked, "What do you make here, comrades?" Said a foreman: "Parts for elevators." "Ah, that's very progressive, something we don't have yet," said the Chinese. "What parts are you making now?" To which the foreman replied proudly, "The signs that read 'Out of Order.'"

A great deal was out of order in East Germany. That its economy continued to grow nevertheless is as much a miracle as East Germany's ability to overcome the penalties of Soviet occupation and the scarcity of raw materials. It explains in part the defiant pride of those who say today: "Sure we made a lot of mistakes, and we're still making them. But they're our mistakes—just like everything else here is ours. We started with less than nothing and look where we are today."

And where is East Germany today?

It has the highest standard of living in the Communist world and is the world's eighth largest industrial power. Its gross national product and industrial productivity are growing faster than Russia's, West Germany's, Britain's, France's and Italy's. It ranks among the world's top ten producers of electric power, artificial gas, chemical fibres and fertilizers, synthetic rubber, railway rolling stock, merchant ships, radio and TV receivers, household appliances, industrial machinery, machine tools, and optical and precision instruments.

Despite the initial disadvantages with which it started, the GDR has built nine new major power plants, one of them the largest in Europe; fifteen iron and steel mills; eight chemical and twelve machine tool factories; four shipyards; seven new electrotechnical and optical plants; six cement works and eight basic complexes for raw materials conversion including the world's only lignite coking combine.

Since the end of 1960 East Germany's national income has increased by 26 percent at an average annual rate of 3.7 percent. The gross national product has increased by almost 46 percent, the industrial productivity by nearly 45 percent.

Though the statistics are East German and the method of compiling them differs from the system used in capitalist countries, West German economists generally agree today that GDR figures are reliable and that Professor Walter Donda, the thirty-six-year-old chief of East Germany's Statistical Bureau, goes about his work with meticulous conservatism.

For 1967 Donda reported a 5 percent increase in the national income—just as projected in the annual plan—and a 7.2 percent increase in industrial productivity. For 1968, East Germany's managers have planned with the same sober conservatism that has typified their approach since 1964. The plan calls for a 5.4 percent increase in national income, a 6.4 percent increase in industrial productivity, a 7.5 percent increase in construction, a 7 percent increase in foreign trade, a 10.7 percent hike in investment and a bare 2.7 percent boost in agricultural output.

East Germany's most dramatic progress falls into that relatively brief period since January 1964 when initial resignation after the Berlin Wall yielded to a new spirit of confidence which persuaded East Germans to make the best of their plight. It also coincides with the introduction of the "New Economic System of Planning and Management"—NÖSPL to those in the GDR who rejoice in bandying about the hieroglyphics of a new alphabet soup. The high priests of NÖSPL are quick to credit it, not the Wall, for at last putting East Germany's rusty economy into gear.

One such suffragan is Manfred Oertel—though in shiny green suit, pink tie, black pointed shoes and wavy blond hair he looks more like a relic of the zoot-suit era. Oertel is an editor of *Die Finanzwirtschaft*, the monthly oracle of GDR industrial investment and financial policy, an organ that makes the *Wall Street Journal* seem like a tabloid in comparison. "Of course the Wall helped," Oertel told me over coffee and cookies in his cramped East Berlin office. "It helped to stabilize the labor force, which was one of our major problems, and it convinced those people with one psychological foot in the West that the time had come to buckle down and make a go of this country.

"But the progress you see today is due to two other important factors. One is NÖSPL, which swept out all the old cobwebs of dogmatism. Furthermore, we are finally getting a return on our investment. We needed years and billions of marks—investments of time, energy and money—to give this part of Germany the kind of industrial base that would make it self-sufficient and competitive. Now, quite literally, we are starting to get our money back."

Stripped of some of the unintelligible Marxist gibberish in which it is couched, the New Economic System is the execution of the iconoclastic theories originally advanced by Soviet economist Yevsei G. Liberman. What is remarkable is that the GDR, by tradition the most conservative and doctrinaire of the satellite nations, pioneered this highly unorthodox approach—and with a speed and determination that has left more liberal countries far behind.

The New Economic System, in its specifically German form, is the creation of Dr. Erich Apel, the planning chief who committed suicide in December 1965, and Dr. Günter Mittag, since September 1966 czar of East German industry. Though the guidelines were spelled out at the SED's VIth party congress in July 1963, NÖSPL was not inaugurated until February 1964, when Ulbricht introduced it at a plenary meeting of the Central Committee.

Ever since then, East Germany has been rushing down an economic path as revolutionary for orthodox Communism as Roosevelt's New Deal was for American capitalism.

Much of NÖSPL's impact is hidden by the veil of ideologically rooted pseudo-scientific language in which the party continues to shroud all economic activity. To understand East German attitudes one should recall the messianic spirit in which socialism and Communism were born. Walter Florath, one of the editors of *Neues Deutschland* once helped to interpret those views when he wrote: "The change from private to socialist ownership is the primary but not the only criterion of a socialist economy. Public ownership by itself does not develop a socialist relationship toward labor and production. Objectively, there is no difference between building an electric motor in West Germany's AEG plant or at VEB Sachsenwerk in Niederseidlitz. That the people's owned factories were really something new, first had to be impressed on the workers by means of intense ideological activity." Thus a Communist cannot simply start speaking of "profit" and "capital" when all along he has held these to be the phraseology of the "imperialist west." Instead he says "self-contained system of economic levers" when he really means profit and incentives, or "industrial fund reserves" when he thinks of the capital needed by people's owned industries for reinvestment purposes.

However, once one has penetrated the ideology curtain, the significance of the changes taking place under the ground rules of NÖSPL becomes apparent.

The traditional chain of economic command ran along military lines with all powers of decision-making a private preserve of the party leadership. All directives were subject to scrutiny and control from the top, and they often involved such details as which kind of button should be sewn on what suits. Lower echelons of the economic bureaucracy were mere transmission belts of policy and directives with no more right to deviate than company commanders have to ignore the orders of their generals. Though the manager of the Wolfen Film VEB, makers of Orwo photographic products, was responsible for $125,000,000 worth of plant and equipment, he lacked the authority to buy a $1000 machine or give one of his workers a $25 raise. Planners at the top were not only concerned with strategic concepts and final objectives, but with actual deployment of platoons and squads. Annual plan directives for individual industrial ministries used to be catalogues, crammed with infinitesimal detail. Everything was centrally determined, from wages to productivity, from stock purchases to detailed manufacturing specifications. Each ministry's primary function was to prepare even more minute instructions and pass these on to individual plants. Fulfillment of the plan, usually based on quantity or tonnage, was the primary goal. The "economic levers"—incentives—were medals, public honors and premiums for producing more than the established norm. The system, innately impractical, was carried to Teutonic perfection in East Germany where traditional roots of a *dirigiste* economy prevailed from pre-Communist days.

The New Economic System relegated all this to the ideological trash heap. Ulbricht probably came closest to describing NÖSPL when he said that it calls for *economic* planning as opposed to the *administrative* planning of the past.

NÖSPL rests on four basic pillars of reform: 1) Machine and equipment parks may no longer be evaluated at prewar prices but at what it would cost to replace them today. 2) Financing of investment and expansion must come from profits or bank loans, not from state grants or subsidy of raw materials out of state funds. 3) Provided they meet social requirements and fulfill the general plan targets, industrial branches and large enterprises may determine their own production goals, the type of merchandise they produce and the scope of their investment activity. 4) Incentives and premiums are to be based on plant turnover and profit so as to encourage both productivity and quality as well as thrift and economy.

In its first four years NÖSPL has dramatically changed the face of East Germany's economy. All capital assets have been revalued at their true worth and depreciation rates have been reassessed. Industrial subsidies have been abolished or curtailed and interest rates have been introduced.

Profits, like individual bonuses for both management and labor, have been related to performance and now depend on *net* output rather than gross productivity in an effort to eliminate the waste of materials which the old system encouraged. The tonnage ideology has been replaced by a pragmatic approach predicated on accounting in financial rather than physical terms. Quality control is being enforced because it has been linked to profits and bonuses.

Profits have become part of each industry's over-all plan. Every year the industrial branches plan not only production targets but anticipated profits. If profits exceed the amount planned—because of greater efficiency, frugality, or good management—bonuses and premiums for management and labor may come as high as 60 percent of the "excess." The rest is plowed back for investment purposes and improvement of social facilities such as cafeterias, reading rooms, plant nurseries, rest homes, and cultural activities.

Profit also depends on quality. All East German industry operates on the basis of five quality classifications. Periodically investigators of the German Agency for Matériel Examination and Economy (DAMW) inspect the output of industrial plants. For goods in the two top quality categories, plant managers may keep a larger share of their receipts, returning a smaller portion to the state treasury, thus increasing their profits. Conversely, for inferior quality, profits diminish because plants must pay the state a higher share of their gross income.

"In theory," admitted Manfred Oertel, "it sounds fine. In practice the inspectors are often lax and tend to grade higher than they should. Quality improvement remains a major problem."

One of the most difficult tasks which faced the innovators of NÖSPL entailed the complete overhaul of the industrial and supply-price system so that every industry now pays the full true value for its raw materials and semi-finished products, just as it can charge a price commensurate with real worth for its own goods.

For many years, prices of raw materials, semi-finished products and consumer goods were set deliberately low—usually by means of subsidies from the state treasury. There were a number of ideological reasons for this. Communists rejected the principle of supply and demand with subsequent rising and lowering costs as one of the cardinal sins of capitalism. Since price is a source of profit, and profit is the root of all exploitative evil, Communist economists attempted to circumvent the price problem. Moreover, there was a more practical consideration: How much should one state enterprise charge another for its products when, ultimately, all receipts flowed back into the state treasury anyway? Some Marxist-Leninist purists even argued that there should be no charge at all when one enterprise delivered—say coal, bricks, or machine tools—to another. After all, had not Marx said that "the price or money-form of commodities is, like their form of value generally, quite distinct from their palpable bodily form. It is, therefore, a purely ideal or mental form?" And had he not also said, "a general rise in the prices of commodities can result only either from a rise in their values—the value of money remaining constant—or from a fall in the value of money, the values of commodities remaining constant . . . Price is the money name of the labor realized in a commodity?"

Ergo, prices were set at the prewar level (1936) on the assumption that the labor value had not changed. Whenever the price seemed too high—because industries were buying equipment from countries where costs rose with wages, the regime stepped in to subsidize out of the state kitty.

During the years preceding the New Economic System all this did not matter. But low prices became a major problem as soon as the economy switched from plan fulfillment to the principle of profitability.

Since the introduction of NÖSPL, industrial users have had to pay increases of 200 to 400 percent on most raw materials and semi-finished products. For example, the price of raw lignite rose from 3.51 marks per ton to as much as 9.20 marks for the best quality (with the least water and sand ballast). Pressed lignite brickettes jumped from 16.56 to 30 and 42 marks per ton (again depending on quality). On the other hand, retail prices have remained constant and will continue to be subsidized by as much as $75,000,000 annually. If industry is forced to pay more for its raw materials and semi-finished goods but prevented from hiking consumer prices—by decree on domestic markets and because of competitive pressure on world markets—how will it meet the cost?

"That," explained Erhard Heyde, a former staffer of *Die Finanzwirtschaft*, now press spokesman for the new Price Office, "is one of the objectives of the whole scheme. Industry will be forced to rationalize. If it cannot raise consumer prices, it must improve efficiency and raise per capita productivity. This is how we intend to trim the fat and the waste off the economy.

"Of course some retail prices may have to increase. Notice how shabby and neglected most pre-war buildings look. Rents have arbitrarily been kept so low—at 1936 levels—that landlords (be they private individuals, municipalities, or cooperatives) cannot afford renovations. Rents are being raised on new dwelling units so as to provide reserves for future repairs and refurbishment, though a final decision about rents in pre-war houses has not been reached."

There are a number of other decisions about prices which have yet to be reached. The regime is averse to hiking retail prices for political and economic reasons and has assuaged the public with repeated assurances that no increases will be forthcoming. But they may turn out to be unavoidable—if only because price plays an increasingly significant role as a regulator in East Germany's economy.

"Eventually," said Heyde, "some degree of price flexibility on the retail market will be permitted—not in response to supply and demand but to channel and control demand. We use price to influence demand instead of vice versa. Automobiles, for example, are kept arbitrarily expensive because the industry cannot match potential demand. Of course we could sell the *Trabant* for 3000 instead of 8000 marks at home just as we sell it that cheaply abroad. But people would break down the showroom doors. Even at the inflated price, delivery time for a car is up to four years and waiting lists are getting longer instead of shorter."

Most likely, the GDR will eventually institute a system of price ceilings and platforms to provide retail outlets with some freedom of maneuver while at the same time guarding against inflation—a word that NÖSPL has injected into the East German economic vocabulary.

The New Economic System has also had a revolutionary impact on the relationship between producers, suppliers and distributors. Under the old system all allocations—the number of shoes produced by Plant X and the variety to be sold by Retail Store Y— were centrally determined. So was the supply of raw materials or component parts allocated to Shoe Plant X from Tannery Z and Rubber Factory A. Today East Germany's state and people's owned factories are legal corporate bodies, free to engage in contracts with other domestic enterprises and (though on a limited scale) with foreign firms. They may sue each other and be sued before so-called "contract courts" for failure to deliver or perform.

They can choose their suppliers and markets, set production in accordance with orders from retail, wholesale, and export organizations. Annual plans now contain a modicum of detail and are limited, instead, to laying down only general targets so as to provide industrial enterprises and the trusts with as much flexibility as possible.

To the experienced observer of East German life, nothing looks stranger than *Neues Deutschland* these days with its classified ad pages where *Volkseigene Betriebe* (VEBs)—People's owned factories—advertise their wares to other VEBs or hunt for subcontractors for some of their products.

There one finds VEB Spezialfahrzeugwerk Berlin (literally: People's Owned Special Vehicle Manufacturing Plant of Berlin) trying to sell its street-cleaning machines, of which Type 20 is available for immediate delivery. As the advertisement emphasized: "Socialist Rationalization will force even you to do away with unproductive manual labor. Ask for our prospectus and let us make an offer."

One of the cardinal principles of NÖSPL is that industrial enterprises must pay their way and must reorganize where necessary. This opens the possibility not only of forcing the shutdown of unprofitable plants—a heretic thought to the doctrinaire Communist—but the introduction of commercial credits for investment instead of direct state grants. To invest, East German managers must now dip into their own reserves or obtain loans from the German Investment Bank. Even more astounding, the bank has instructions to *look* for customers. Thus far it has not yet advertised in *Neues Deutschland,* but at the rate things are changing in East Germany, even that is possible. Except for major projects of national interest or importance—construction of a dam for instance—investment decisions need not be cleared with either the party or industrial ministries.

As creditor, the Investment Bank has extensive powers. If an enterprise is found to be operating at a loss or producing goods below standard, the bank may not only suspend all credit but put in a commission to investigate the situation and reorganize the factory. One of the first enterprises to be disciplined in this way was the state-owned Textile Machinery Works at Karl-Marx-Stadt, a plant employing 2500, whose credits were suspended in September 1967 because it was in debt to the tune of "millions of marks." The plant was given an ultimatum in which to set its affairs in order. Failing that, the bank would appoint compulsory management.

Of course, the GDR is not turning capitalist. But it is within the realm of possibility that some day East Germany's will be a free market economy with state and cooperatively owned industry instead of private enterprise.

Though the New Economic System rests on four columns of profitability and pragmatism, its keystone is the network of VVBs or *Vereinigungen Volkseigener Betriebe* (Associations of People's Owned Enterprises). VVBs—there are now eighty-five on the industrial sector, seven in the construction field—are hybrids of the old-fashioned cartel, trust and combine. Although the term is not new—VVBs with varying responsibility and power have been part of the economic hierarchy since 1948—it was not until the introduction of NÖSPL that the trusts were accorded the unique role they have today.

"We have as much authority and independence as executives in a large American concern or holding company," said Reiner Stähr, the dark-haired, easy-mannered, thirty-five-year-old managing director of VVB Office Machines and Data Processing Equipment in Erfurt. Judging from his salary or the simplicity of his office, one would never suspect it, though.

Stähr—second-in-command (to General Director Dr. Wolfgang Lungershausen, 42) of an enterprise that employs 33,000 people in fifteen small and medium-sized plants spread over the country—earns a basic salary of 1700 marks ($425) monthly plus premiums and bonuses which average an additional $50 per month. In West Germany he could make four to six times as much. But Stähr told me candidly: "It's a small fortune, here. You have to consider that I spend only $25 a month for rent."

Stähr works in a nondescript turn-of-the-century office building on Erfurt's Karl-Marx-Platz. Brown and dingy on the outside, hastily refurbished inside, it is easier to miss than notice. Only an eight-by-ten-inch aluminum plate on the door identifies it as the nerve center of a Communist industry that exports 180,000 typewriters and 100,000 calculating, invoicing, and accounting machines and has just entered the computer market with its Robotron 300.

"We are the economic, financial, planning, and research center of our branch," said Stähr. "That means we are responsible for all investment, production sales and export goals, and for development coordination."

Like other VVB managers, Stähr can hire and fire, open new plants, close old ones, shift production from one to another, borrow money, allocate capital for investment, distribute profits and deal directly with foreign and domestic customers. He is as much at home running exhibits at trade shows in Moscow as he is at programming conferences in Paris. Were it not for Allied travel restrictions, he insists, he would also be representing his plants in the U.S.

There are VVBs to cover every conceivable branch of manufacturing and distribution: motor vehicle manufacturing, optical and precision instruments, pharmaceuticals, industrial chemicals, heavy machinery, electro-technical goods, furniture, clothing, leather products, shoes, housewares, and agricultural implements.

Eighty-seven percent of East German industry run by these trusts is socialized. The remainder is privately or partly state owned and progressive socialization notwithstanding, continues to play an important role in East German manufacturing, especially on the textile, light industrial and light construction sectors.

At last count, East Germany had 5100 semi-state owned manufacturing firms with 340,000 employees—13 percent of the industrial work force—which produced 9 percent of the gross industrial product and accounted for 21 percent of light industrial output.

In addition to semi-state, East Germany still has 4500 privately owned industrial enterprises which employ 110,000 workers and produce 3 percent of the gross industrial product. Most of these are shops engaged in specialized work on a consignment basis for big nationalized industries. An Eisenhüttenstadt manufacturer of anchor winches and motors represents a typical case. As one of only three producers in this field, he and three employees make nearly half the winches and motors installed on small East German boats and river barges. "It's a trade I learned from my father, who started this business," he explained. "I'm sure I would have been shut down or nationalized years ago if I weren't making something on a commission basis for the shipyards which no one else can make. It's tough work though. Countless laws and regulations prevent me from paying enough to attract help and if I had more than three employees my taxes would go up. I manage to clear out about twelve to fifteen thousand marks ($4000) per year from the business—but mind you, only by working twelve to fourteen hours a day. Yet, it's better than being on the assembly line or collectivized in a craft cooperative."

Craft collectives—called *Produktionsgenossenschaften des Handels* (PGH)—are the regime's way of socializing the trades. They claim 205,000 of East Germany's 573,000 shoemakers, watchmakers, plumbers, carpenters, plasterers, painters, roofers, chimney sweeps, tailors, electricians, auto mechanics, and television repairmen as members.

The craftsmen, whether organized in cooperatives or still in business for themselves, are the GDR's most sought-after workers and members of its pampered delight. Because there are so few, they benefit handsomely from the old law of supply and demand. They have gotten rich on the gray labor market and are coddled at income tax time.

The cooperatives, created under intense political and propagandistic pressure in the period from 1958 to 1960 when the GDR also forced collectivization of agriculture, represent one of East Germany's most unusual and controversial social experiments. Feelings about them are strong and mixed. Most of the artisans who have joined a PGH, wax enthusiastically over the system. The 64 percent who have thus far stayed out, fulminate against it and speak proudly of the independence they have managed to preserve.

"I was a self-employed house painter," explained forty-six-year-old Günther Leonhardt, "and the going wasn't rosy. It seemed to me I was working twenty-four hours a day, I had a tough time getting materials because the allocations all went to the cooperatives and I just wasn't getting ahead. I closed my business, worked in a factory for a while, then joined the cooperative in 1960."

Today Leonhardt is the salaried secretary of the main craft cooperative in Eisenhüttenstadt, a job that pays him 1100 marks per month plus a share of the profits. "When I joined," he said, "I paid in my share of 1000 marks like everyone else and swung a paint brush for quite a number of years before I was elected secretary by the members."

The cooperative includes eleven trades and services: tailors, shoemakers, carpenters, painters, electricians, barbers, beauticians, portrait photographers, watchmakers, opticians and television-radio technicians. Its 300 members—all journeymen or masters—have set up their business in strategically located, cooperatively owned or rented stores and buildings around town. PGH property—which includes everything from the tailors' needles and thread to hair drying machines for the beauticians—is worth 1,900,000 marks.

Any journeyman or master can join for an admission price—tantamount to capital investment—of 1000 marks. The capital draws no interest and members are liable for losses incurred by the cooperative though, as Leonhardt explained, "that's an eventuality with which we'll probably never have to reckon." Each member draws a monthly salary averaging 750 marks, though this varies from one trade to another and can be bolstered by premiums, overtime and high productivity. All profits, over and above wages, premiums, materials and other running costs, are banked and split at the end of each year: 55 percent for capital investment, accumulation of reserves, repair of plant and equipment and amortization of property; 15 percent for apprentice training, recreational and social facilities. The remaining 30 percent are distributed to individual members, and averages 1500 marks per year—give another 1000 for the electricians, take another 700 for the tailors who are among the lowest paid.

Each craft or trade elects its own shop or department foreman. The board of directors, only one of whom is a full-time, salaried professional, is elected annually by secret ballot. Major decisions such as acquisition of property, changes in pay scale and service charges, require the approval of two-thirds of the membership.

The inducements are obvious. Equipment is better, productivity higher, and remuneration more lucrative than on an individual basis. Moreover, the cooperatives have a privileged position in obtaining materials and tools with which to work. "As a self-employed painter," Leonhardt explained, "I'd be an old man before I could afford the scaffolding and elaborate spraying apparatus we have at our disposal here."

Though Leonhardt paints an enticing picture, the majority of artisans and craftsmen continue to resist collectivization. Even in Eisenhüttenstadt, vaunted as East Germany's "model socialist city," 144 artisans remain in business for themselves and the more prosperous ones even have journeymen and apprentices working for them. Nearly all of them, however, have their shops in Fürstenberg, the old part of town.

If private enterprise still holds its own among the trades, it is fighting a losing battle on the retail sector of the economy. But the reasons have less to do with capitalist versus socialist ideology than with a trend common to both East and West Germany: the inevitable demise of the corner grocer in the face of mounting competition from the supermarket. The difference in the GDR is that the supermarket is state owned.

Of the GDR's 205,000 retail shops and restaurants no less than 81,000, or 39 percent, remain privately owned, though their number decreases by 2000 to 3000 annually. However, they account for only 11 percent of yearly retail turnover. No significant attempt has ever been made to legislate them out of business. They are being squeezed out by the state-run enterprises which have all the advantages of lower overhead, better selection of merchandise, and tax privileges.

It is a trend which even doctrinaire Communists mourn, for

they have learned from experience that all the "economic levers" and other incentives they invented will not substitute for that added touch of service, that wider smile and cheerier "thank you" which only an economic underdog delivers. Even in the mammoth state-owned department stores, supermarkets, service outlets, and restaurants, now that East Germany is moving from a seller's to a buyer's market, customers are no longer treated as supplicants but as customers. In the privately owned stores, however, they are again kings. Despite the handicaps they face in filling their shelves with as plentiful and varied a selection of merchandise, East Germany's private stores and restaurants invariably look brighter, and more inviting than the grandest of state-run emporiums.

In apparent recognition of this phenomenon, the regime, with a minimum of fanfare and publicity, has turned to encouraging private ownership of restaurants, cafés, and bars. As one Erfurt resident told me: "All those nice taverns, beer gardens, and cafés in the Steiger Forest" (a popular Sunday outing area) "were nationalized and got so run down that no one patronized them any more. The *Gemütlichkeit* went right out with the owners. Now the government is inviting private management back on a lease or commission basis. And would you believe it? The atmosphere is changing completely and the customers are starting to return."

Even a top VVB executive admitted: "I am convinced that when we get the kinks out of it, a planned socialist economy will prove more efficient than capitalism. But you know, for all my confidence in socialism, I cannot understand why the tablecloths in West German autobahn restaurants are always clean and those in our roadside cafés invariably dirty."

Though the SED has sacrificed principle to public morale by inviting private ownership of restaurants and taverns, the final demise of private enterprise is but a matter of time. Its greatest enemy is not the all powerful state with its ubiquitous control over every facet of commercial activity, but attrition. No East German law bars the corner grocer from passing his store on to his son except the uncodified rules of social custom, convenience and accomodation. "My boy helps me run the shop now," an Erfurt confectioner said, "but he's already told me that once I'm gone, he'll close it down and go to work in a factory instead. You know what he told me? 'I'll not only make more money but I'll feel like I'm helping to build the country.'"

It is with this kind of attitude that a lot of East Germany has already been built. And it keeps the chimneys belching at those state-owned mammoths which—in the face of incredible obstacles —forged the GDR into a major industrial power.

For seven centuries—since the first fishermen settled on its sandy, silty flats, Eisenhüttenstadt on the Oder has experienced all the vicissitudes of German history. Wars ravaged and destroyed it many times and thrice within one generation the town has had different names. To old-timers, and on most international maps, it is Fürstenberg. For one decade, from 1951 to 1961, it was known as Stalinstadt. But like most things in East Germany, it, too, was renamed when the dead dictator's remains were evicted from the Lenin mausoleum and reburied along the Kremlin wall. Then, Germany's "first socialist city" became known as Eisenhüttenstadt—literally, Iron Works City.

Iron has been Eisenhüttenstadt's business since January 1951, when the cornerstone of its first blast furnace was laid. Until then, Fürstenberg had been an insignificant dot on the German landscape with 6800 inhabitants. Its only industries were a small glass smelter, a few open pit lignite mines and a river port. When the SED announced its plan in July 1950 to build a smelter and give East Germany independent industrial muscles Fürstenberg seemed the most unlikely site. Its soil holds no mineral riches. It is part of the flat, sparsely wooded, generally barren land southeast of Berlin which the inhabitants derisively call the "Brandenburg Sandbox." The area around Fürstenberg, where the flooding Oder deposits its silt, is the sandiest of all. But it had two important waterways—the Oder itself and the Oder-Spree Canal which links the town with Berlin. Moreover, it was conveniently located for receipt of the Soviet ore and Polish coke which a smelter would need.

Once the choice had been made, Eisenhüttenstadt literally burst into existence. It required only 262 days before the first blasting furnace was fired by Premier Otto Grotewohl in September 1951. The second was in operation three months later. The iron workers were, for the most part, former farmers, basketmakers and riverboat men, hurriedly trained in crash courses. They soon ran into trouble and in 1952 called Soviet experts to help. But despite early setbacks, production grew steadily until today, with six furnaces and 5700 workers, the combine produces more than 1,500,000 tons of pig iron: three times its planned and two-thirds of the GDR's total output—more in eight days than all the iron smelted in 1938 on East German territory. Its by-products include gas to feed a power plant which generates 800,000,000 kilowatt hours annually, and a cement plant.

Eisenhüttenstadt today has a population of 37,000—most of it concentrated into a spacious, airy "dwelling and shopping" complex punctuated by new apartment houses, playgrounds, schools, restaurants, and community centers just west of the old Fürstenberg city limits.

Its main street—Lenin Allee—offers some of the nicest window displays found anywhere outside of East Berlin or Leipzig. Stores are filled with merchandise and shoppers. The streets are light, wide and cheerful with rows of young trees, large spaces of lawn, and countless flower beds meticulously cultivated and tended by a platoon of municipal gardeners. Architecturally—except for several blocks of apartment houses built in days when Stalin's taste still dictated construction style—Eisenhüttenstadt looks like any small West German city. Despite an air of sterility surrounding it —common perhaps to any large "company" town—East Germans have ample reason to be proud of it. Living conditions—most families rent or own four and five room apartments with sunny balconies and all conveniences—are the best in the GDR.

Eisenhüttenstadt even has a future. Since 1963 work has been in progress on a $750,000,000 steel plant which eventually will employ an additional 6000 workers and produce, so says the plan, 1,800,000 tons of crude and rolled mill steel annually by 1972. It is to be "the most modern steel plant in Europe," complete with an oxygen blasting furnace and automated rolling mills and foundries. With the plant Eisenhüttenstadt's population is expected to grow to 60,000.

CHEMIE IST TRUMPF, says the white-on-red banner over the main gate of nearly every East German chemical plant. Chemistry is indeed a trump card in this land where the only natural resource of importance—other than lignite—is the diligence and inventiveness of its technicians and dwindling labor force. "Eighty percent of the world's chemical products originate in only eight countries," boasts Günter Wyschowsky, the thirty-eight-year-old Minister of Chemical Industries. "That the GDR is one of them is to the credit of the economic wisdom of our party. Next to the United States we are now the world's largest per-capita chemical producer."

For eighteen years—from 1945 to 1963—this remarkable achievement depended primarily on the lignite output of East Germany's soft coal miners. Since then, however, the GDR has been able to turn to oil which is now being delivered at the rate of 4,000,000 tons a year from deep in the heart of Russia via the 2500-mile-long "Pipeline of Friendship" to Schwedt on the Oder. Hopeful East Germans call this once unimportant tobacco-growing center their "rendezvous with the future."

The chimneys and burn-off vents are visible for miles across the sandy plains of this desolate region in the Uckermark, thirty miles upstream from the Polish controlled port of Stettin. Although documents dating back to 1265 mention it, Schwedt slept through generations of lords and landholders who sold it to one another at will. It hit the history books only once: during the Thirty Years' War when, setting a record of sorts, it was plundered thirty-two times alternately by Wallenstein's mercenaries and the Swedes. Schwedt's selection as the terminal point of the pipeline from Russia and as a site of East Germany's largest refinery put it back on the map.

Since December 18, 1963, when Walter Ulbricht gave the command: "The oil is here. Turn the automatic to 'Spigot open,'" and Schwedt's tanks began to fill, the refinery has become the heart of East Germany's petro-chemical industry.

Schwedt already produces all of East Germany's diesel and heating oil plus half its gasoline—a 79-octane product. It is a tremendous improvement over the 72-octane, lignite-based variety which for years made automobiles sound like threshing machines and pervaded the whole GDR with an acrid odor of ether mixed with floor wax and sulphuric acid. One ancillary factory produces a half million tons of calcium-ammoniac saltpeter from waste refinery gases. Nearing completion are several petro-chemical installations which will refine basic products for the manufacture of synthetic fibers. Among these is a plant and process for making acryl-nitril, a base for orlon, which was purchased for $25,000,000 from Litvin Engineering Co. of Kansas and Standard Oil of Ohio in November 1964. When news of the deal leaked out there was an understandable uproar in West Germany. But as one Schwedt refinery official said defiantly: "We are going to have the most modern equipment—regardless where it comes from."

Schwedt's most recent contribution to the GDR's economy is a pipeline, completed in July 1967, that is delivering refined petroleum to the imposing Leuna petro-chemical complex.

The mastodons of East Germany's chemical industry are VEB Leuna Works-Walter Ulbricht in Merseburg and VEB Buna Chemical Works in Schkopau. Both well known as I. G. Farben subsidiaries before 1945, they are now so substantially enlarged in both capacity and variety of output that prewar customers would not recognize either one.

Leuna, with a payroll of 30,000, is the largest single industrial enterprise in the GDR and one of the biggest chemical plants in Europe. With 450 products, 90 percent of which are still produced on a lignite, not a petroleum base, Leuna accounts for one-tenth of East Germany's chemical production.

In 1945 more than 25,000 Allied bombs had reduced it to a twisted jungle of rubble. Eighty percent of its productive capacity had been destroyed. What was salvageable ended up on flat cars headed toward the Soviet Union. Reconstruction—as a

Soviet stock corporation—was slow and painful. In 1953 when the plant had not yet reached its highest prewar production, it became one of the centers of the June insurrection. Leuna workers demanded that Walter Ulbricht's name be dissociated from their plant and pushed over his portrait, mounted on a huge board near the combine's main entrance.

For Leuna's workers this is ancient history today. Coddled with countless social institutions,—modern low-cost housing, plant-owned swimming pools, tennis courts, chartered vacation resorts, kindergartens, and nurseries—they rank today among the regime's most loyal and productive adherents.

Leuna consists of two major plant complexes, one of which is still under construction. Situated on the flat bank of the Saale River between Merseburg and Weissenfels twelve miles west of Leipzig, they are intricate laceworks of cooling towers, chimneys, silvery gas and oil tanks, cracking turrets, hydration columns and a filigree of countless catwalks and railway track. Leuna is recognizable in daytime by the blue-gray haze that hangs over the complex like a finely woven veil, at night by the putrid odor that pervades the smoggy atmosphere.

The plant's most important products now are ammonia, methanol, gasoline, nitrogen and phosphorous fertilizers, herbicides, insecticides, detergent bases, adhesives, lubricants, phenolic acid, cresolxylenol, plastics, and catalytic agents. Output today is twice what it was in 1943 before the first air raids. When the new plant is completed, late in 1968, Leuna's production will double again. Leuna II will concentrate on production of petro-chemicals— ethylene, polyethylene, and carolactam—dramatically changing the basis of East Germany's chemical industry.

"I know what a modern automobile plant is *supposed* to look like," said thirty-four-year-old Hellmut Uhlig, director of technology at VEB Sachsenring in Zwickau, makers of the Trabant— East Germany's Volkswagen. "It consists of one huge assembly hall with three large doors. The raw material enters through one, the workers through another and the finished cars come out of the third door. It's the kind of installation we dream of."

VEB Sachsenring, makers of 70 percent of East German passenger cars, is anything but modern. The plant consists of nearly
a dozen assembly halls isolated from one another in different sections of this cheerless Saxonian coal mining town. Twice, in the
course of their production process, half-finished automobiles must
be transported by truck from one building to another and back
again. Despite such obstacles, VEB Sachsenring, with 9000 employees, managed to produce 80,000 little Trabants in 1967 and
expects to have an annual output of 100,000 cars by 1970.

"Our dilemma," explained Uhlig, a former mechanic and pro-
duction-line worker who studied engineering and became an
executive, "is that automobile production took a secondary position. More important things had to be done first."

Consequently, Sachsenring today continues to operate in the
old Audi and Horch plants, once part of the pre-1945 Auto-Union
complex, as famous for its representational limousines as it was for
the three-cylinder, wood and wax-cloth DKW which threatened
to revolutionize automobile making in the 1930s. In 1945 most
of Auto-Union's engineers and technicians fled to Ingolstadt, West
Germany, where the company owned a small motorcycle plant.
There they continued to make the DKW. In East Germany automobile makers initially produced their own version of the DKW
using the same dies but a different name. Patent infringement
suits halted production in Zwickau and forced a shift of the operation to a plant in Eisenach where, since 1958 a modified DKW
called the Wartburg has been produced.

The Trabant (it means Satellite), on which production started
in Zwickau in 1958, was designed as a small, simple, robust
"people's car" which would last a long time and be cheap to
operate. "We are convinced," says Uhlig, "that we have succeeded
in producing just that."

The Trabant won't win any beauty or design contests and it
leaves plenty of comfort questions unanswered. It is loud and
only slightly larger than a small Fiat. But it is, indeed, robust,
simple and cheap to operate. Its air-cooled, two-cylinder, valve-
less, two-cycle 600 cubic centimeter engine delivers 27 horse-

power and a top speed of 63 mph and uses only a gallon of gas (cost $1.40) every thirty-five miles.

East Germans derisively call their "people's car" the "plastic bombshell." And for good reason. Most of the body—hood, fenders, roof, doors, trunk, and trunk lid—are made of plastic, an innovation of which Sachsenring engineers are defiantly proud, not apologetic. "It's called 'toroplast' and the formula, of course, is secret," said Uhlig. "But I can tell you it has halved maintenance costs and doubled to tripled the longevity of our automobile."

Various exigencies led to the invention and use of toroplast. Uhlig said candidly: "We were short of sheet metal and didn't have the money to import it. Moreover, we had to try and build a car that would last longer. Since body corrosion is the chief cause of an automobile's obsolescence we hunted for a material that would have all the advantages and none of the disadvantages of sheet steel."

Toroplast seems to meet those specifications. One favorite Sachsenring public relations stunt is to ask three burly assembly-line workers to stand on a Trabant roof. There is never a dent. And, insists Uhlig, toroplast is completely corrosion resistant. "We have put it into water for periods of up to a year and it wasn't affected at all," he said. "It also insulates better (fortunately, for otherwise the Trabant would sound even louder than it does)." Toroplast's greatest advantage for Trabant owners: it is cheap. A wrinkled fender costs only 13 marks ($3.25) to replace.

Because the GDR has no tool and die industry, Sachsenring had to develop and make its own. Some six hundred of its employees work in the plant's own machine factory, where not only tools but automation equipment are produced.

Sachsenring's greatest problem, however, is the geographical fragmentation of its production process into shops located in the most diverse parts of Zwickau. This Henry Ford's nightmare is an obstacle which ultimately will limit output to the maximum of 100,000 units projected for 1970 and vitiates the management's ambitions of some day competing with Volkswagen. "Automobile manufacturing has had to take the back seat in our country," said Uhlig. "We cannot afford the investment a large, really efficient plant would require. And even if we could, we wouldn't be able to find the property in this area. Our current plans do not go beyond 1970. What will happen after that remains speculation."

One speculation is that Sachsenring and all other automobile production will be shifted to the town of Ludwigsfelde just south of Berlin. A truck factory, with an annual capacity of 20,000 units by 1970, is already in operation there and some day the town may be turned into an East German Dearborn or Wolfsburg.

One-fourth of Zwickau's cars are exported: to Holland, Finland, Belgium, Norway, Iceland, Austria, Switzerland, Hungary, Czechoslovakia, Bulgaria, and Poland. Trabants participate in many rallies and with considerable success at that. "We've won most of the gold and silver cups in our class in the Finnish Thousand Lakes Rallye, the Semperit and the Alpine Rallyes," boasted Uhlig.

Though output seems insignificant in the face of such European competitors as Volkswagen and Fiat, each of whom produce more cars in a month than Sachsenring does in a year, enough Trabants have been built to dramatically change the East German landscape and ignite the inevitable movement from two wheels to four. Since 1960 the number of automobiles registered in the GDR has more than doubled to 740,000, so that there are now 40 cars per 1000 inhabitants compared to 164 per 1000 in West Germany.

The effect of motorization is ubiquitous. The accident rate is climbing, parking places are sometimes hard to find and a string of autobahn motels is under construction. But at current production rates it will take the GDR until 1985 to reach the 1967 level of West German motorization—assuming, of course, that all the cars registered today will still be serviceable.

Traditionally, East Germans are landlubbers. Between Luebeck in West Germany and the Free City of Danzig, eastern Germany had only one significant port on the Baltic: Stettin. Like Danzig, it also belongs to Poland now.

Rostock, for all its fame as a member of the Hanseatic League, lost all importance as a harbor when four-masters went out of fashion. A total of seventy-five ships with a gross tonnage of only 60,000 were registered there in 1939. The city had one ship-yard—the old Neptune Wharf—which built fishing cutters and vessels of up to 8000 tons. The only yard on what is now GDR territory, it accounted for a scant four percent of Germany's entire oceangoing vessel production before the war.

Since then the change has been dramatic. East Germany has become one of Europe's leading maritime powers. Rostock harbor, where construction began in 1957, is now one of the leading ports on the Baltic. In 1967 it turned over 7,150,000 tons of goods. East Germany's shipbuilding industry, strung along the coast from Stralsund to Wismar, accounts for one-fourth of all sea-going vessels now built on German soil and in 1966 launched 175 vessels with a total tonnage of 325,000—among them two 20,000-ton ocean liners.

Shipbuilding began by Soviet edict in 1945 and had but one purpose: to repair and convert former German merchant and naval craft as reparations. Until mid-1954 all the German yards were Soviet stock corporations.

Today, though they still produce heavily for the Soviet Union, the GDR's yards are important sources for foreign exchange. Freighters, trawlers, fish-factory ships and liners built in the GDR sail for Switzerland, Sweden, Denmark, Norway, West Germany, Tunisia, Czechoslovakia, Poland, Red China, and of course, the USSR. The five principal yards—Mathias Thesen at Wismar, Warnow and Neptune at Rostock, the Volkswerft in Stralsund and the Peenewerft in Wollgast employ more than 37,000 workers. Total sales in 1966 exceeded $450,000,000.

"We are getting bigger and bigger in the shipbuilding business," said a young executive of VVB Schiffsbau. "In 1963 we were in thirteenth place in the world and for 1967 we will probably be eighth or ninth."

The Warnow Werft is the pride of VVB Ship Building. "Twenty years ago," says one of the yard's officials, "there was nothing here but a small aircraft plant and weeds. Now we turn out 10,000 and 13,000 tons automated freighters almost on the assembly line." Its 200-foot-high, 1000-foot-long cable-crane installation which transports finished parts from the assembly line to the four slipways like a conveyer belt, is one of the most modern and efficient operations in Europe.

The industry is fired by the élan of its youthful workers and executives. Average age of the employees is thirty-two and Gerhard Zimmermann, the VVB's top executive until he was appointed Minister of Heavy Industry in December 1965, was only thirty-four when named general director in 1962.

The development of East Germany's maritime fleet and the construction of Rostock harbor are no less spectacular achievements. It was the lure of the sea's prestige and the common sense economics of too much money being lost in foreign holds which prompted the GDR to embark on its ambitious maritime expansion program. Its merchant fleet, launched in 1952 with a forty-year-old, 917-ton coastal freighter, symbolically christened *Forward*, now consists of 162 bottoms with a total tonnage of 1,000,000. It owns two pleasure liners, both used largely to give activists and other deserving workers vacations at sea, runs two ultra-modern, 1000-passenger car-and-railway ferries to Denmark and Sweden.

To handle this traffic and at the same time become independent of both Hamburg and Stettin, East Germany began developing Rostock as a harbor in 1957. The old port in the town itself, was too small to accommodate massive international tonnage, so a site near Petersdorf, a little fishing village on the heath-covered banks of the Breitling, a lagoon formed by the Warnow River, was chosen. The harbor, which required digging two main basins, each nearly forty feet deep and an artificial water channel paralleling the Warnow to the sea, was a massive job of "socialist construction" for which thousands of youths were drafted and induced to enlist. Party propagandists called it a special project of youth and to build the artificial mole that protects the channel, more than 50,000 tons of rock and stone were transported to Rostock—from all corners of the GDR where they had been collected by school classes and loaded on trucks, freight cars, and barges. The job was finished precisely on schedule and on April 30, 1960, the GDR freighter *Schwerin* docked in Rostock.

Today Rostock boasts three 4000-foot quays and the capacity to load and unload 5000 ships annually. New warehouses, new switch yards, new cranes and quays are being added every year and by 1970 annual tonnage turnover is expected to exceed 16,-000,000—more than twice that of San Francisco.

Yet, Rostock has a problem. It has no inland waterway connections. The Warnow, a small stream only sixty miles long, is neither navigable nor does it lead anywhere except into the flatlands of Mecklenburg. A massive railroad terminal backs up the port, its powerful floodlights on tall steel towers providing twenty-four-hour switching and loading service. But the single trunk line between Rostock and Berlin and the country's industrialized south is not even electrified. Plans do not call for its conversion from steam until 1977. Numerous projects for a canal to link Rostock with the Elbe or the Oder-Havel Canal and the rest of East Germany's inland waterways have been discussed and discarded, either because they were too expensive or technically unfeasible.

When pressed on this matter, East German authorities are surprisingly uncommunicative. But they nod agreement when reminded that the freight yards now backing up Rostock cannot possibly handle the volume of cargo expected to move through the port by 1970. More than likely a canal project will be announced within a year or so—doubtlessly with the usual propagandistic flourish.

Rostockers, meanwhile, do not sound worried. They lose no opportunity to boast of their "Gateway to the World." To visit this bustling city with its acres of new apartment houses and meticulously curated remnants of Hanseatic days and not take a harbor sightseeing trip, is considered an unforgivable affront. "One of these days," said a longshoreman with pride and confidence, "we're going to be even more important than Hamburg."

That is the kind of self-confidence that is making the GDR a factor to be reckoned with on every front.

CHAPTER VI

Made in the GDR

For several weeks in February 1965, more than forty of East Germany's top trade experts and senior industrialists went back to school. Dutifully, at nine each morning, they filed into the new steel and glass Foreign Trade Ministry Building on East Berlin's Unter den Linden to hear lectures on the economic condition of dozens of Middle Eastern, African, Asian, Latin American, and West European countries. They studied scholarly analyses of infrastructure, foreign aid requirements, financial capabilities, and export-import potentials.

Then the experts and executives converged on freshly scrubbed and newly painted Leipzig to reap the harvest of their schooling. Each man attended the leader of one of dozens of buying and selling delegations registered at the spring fair. The mission: to act as gracious and deferential hosts while bending the ears and gently twisting the arms of their charges and extol the benefits of doing business with the GDR.

Such meticulously planned assaults on non-Communist businessmen and government officials are indispensable to the new look of East Germany's broad-fronted economic offensive. They are the other side of the NÖSPL coin. A country struggling for social acceptance rarely distinguishes between trade and diplomacy. Commerce, East Germany is convinced, is the best foot in the diplomatic door.

The GDR pursues business abroad with tenacity. Its diplomats and commercial representatives hustle on the international scene and knock on neutral and Western doors with the zeal of Fuller brushmen. The effort is remunerative. The annual volume of total foreign trade increased by 30 percent from $4,600,-

000,000 to $6,500,000,000 during the last six years. During the
same period business with the non-Communist nations nearly
doubled and now accounts for one-fourth of the GDR's exports
and imports.

East Germany today sells office machines to ninety-six countries; seagoing freighters, trawlers and passenger liners to every
continent; cameras and porcelain to the United States; synthetic
rubber to France; printing equipment and musical instruments
to Britain; automobiles to the Netherlands; oil and steel to Austria; household appliances to Sweden; machine tools and paraffin
to Colombia, chemicals to India and power plants to Greece.
Until December 1966 the GDR had sold franchises on 250 patents and processes abroad, including a $20,000,000 license to the
U.S. for the manufacture of a GDR patented hydrometer.

"Made in the GDR" has become a meaningful symbol around
the world.

Buoyed by a new sense of self assurance and imbued with remarkable poise, GDR representatives in 1966 participated in
twenty-five international trade shows and three hundred fairs in
fifty countries—from Cambodia to Colombia, from Sweden to
Tunisia. And to the East Germans' smug satisfaction, their own
biggest show, the Leipzig Fair, has long ago lost its odious reputation as a Communist propaganda pageant to which West Germans rushed merely in the hope of meeting their cooped-up
relatives. Leipzig, where nearly eighty countries, including the
U.S., now exhibit regularly, has become the principal rendezvous of capitalism and Communism. Between 1950 and 1967 its
number of non-Communist exhibitors increased from 106 to
nearly 3000 and they now account for one-fourth of all displayers.
During the same period the number of visitors and buyers from
western and non-aligned countries, has quadrupled from 3000 to
12,000.

Even the usually staid *London Times* once said: "East Germany's status as a leading industrial power and as an economic go-
between for East and West is more striking with every year that
passes and finds palpable expression at the Leipzig Fair. One has
only to see the impressive rush of West German businessmen in

glossy cars to reach a country whose existence their own government still officially denies."

The rush of English businessmen is no less significant. Each spring, British Rolls-Royces vie for Leipzig parking spaces with West German Mercedes. Two-way British trade with the GDR topped $72,000,000 in 1966 and nudged $80,000,000 in 1967.

The British also compete hotly with the French who have become the biggest non-German capitalist exhibitors at Leipzig. British businessmen frequently complain that they receive no government backing while Paris officially supports French trade with East Germany—$60,000,000 in 1966.

Nor are businessmen from other western countries standing still. Trade with Italy reached nearly $50,000,000 in 1967, with Denmark $52,000,000, with Sweden $70,000,000, with the Netherlands $75,000,000 and with India $65,000,000.

Perhaps even more significant than the tenacity and scope of the East German economic offensive is the skill with which GDR traders now attempt to carve their share of world markets. Just as the pragmatists have jettisoned the old "tonnage ideology," so they have learned to design, package and advertise their products to meet modern criteria and "the highest world standards."

East Germans delight in telling the story (some insist it is true) of the day Walter Ulbricht visited the Optima Typewriter plant in Erfurt, frowned and with patriarchal severity asked the plant director: "Now why are the typewriters so angular, Comrade? Rounded, elegant designs would be much more attractive. Our women ought to find cultural surroundings in their offices, too, shouldn't they? And here you are turning out square, dull-looking boxes." Dryly, the director replied, "Perhaps, Comrade Ulbricht, but the typewriters sell better when they are square, especially abroad." Ulbricht who allegedly purports to know something about everything and once even told physicist Manfred von Ardenne how a Russian atomic reactor works, was taken aback when so blatantly contradicted. But then he added in a conciliatory voice, "Well, you know more about selling than I do. You are probably right." He was, and the angular look of functional design has now invaded every branch of German industry.

East German radio and television receivers, now look like those made in West Germany. Household appliances now flat and angular, come in shells of gray and white plastic that fit into any modern kitchen instead of the one Mother used to have in the 1930s. Even the trusty old Wartburg sedan, of which the GDR produces and exports so few that it hardly seems worth the trouble, made its debut in a sharp, angular, obviously Italian-influenced body style in September 1966. "Everything looks a little more Western today," one East German told me, "even the cars on our highways look like those we watch on TV—until you come closer." It is true. The GDR can compete. So well, in fact, that West Germans did not realize, until told by *Der Spiegel* several years ago, that the up-to-date-looking television sets, sewing machines, refrigerators and washing machines sold by their two largest mail order houses had actually been made in the GDR.

Even sex has been injected as a persuasive element of East German advertising and sales techniques. Chesty, pretty, young hostesses woo Leipzig buyers into ordering everything from complete chemical plants to ladies' lingerie. And brochures for the Trabant cars show more leg art than automobile.

"With each trip to the GDR," said one West German businessman, "the advertising materials, the sales techniques, the packaging and the industrial design appear a degree or two more professional, a little more Western, a little slicker and eye appealing. It used to be that everything in the GDR, from the fountain pens sold in stationery stores to the way executives conducted business, reminded me of prewar days. The GDR seemed to have stood still in 1939 in both attitudes and appearance. But not any more. They are catching up so fast you can see them run."

Never was this more apparent to me than in the spring of 1965 when Soviet Premier Aleksei Kosygin made his first visit to the GDR and I followed him, Willi Stoph and Erich Honecker from exhibit to exhibit, from stand to stand for two grueling days at the Leipzig Fair.

Kosygin inspected electronic computers, tested foldaway bed couches, looked into bedroom wardrobes, shaved with an electric razor, sat under a hair dryer, peeked into pressure cookers and accepted, as a souvenir from a notions manufacturer "the only lightweight, two-way, non-rusting, non-catching zipper produced in the socialist world."

Occasionally the routine was broken by a bit of entertainment or some refreshments. At the stand of East Berlin's semi-state owned Otto Bengtson Co., manufacturers of coffee, tea, and lemonade dispensers, Kosygin sampled a cup of Bengtson's coffee, then said gravely, "Your product is of interest to us. It is ideal for plant canteens and cafeterias."

The climax of his tour came at a sample-kitchen established by the GDR's IKA Elektrika works, makers of a complete range of attractively designed household appliances. Seated on kitchen stools, Kosygin, Stoph, and Honecker watched a classically Western demonstration of housewares equipment, conducted, of all things, by Nigerian students from Leipzig's Karl Marx University who were earning pocket money at the fair. One of the boys, a microphone attached to his IKA Elektrika uniform, a chef's cap tilted jauntily on his head, showed the Soviet premier how to make Nigerian fruit punch in an all-purpose mixer. With each ingredient he made sure he got in a plug for his product—strictly American TV fashion. It was IKA Elektrika here and IKA Elektrika there. No sooner was Kosygin served the fruit punch when a Nigerian co-ed demonstrated how to make breaded yam balls on an IKA Elektrika automatic range. Before Kosygin moved on to a display of pots and pans, he munched two of the yam balls and listened patiently as the students sang a jingle praising— naturally—IKA Elektrika. Madison Avenue could not have done better.

This kind of hard sell, underscored by techniques borrowed liberally from West Germany and the United States, delineates the GDR's new approach to trade and business. Little, if anything, remains of the deliberate ideological obduracy, the surreptitious obfuscation or the open-collared proletarian mannerisms so typical a few years ago.

One man who really wants to sell, and by doing so has shaken preconceived Western notions about GDR life, is rotund, balding, forty-nine-year-old Heinz Bormann, the "Red Dior" from Magdeburg. Until the spring of 1966, when he drove across the border at Helmstedt with six svelt, sexy Saxonian mannequins to show his collection in such capitalist fashion strongholds as Munich, Düsseldorf, and Hamburg, East German styles had been equated with flat-heeled shoes and calf-length skirts. But to the *grandes dames* of Communist society in Moscow, Warsaw, Prague, East Berlin, and Dresden, Bormann has long been a symbol of good haute couture.

Bormann started in the debris of his father-in-law's dress factory after the war with thirty seamstresses and, as he puts it, "the most primitive equipment and supplies." Today his business is owned partly by the state but has grown to a payroll of three hundred. Bormann produces some 140,000 ready-to-wear dresses in the top-price and quality brackets annually plus 10,000 haute couture pieces.

"We export about half of what we make to thirty countries, (including some 25,000 dresses a year to West German department stores and mail order houses)," he explained. "Unfortunately, our West German customers insist on sewing in their own labels so that no one in the Federal Republic knew about us until I decided to introduce my collection."

Bormann's complaint focuses on the most problematic aspect of East Germany's economic offensive and trade policy: interzonal trade with the Federal Republic which, in 1967, amounted to $712,000,000—more than the GDR's exchange with any other country except the Soviet Union. But it is an arrangement of mutual convenience fraught with mutual recriminations, a deal in which both sides participate reluctantly, an agreement in which both Bonn and East Berlin seem to find only fault and never mention the advantages.

Interzonal trade—East Berlin calls it inter-German trade—grew out of the inherent interdependence of an economic entity artificially divided after Germany's defeat. But as time passed, Bonn tended to view the agreement, as a two-pronged political tool. One prong, in Bonn's eyes, served as a clamp to hold the two parts of Germany together economically: the other turned into a lever to apply whenever the Ulbricht regime became politically truculent. For example, in 1960, West Germany threatened to cut off deliveries of critical goods in retaliation against the GDR's forced collectivization of agriculture. The effect was a boomerang whose reverberations are felt to this day. The GDR accelerated its efforts to become independent of West German deliveries and interzonal trade degenerated into a mutually unproductive and unprofitable love hate relationship in which both sides seem to prefer out-trumping the other and have lost complete sight of the potential economic advantages.

For fifteen years, from 1952 to 1966 interzonal trade tripled in volume, though its importance to the GDR diminished steadily. In 1960 it presented 16 percent of East Germany's total trade, in 1966 only 11 percent. Then, in 1967, this German-German trade began dwindling in volume as well: turnover dropped by 5 percent compared with 1966. East German officials give the impression they could not care less if trade with West Germany dried up completely. "We are interested only if Bonn will give us long-term commitments and is willing to cancel revocation clauses which it threatens to invoke every time it has a political fancy," Wolfgang Schober, an editor of *Aussenhandel*, the East German foreign trade journal, once told me. Foreign Trade Minister Horst Sölle has said flatly that an increase in inter-German trade must be predicated on a "modicum of normal relations between two states," a remark with which he obviously meant that Bonn should recognize the GDR.

East Germany's growing importance as a lucrative and attractive market, on the other hand, has caused friction between West Germany and its allies—notably France and Britain—who claim that Bonn has a privileged position in trading with the GDR because the relationship is on a barter basis and counts as internal German, not foreign trade. West Germany has repeatedly cautioned other Western countries against extending long-term credits to the GDR (in keeping with NATO trading-with-the-enemy regulations) though it has given de facto credit to the GDR for years.

Until August of 1967, part of the trouble with interzonal trade was in the nature of the agreements and their failure to keep

pace with economic changes. The system operated on two accounts—one "hard" (for raw materials and industrial goods) the
other "soft" (for consumer goods). Credit for deliveries on the
one account were not transferable to pay for receipts on the other.
In 1966, for example, the GDR could not "pay" for West German
raw materials and hard goods with consumer products because
of the West German business slump and slackened demand.
As a result, the GDR ended 1966 with a $100,000,000 "deficit"
on the books. A similar development in 1967 has brought the total East German deficit to nearly $150,000,000.

For years many West German businessmen, anticipating such
developments and predicting the eventual deterioration of interzonal trade, had argued for a complete revision of the agreements
so as to take political considerations out of the pact and place
it on a more businesslike basis. In fact, Kurt Leopold, the former
West German representative on the Interzonal Trade Agency, resigned in 1965 because he could not persuade ex-Chancellor Ludwig Erhard in this vein. Leopold, who recommended giving the
GDR long-term investment credits, argued: "The way the agreement runs now, the GDR is making all the economic concessions
and sacrifices and we are reaping all the benefits. No wonder they
are looking for other markets and suppliers."

Like so many other Bonn policies toward East Germany, attitudes on interzonal trade changed significantly with the inauguration of the new coalition government of Social and Christian
Democrats under Chancellor Kurt Georg Kiesinger in December 1966. During the course of the following year Bonn established
an interzonal trade bank to provide East Germany with long-term
credits, raised the contingent for the import of East German machinery, abolished the political revocation clause and fused the
"hard" and "soft" accounts into one.

But these concessions, like so many Bonn has made to the
GDR, came too late. Not only has West Germany's continuing
business slump crimped the market for East German products, but
the GDR has continued to raise the ante. Confident of its growing economic prowess, East Germany has made any improvement
in the interzonal trade relationship conditional on political

recognition. The GDR now wants trade with the Federal Republic based on a new agreement that would be tantamount to a formal treaty between two sovereign states. It is a price which Bonn is not likely to pay.

CHAPTER VII

The Shackles of Pragmatism

East Germany swaggers with the pride and confidence of achievement and enjoys flexing its muscles before the mirror of world statistics. But for all its economic progress, the GDR is not yet a 97-pound weakling suddenly transformed into a Charles Atlas of economics. A lot of agonizing hours on the body-builder will have to be spent before the inefficacies caused by overage equipment, shoddy workmanship and the indulgence of bureaucracy have been overcome.

The effectiveness of capital investment has lost momentum, and returns on dollars spent are diminishing. Ulbricht once pointed out acrimoniously: "Between 1956 and 1960 our total investment on all sectors of the economy amounted to 33,000,000,000 marks ($8,250,000,000) and the net national income rose by 21,000,000,-000 marks ($5,250,000,000). But from 1961 to 1965 we invested twice as much—66,000,000,000 marks ($16,500,000,000) though our return in growth of national income was only half as high—10,700,000,000 marks ($2,700,000,000).

One reason may be the top-heavy bureaucratic structure which continues to plague the economy, another that GDR executives are still not paying as much attention to quality as they should.

At one recent plenary meeting of the SED Central Committee, Günter Mittag shocked his party comrades with a display of inferior industrial products. He showed them cameras that could take no pictures, transmissions that would not shift gears, electric mixers that wouldn't mix, washing machines that refused to wash and lathes that turned balkily.

And at another such meeting, in November 1967, Mittag bitterly attacked the failure of many industries to put new processes and innovations into practice and production, thereby losing out on important world markets. "In 1961," he said, "a research team at the Institute for Chemical Fibre Research developed a new technique for the polymerization of acrylnitrate. Although it was a world precedent-setting procedure, its practical introduction and the production of installations to employ this process were repeatedly delayed and are not scheduled until 1970. Meanwhile, a British concern has now developed and marketed an even more efficient method, depriving us of sales and franchises.

"In fact," said Mittag, "there are some 400 patents and processes, on which 35,000,000 marks of research money were spent, but which have not been applied or put into production yet because no decision has been made on which enterprise is to produce or use which of them."

For the energetic young pragmatists who today run most of the GDR's important industries, ideological drag on the ministerial level and bureaucratic friction in plants and factories are the chief irritants. They speak of it with rancor and admit candidly that they have yet to find the appropriate lubricant with which to negate its vitiating impact on productivity.

"All too often good managers and executives are surrounded by staffs of bureaucrats and party hacks who cannot tell a nut from a bolt," lamented one ranking executive. "The battle against ideological restriction requires time, energy and ingenuity which could be applied more profitably elsewhere."

One weapon on which the technocrats count is the computer. "Why just imagine how efficient a planned economy will be when it begins to operate with computer-processed data," one manager said. "All those inequities of supply and demand, distribution and consumption which hamper us today because of the unwieldy bureaucratic apparatus, will be solved instantaneously by data processing equipment."

However, before the computers arrive to displace the bureaucrats, a lot of water will flow down the Elbe. Reiner Stähr of Erfurt's Office Machines and Computer VVB, said, "Initially, our production of the Robotron-300 will be solely for domestic use. We will build between 100 and 200 to be utilized exclusively by

East German industry." But, by January 1967 production had not yet started and the GDR's biggest enterprises began importing Soviet and Western data processing machines. One year later, a total of 30 Robotrons and a few foreign computers were in use. None less than Ulbricht fulminated: "Computer production is not keeping pace with requirements."

Nor is automation. As Mittag pointed out, East Germany's automation coefficient rose from only 4.2 to 4.8 percent between 1963 and 1966.

In December 1965 priority was finally attached to rationalization and modernization of the production process and the economy after Ulbricht had told the Central Committee: "The effects of our investment activity are being dissipated by poor workmanship, indifferent management, and lack of coordination. Future productivity is being impeded by rising costs. We must learn the techniques of modern management if we are to succeed."

Since then the GDR has been on a crash efficiency and rationalization program whose three main points, according to Premier Willi Stoph are: "economic management, reduction of costs, precise calculation. In other words, efficient production in all branches of industry. If plants have costs that are too high, the New Economic System and the industrial price reform will force them to modernize or lose profits. Failure to operate economically or to produce high quality goods will have but one effect: a reduction in sales and profits. Our goals are simple and clear: to produce world marketable goods in accordance with the highest standards of science and technology at the lowest possible cost."

"Socialist rationalization," as Ulbricht called it, encompasses all phases of the productive process and begins with its planning and management. He outlined its principal components during a "standardization and rationalization conference in Leipzig in June 1966: (1) transition to modern management methods with the assistance of computer technology; (2) rationalization research work for development of products which will be fully competitive on world markets; (3) standardization, specialization and concentration of production in accordance with optimal economic criteria; (4) mechanization and automation of production processes, transport and management; (5) flexible cooperation between suppliers, manufacturers of semi-finished products and makers of final goods.

The campaign, like any in East Germany, naturally has its ideological overtones. *Neues Deutschland* and the local SED papers strive to use the terms "rationalization," "cooperation," "world standards," "highest technological criteria" and similar phrases of the new economic catechism in at least every other paragraph. Factory bulletin boards no longer exhort workers to produce more but to produce better.

The rationalization campaign even has its own peculiar version of the "Stachanov" or "Hennecke" movement. Adolf Hennecke, the Zwickau miner, paragoned in 1948 as the GDR's first "activist" because he had dug nearly four times his daily quota of coal, was the personified pacesetter of tonnage ideology. The "Hennecke" of rationalization is Gerhard Kast, a thirty-three-year-old Berlin electrician who wrote a letter to the editor of *Neues Deutschland* in December 1966 saying: "Our plant must no longer profit at the expense of others." Pledging to support the rationalization program, Kast said, "I feel I share responsibility for seeing to it that our plant earns its profit in the future and contributes to the benefit of the whole economy." Ever since, the columns of *Neues Deutschland* and all other East German papers have been filled with interminable rumination of "Comrade Kast's excellent suggestion." He is a new kind of "activist," tailor-made to East Germany's changed society. Hennecke was the embodiment of the philosophy which taught: "Keep your mouth shut and work harder." Kast represents the new slogan: "Think, criticize, and work better."

Fortunately for East Germany's economy, the "Kast" movement and similar charades of rationalization are primarily sops to those ideologues who still believe there can be no progress without the heady brimstone and fire of yesteryear.

The hard-headed young managers of industry, party and government know better. They smile patiently at this revolutionary folderol, ignore it and go about systematically enacting the new principles of rationalization with a modicum of fanfare.

When the GDR's pragmatists speak of rationalization they mean not only modernization of industrial techniques but improvement of efficiency through "cooperation," a system of concatenating industries involved in the various production stages of a final product or group of commodities. For example, cooperative agreements are now being worked out between plywood suppliers and furniture manufacturers to deliver the wood according to certain standards and in certain dimensions so as to accelerate and facilitate the manufacture of furnishings. Cooperation is a relatively new scheme, first outlined in December 1966, and East German industrialists are still experimenting with it. Hans Wittik, the Minister for Light Industry, explained it as "chains or cooperative associations between plants of different categories involved in the production of goods and commodities that lead to one final product."

The system, as it began to work in its early stages, called for surprising flexibility and accorded VEB managers far more autonomy than they had before. They have been encouraged to enter into contracts with each other as well as with semi-state owned and privately owned firms, to look on the market for the suppliers they need. Even the old maxim that socialist industry should not go out soliciting help on the labor market—because it denigrates the worker—has now been silently dropped. The help-wanted ads in East German papers are not only becoming more numerous but more elaborate and alluring. In 1966 it was still heresy but in 1967 the Black Pump Combine at Hoyerswerda thought nothing of advertising in *Neues Deutschland*:

"The world's largest and most modern coal processing plant needs machinists, electricians, mechanics, assembly-line workers and unskilled laborers for its expanding industrial program. Our plant academy offers numerous training and qualification opportunities. The combine will provide free quarters and a daily family separation allowance until apartments, in buildings now under construction, are completed. Send written applications to the personnel department."

The new methods also call for more decentralization of management responsibility and in November 1966 Ulbricht heralded the establishment of "advisory councils" comprised of plant fore-men, technicians, engineers and economists who will consult with VVB managements in meeting production goals, implementing rationalization programs and improving efficiency and quality. Though a long way from the Yugoslav system of works councils which, theoretically, are responsible for plant management, it is a major step away from narrow, centralized hierarchical manage-ment.

One problem cannot be unilaterally resolved by either Ulbricht or the spirited band of technocrats who today sit at the switch-boards of industry. This is the intricate matter of East German economic vulnerability to pressures arising out of its relationship with Russia.

The West's attention was first drawn dramatically to this prob-lem at ten o'clock on the morning of December 3, 1965, when forty-eight-year-old Dr. Erich Apel, the chairman of the State Planning Commission and architect of the New Economic Sys-tem, pulled a pistol from his desk drawer and fired a bullet through his head.

Said a terse government and party bulletin: "He suffered from circulatory disorders and nervous strain which, despite all efforts by doctors, led to a complete nervous breakdown." To date, no one has accepted the official version.

Apel's first wife, who now lives in West Germany, charged that he had been murdered.

West German Social Democratic Party leader Willy Brandt, then mayor of West Berlin, now West German foreign minister, announced ominously that "Erich Apel did not go silently to his grave," but had left behind a "political last will and testament" which would surprise the world.

The left-leaning *Frankfurter Rundschau*, suggested that Apel was Moscow's golden boy in East Berlin, a new Schirdewan-Zaisser-Wollweber who had the Kremlin's blessings, aspired to the premiership and thought of himself as an East German Lud-wig Erhard. Allegedly Apel enjoyed Soviet protection until Sep-tember 1965 when Moscow dropped him in favor of grand prom-ises of machinery, chemistry plants and other finished goods which the GDR was to deliver from 1966 to 1970. According to the *Rundschau's* anonymous article, purportedly written by a highly placed source in the East German apparatus, Apel was scheduled for severe criticism at the December 17–19 Central Committee plenary meeting because certain evidence of his disloyalty to Ulbricht had become known. Rather than face the embarrassment of a public upbraiding and possible ouster from party and government, he killed himself.

According to Stephan Thomas—the SPD's East Bureau chief —Apel and the team of technocrats with whom he surrounded himself, had been caught cheating the Soviet Union (with Ulbricht's tacit approval) on deliveries of finished goods and machinery. Apel had used Soviet raw materials to fuel the GDR's economy, then sold manufactured goods on Western capitalistic markets for hard foreign exchange, keeping the Soviets waiting on promised deliveries.

According to Thomas, the Russians confronted Ulbricht and Apel with intimate knowledge of this economic subterfuge at a September 18, 1965, meeting in Moscow. In addition to even more favorable trade terms in the future, the Russians allegedly insisted that all outstanding orders be delivered by 1966 without further shipments of raw materials. Apel knew he would seriously crimp his New Economic System if he bowed to the Soviet demands. He bargained for time, and negotiations dragged on until the morning of December 3 when the new trade treaty was due to be signed in East Berlin. Apel is reported to have telephoned Willi Stoph about twenty minutes before 10 A.M. and told him, "If you go ahead with the treaty it will be over my dead body." When Stoph told him there was no choice, that the Russians were demanding approval, Apel hung up, then shot himself. Several hours later the pact was signed in a short ceremony.

Though the truth about Apel's suicide may not be known for years, if at all, his death called attention to the new treaty whose terms—a $15,000,000,000 two-way trade agreement for five years from 1966 through 1970—ties the GDR inextricably to the USSR.

West German sources have equated the treaty with exploitation and likened it to a neo-reparations policy designed to fatten Soviet coffers at the expense of East German labor. The Soviets have been described as keeping the GDR in economic servitude by selling East Germany raw materials at inflated and buying East German goods at below world prices.

Though the treaty is indeed discriminatory it is no worse than any other agreement between a very powerful trade partner who offers absolutely essential raw materials and a weaker partner who needs and is willing to pay an inflated price for them. It is the law of supply and demand at work between two countries sworn to an ideology which spurns that law. The pact may impede East Germany's economic miracle but it will by no means curtail it insufferably. In essence it will restrict the GDR's westward trade effort or force the regime to get even more out of its industry as compensation.

In volume the treaty represents a 20 percent increase in Soviet-East German trade which totalled nearly $12,500,000,000 during the preceding five-year period from 1961 to 1965. During those five years, trade with Russia accounted for approximately half of East Germany's exports and imports, a ratio that is more likely to diminish than increase between 1966 and 1970.

Far more problematical is the question of price disparity which suggests that the USSR is milking East Germany for raw materials that sell cheaper on world markets. The GDR will get 7,000,000 tons of Soviet crude oil annually, 67 percent more rolled steel products and aluminum and more than six million tons of anthracite per year. In return, East Germany will supply two hundred chemical plants, 399 seagoing ships, and approximately 29 percent of the Soviet Union's imports of machinery.

It has been reported that the GDR is committed to deliver the ships at 1949 or 1950 prices but must buy its coal at 83.6 percent, oil at 80 percent, chromium ore at 113 percent and its pig iron at 86 percent *above* world market prices. The allegation is easy to make but hard to prove as the bulk of Soviet-East German trade is carried on by barter and determined in "settlement marks" rather than cash. Actually the disparity has never been that great. One recent survey covering the period from 1955 to

1961, was conducted by Oliver von Cjzago, a West German economist, who revealed that the GDR had paid the Soviet Union an average of only 8.4 percent more than Western countries were paying for 62 selected commodities and raw materials.

As recently as 1966 East German managers admitted to me that Soviet prices for coal and oil were higher than current world market levels, "but not so much higher that it really makes a great difference." One chemical industry executive said, "The price we pay for Soviet crude oil was established in a Comecon agreement of 1962. It was to prevail for five years, then be revised and prices readjusted to match world market levels. In the meantime the world oil price dropped substantially so that we are actually paying too much."

Since then, however, and as a consequence of both the Middle East war and a retroactive Comecon agreement, the GDR has been in a very advantageous position. According to statistics released by West European sources in January 1968, the East Germans are actually paying 8 to 10 percent less per ton of crude than Great Britain is paying for oil from Kuwait.

Moreover, though the Soviets obviously take advantage of the GDR and strike tough bargains, they are not implacable. To move them just takes time and patience, of which Ulbricht showed plenty in August and September 1966 when he journeyed to Moscow twice to make a more equitable arrangement. At first the Russians were truculent and argued they were entitled to advantageous trade agreements because they were bearing almost the entire load for Warsaw Pact defense. Moreover, Soviet Premier Aleksei Kosygin is reported to have told Ulbricht that he was under mounting domestic pressure from the Russian people who resented the meteoric rise in the GDR's standard of living at what they considered Soviet expense. Though negotiations with Moscow dragged on for months, Ulbricht's appeal apparently produced results. When Horst Sölle, the minister for foreign and intra-German trade went to Moscow in December 1966 to work out the 1967 protocol to the long-term treaty, he won numerous concessions from the USSR, including promises of deliveries that would exceed German exports to Russia by $125,000,000.

Consequently 1967 was the first year since 1962 that GDR imports from the Soviet Union exceeded exports.

In addition to raw materials, the Soviets delivered a vast array of machine tools, electronic equipment, modern textile machinery, 650 road surfacing and construction machines, 85 diesel locomotives, 1300 heavy trucks, 15,000 passenger cars, 2855 tractors, and an undisclosed quantity of industrial diamonds and even some computers.

Thus, Ulbricht's pilgrimages to Moscow and the favorable trade terms obtained by Sölle, dispelled some of the worries generated by Erich Apel's death. In fact, East German officials now sound as if they were genuinely pleased that so much of their trade is with Russia. Said Werner Jarowinsky after the November 1967 devaluation of the British pound: "The ruble is proving to be the most stable currency in the world during this crisis of the capitalist monetary system. It is a blessing for us that 75 percent of our foreign trade is based on it." The five year trade treaty with the USSR, it seems, shows no signs of stifling East Germany's economic miracle.

Oddly enough, it is Ulbricht himself who is primarily responsible for giving the pragmatic reformers the opportunity to perform their miracles. Out of character? Not at all. Ulbricht has merely understood that his prestige and authority depend on economic progress and that it cannot be achieved with ideology and doctrine. Thus it was he who once exhorted industrial ministers and top executives to do more thinking for themselves. "Some comrades," he said, "still expect the party to spell out instructions the way a computer might spew out specific details. Those days are over, however, and it is time some of these people learn to stand on their own two feet."

CHAPTER VIII

Revolution Rides a Tractor

The huge, orange disk of the September sun had just sunk behind the rolling, green Thuringian hills. The chilly hint of an autumn evening wafted in from the east and settled over the countryside. Though dusk was yielding quickly to night, the big Rumanian-built tractors, continued to pull their harvesters noisily through the fields of corn which belong to the agricultural production cooperative—LPG—at Eckartsberga.

We were standing by one of those outsized, rackety machines— the LPG chairman with the SED party button in his lapel; a rawboned, angry, vociferous tractor driver named Harald; a dozen excited and jabbering collective farmers with faces lifted from a Breughel painting.

"Yes I would, you bet I would," staccatoed Harald at the top of his larynx to drown out the clatter of his tractor engine. "I'd go back to farming my own land tonight if they'd let me. I'd earn just as much, work no harder but I'd be my own boss."

The derisive laughter of the little crowd of men and women cackled out his angry shouts together with the din of the machine.

"You don't believe that yourself," insisted one dumpy, leathery-faced, bandanna-wearing woman. "With the forty-five acres you brought into the cooperative you'd be lucky to afford that tractor you're driving. You wouldn't have a combine, a thresher, a harvester. Your cows would be tubercular again in a year. The only way you could make a go of it would be to exploit hired hands at 18 marks ($4.50) a week the way you used to. But nobody'd go to work for scraps like that any more."

"I could do it alone, the way I always did," countered Harald "I'd make out and I can name a dozen others who feel the way

I do. Kurt and Hans want their land back. Don't you Kurt," he said turning to a blond, heavyset man leaning against one of the tractor wheels. But Kurt just shook his big head, touched a fore-finger to his brow and said, "Me, with my twelve acres? I'd be crazy, and I know you are. You could no more apply technology on those four lousy strips of land you own than I could raise the feed for a horse."

Furiously, Harald hitched up a trailer full of corn silage, swung into the seat, jammed the tractor into gear and roared off the field onto the blacktop road leading into town. The laughter of his neighbors and partners followed him down the highway.

"It's like I told you," said the chairman, pushing his oily tweed cap to the back of his head, turning up the collar of his brown jacket against the evening mist that was starting to roll over the 1350 acres that comprise the LPG of this village twelve miles east of famous old Naumburg. "Ninety percent of our members wouldn't leave the co-op to go back to individual farming even if they were paid a premium. Of the ten percent who say they would prefer to farm by themselves again, I'm convinced, more than half don't believe it themselves. They've griped and com-plained all their lives and they'll go right on griping.

"Look, in the beginning I was against collective farming too. Very much against it. I contributed more land to the co-op than Harald did—forty-seven acres—and it was good land. My plots were close together, not spread out all over the area. I owned a lot of machinery and I really resisted collectivization. But the system finally convinced me, and when it did, I joined the party, too. In 1963. Not before.

"It's simple arithmetic," he added. "What we earn in the LPG really belongs to us, it's our private income. In the old days most of us figured we had made so much and never bothered to realize that we had to plow 70 percent of our earnings back into the farm—for a new horse, a cow or a barn—and had only 30 percent left as real profit or income. By pooling our land, our equipment, our labor and our brains, we have to invest only 30 percent and we keep the remaining 70 for ourselves. That's the difference.

"Of our sixty-four families, thirteen own automobiles and ten more have cars on order. Most of them own television sets, refrigerators, washing machines and all kinds of kitchen and household gadgets. We work less and earn more than we ever did before. That's the reason most farmers favor collectivization today."

They do—despite the bitter, tearful and bloody resistance with which East Germany's peasantry fought forced collectivization seven years ago. The initial period of stagnation which followed collectivization in 1960 to 1962 and threatened the GDR with catastrophe, has given way to sharply increased productivity. In 1965, for the first time since the war, East Germany's per-acreage yield of such key crops as wheat, rye and barley surpassed the Federal Republic's. Though yields for such other vital crops and products as potatoes, sugar beets, fodder pulses, fruit and milk still lag 20 to 30 percent behind the Federal Republic, East German agriculture is closing the gap.

More than any other sector of the economy, East German agriculture has been misunderstood and misrepresented in the West. Just as the GDR's peasantry suffered more than any other group from the regime's pertinacious determination to set ideology before common sense. But both these developments are rooted in a history that made the German peasantry at once the most obstinate and the most romanticized class of society.

To this day, West German agriculture is hampered—and hampers the economy—because of a mythology that depicts the independent farmer as the backbone of the nation. This view of agriculture, spiced with notions of super nationalism and some of the blood-and-soil ideas of the Nazi era, has already cost the Federal Republic a fortune in subsidies to its inefficient farmers and in bad will within the Common Market. The same mythology, moreover, led to systematic vilification of East German agricultural experiments as a monstrous tragedy of socialist mismanagement which transformed an independent peasantry into wage slaves and the country's bread basket into an underdeveloped barrens.

The truth looks only half as wild. While Communist abuse was

[12] East Berlin's Karl Marx Allee with Hotel Berolina in background and International Cinema in foreground (film advertised on movie house is *Around the World in Eighty Days*).

[13] Outdoor cafe on East Berlin's Karl Marx Allee.

[14] *Gammler* (GDR beatniks) posing for author in front of East Berlin's *Lind Corso* cafe. In case there are any doubts, all four are boys. One on right rece had hair shorn by the *Volkspolizei*.

] Soldiers marching to anti-fascist demonstration on East Berlin's Marx Engels
tz.

Anti-fascist rally. Sign says: "For Freedom and Humanity, Against the Re-
ism of Bonn."

[17] Sign on lawn in front of Eisenhuettenstadt apartment houses reads, "Americans get out of Vietnam."

[18] Rostock harbor, East Germany's largest port.

indeed virulent—and sometimes violent—East Germany's peasantry was neither as independent nor its agriculture as lucrative and efficient as Bonn has suggested.

Until the September 1945 land reform, Soviet Zone agriculture was primarily a cake from which only the landed gentry—the Junkers who survived feudal days—could cut slices large enough to taste. A mere 6000 of them owned one-and-a-half times as much land as 300,000 small peasants combined. In 1939 East Germany had only 14,400 landowners—2.5 percent of the total number—who owned farms larger than 125 acres, though these accounted for nearly 40 percent of the agriculturally useful land. The majority of East Germany's independent farmers—320,000 or 56 percent—owned plots ranging from 1.25 to 12.5 acres and controlled only 10 percent of the useful area. These were the farms which had become progressively smaller through divisive inheritance, a practice not halted in Germany until Hitler came to power in 1933. It mosaicked the countryside and led to farm earnings so skimpy that most smallholders were usually caught between the pillar of privation and the post of bankruptcy. The only independent and economically viable peasants were those 238,000—41.5 percent of the farmers—who owned plots ranging from 12.5 to 125 acres.

Even before World War II the territory comprising East Germany was not agriculturally self-sufficient. Only Mecklenburg, Western Pomerania, parts of Brandenburg and northern Saxony-Anhalt were significant agricultural regions. But their soil was poor, and their harvests never sufficed to feed the industrial populations of Saxony, Thuringia, the area around Halle, Berlin, or the Lausitzer industrial region. The real German granary lay further eastward, in those areas now controlled by Poland.

Moreover, East German agriculture was hampered by many of the same troubles which for years afflicted Soviet Zone industry. The Russians plundered the land of livestock, draft animals, agricultural machinery, and implements: an adjunct to the "trophy action" that cost East German farmers $250,000,000. Furthermore, the East Zone lacked the investment resources to mechanize and modernize its agriculture and to fertilize the fields which had been drastically depleted of mineral content during years of wartime neglect.

West German critics allege that land reform, as it was practiced by the Russians and Ulbricht, could have had but one ultimate aim: to prepare the countryside for collectivization at some later date. They argue that the holdings of the Junkers and other larger farms were chopped up into parcels so small they could never have become viable. In fact, land reform affected about 14,000 farms with 8,245,000 arable acres, or approximately 35 percent of all of East Germany's countryside. Except for some state-owned farms and a few early cooperatives, most of this land was divided into parcels of 12.5 acres.

On the other hand, Professor Hans Apel, in his study of the East German economy, contended that parceling the big estates was not only economically justified but probably the soundest approach under the circumstances. The lack of draft animals, machinery, tractor fuels, and fertilizer necessitated dividing the Junker holdings into plots small enough for a family of two or three to cultivate with maximum efficiency. The new farms were no less profitable than the majority of West German farms, more than half of which still comprise only two to twelve acres.

Although land reform provided some mechanized equipment, there was little enough to distribute. For 210,000 new farmers there were only 6000 tractors, 5000 threshers, 11,000 plows and 18,500 hay mowers. For every one hundred farms there were only 24 draft horses, 59 cows, 24 pigs, 87 goats, 25 hand plows, 2 sowing machines, 7 mowers, and 4 beet and potato harvester combines. Fertilizer was so scarce that the per-acre supply of nitrogen, phosphoric acid, potash and lime in 1945 and 1946 was approximately half of what had been available in 1938.

As supplies of machinery and fertilizer increased, the small farm lost its *raison d'être*. Mechanization literally invited consolidation—a phenomenon by no means restricted to East Germany. After all, though the independent farmer is considered the salt of the earth and the bread of the nation's dinner table, there is hardly an industrialized country in the world where he still prospers unless protected against the icy winds of competition by many mantles of subsidy.

The argument, that freedom and private initiative are the principal drives behind successful agriculture, depends on the view that only private ownership can generate the necessary interest and incentives. In farming this is generally considered optimal if the enterprise consists only of the owner and his family without outside help. This theory may have been applicable for the period up to World War II. But conditions and requirements changed radically once the technological revolution spread to the countryside. Since then the best farms have turned out to be the biggest —regardless whether they are owned cooperatively or depend largely on hired help. This has been an incontestable fact of farming life in the U.S. where agriculture has become big business. It has been recognized in West Germany where the ministry of agriculture has already spent $600,000,000 (and will spend as much again in coming years) to replot atomized farmland and make it more conducive to mechanized cultivation. The same principle applied in East Germany.

Collectivization of East German agriculture was economically justified. Not justified was the fanatic zeal with which the regime enforced and accelerated it in the spring of 1960. By resorting to its total arsenal of propaganda, agitation, economic pressure, and political terror the SED produced cataclysmic results.

Thousands of farmers fled the GDR and there were instances of entire villages which defected to West Germany—complete with livestock, implements and draft animals. Lowered morale in the countryside contributed to the food shortages in 1960 and 1961. These in turn exacerbated the mass flight of city and industrial populations which obliged the regime to build the Berlin Wall.

Yet, in 1952 when collectivization first began, it seemed a benign movement. Virtually no pressure was exerted and farmers were merely encouraged to join one of three distinct types of LPGs—agricultural production cooperatives.

In Type I, only the fields were to be tilled collectively: everything else remained private. In Type II, fields, grazing land, machinery and draft animals were to be held collectively: livestock ownership and production of milk, meat and eggs remained private. In Type III, all farming was to be cooperative and collective, with membership open to all, including landless hired farm hands, though each farmer was to retain 1.25 acres, two cows, pigs and poultry for private use and profit. These basic distinctions still apply today to the GDR's 15,000 LPGs. Though 8900 are Types I and II, and only 6100 of Type III, the latter type has twice as many members as the other two and accounts for three times as much useful land.

To drum up enthusiasm, for collectivization the SED initially resorted to the carrot of economic advantages, not the stick of terror and exhortation. Collective farmers were promised eight-hour working days and a plethora of benefits ranging from tax exemptions to low interest, long term loans for modernization and renovation and virtually exclusive use of equipment at the machine-tractor stations. Notwithstanding these patent advantages, initial enthusiasm ran lukewarm. After the first year of the program merely 128,000 members—one-eighth of East Germany's total farm population had joined collectives. The LPGs seemed to attract only the weakest, most inefficient farmers and were ridiculed as "agricultural unions of incompetents."

Though the party continued to propagate the virtues of collectivized agriculture, the program limped along through the 1950s as the stepchild of the East German revolution. A new drive to attract more farmers and establish additional LPGs was launched in 1955. By the end of 1956 about a fourth of East Germany's farmers had joined LPGs and cooperatively tilled land accounted for slightly more than 20 percent of the nation's agricultural acreage.

By December 1959, when the SED placed top priority on collectivization, nearly half the GDR's farm land was being tilled collectively, though 343,000 farms remained individually owned. Thus far the program had not been a smashing success, though the extent of progress should have given the party hope that patience, education, and circumspect agitation might bring nearly complete results within a few more years. But circumspection was not in demand that year. The summer drouth had wreaked havoc in East European agriculture and Nikita Khrushchev had exhorted all satellite leaders to consolidate their agriculture, make it self-sufficient and protect it against the vagaries of nature. Though he never insisted on forced collectivization, East Germany's ideologues, eager to transplant the Russian experience stereotypically on the GDR, read him that way. Mindful of Lenin's admonishment that the peasants were the last Mohicans of the class struggle, the SED launched its own "Kulak" war to create a classless society by eradicating distinctions between farmers and industrial workers.

The drive began in February 1960 under tough, ambitious, and dogmatic Karl Mewis, then the First Secretary of the Rostock District, who dispatched hand-picked cadres—industrial workers, trained agitators, secret police, and activists—to the Mecklenburg countryside. Riding loudspeaker trucks, and equipped with mimeograph machines, the personal histories of every farmer in the district and an overdose of fanaticism, these men in dark leather coats entrenched themselves on picturesque village squares and refused to leave again until the last farmer had signed on the dotted line. In less than a month, on March 5, Mewis reported the complete "socialization of the Rostock District." Then the campaign got underway everywhere else, ending on April 14 when Karl-Marx-Stadt, the last and slowest district, also reported total compliance. In the meantime, 250,000 farmers had been forced into collectives, thousands more had simply sold out and retired, thousands of others fled to West Germany and hundreds committed suicide.

Upholding stringently the fiction that membership in LPGs was strictly voluntary, the regime resorted to every conceivable means of "persuasion." Propaganda, agitation, political terror, blackmail, physical pressure, bribery, and prosecution for hastily contrived or long forgotten misdemeanors.

For interminable days and weeks, the loudspeakers of the SED badgered East German villagers with cajolery, threats, promises, and obloquy. Village was set against village, farmer against farmer, wife against husband, father against son. Agitators bandied about promises of washing machines, refrigerators, and Wartburg sedans. Farmers who refused to join were publicly defamed on bulletin boards and in handbills. Houses of holdouts were bathed in floodlights at night and surrounded by loudspeakers shouting invectives per day. When those methods failed, farmers were lured to public meetings with subpoenas, then physically restrained by SED bullies until they signed LPG membership contracts just to get home. And always the thrust of the argument was the same: "Are you for peace or war?" Peace was the road of the LPG, war the path of individual ownership.

"I was visited by six or more agitators daily," one farmer said. "Sometimes each man came two to three times a day. They sent the police, the SED secretary, the district attorney and the school teacher. They distributed handbills, set up loudspeaker trucks on the village square, paraded through town with bands. In three weeks they called me in for 'discussions' at least sixty times. They threatened me with jail for tax evasion, for failing to pave the driveway, for anything they could think of."

Another farmer, from somewhere near Weimar reported: "My neighbor suffered a heart attack, one man's wife from a neighboring village hid in the hayloft when they came; four fellows from our town just ran for the woods. But the agitators wouldn't let up. They found them even in the forest and began badgering them with propaganda."

Nothing stings more than public embarrassment, especially in small towns where conformity is the common denominator of life. The SED agitators who spread over the countryside to collectivize East German agriculture, were experts at making use of this human weakness. Their language was vituperative, the effect persuasive.

When public embarrassment failed to produce results, the agitators turned to outright blackmail and extortion. "Years ago," said one farmer from Mecklenburg, "there was a barn fire in our town. The causes were never determined and there was suspicion of arson. I was told bluntly that I would be charged with setting the fire unless I signed up for membership in the LPG."

It was a campaign so venomous and rabid, so base and obtuse

that even Politburo members conceded later that the propagandists had gone too far. Alfred Neumann, himself no exponent of kid-glove methods, admitted in May 1960: "There were districts in which the power of persuasion was ignored and collectivization was achieved by pitting the power of the state and the party against the farmer. We are going to have to do much to restore confidence in socialism during the next few months."

Despite the rush to collectivize by April, most of the LPGs did not begin operating until the fall of 1960 so that the results of the drive first became apparent during the 1961 harvest. It was catastrophic. A massive slowdown, as much deliberate as the product of complete confusion generated by lack of proper LPG management, sent the GDR's agricultural productivity plummeting. The potato yield dropped by 37 percent; sugar beets and forage root crops by 25 percent; cereals by 20 percent.

"They held so many planning and production meetings, there were so many propaganda sessions, that we couldn't have gotten anything done even if we had wanted to," one elderly Neubrandenburg farmer admitted to me. "When we weren't being badgered by the agitators we were at the corner *Gasthaus* to commiserate with one another or watch the army and the city kids, who had been trucked to the countryside, work the fields and bring in the harvest."

Food supplies had become so scarce that by the fall of 1961 butter was put back on ration and housewives complained bitterly that they could get no potatoes or meat—unless they queued in front of shops three and four hours before the start of business each day. By 1962 East Germany was trading automobiles for Polish potatoes and chemical plants for Soviet wheat. Vopos and soldiers of the National People's army were sent out to scavenge the cellars of city dwellers in search of seed potatoes with which the farmers could start the 1963 crop, while in the countryside, other police and army units were scouring farmers' potato bins to help alleviate the shortage in cities.

The turning point came in late 1963 or early 1964 when the advent of the New Economic System compelled both farmers and the regime to take the long and pragmatic, instead of the short and ideological view of agriculture. Since then, as farmers realized that they had not become modern serfs and that their personal incomes stood a good chance of doubling if they worked, collective farming has moved on to become one of East Germany's most striking successes. Even Mewis, who is now East German ambassador to Poland, says confidently: "I was hated, I was the bête noire in those days. But now I could visit any village in Mecklenburg and sleep quietly without fearing retributions."

Compensation in LPGs is based on a complicated system whose common denominator is the so-called *Arbeitseinheit*, or labor unit, an arbitrary measure applied to various kinds of work. For example, eight hours in the fields or milking 100 kilograms of milk equal 1.2 units while a tractor driver who has plowed 7.5 acres—an eight hour job on the average—has earned 1.6 units. The value of the unit depends on the over-all productivity of the collective and is determined at the end of each year when an LPG's expenditures—operating costs, amortization of plant and equipment, insurance, social welfare programs and investments—have been balanced against total receipts. The *Arbeitseinheit* on profitable farms may range from 13 to 18 marks, on inefficient and poor farms from 4 to 5 marks, in which case the state steps in with a subsidy to bring compensation up to the legal minimum of seven marks per labor unit.

In practice the system works this way:

LPG members are paid an advance of seven marks per labor unit in the form of a monthly salary. Thus, a field worker who has amassed 60 labor units per month will have received a monthly take home pay of 420 marks ($105) or 5040 marks ($1260) by year's end. If, when the books are balanced, it turns out that the LPG can afford to pay 10 marks per unit, the field worker will receive the difference owed him in a lump sum cash payment. In the case of our hypothetical field worker that would amount to an additional 2160 marks or $540. No distinction in pay is made between the work of men and women so that a married couple, each of whom has put in 60 labor units monthly at an LPG able to pay its members 10 marks per unit, will have drawn 840 marks per month as advance pay and received a year-end cash payment of 4320 marks or $1080.

Members are entitled to two weeks paid vacation per year as well as all the social welfare benefits—free medical care, old-age pensions, child support payments—which accrue to industrial workers.

In addition, farmers who contributed land to the collective—in contrast to members who are landless field workers, tractor drivers, or professional agronomists who may have joined the LPG without contributing to its actual acreage—receive an annual rental fee of 20 marks ($5) per acre.

Most LPGs also pay their members the equivalent of a year's supply of potatoes, grain and meat so that personal food costs are minimal. Private houses brought into the LPG remain the property of their owners. Most LPGs now provide apartments at monthly rents that rarely exceed 30 marks ($7.50) for those members who joined without property.

All earnings from privately kept livestock, chickens, and the private plot to which each family is entitled, are added to advances and the annual profit. These average 4000 marks ($1000) per year.

Production quotas are determined by district agricultural councils in accordance with the general plan targets set by the Ministry of Agriculture. LPGs are required to sell the state at least half of their grain harvest at prices determined by the government. They may keep the remainder, if they wish, for fodder to improve livestock breeding. State prices are flexible and depend on quality as well as on delivery time.

Of all East Germany's institutions, the collectives come closest to being democratically run. Once a year the members meet to elect a 17-man board of directors which in turn elects a chairman who is responsible for day-to-day operations. The chairman, who functions as a manager, is paid for his full-time service on a labor-unit basis like all other members.

LPG members retain title to the land they contributed to the collective and have the right to sell it to the state, the LPG or to other LPG members and prospective members. Land can also be inherited and those farmers who retire or are incapable of working, may lease their land to the LPG.

Each LPG is entitled to hire or attract as members whatever professional help—accountants, agronomists, breeders—it wants and can obtain. In fact, the movement of scientifically and technically trained specialists to the countryside has contributed immeasurably to the transformation of East German agriculture. Old, experienced farmers as well as professional agronomists have taken the place of the party functionaries who ran many LPGs in the chaotic days of 1960 and 1961. Nearly one-fourth of all LPG members today have either attended college, technical schools or agricultural training programs. Of 15,000 LPG chairmen, more than one-third have university or agricultural college degrees and another 3500 have taken advanced training at special agricultural institutes. With the specialists and technicians have come technology and mechanization. Supplies of chemical fertilizers have been doubled since 1960 and now either equal or exceed the West German per acre supply of nitrogen, phosphoric acid, potash and lime. Mechanization of agriculture has doubled and tripled since the great peasant siege of 1960. The GDR now has 117,000 tractors, more than twice as many as in 1960, though, as Ulbricht himself admitted a few years ago, those produced in the GDR are three to four times as susceptible to breakdown and repair as the models imported from Rumania and the Soviet Union. The number of harvester-combines has increased from 3241 in 1960 to nearly 16,000. There are twice as many potato planting machines, potato harvesters and beet harvesters.

The results are ubiquitous. East Germany's per acreage grain yield now matches West Germany's, the root crop gap is being closed. Though the GDR's human population is less than one-third that of West Germany's, its livestock population is almost half as large. Meat production is now high enough to provide each East German with 128 pounds per year—just five pounds less than the per capita West German consumption. Though butter remains rationed in East Germany, the actual annual per capita consumption in the GDR—27.5 pounds—is higher than West Germany's—18.7 pounds. American doctors would say this is a fast way toward mass East German arteriosclerosis, but medical considerations aside, butter consumption remains a status symbol in European countries and East German propagandists never fail to mention that they eat more of it than their "margarine cousins" in the Federal Republic. Even the mystical "milk barrier," long a source of agricultural criticism and self-criticism, has at last been broken. It is true that capitalist cows still produce more milk than Communist bovines. But for the first time in 1966 the East German milk yield surpassed 3000 kilograms (6600 pounds) per cow. It was a goal toward which GDR agronomists and dairy farmers had been striving for years and when they reached it, *Neues Deutschland* devoted front-page space and big black headlines to the news.

It is out in the countryside, however, where the story of the GDR's agricultural transformation is being told graphically. The change becomes apparent the minute one crosses the border. Fields that until a few years ago caught my eye because of their neglected appearance, now sprout a neatness so characteristic of traditional German landscapes. Villages that until 1964 and 1965 were drab and shabby eyesores, now glisten with coats of new paint on their farmhouses and barns.

"Just look around and you'll see the change," said a building contractor in Grumbach, a village near Dresden. "There isn't a shabby-looking house or barn left in town. Every farmer belongs to the LPG and everyone has had the money to paint, plaster or stucco his place within the last year or so." With a sweep of his arm he took in the little hamlet, then pointed to a trim, half-timbered house right behind us. The beams glistened with fresh varnish, the white stucco patches between them dazzled in the summer sunlight. "The owner is a widow," he said. "She has about eighty acres which she contributed to the LPG. She's too old to do any of the heavy work, but still takes care of the LPG poultry and keeps her own two cows and some pigs. Before the war she and her husband didn't earn enough to make ends meet and I wouldn't have thought of her as a customer for a refacing job on the house. Now the money is rolling in. We have ninety farm families and they're all LPG members. I know them all and what they think. Seventy of them will tell you they'd never want to go back to individual farming. They're all better off today."

"Of course we have problems," admitted Kurt Strobel, the chairman of the LPG in Oberrossla, a wide spot on the road between Weimar and Apolda. "We have 625 acres and forty-nine members. But only twenty-one of them work full time. Six are pensioned and too old to work, so they only earn a profit on the land they brought in. Three more work half days. Seventeen of the members are between sixty and sixty-five years of age—not old enough for a pension but too old to pitch in full strength. Despite this, we've managed to become completely mechanized and to reduce our total debts—on buildings and equipment—to 85,000 marks ($21,250). By the end of 1967 we expect to have it all paid off. When we started in 1959, our collective and individual debts topped 500,000 marks.

"There was a lot of resistance to collectivization at the start and we have members who still don't like it," said Strobel. "But those are mostly older people. They don't see the advantages. They don't seem to realize how much more they're earning.

"The average member makes 5700 marks ($1425) per year plus 2000 ($500) marks on privately owned livestock and land. We have several families of milkers who earn nearly 20,000 marks plus 4000 from their private plots and animals," Strobel insisted, and just to make sure I believed him, opened the dogeared ledger books and showed me the previous year's total payoff to each of the forty-nine members. There were, indeed, two families whose earnings had come to between 19,000 and 20,000 marks—a sum that is close to a fortune in East Germany and nothing short of respectable in the Federal Republic. "Every member," added Strobel, "gets 180 kilograms of pork, 18 hundredweight of grain for personal use each year. We Germans like to eat a lot of ham but 180 kilograms (396 pounds) is a little too much even for us. Don't ask me what happens to it. Most of us have relatives in town and give some away."

For all the prosperity of Saxony's and Thuringia's farms, agriculture in the GDR continues to face problems. The biggest ones, surprisingly, are in the Rostock, Schwerin, and Neubrandenburg district where the new agricultural technology could be most profitably applied, but per acreage yields are consistently below the national average.

"We're still fighting the transition problems," said a member of LPG New Life in Mestlin, a desolate, forsaken village twenty-five miles east of Schwerin. "We're short of fertilizer and much of our machinery is not suited to our ground. We're using Russian equipment which seems to be made for the dry, hard earth of the Ukrainian prairie. In our damp soil the combines sink up to their axles, then get stuck or tear up half the crop."

It is to Schwerin and Neubrandenburg, the GDR's Appalachia in the underdeveloped, backward, unindustrialized north, that thousands of high school and college students are sent each autumn to help with the harvest. "Oh, it's good for the youngsters," said one sarcastic LPG chairman, "and they don't mind. But we do. They're more trouble than help. City kids just seem to get in the way when there's work to be done, though we tolerate them and appreciate the spirit with which most of them pitch in."

This annual pilgrimage of East German youth to the countryside is symptomatic of East German agriculture's chief problem: the harvest dilemma. For years the regime attempted to solve it with exhortations to the socialist conscience or public embarrassments. The results were negligible. Then in 1965, agricultural boss Georg Ewald borrowed liberally from the arsenal of "economic levers" introduced in industry. He lured the farmers to market with prizes, premiums, all-expense paid vacations on the Black Sea and a gala harvest festival in Neubrandenburg. While *Neues Deutschland* banner headlined the slogan *THE HARVEST IS EVERYONE'S BUSINESS—DON'T LEAVE A KERNEL ON THE GROUND,* farm workers were lured to the finish line with cash.

Premiums occasionally equaled four and five times the basic pay rate and, perhaps most important, were paid out on a daily basis instead of after weeks of meticulous calculation by LPG auditing commissions.

To attain maximum utilization of manpower and machinery, combines and harvesters from several LPGs were joined into teams of ten and more, backed up by gasoline trucks and mobile repair stations, then dispatched to harvest an entire county or two. Machinery moved from one farm to the next according to schedules drafted weeks in advance. Drivers were quartered in the villages so they could get as early a start each morning as possible. Maintenance on machinery was performed at night when the mechanics, allowed to sleep during the day, inspected and repaired each combine to make sure it would perform flawlessly by dawn.

Frequently the machines and the drivers were imported from Thuringia and Saxony where the grain fields are smaller and the harvest sets in sooner. They joined brigades in Schwerin and Neubrandenburg and hired themselves out to various collective farms.

"It's the harvest technique of the future," said Fritz Jeschke, a Ministry of Agriculture official, who supervised one such brigade which shaved its way across the grain fields of Strassburg county in Neubrandenburg. Jeschke, a squat, fleshy, forty-three-year-old county agricultural agent, hired twenty-five threshing machines and their drivers from various LPGs in the district of Cottbus, 180 miles to the southeast, promised them top pay and premiums and lured them to the north after their own harvest had been completed. Then he divided the machines into two teams and sent each out across the county accompanied by a repair station, a mobile canteen and a fuel truck. Jeschke arranged for housing in each village and guaranteed that LPG chairmen were on hand each day to pay out wages and premiums in cash. The results: each team cut between 125 and 150 acres daily.

"It's the best organization I've ever seen," said one of the drivers. "Everything seems to roll just right. The combines, the fuel trucks, the repair station, the canteen and above all the cash."

In other districts enthusiasm was generated with team competition in addition to cash. Combine crew members stenciled such honors as "district winner," or "county champion" on their shirts, painted the names of girls on their machines and imbued the project with the air of a mammoth threshing bee.

The results were astounding. Despite a rainy summer and harvest season, the GDR's 1965 cereals crop exceeded 6,700,000 tons—the biggest in its history. Unfortunately, much of the wheat was too damp for use and the shortage of drying equipment turned thousands of tons to waste. In fact, the GDR had to buy $3,470,-000 worth of wheat from the U.S. Nevertheless for the first time a harvest had been at least a quantitative and organizational if not a qualitative success.

In 1966 the approach was less colorful and dramatic, and the grain harvest was not as good: only 26.1 quintals per hectare compared to the 1965 yield of 29.2 quintals. But the quality of the crop was better. In 1967 the yield was the highest ever—31 quintals per hectare, a bumper crop that compares favorably with West Germany's.

Though East Germany will face more such fluctuations, it is evident that the GDR's agriculture is at last in gear. Cultivation and harvest of all other major crops—potatoes, sugar beets, forage roots, and silage corn—have improved steadily along with mechanization and the supply of chemical fertilizer. Above all, sound economic principles rather than ideology now provide the main drives.

Some of the rudimentary problems common to agriculture in all countries remain unsolved. The farm population at an average of fifty-six, is critically overage and the flight of farm youths to the city remains unabated. The only solution appears to be even greater rationalization and increased efficiency, for which East Germany's agricultural experts are striving with more intensive cooperation between LPGs.

Some Western analysts view the drive for increased cooperation between LPGs as a new campaign toward ultimate socialization. They point with alarm to what they fear may turn into industrialization of the agricultural sector. Düsseldorf's influential *Rheinische Post*, for example, wrote that the ultimate aim of the Ulbricht regime is to establish some 1600 super collective farms, each with around 700 workers, who would be paid salaries in the manner of assembly line workers. There is no evidence to support this assertion.

Though the semi-socialist Type I and II LPGs are regarded with displeasure by the regime, no effort to force their disbandment or adoption of LPG III statutes is known. Their number and importance do continue to diminish—from 13,000 in 1960 to 8200 by mid 1967—but this appears to be without prodding.

The national agricultural council and the Ministry of Agriculture propagate cooperation between large and small LPGs, specialization of crops, more efficient and productive use of machinery, but it is evident that the basic guideline is flexibility. Cooperative schemes are praised as the ultimate ideal and goal but the new managers of agriculture insist there must be no coercion and that local individual conditions should determine both the speed and the extent of further collectivization.

Georg Ewald, the Minister of Agriculture, made the position clear when he said: "Farming can have but one purpose: to meet consumer demands and wishes."

That may be *Sauerbraten* Communism. But it works.

PART FOUR

TIMID
NEW
WORLD

CHAPTER IX

The Sufficient Society

Once it was one of the world's most elegant and celebrated boulevards. Like the Champs Elysées, Fifth Avenue, or Regent Street, Berlin's Unter den Linden was a place to see and be seen. Here Napoleon commemorated his triumphs over Prussia, Heinrich Heine promenaded, and Kaiser Wilhelm tooted the horn on his first automobile. Here ambassadors met the rulers of the Reich to remake the globe and the literati expounded views for remaking mankind. It was where Germany's most influential men strutted to catch the glimpses of Germany's most beautiful women.

But like so many other German dreams, by 1945 Unter den Linden smoldered in rubble of defeat, its 246 stately linden trees merely toothpicks splintered by American bombs and Russian artillery shells. For nearly two decades the street was the city's saddest scar. Where elegant foreign embassies had once played host to the mighty of the world, weed-grown ruins lay in desolate shambles. From the gutted husks of old buildings, empty windows gaped like the eye sockets of skulls. On the sites of Unter den Linden's most famous cafés—the Bauer and the Kranzler—stood tar paper shacks selling the shabby goods of Communism's spartan beginnings. For reasons which neither architects nor ideologues can now explain, the neo-classical castle which had marked the street's easternmost terminus, was razed. The renowned Lustgarten that surrounded it was turned into barren Marx-Engels Platz where Walter Ulbricht and his satraps can summon a half million of the faithful to demonstrate for Germany's first "workers' and peasants' state."

Though Ulbricht ordered the planting of 370 saplings in the

spring of 1950 and the Russians rebuilt the Staatsoper as well as their own embassy—a monument to tasteless Stalinist baroque—Unter den Linden remained a ravished symbol of the rest of East Berlin life. It was a wasteland—an impression left indelibly at the avenue's intersection with Friedrich Strasse. This corner, once one of the liveliest in Europe and roughly comparable to 42nd Street and Broadway with a liberal dash of Park Avenue elegance, was dead. Only sewer rats said goodnight to each other. At this hub of a city, once the largest metropolis between Paris and Moscow, traffic was so sparse that the lone signal light stood like a sentinel on a moonscape.

In 1965 East Germany's rulers started to change all that and today the East German capital's ugliest duckling again looks almost like a swan. Sidewalk cafés, posh restaurants, a luxury hotel, boutiques, gift and jewelry shops, furniture stores, government ministries, foreign embassies, museums, libraries, art galleries, two opera houses, and apartment houses for the privileged élite of the regime have mushroomed from the debris.

Once the preserve of aristocrats and plutocrats, Unter den Linden is now the mecca of the new upper classless. Its "Havana" shop features Johnny Walker's Red Label and Vat 69 at $20 the fifth, American cigarettes at $2 per pack and Cuban cigars at 50 cents apiece. In the "Delikat" shop just around the corner there are mountains of French cheeses, Polish hams, Swiss chocolates and Moroccan oranges at prices that would cause even a capitalist to wince.

The intersection of Friedrich Strasse blooms again. On the site of the gingerbreaded Hotel Viktoria an opulent, 340-room, air-conditioned hostelry vies with the best hotels in the West. Across the street, where once the Café Bauer claimed a clientele that ranged from Thomas Wolfe to Marlene Dietrich, the GDR's most elegant restaurant and café complex—the fountain ringed Linden Corso—plays host to a new élite. It even features a bar open until dawn.

But the most dramatic change of all: Unter den Linden is again alive with people who stroll, window shop, sightsee and, when the weather allows, just sit on the benches or at sidewalk cafés. Once again the place for Berliners (East) to meet is under the linden trees.

The boulevard's renaissance is symptomatic of the industrious reconstruction which is transfiguring the GDR's cities into modern metropolises with shiny new faces of neon, concrete, and glass. Leipzig, long privileged because of its fairs, is a throbbing cosmopolitan synthesis of modern and old. Dresden, once famed as the "Florence on the Elbe" has recaptured much of its former elegance though many ugly sears still distort it. Even sooty, odiferous Halle, the capital of the GDR's smoggy chemical triangle, boasts a flashy, palatial 300-room hotel and its downtown section is being completely revamped. Modernity, simplicity and functionalism take precedence over more esthetic values. But at least the new architecture is a welcome departure from the pompous Stalinist style which dominated so much of the East German landscape until the Soviet dictator's sudden secularization in 1956.

It is in East Berlin, however, that the most grandiose project is underway. For many years this city repelled instead of attracted. Gray, desolate, impersonal and with vast barren wastelands, it was Communism's worst foot forward at a front where image counted most. Now, bulldozers, steamshovels, and cranes are remaking the old heart of Berlin at Alexander Platz. Apartment houses, office buildings, a new thousand-room hotel, stores, and movie theaters are jutting skyward. More than 1200 feet up, workmen are completing the most unique edifice of all, the television tower—a steel and concrete structure which East and West Berliners, renowned for labeling every landmark in town, have dubbed "Ulbricht's Zeigefinger"—("Ulbricht's warning finger"). It'll be as famous as the Eiffel Tower (which it dwarfs) or the Empire State Building (which is only 50 feet taller). When completed—in 1968—a restaurant and café on the top platform will afford a spectacular panoramic view of the city. And, one should add, a cartographic bird's-eye glimpse of the wall that bisects it.

From that lofty vantage point the disparity of affluence between the two Berlins will become provocatively apparent. In the

West, the opulent glitter and dazzling brightness of Kurfürstendamm; in the East the somewhat darker realities of Communism.
Is it a chance the GDR's rulers can take? They have already calculated the risk and no longer fear, for they know that the prosperity gap, though still wide, is narrowing. Already the East has
attained a standard of living that has robbed the West of some of
its magic lure. The difference between the two has become more
sophisticated. East Germany is on the threshold of the whipped-
cream era. West Germany has progressed to a diet of reducing
pills.

It is a transformation I have found more perceptible with each
trip I have made to the GDR since 1961. The shops and markets
abound with merchandise in quantity and are beginning to hint
of quality. Suits now hold a press, sacks no longer substitute for
dresses, advertising and packaging seek to generate wants and
sales clerks try to please the customers.

East Germans now take such amenities of life as television
sets, modern and attractively styled furniture and a plethora of
household appliances for granted. They have begun to hunt for
fashion and style, to shop discriminatingly and to demand a selection. They are even inching up on that ultimate bench mark
of civilized prosperity—motorization. The GDR is shifting from
two wheels to four so fast that motorcycles, mopeds and scooters,
of which every third East German family owns one, have now
become so hard to sell that dealers have slashed prices by 10 to
15 percent in addition to seasonal winter discounts.

East Germany is a land of unusally sharp contrasts that make
it a propagandists' paradise. It can be portrayed in the optimistic technicolor of East Berlin's Unter den Linden as easily as in
the harsh grays of the shabby tenements behind Karl Marx Allee.
But where is its true face today? Is it the neat, glittering façade of
downtown Leipzig with its bustle of traffic and worldly mien? Or
is it the maze of sooty, grimy dilapidated brownstones of Berlin's
Prenzlauer Berg, one of the city's oldest working class districts?
Perhaps it is the bright, colorful, spacious cheerfulness of Eisenhüttenstadt. Or perhaps it is the depressing disrepair of Crim-

mitschau, an ugly Saxonian textile town, the smoke from whose 120 factory chimneys have turned it into an elegy of gray.

The GDR is all these and many more. It is Dresden whose reconstructed Zwinger makes the erstwhile pearl of the Elbe again a city of beauty, though its other scars may take additional decades to heal. It is also Erfurt, a medieval gem untouched by war and unchanged by the ups and downs of political ideologies. It is certainly Schwedt whose bonanza spirit persuaded one American visitor to describe it as "a little Texas in Brandenburg." Yet, the GDR is also Zwickau, oppressive with the industrial grime of decades and chuck-holed streets being sucked down by abandoned mine-shafts into the disemboweled earth. And it is Rostock with the crisp salty, Baltic air, bustling fever of trade and a proud, lusty confidence mirrored in the red brick of its Hanseatic architecture.

To understand East Germany one must bear in mind that only eleven of its cities have populations of 100,000 or more, that only one-fifth of its 17,000,000 inhabitants are privileged to live in them. For the remainder "home" is a Mecklenburg hamlet, a Thuringian village or one of hundreds of small Saxonian industrial towns. Here, where the prosaic spirit of Lutheranism melded with the Philistine earnestness of mercantilism and the grimness of the proletarian revolution, the real GDR is to be found. This is where life revolves about a television set, where doilies on the parlor sofa are a symbol of respectability, where gossip—not ideology—is what people discuss at street corners. Here entertainment means going to a stuffy, airless cinema or shuffling aimlessly across a dance floor as a tired, shirt-sleeved band plays the out-of-tune foxtrots of yesteryear's Saturday nights. Little if anything has changed in these tedious huddles of prosaicness, most of which escaped the architectural catharses of war and reconstruction. Away from the cities, East Germany is a land unchanged since the 1930s. In the provincial manufacturing and marketing towns, time and neglect have turned the aging façades, the bumpy cobblestoned streets, the cheerless veneer of petit bourgeois respectability into strongholds against time. In Arnstadt, Neustrelitz, and Meuselwitz, in Mittweida, Apolda, and Zittau

—names barely perceptible on a map—life retreats behind shutters at dusk. The timid new world of Berlin's Unter den Linden or Leipzig's after-hours bars is as remote as Kurfürstendamm or Piccadilly. It is unlikely that these towns will ever change, no matter with how many Wartburgs or refrigerators the Communist cornucopia some day overflows. They are one reason why for years to come the GDR will lack the luster of the West.

But it is not the only reason. The West glitters with an amalthean superabundance of wealth, with an amplitude in which only a minority, albeit a very large one, can partake. It is the sparkle of an economic system which must sell fashion, obsolescence, prestige, and status—not just utility—to survive. In principle, Communism spurns neither beauty of design nor variety of merchandise, but it is ideologically opposed to the built-in obsolescence and artificially created desire which contribute to Western society's affluent look. East German cities, I am convinced, will never display the West's overt, ostentatious wealth, because the regime rejects it as symbolic of capitalist decadence. "It is wrong to say we strive merely for austerity," an East German journalist argued defiantly, and he was undoubtedly right. But for many years the GDR's goal will be limited to achieving comfortable prosperity for the mass instead of extravagance for a few.

Approximately 19 percent of all West German families are in an upper income bracket earning more than 1200 marks ($300) per year. In the GDR this privileged category is only half as large and represents merely 9.5 percent of the population. Neither country has real poverty. Slums and ghettos, hunger and privation have been long erased on both sides of the border. That the GDR lacks the icing of lavishness is not just an accidental product of economic exigencies but the result of ideological intent.

Where the disparities between the two systems are being systematically erased, however, is in the standard of living of the lower and lower middle class. "Of course the West seems shinier," one East German executive told me. "Everyone knows the really well-to-do live much better in West Germany than here. But they are a minority in both societies. We're concerned about the lower income groups," he said, "and you have to admit they fare better here than the working class in the Federal Republic. Just compare a family of four earning 600 marks a month here and 800 marks a month in West Germany and you'll see what I mean. Our rents are a fraction of those in the West and the price of all basic commodities—coal, potatoes, bread, milk, transportation, entertainment, medical care, and education are substantially cheaper and the common man lives better."

Well, almost. But there is a measure of truth in these claims which no statistical comparison of prices and wages can dispute. On a back country road near Dresden I once met a grizzled old-timer, still wearing the railway conductor's cap that identified his erstwhile profession in life. He had a huge basket in his hand which he was filling rapidly with currants picked surreptitiously off a neighbor's bushes. The subterfuge was to him the source of primary delight. At first our conversation was hopelessly lopsided, I asked the questions and got only grunts and mumbles in reply. Just as I was about to give up and search for more responsive subjects, he became reasonably communicative, told me he had a monthly pension of 370 marks ($92.50) on which he and his wife got along comfortably. A three-room apartment in an old farmhouse, he explained, cost him only 18 marks ($4.50) per month. Finally, in one burst of loquacity that took me by surprise, he blurted out: "Look, young fellow. I was never a Sozi and never a Commi and I'm neither now. But this'll probably bowl you over. I want for nothing. The state cares for us well. My woman and I are well off, better than we would have been under a different system. I've got no complaints."

The average gross monthly earnings of all workers in East Germany is 660 marks ($165) monthly—almost 900 marks ($225) in West Germany. But because of the high percentage of working wives, an accurate analysis should be based on family income which in 1966 averaged 936 marks ($234), after taxes, for a four-person household.

Rent, including heat and utilities, consumes 5 to 10 percent of income depending on size, location, ownership, and condition of the quarters. Food will account for another 40 to 45 percent of monthly income. Clothing and household purchases take up 30 percent, services and repairs about 6 percent, alcohol and tobacco almost 10 percent.

The major difference between East and West German life is to be found in that varied interpretation of the meaning of luxury goods. To the steel worker in Essen, a 5000 mark ($1250) Volkswagen has become almost a right. He grumbles about the 150 ($37.50) marks he must pay for rent out of a monthly income of 800 marks ($200). For the Eisenhüttenstadt foundry worker, earning 660 marks ($165) a modern three-room apartment at 54 marks ($13.50) is a "Socialist achievement," a two-door plastic-bodied Trabant sedan which cost 8000 marks ($2000) remains a luxury. He grumbles, with understandable justification, at the 40 marks ($10) he must pay for a pound of coffee, but takes it for granted that he can ride the bus to work for 20 pfennigs (five cents). His West German counterpart pays only six to eight marks ($1.50 and $2) for a pound of far better coffee but is likely to shell out 60 to 80 pfennigs (15 to 20 cents) per bus ride, provided of course, that he does not own a car.

Most East Germans now accept—if not graciously, at least with equanimity—the outrageous disproportion between the cost of "basic commodities" and the usurious prices for "luxuries." I can recall hearing only isolated complaints. "They charge us extortionately for anything out of the ordinary," complained an Erfurt physician, pointing to his imported Italian shoes which had cost 135 marks at an Exquisit shop. But then he reflected a moment and admitted, "Well, back in the days when I could travel to the West, my wife and I spent almost as much. We have expensive tastes and buy the best wherever we are. The only difference is that the best here is inferior to the best in the West." Once I heard a man denounce this double-price standard with uncontrolled rage. It was on Unter den Linden where I was conversing with a group of students. He approached us, noticed I was a foreigner and began complaining loudly and bitterly about the "black market prices" being charged in the Havana and Delikat shops across the street. "Sixty marks for a pound of West German coffee which comes to six marks in Munich. Eighty marks for a bottle of scotch which they sell for 15 to 20 in the west. Seventy marks for the same nylon shirt my sister can buy for twelve in West Berlin. And they call that socialism?" he screamed. "I'll tell you what it is, it's legalized black marketing, legalized exploitation of the masses they profess to love in this rotten concentration camp." But such views are rare. The majority of East Germans accept the high cost of affluence with a shrug or attempt to rationalize it. "Of course I'd rather have a Volkswagen at 5000 marks than a Trabant at 8000," said a Berlin executive. "But we can't have everything at once. We have to wait until we can afford it. First we had to build up our basic industry."

If the GDR's is not yet an affluent, it is undeniably a sufficient society and in the years since the Berlin Wall, its most striking transformation has been from a seller's to a buyer's market. Shop windows, at least in larger cities, once the brunt of caustic humor because they displayed only portraits of Ulbricht and promises instead of merchandise, now burgeon with handsome goods arranged attractively to lure customers.

Even advertising has become respectable and there is nothing extraordinary about opening one's copy of *Neues Deutschland*, to find state-owned soap manufacturers and socialist-run supermarkets competing actively for reader attention against the unabridged texts of five-hour speeches by Ulbricht. East German women are being exhorted to buy Mintox home permanent solutions, Riwa toilet soap and Chlorodont toothpaste. East German husbands and fathers, conscious of their "family responsibilities," are regularly reminded that supplementary health and life insurance is the "best protection against unexpected calamity." Just fill out the coupon, says an ad, and a "people's-owned salesman" will come running like the man from MONY. State and cooperatively owned supermarkets advertise their specials just like the A & P. Once I even spotted Erfurt's Konsum (co-op) chain advertising telephone orders and home deliveries on poultry which it was selling at 30 percent off. Even sex—with reservations —has joined the battle. The shapely, barebacked blonde who purrs with satisfaction at the marvels of Diplom scented toilet soap on the pages of East German magazines could have been transplanted from Vogue.

East Germany has indeed come a long way from the era of shortages and planning blunders when there seemed to be nothing but left-footed shoes, buckets without handles, tires without tubes and nails without hammers. Those were the days when people shopped, not for what they wanted, but for whatever happened to be available. The classic story of those times tells of a man walking across the town square, toting a huge funeral wreath. A friend stops and asks him who died. "Oh, no one. But they're selling wreaths today and I thought I'd better get one to keep until I need it." It was the time when everyone knew the Leipzig fair had started because shop shelves elsewhere suddenly emptied. East Germans will bend any willing ear to tell about the year there were no screws but a glut of screwdrivers, about the time Dresden nearly suffocated in an over-supply of onions while residents of all other cities had to write relatives in the West to send them one or two. Shortages still exist and plans still go awry, but increasingly they are becoming the exception instead of the rule. "Sure it's irritating when our oil refineries produce lighter fluid but the bottle industry louses up the plan and the tobacconist tells you he has no fuel in stock," said a Berlin economist. "But we're doing everything to prevent such bungles and I think we've made progress." Not enough for some people, though. A Zwickau housewife told me: "Right now you won't find a sheet of carbon paper in town and in some offices they've blackened their own." I couldn't test her charge because it was a Sunday, but the next day, in Erfurt, I found stacks of carbon paper in stationery stores. In Erfurt there was a shortage of paper clips.

"It's gotten better," a Fürstenberg craftsman told me, "but something is always missing. Usually it's the little item that you think you never need. Sometimes there'll be weeks when you can't get a tube of toothpaste. Right now there's no washing-machine soap powder. My wife waited three years to get her washer, now she can't use it because she can't locate a box of detergent within fifty miles of here. A friend of mine broke the starter switch on his wife's mixmaster. For three months he has been trying to obtain a replacement part. Nothing doing. The factory dealer wrote the wholesale organization, the wholesaler wrote the factory and all my friend got back was promises. Sure they're making the spare parts but nobody seems to know where they've been shipped."

Added his wife: "There's no real shortage of food. It's just that the selectivity is so limited. When you see people standing in line in front of a butcher shop it doesn't mean they're queuing for meat but that every housewife knows the earliest bird gets the fattest—in this case the leanest—worm. I do my weekend shopping on Thursdays, not Fridays, or Saturdays. That way I know I'll get a good roast for Sunday. I have a refrigerator to store it. But what does the poor woman without one do. She has to wait until Saturday morning to shop and then she'll probably find nothing but gristle left."

The lack of selection coupled with intermittent shortages of some goods and the sudden profusion of others often makes shopping a source of irritation. A young Dresden mother of two said: "A West German or American housewife can sit down in the morning, make up a shopping list and plan her meals, then go to the grocery store and buy everything her budget will allow. Not I. My meals are dictated by what I happen to find on the shelves. If I intend to make steaks tomorrow I may end up serving schnitzel because all the butchers are out of beef though inundated with veal. We don't have real shortages, but invariably I find myself shopping for what's available, not what I want or need. It is simply impossible to find everything all of the time. I fill my wardrobe, my refrigerator and my pantry according to the dictates of some distant planning expert or wholesale buyer. He determines what I set on the table tonight." In this particular case, he must have planned well. I was an unexpected guest for supper who arrived after the shops had closed. Nevertheless I was offered four kinds of cheeses, three varieties of sausage, ham, three types of bread, a choice of butter or margarine and wine.

The shortage of certain critical materials—notably steel—is omnipresent. Even in the best hotels, not to speak of modern new apartment houses, all bathroom fixtures, door handles and knobs on furniture are made of plastic. To Western eyes, accustomed to the sparkle of chrome and brass, it lends East Germany an aura of *ersatz*. Cotton and linen, which must be imported, are so scarce that restaurant tablecloths—even in the poshest establishments—are so small they look like outsized napkins.

Bad customer service remains one of the chief abrasives of socialist living—despite such innovations as eighty-day trials on refrigerators and same-day delivery of television sets. Getting a roof repaired, a house repainted or a leaky pipe fixed is a test of will and endurance which the handyman usually wins. Persuading a state-owned store or factory to make good on the guarantee for its merchandise involves struggling through a maze of bureaucratic obstacles with little hope of success. Automobile repairs may take weeks because garages are short of mechanics and spare parts. The average time a suit or dress spends at the cleaner's is fourteen to twenty-one days.

The handyman problem is now being solved by means of legalized moonlighting. Community councils have resorted to organizing "craft brigades" whose members, recruited from offices and industry, are dexterous amateur house painters, paperhangers, roofers, plumbers, carpenters, plasterers and electricians. Their rates match those of professionals but they are quick to respond to a call and motivated by that most decadent of all incentives: personal profit. It gets the job done.

"Three years I waited for a roofer," an elderly Zwickau home owner once told me. "Finally I heard about the moonlight brigades. I called one and could hardly believe it. The men were on the job that evening."

Public pressure and embarrassment, usually in the columns of local newspapers, has also managed to overcome some of the apathy that for years made the niggling problems of daily life a source of constant disgruntlement.

"We know these are aggravations," an SED city official in Eisenhüttenstadt confided, "but the only way we can find out and do anything about them is when people take the trouble to complain. Just grumbling in private or writing relatives in West Germany won't help."

East Germans are learning to deal with the daily frictions of a collectivized society. However, no torrent of party palliatives will erase the discontent engendered by the lack and high price of automobiles or the shortage of housing. Production of both, though brisk, continues to lag critically behind demands which become more sophisticated by the day.

The beetle-shaped Volkswagen is a tribute to West Germany's industrial prowess, just as the crowded autobahn highways are noisy proof of its high standard of living. Postwar motorization has become the criterion of the Federal Republic's economic miracle, just as East Germany's critics ineluctably point to its dearth of cars as evidence of the GDR's impotence. Yet, despite the automotive gap, the two Germanys have a lot in common: both are hopelessly car crazy.

Sometimes it seems the automobile, not socialism, has become the common denominator of East German life. Everyone talks about it—either wistfully because he doesn't have one, or ebulliently because it is about to be delivered. All newspapers and magazines write about it—either disparagingly because it has become a yardstick of false values, or optimistically because production continues to increase. A conversation in the GDR, be it with a party ideologue or a laborer, a pampered scientist or a schoolboy, inevitably reduces to a discussion of horsepower, acceleration, fuel consumption, the price of gasoline and which polish is best for which kind of chrome. Among knowledgeable Western journalists it is a favorite sport to travel through the GDR with the flashiest, most ostentatious car available. They know it is the quickest start to conversations which, hopefully, will get around to more newsworthy subjects. Even *Neues Deutschland*, which doggedly fills its tedious, boring pages with all the non-news unfit to print, finds space once weekly to publish results of car tests or dabble in accessory and cylinder talk. Traffic and cars have become the standards by which East Germans measure their progress. I have heard party functionaries boast about the growing parking problem as proof of the nation's progress.

As the most coveted symbol of modern civilization, the automobile has become the source of a flourishing black and gray market. Though the courts judge "auto speculators" harshly, this breed continues to thrive handsomely. Managers of state-owned automobile distributorships have been sentenced to prison terms for manipulating waiting lists and accepting bribes to speed up delivery time. Recently East Berlin police cracked a ring of mechanics who had been buying up used cars, repairing and refurbishing them in backyard garages and reselling them—mostly to well-heeled collective farmers—at outrageously inflated prices. Within a few months, according to testimony before an East Berlin court, the group had sold 107 cars at more than one-and-a-half times their actual value.

So long as new cars remain a scarce commodity, the used-car market will prosper and in the GDR "used" means anything that still has four wheels and an engine. Most of these are advertised in *Neue Zeit* the official organ of the East German CDU, and in the "independent" *Berliner Zeitung*. Both are treasure chests for Old Timer buffs. Prewar Opels, for example, still sell for up to 1000 marks ($250); Wartburgs and DKWs nearing the end of their second decade, with speedometers that have passed the 100,000 kilometer mark several times, continue to bring $1000. Once I spotted an ad for a 1952 Nash (How did it ever find its way into East Germany?) selling at $1250 and a 1940 Mercedes offered for $600. Hundreds of such jalopies change hands every weekend. They keep running on ingenuity and spare parts slaughtered from the innards of even older models. Though mechanics are slow they are undoubtedly among the most inventive in the world. With wire, pliers, and imagination they seem able to keep even the most archaic relics sputtering along for decades.

To meet the growing demand for automobiles, rental car services have started in nearly all major cities. Standard rate: 30 marks ($7.50) per day for a Trabant plus 10 pfennigs per kilometer exclusive of gasoline. One of the largest agencies—with 120 vehicles —is owned by East Berlin's VEB Taxi Dienst. "We started in 1961 with eight sedans, eighteen motorcycles, and two motor scooters," said Klaus-Peter Siebert, the manager. "It took awhile for the idea to catch on. Now we have to turn customers away almost every weekend. With ten times as many cars we would still fail to satisfy demand."

Roads and highways are better than their reputation. The autobahns which Hitler built are generally in excellent condition. One reason may well have been the dearth of traffic until a few years ago. Secondary roads—most of which are cobblestoned, not asphalt-covered—are more problematical though an intensive resurfacing program has been under way since January 1966, including expansion of the 875-mile autobahn network. Good springs and shock absorbers, however, will remain an important requirement of cross country travel in the GDR for many years.

Roadside restaurants and snack bars are spaced far apart and they leave many wishes of comfort, cleanliness and service unfulfilled. The opening of the GDR's first motel in 1967 near Dresden made front page headlines in all newspapers. Gas stations, of which the GDR now has 1600 are as hard to find as Eskimos in Africa, and once found, will either be closed or have long lines of cars waiting to be served.

Considering the price of gasoline—$1.40 per gallon—it seems surprising anyone drives a car at all. "Most people buy theirs to use on weekends," a Dresden acquaintance confided. "They keep their automobiles garaged or under plastic covers all week, then spend Saturday afternoons washing and polishing them like family idols (a practice common in West Germany, too). They'll run it over to the nearest gas station, put in enough fuel to last over Sunday (when most gas stations are closed), then park in front of their houses so all the neighbors can ogle. Actual driving is done on Sundays. We are a nation of Sunday drivers."

The car has become a status symbol and East Germans promenade it on the highways just as they take their Sunday suits and dresses "for a walk." Indeed, the car's role already has socialist moralists worrying. They fear it may corrupt what the party has set as the goals of East German society. "There is a dangerous tendency on the part of many comrades in our workers' and peasants' state to attain status and respect through acquisition of a Wartburg or a Skoda," wrote East Berlin's *Wochenpost* in September 1966. "These citizens of our republic seem to have lost sight of the real purposes of automobiles. Are cars not means of transportation, vehicles with which to enjoy the fruits of our labor, with which to tour our country and enjoy its scenery and historic sights? Are they not tools of convenience to make our life easier and more pleasant? Automobiles are all these things, but they should certainly not be considered symbols of rank, power or station." With that, the management of *Wochenpost*, a Sunday paper which carries columns upon columns of marital ads (an old German custom), announced that it would no longer accept advertisements from eligible bachelors trying to lure girls by referring to the cars they owned. Nor would girls advertising for mates be permitted to specify possession of an automobile as one of the pre-conditions for a trip to the altar.

Wochenpost personal columns used to be full of such ads as: "Artistically inclined blonde, 25, tall, good figure, well groomed, good natured, seeks acquaintance of academic, technician or naval officer for eventual marriage. Must have car." Or, "I am 27, have an engineering degree, my friends call me handsome and kind. Which young blonde or brunette not over 24 would like to correspond with me? Eventual marriage possible. I own a Wartburg."

Said Dieter Kerschek, *Wochenpost's* managing editor: "Readers who have a car for sale or want to obtain one should go to a distributorship or advertise in newspapers which carry automotive classified ads."

Whatever their attitude toward the automobile, East Germans consider a modern apartment at ridiculously low rent, as a right. And they grumble when they have not yet been granted it. The regime has done much to meet that right, but quite obviously, not enough. Thousands of East Germans complain that they still live in quarters too old or too crowded. Only 775,000 new apartments have been built within the last decade—about one-tenth as many as in West Germany, and officials admit that the housing shortage will not be alleviated until 1970.

Life in East Germany is a curious mixture of incongruities and inconsistencies which seem to find their ultimate expression in housing. Rents—too low to pay for even the most essential repairs

—have not been raised on prewar apartments, which account for 80 percent of all units, since 1938. This gives low- and middle-income families an attractive compensation for the high cost of luxuries, but lends to most East German cities an air of Kafka-esque, ramshackle, grimy decay. To brighten up East Germany's façade, rents in prewar buildings would have to be doubled, a politically untenable move. Consequently landlords and munici-palities skirt the issue by putting up signs warning pedestrians to "beware of falling stucco." Though that is cheaper than refacing exteriors, if this policy of postponement is continued the bulk of East Germany may collapse in one huge rubble pile of decaying brick.

Sixty percent of the GDR's new apartment houses have been built with state funds and are managed by municipal housing authorities. These light, airy but small three- and four-room apartments rarely cost more than $20 per month—utilities in-cluded. The remaining 40 percent are cooperatively built units. To obtain one, each tenant must have contributed 500 to 600 hours of personal labor plus a lump-sum payment of 1600 to 2400 marks ($400 to $600). Title to co-op apartments may be inherited by children and close relatives. Rents for units of three and four rooms in co-op buildings rarely exceed $15 per month. The hours spent on construction are a lost labor of love. The cash payment, however, is repayable on cancellation of member-ship.

For years the regime capitalized on the low cost of housing as one of those socialist achievements which the West could never match. Now it has realized that rock-bottom rents were a bad investment. It not only cost the state an annual $200,000,000 in construction subsidies but many of the new structures are al-ready in such a deplorable state of disrepair that vast sums will have to be pumped into their maintenance and refurbishment. Rent increases of up to 40 percent were finally decreed in Sep-tember 1966, but apply only to units constructed or completed after January 1967. Even then, apartment living in the GDR will remain a bargain.

Private home construction and ownership, though not propagated, are perfectly legal. By tradition, home ownership in Germany has always been an exception. In a land where population density is seven times greater than in the United States and three times that of China, there has never been much room for the single or double-family dwelling. Apartment living has become the rule. The common man's escape valve from the confines of the flat are the garden plots or *Schrebergärten*, sometimes only a few square meters, wedged in between industrial sites or on the outskirts of larger cities. East Germany has 754,000 weekend cultivators, most of them organized in clubs and cooperatives. Nearly 75,000 live in East Berlin. Nevertheless, there has been an increase in home ownership and construction. Money is all that counts. On the edge of Eisenhüttenstadt, for example, extensive colonies of private single-family houses have been built on state-owned land. Because labor is short and materials scarce, private homes often are the product of years of weekend work and ingenious hoarding of building supplies.

With neither enough automobiles nor enough houses and apartments on which to spend their money, what *are* East Germans doing to get rid of their excess cash? One problem is that they cannot do enough and that accumulated savings and purchasing power are again too high. Nevertheless, there are plenty of safety valves. Thousands, for example, own boats—from raft to yacht size—though where they sail them is anyone's guess. The country is short on rivers, canals and coast line. It has only nine lakes with a surface area of five square miles or more, and on any summer weekend they are as crowded as Times Square on New Year's Eve. Rostock has a yacht harbor—an anachronism if ever there was one in an egalitarian socialist society.

Travel and tourism also help to blot up some excess marks, though rates for group vacations and excursions, especially within the GDR, are generally so low that a thrifty man can spend less on holiday than at home. It may not be everyone's cup of tea, but hardy souls willing to travel with their co-workers on plant-supported journeys or to factory-owned hotels can count on paying no more than 200 marks ($50) per person for two weeks—room, board and travel included. Each year more than a half million people go on vacations sponsored by the GDR's federation of trade unions which owns or controls nearly 250 once-posh hotels and rooming houses on the Baltic Sea, in the Harz mountains and the Saxonian Jura. Accommodations range from just bearable to luxurious and the atmosphere is strictly collectivist. But prices are bargain basement. For transportation, room and board, rates range from a minimum of 30 ($7.50) to a maximum of 100 marks ($25)—not per day but for the entire two weeks.

The more discriminating who prefer privacy or companions other than fellow employees, must pay more for a vacation, although by Western standards rates are ridiculously low. The GDR's state travel agency features three-week all-inclusive trips to Varna on the Black Sea for 1100 marks ($225), two-week tours of Poland's highlands for 750 marks ($187.50) and 14-day round trips of the Soviet Union by air for $300.

East Germans can have the cheapest winter vacations in Europe in some of Europe's best skiing areas: Poland, Czechoslovakia, Bulgaria, Rumania, the Soviet Union, and their own Thuringian and Saxonian hills. Fifteen days in Czechoslovakia's rugged and idyllic Tatra Mountains cost only 600 marks ($150)—train transportation, room and board in first-class hotels, rental skis, lessons, and lift fees inclusive. Two weeks in Bulgaria's Rila Mountains, fifty miles from Sofia, come to 800 marks ($200)—including air transportation, American plan, room with private bath and all incidentals. And winter vacations in the GDR's Erzgebirge or Thuringia generally run no more than 150 marks ($37.50) for two weeks. Those who insist on making their own arrangements to keep away from the mob pay just slightly more. A Dresden bookkeeper estimated that two weeks of skiing in Oberwiesenthal cost him 400 marks ($100) for himself, his wife and ten-year-old son. "I took a room in a private inn and we ate our meals in restaurants." Where could a family earning 900 marks monthly do better?

The regime boasts that its cut-rate holiday program is one of socialism's major achievements. But socialist tourism has its dark side too. Trips to countries outside the Soviet bloc are taboo for all except the lucky few who get berths on one of GDR's two cruise liners, the *Fritz Heckert* and the *Völkerfreundschaft* which sail the Mediterranean and the Caribbean. Even Yugoslavia is off limits because there have been a number of embarrassing escapes and defections. For the GDR's élite who could afford vacations in France, Italy, and Greece, the restrictions are a perennial abrasive. "I'd be the last man in the country to defect," said one plant manager. "Why shouldn't I have an opportunity to see Paris or Rome, not to mention Dubrovnik?"

Even more demoralizing than the ban on travel to the West is the pervasive spirit of togetherness which pursues East Germans to the beach. In Heringsdorf, once the most exclusive resort town on the Baltic, workers now enjoy 12 days at only 115 marks ($38.25) in the opulent Hotel Atlantic, famous in the 1920s and 1930s as one of Europe's best. But it has been renamed Hotel Solidarity, which says just about everything. "Once a year," explained a Dresden teacher, "I'd like to get as far away from solidarity as possible." It's not easy. In the best and cheapest hotels—those owned or controlled by the Trade Unions—everything is organized from breakfast until the evening dance. Propaganda is never far away, though it is becoming more sophisticated. The only way to avoid it entirely, is to travel alone: a risky venture, as the best hotels and inns belong to the unions or have been chartered for the season by large industries.

Improvements are planned by 1970, however. Said Adolf Knipper, a Rostock district functionary, in 1966: "Within the next decade we intend to build dozens of new hotels with the best facilities so there'll be something for every taste, for the people who enjoy vacationing in groups at minimum cost and for those who prefer to be alone and to pay a little more. These things take time. Eventually we'll be able to deal with all the complaints we hear nowadays."

Most East Germans confidently expect today's complaints to be met on some tomorrow. I have heard countless people say: "A lot remains to be done but we know exactly where we stand and our perspective"—a popular word to describe future plans, public and private—"is clear."

Life in the GDR today is this curious mixture of complacency and crass materialism. Complaints come mostly from the very well to do—the intellectuals and members of the technical intelligentsia—or the older generation which can recall the prewar days that were better than the regime portrays them, worse than most people like to remember. For the vast majority, however, there is a sense of naïve trust in the future which, they have been advised by the SED, will be better if only everyone will work a little harder.

Most East Germans heed the advice. It is a beehive of a country in which production plans keep climbing, productivity increases steadily, more than half of all married women help supplement family income and nearly everyone and his grandmother is engaged in some form of study for self improvement. More than 675,000 East Germans are enrolled in university correspondence courses or adult education and qualification programs. Nearly every mechanic, it seems, is taking a correspondence course in mechanical engineering and announces: "When I finish, in about five years, I'll have a degree and my income will jump from 700 to 1500 marks a month." East Germany's is a dizzying atmosphere of aspiration in which the regime's collective goals are inextricably mingled with personal ambition. Women are exhorted to work because the economy desperately needs their labor. Most women do work, but usually to help their families acquire the gadgetry of modern living.

To entice women to the assembly line, the regime has offered persuasive inducements ranging from inexpensive, scientific child care, to complete equality—including male wages. Women are everywhere: they rivet, run chemical plants, drive bulldozers, streetcars, trains, busses and tractors, they regulate traffic, design dams and hydroelectric plants, run hospitals, schools and nurseries, supervise collective farms and preside over courts as judges. Discrimination exists only in government and politics, it seems. Of the Politburo's fifteen members all are men and only one of its six candidates—thirty-five-year-old Margarete Mueller—is a woman. The ratio on the Council of Ministers, only one of whose thirty-nine members is a woman, is not any better. Nevertheless,

East German women today have a sense of confidence and enjoy an equality undreamed of in a society which barely a quarter of a century ago counted as one of Europe's most patriarchal. On the other hand, this is a highly problematical development, for the GDR is turning into a country desperately short of the influence of full-time motherhood.

Half of the GDR's pre-school children are being raised in day nurseries and kindergartens. No force other than money compels East German mothers to place them there and the nurseries are all models of child raising where toddlers are supervised by trained teachers, cared for scientifically, fed perfectly balanced meals, examined monthly by dentists and pediatricians and taught games and group living in antiseptically clean and modern surroundings. But the program is fraught with dangers which no East German pedologist has yet dared to examine closely. The effect may well be a whole new generation of neurotics raised without love.

"You should go to a streetcar stop early some winter morning and see all the mothers with the waifs they're about to deposit for the day," an elderly Dresden woman once told me. "The kids are yanked out of bed with not enough sleep, rushed through the cold and the crowds by mothers in a hurry to get to work, then dumped unceremoniously with strangers for the day. Children are subconsciously aware of the love they receive or don't receive. These kids must sense they are in someone's way and I'm sure they'll grow up reacting accordingly. But mothers are so essential to the production process that no one would dare raise the question publicly."

"It is a problem," an East German physician told me once. "A child psychologist or pediatrician can tell you right away which children have been raised in day nurseries, which ones grew up at home. The ones from kindergarten are, comparatively speaking, retarded. They have been systematically deprived of the impulses that come from adult surroundings. No matter how well trained or willing the teachers and supervisors may be, they will never have the time to influence each child as intensively as its mother. No amount of scientific child care is going to substitute for the attention which only a mother can devote. I'm afraid it is a lesson for which we shall have to pay dearly some day."

Until the bill is presented, however, East German propagandists will undoubtedly laud the nurseries as one of socialism's major achievements, and the women will continue to rush to the assembly line.

Only a third of East German families earn more than 1000 marks ($250) per month, but when they do, they can live in considerable comfort. The GDR purports to be a classless society, which it is, if one interprets class in the narrow sense to mean exploitation of one group by another. But East Germany certainly has strata of society almost indistinguishable from traditional classes. Among the upper strata, life borders on affluence. If East Germans are not yet openly resentful of the disparities, they are certainly caustic about them. Strange as it may seem, some of the sharpest criticism emanates from the new élite itself.

"They call this socialism and equality," an East German surgeon told me disgustedly, "but it's as unequal a distribution as anywhere else in the world. Where's the classless society we're supposed to have? Look, my wife and I earn about 2500 marks ($625) and we can afford almost everything. But there's something wrong when we're constantly subjected to propaganda about the decadence of capitalism, yet all those decadent symbols from shoes to whisky at twenty dollars per bottle are sold right here. Prestige and class consciousness prevail here just as they do in West Germany with one difference: we're afraid to call it by its name. What infuriates me is the hypocrisy."

Nowhere is this hypocrisy more ubiquitous than in the GDR's Intershops—duty-free stores, usually located in large hotels, where smartly uniformed salesgirls sell anything from nylon hosiery to Swiss chocolates and French cognac at cut-rate prices. The only catch: all purchases must be made in foreign exchange—American dollars and West German marks preferred. Theoretically, Intershops are a convenience for tourists whose hard currency the GDR needs. In practice no customer is ever asked his nationality or required to show any passport except his cash. Consequently they are patronized by East Germans who possess West German marks or dollars illegally and have a furtive speakeasy atmosphere which is heightened by the location of most Intershops in hotel basements or dark corners behind the washrooms.

The regime is far from niggardly toward the new upper class-less. Physicist Manfred von Ardenne, lives in resplendent comfort in Dresden's upper crust suburb of Weisser Hirsch. From his villa—furnished with Oriental rugs and valuable antiques—he has a panoramic view of the Elbe and the city below. One of the richest men in the GDR, his fortune derives as much from salary as from royalties on his patents.

Iris Dullin-Grund, thirty-three, is the GDR's most successful architect and city planner. She caught Ulbricht's eye and the party's attention in 1959 when she designed an ultramodern fifteen-story cultural and community center for the town of Neu-Brandenburg. Now Frau Grund is city planning director for the district of Neu-Brandenburg and busy putting her novel ideas into practice in smaller communities. The Grunds—her husband is a construction engineer—have two children and a monthly income that nudges 4000 marks ($1000). They own a modern single-family house on state-owned land, and collect antiques at bargain prices from farmers who don't know the value of the furniture in their attics. Even among the GDR's upper crust, the Grunds are unique. They own *two* cars: a Wartburg sedan and a convertible.

Life for Erika Radtke would be just as beautiful if she weren't so frugal and thrifty. Fräulein Radtke—or Frau Urban to be exact —is a tall, leggy, blue-eyed blonde whose face is more familiar to most East Germans than Walter Ulbricht's. She is GDR Television's star announcer—a role she has played with spectacular success since she, her equally stunning sister Annemarie, and six other girls were selected from among 680 applicants ten years ago. Erika Radtke's career is virtually a cliché success story. The daughter of a locomotive engineer, she worked as a stenographer in East Berlin's Foreign Ministry and financed the dates with her boyfriend, Peter Urban, a medical student. When television discovered her, Erika became rich by East German standards. Her salary climbed to over 1000 marks—enough to get married to Peter. Their first home was a one-room garden hut with a kitchen nook. "It was terribly crowded and primitive," she recalls, "but we were alone and that was all that mattered." Today Erika brings home 1700 marks ($425) a month; Peter, now a surgeon, earns 2000 ($500). But the Urbans continue to live modestly. They have a four-room East Berlin apartment which rents for 42 marks ($10.50). Now that they have Cathrine (their three-year-old daughter) it may be a little small. "But," says Erika, "we find it cozy and see no reason to move." They do own a car, though Dr. Urban has first and permanent call on it. Erika, one of the GDR's highest-paid television personalities, rides the subway or elevated to the studios each day. Their only real extravagance: gourmet food, which both relish when dining out (which is often) and both can prepare in their tiny kitchen with remarkable professionalism.

Judged on the East German norm, the life of the Urbans, von Ardennes, and Grunds seems extravagant. Clearly, the SED has relegated to the dustbin of history that old Marxist maxim: from each according to his abilities, to each according to his needs. But even if the von Ardennes, Urbans and Grunds receive more than they need, no one can deny that they contribute to the best of their ability. Von Ardenne is a brilliant innovator who has dozens of patents to his credit and is convinced that he has discovered a means of controlling cancer by treating it with extreme heat. Iris Dullin-Grund is an architect with a refined taste and common-sense practical ideas. In a capitalistic society she would earn five to ten times her present salary. Erika Radtke has more than a pretty face. She is multi-lingual, memorizes scripts in English, French, Hungarian, Czech, Russian, and Polish and has been offered twice her present wage by West German TV if she would defect.

Clearly it is ability that counts, and that is the crux of the East German argument. Wealth and affluence are no longer the privilege of chance or birth, the SED insists, but the reward of talent. East German society is "classless" in the Marxist sense but stratified. Its élite is a strata of scientists, doctors, engineers, technicians, architects, entertainers, writers, composers, journalists, and—one must not forget them—top-echelon functionaries. The upper crust is a sensitive subject among Communist ideologues who are clearly embarrassed by the new affluence. But in a moment of complete candor one apparatchik once said to me: "Make fun of us if you wish. However, ours is at least an 'upper class' which cannot perpetuate itself. Money can be inherited all of the time: talent and ability only some of the time." Perhaps. Only the future will determine whether in the GDR, as in the Soviet Union, the progeny of the new class is also privileged. A functionary as a father does not yet mean an automatic ticket to college.

Yes, East Germany is prosperous today. It is the envy of its neighbors in the Soviet bloc. But its socialist togetherness has eliminated privacy, and efficiency supersedes human sensibilities. The SED's ideologues never weary of propagating the postulate that socialism has but this aim: to benefit man, to concern itself with human welfare. But in order to reap such benefits the East German must be willing to give up individuality.

CHAPTER X

The Making of Collectivized Man

Germany's repudiation of Hitler was not a spontaneous domestic uprising against tyranny but a renunciation forced upon it in the throes of defeat. In the wake of conquest each victor attempted to rebuild Germany in his own image.

In the West this has been an endeavor to transplant the great tenets of Anglo-Saxon democracy and the ideals of the Enlightenment upon a society that had misunderstood the Age of Reason and turned its own century of nationalism into an aberration of myths. It has been like placing a frail sapling in fallow ground. Though the young tree bloomed in its first spring and may even bear fruit, no one can vouchsafe whether it will take healthy root. "Clothes often *do* make the man," a senior Bonn official once told me, "and we can only hope that by wearing the mantle of democracy long enough, democratic behavior will come to us naturally."

In the East the situation is analogous. East Germany's population did not stage a revolution. It neither rose against the Nazis when they were in power, nor did it participate actively in the reformation of society imposed upon it by the Soviet conquerors and the German Communists who assisted them. Supported by Soviet tanks and bayonets, Walter Ulbricht, Wilhelm Pieck, and their politruks expropriated the Junkers and industrialists. They subjugated the upper middle class. They convulsed the civil service and judiciary, both of whom were infested with the mold of reaction. But it was, at the most, the exterior shell of a revolution.

However, the instability of his position as Moscow's proconsul in a Germany whose ultimate fate remained in abeyance, and the messianic spirit inherent in Communism itself, behooved Ulbricht to attempt a revolution of his own. It demanded more than merely expropriating capitalists, nationalizing the means of production, collectivizing agriculture and fortifying the SED's monopoly over the state. Instead, it required an encompassing metamorphosis, not merely of social structure but, of the character of East German man. His sense of values, views on property, notions about God, perspective of history, relationship to fellow beings, concepts of morality and his attitude toward authority all had to undergo transformation and conform to the pseudo-religious tenets of modern-day Marxism. This transmogrification, based on the Marxist-Leninist maxim that ideas serve not merely to explain but to change the world, began with a reorientation and re-education of East Germany's *Weltbild*. Eventually it may produce a novel man and a new pattern of social relationships.

Ulbricht's "ten commandments of socialist morality," coined in 1958, portray the ideal of this "new man" succinctly.

1. Thou shalt honor the international solidarity of the working class and the proletariat and strive for friendship and alliance between all socialist countries.

2. Thou shalt love thy fatherland and always be prepared to defend the Workers' and Peasants' State with all thy strength.

3. Thou shalt help to eliminate exploitation of man by man.

4. Thou shalt strive to perform good for socialism, for it leads to a better life for all members of the working class.

5. Thou shalt act in a spirit of comradely cooperation and mutual help in the construction of socialism and respect the collective and take to heart its criticism.

6. Thou shalt protect and help to multiply the people's property.

7. Thou shalt strive to improve thy productivity, to be thrifty and frugal and to strengthen socialist discipline of labor.

8. Thou shalt raise thy children in the spirit of social-

ism and peace and help them to become well-educated, healthy and strong persons in body and mind.

9. Thou shalt live cleanly and decently and respect thy family.

10. Thou shalt practice and observe solidarity with those peoples of the world fighting for their freedom and struggling to defend their national independence.

The Communists' attempts to remake East Germany in this image sometimes bordered on the comical, more often on the macabre and repeatedly justified Stalin who once said: "Communism suits the Germans like a saddle suits a cow."

Western democracies are predicated on the theory that one never knows in advance exactly which social and communal policy will function best. Men of varying and often conflicting persuasions attempt to demonstrate the verity of their views and elicit the electoral confidence which is the prerequisite for leadership. Power is deliberately limited in duration to allow the community to confirm or reject the course and select a new group which may bend the experiment of human association in a different direction. The Communists, on the other hand, believe they know precisely what is best for society. Marxism-Leninism, which holds its truths to be self-evident and infallible, abhors a permissive social order in which everyone follows his own pursuits and impulses. The problem of reconciling the wishes and interests of individuals and groups assumes insignificance. Instead, primary attention is paid to inducing individuals to accept the neo-Benthamite dictates of the regime. Even more, the Communists demand inner approval of the experiment and badger their subjects until they embrace their new world voluntarily.

In this context, propaganda—designed to foster innate acceptance and nurture the new socialist consciousness—has been part of East German life for more than two decades. It is no longer as obtuse as it used to be. The red banners, which once exhorted East Germans to grow more potatoes, resist imperialism, build more tractors, fight revanchism and live cleanly, have been replaced by more variegated spots of color: neon signs, modern architecture, and automobiles. Gone, too, are most—though not all—of the loudspeakers which used to drone out the regime's views and arguments to the inhabitants of provincial hamlets. Propaganda has become more subtle, but it remains omnipresent.

East Germany's is a society in which labor, the factory, the collective, the building of socialism have become *raisons d'être*, the end—not the means of a better life. Acquiesce, society seems to say, and you shall be welcomed and embraced. Demur, and you will be ostracized and denied the absolution of socialist salvation. This promise and warning run thread-like through East German life and literature. "Your brigadier, your steel plant, your workers—that is all you can ever say," sneered Ullrich, about to flee to the West, at Elizabeth in Brigitte Reimann's novel *Brother and Sister*. And in Christa Wolf's *Divided Sky*, best-selling tale of love in the two Germanys, Manfred, a chemist, has escaped to West Berlin. He implores Rita, his "little brown-haired love," visiting him once more in his new world, to stay and not return to East Berlin. "Here I can work," he explains. "All those pointless difficulties, the exaggerated self-praise when there is a minimum of success, the tortured self-laceration when there is another failure—that's all behind me now. I have gotten a job where others are paid especially to shield me from unnecessary disturbances and hindrances in my research. It's what I have always dreamed of." But all Rita can think of, as they walk hand-in-hand down glittering Kurfürstendamm are the tribulations of "my brigade, my comrades, my plant." She sacrifices Manfred's love for love of socialism.

East German society exudes finger-wagging moralism, puritanism, conventionality, and strait-laced Philistinism which the proletariat has inherited unadulterated from the petite bourgeoisie. The GDR also burgeons with positivism, an embryonic patriotism and nationalism, self-righteousness and a naïve confidence in the infallibility of socialism. Above all, East Germans practice a new philosophy of togetherness which holds that society should be of the collective by the collective and for the collective.

Newspapers are published by "editorial collectives." Waiters in restaurants are organized into "service collectives." Work in sci-

19] Assembly line in Sachsenring automobile plant in Zwickau, where plastic-odied Trabant is made.

] Professor of Engineering Gerhard Kosel shows visitors what Alexanderplatz the center of East Berlin will look like when completed in 1970. (Credit: Zen-ild)

[21] Interior of new self-service supermarket in Berlin-Lichtenberg. (Credit: Zentralbild)

[22] Downtown and residential Leipzig. (Credit: Zentralbild)

] Women have equal rights and equal responsibilities like these gardeners ployed by the city of Eisenhuettenstadt.

[24] Pre-school children in Eisenhuettenstadt.

[25] These collective farmers from village of Ziesluebbe, Parchim County, being instructed in use of milking machine by agricultural expert who makes rc of collective farms with classroom housed in a truck trailer (Credit: Zentral

entific institutes is conducted by "research collectives." Apartment
houses are run by "housing collectives." Production in industrial
plants is organized among so-called socialist brigades whose leaders are like foremen. An attempt has even been made to organize
artists, writers, and composers into "collectives" but the result has
been abominable.

Alien as the terminology may sound, repugnant as collectivism
may be in the eyes of societies nurtured on the principle that the
rights of the individual are inviolable, the collective has introduced a spirit of teamwork which had been alien to German
life. Collectivism has imbued East German society with a climate
of cooperation and mutual respect for fellow men which is almost
second nature to Americans but completely foreign to German
tradition. In this respect, despite the extremes to which collectivism has been—and still is—carried in the GDR, most Americans would be able to adjust to life there more readily than the
majority of West Germans.

Class distinctions play a far more influential role in West Germany than is generally recognized. Family background, education,
financial status and profession all create worlds in which various
social groups move, just as they create the abysmal moats that
divide them. Titlemania is but the most annoying symptom of
this. Whether academic or professional, titles are jealously coveted and proudly paraded in front of each name. It is not just
Herr Schmidt but Herr Managing Director Schmidt who may
wish an appointment with Herr Professor Doctor Schultz for a
check of his sacroiliac. It is Herr Locomotive Engineer Krauss
who is at the controls of old No. 999 and Herr Stationmaster
Maier who gives him the signal to head down the track.

East Germany is not entirely free of this and after nearly two
decades, during which everyone called everyone else *Genosse*
(Comrade), the use of some titles has come into vogue again.
Nevertheless, the GDR's is a more egalitarian society with elements faintly reminiscent of life in the U.S. Raised on a strict
diet of proletarian equality, no young East German would think
of bowing and scraping before his professors or employers as so
many West Germans still do. The title *Herr* has virtually dis-

appeared from the language and been largely replaced by *Genosse*, which is always used among SED party members, or the more universal *Kollege*, which means colleague. The effect is often farcical, such as when high-ranking army officers are addressed by their subordinates as Comrade General. But it is also beneficial. No East German would think of stammering to a cop whom he has learned to address as Comrade Policeman. In fact, for all East Germany's reputation as a police state, the relationship between citizens and the *Volkspolizei* is far less strained than that between West Germans and *their* policemen whose uniform commands deferential respect and whose manner is usually supercilious. It is one of several signs that in this undeniably autocratic state there are more symptoms of grass roots democracy than in West Germany with its incontestably democratic system of government.

The collective spirit has enabled the regime to create useful artificial competition as a productive stimulant. Sportive rivalry between factory brigades, in an atmosphere reminiscent of grade school field and track days, helps to keep the wheels of industry turning. It works in a dual fashion. Because premiums are paid for both exceptional individual and collective performance, workers are induced to raise their own as well as the brigade's production.

For all the changed attitudes which the collective system has already spawned, its influence would be far more pervasive if the regime left well-enough alone, if instead of foisting it upon the mass of East German society, it were allowed to grow roots spontaneously. But organic and spontaneous development are anathema to the apparatchik mentality. Consequently the SED periodically spreads the good word by whipping up campaigns designed to press more activists into company oriented recreation programs such as plant movie theaters, factory clubs, factory libraries, and social centers. With each such effort, which East Germans see as an invasion of their private life, resistance mounts. As it does, the party calls for more agitation.

An agitator to most Westerners is a political troublemaker. The term evokes unpleasant associations and fleeting glimpses of bomb-throwing anarchists or haranguing pamphleteers. Not in the GDR, where to be an agitator is to be a peer of the community. East Germans have gotten accustomed to finding ads like this in their newspapers: "Agitators' Forum on January 26 at 4 P.M. in the dining room of Pankow City Hall. Subject: Problems Arising from the 14th Plenary Meeting of the Central Committee: Speaker: Comrade Neubauer. All agitators are cordially invited."

Agitation, according to East German dictionaries, is "to influence the consciousness and attitudes of the masses politically through dissemination of various ideas and slogans." The SED practices that profusely though, apparently, not yet to perfection. Party meetings and conferences are usually laden with discussions about the methodology of agitation and the consensus seems to be that the majority of agitators are still too heavy-handed to meet the demands of a sophisticated and enlightened society.

As Albert Norden, the chief of the Politburo's Commission for Agitation, put it in November 1963: "In making our policies clear, party agitators should talk in terms everyone can understand. We must discuss the problems facing us with maturity and compassion for the problems of others."

Failure to heed Norden's advice has been one of the two major problems facing organized agitation in the GDR. The other is that the SED just tries to agitate too much and too often.

The purpose of agitation is to proselytize the SED's views and policies and to cultivate the "socialist awareness and attitude" of the East German people. So long as this was accomplished on factory property—albeit on the workers' own time— East Germans accepted it with equanimity as one of those inevitable aggravations of Communist life. But once the party sent out its minions to sell the faith of socialism like Fuller Brushmen at the doors of people's homes, a dangerous reaction set in.

One such campaign began in August 1963 and had but one aim: "to get the party's word and message and the view of the government into every living room." As Norden put it: "An agitator should be at work in every apartment house, on every block to overcome indifference and accomplish what years of countless appeals to socialist awareness have failed to do."

Hundreds of the agitators themselves balked. They were so busy propagandizing their fellow workers in factories by day, they argued, that they had no time and were in no mood to also go knocking on doors at night. After all, even agitators are entitled to relax with a beer and watch TV sometimes. The party wouldn't hear of it. Said Halle's Horst Sindermann, "All comrades must understand the importance of helping socialism's growth. The republic needs the help of the entire population in solving political and economic problems and it is the duty of every party member to assist them in becoming part of our new socialist way of life."

The results were meager. Despite some upbeat reports to the Central Committee, most people neither wanted to bother nor be bothered. In the rush to field an army of agitators, the party had recruited far too many who knew nothing about salesmanship or human psychology.

One obviously successful agitator found the key: subtlety. "When I visit my neighbor and see him watching West German television," he explained, "I never wag my finger. Instead, I watch with him for a while and wait for the right opportunity. For example, there's the map used by West German weather forecasters. It includes, as part of Germany, the territories east of the Oder-Neisse border which now belong to Poland. That's the time to show that even the weather map is an instrument for Bonn's revanchism."

Among the legions the party dispatched, such propagandists are rare. Far too many went knocking on doors and, if they got responses at all, would often say, "Good evening, comrade, I want to agitate you." Locks usually clicked hard and fast. Only a minority of agitators came in from the cold and after a year or so, the agitation-by-the-hearthside campaign sputtered to an end.

"Ach, our agitator is my neighbor Schmidt," said an elderly man in Halle. "He has been agitating all his life. But we are still good friends. He doesn't bother anyone except for a cup of sugar or a schnaps when he's thirsty. The whole thing was a farce."

As much of a farce was the attempt to dissuade East Germans from watching West German television. Thanks to special high-powered transmitters along the border and in West Berlin, Western TV can be received clearly in most East German towns with a modicum of gadgetry. All it usually requires is a special arm on a roof antenna, easily detectable from the street. This is not illegal: though watching publicly—for example by inviting neighbors—or disseminating information obtained from Western broadcasts is a violation of East German law.

Only a German could have construed such a nomistic interpretation but for hundreds of thousands of GDR citizens it opened the door to Western TV which they could watch in the privacy of their living rooms. Incapable of producing programs that would lure viewers away from decadent capitalist to Communist channels, the regime tried other means of persuasion. The most infamous of these was Operation Ochsenkopf (Oxhead), a campaign that sent thousands of teenaged Young Pioneers and junior apparatchiks of the FDJ up to the rooftops with orders to haul down the "west antennas." The drive won its name from several sources: Ochsenkopf is the name of the mountain along the border on which the strongest West German transmitter is located. But "oxhead" was also vernacular for the antennas themselves. And no doubt the party thought of "west viewers" as oxheads—too stubborn to see the light of Communism's promise.

The reaction to this teenage invasion was violent, and citizens who refused to bow to the noisy entreaties of the kids, usually got by with their antennas intact. At worst they were forced to move them from the roofs into the attics so they would no longer be visible from the street.

When resistance prevailed, Operation Oxhead eventually got hung up on its own antennas. For a while, in 1963, the regime attempted jamming the Western channels, this backfired, however, because frequencies were so close that East German TV was also being disrupted.

In a more subtle approach, the regime tried to dissuade parents from watching by embarrassing their children at school. Deviously teachers would ask pupils in the morning what they had seen on television the night before. It forced parents to either teach their children to lie, see them embarrassed before the whole class, or pack them off to bed before switching on the set.

Finally, in December 1964 the SED capitulated. Writing in *Junge Welt*, the official organ of the Free German Youth (FDJ), radio and television czar Gerhart Eisler pontificated: "We cannot permit public listening to the militaristic, capitalistic West German network. But on the other hand, we cannot forbid every young person from tuning in personally. Though radio and television are major weapons in the reactionary, revanchist Federal Republic's campaign to destroy us, all we can do is offer our friendly advice not to listen or watch. The programs are detrimental to the intellectual and moral development of every young person and the stations are a scandal even if they do, occasionally, broadcast good music. Their aim is to make the West's policy of murder and aggression more palatable."

If East German TV were to reduce its own propaganda the SED would have fewer problems. East Germans tune in on Bonn not so much for political information as entertainment. Western TV is not really what Bonn calls "The Soviet Zone's last remaining window on freedom," but an escape from the undertone of agitation and propaganda which East Berlin's Adlershof studios weave into almost every show.

"We aren't that eager to hear Western political views," said a Leipzig woman, "Western television just gives us a chance to get away from the humdrum of politics and propaganda." West German programs designed specifically for East German listeners— unadulterated Western propaganda—enjoy the smallest audiences east of the border. "It's what we want the least," said one industrial executive. "People recognize these shows tailored to the 'Soviet Zone' for what they are. They don't want propaganda but entertainment and straight news. I feel the only way to be informed is to listen to both sides. I watch our evening newscast at 7:30 P.M., then turn on the *Tagesschau* from Hamburg at 8 o'clock. I take it for granted that both exaggerate wildly and form my political opinions by distilling the extremes."

Millions of East Germans, of course, do not have such a choice.

Either they do not own a receiver or live in areas where the West's picture is but a fuzzy shadow on the screen. Except for West German radio, they are relegated to life in an intellectual vacuum. They depend on "newspapers without news," as Franz von Nesselrode called them in his book *Germany's Other Half*. State-guided thought control distorts the East German's image of the outside world. Largely responsible for distorting it are the GDR's thirty-nine daily newspapers—hybrids between company house organs and missionary tracts. Though there are two independent papers (*Berliner Zeitung* and *BZ am Abend*) and several published by other parties than the SED, virtually all are carbon copies of the official organ, *Neues Deutschland*. And just as boring.

Neues Deutschland's front page banner headlines can range from vituperative epithets against Bonn to glowing announcements about the overfulfillment of the turnip plan in Dippoldiswalde county. Inside pages may be crammed with the full texts of six-hour speeches by Walter Ulbricht and the anti-Western fulminations of Albert Norden. The only thing East German papers rarely contain is what most rational people call news. Instead they abound with liturgical banalities told in twaddly gobbledegook which only the party cabalists understand and no one wants to read.

On the morning I wrote these passages, my copy of *Neues Deutschland* featured such headlines and articles as: "Paper Factory Calculates Competitively, Compares and Rationalizes Production"; "Parchim's LPG Milkers Set Goal of 4300 Kilograms per Cow"; "New Warnowwerft Freighter to be Finished Three Days before Election," and "Walter Ulbricht, Willi Stoph Journey to Budapest."

There was not a word about French President Charles de Gaulle's press conference, the mounting Middle East crisis, the successful completion of the Kennedy Round tariff talks and a half dozen other events of world significance which filled the columns of such newspapers as the *New York Times*, the *London Times*, *Le Monde*, or the *Frankfurter Allgemeine* that day. Nor can East Germans—except a select group of functionaries and executives—obtain those papers. Even large international news-stands in the GDR's leading hotels carry mainly the organs of other Communist countries. Western Communist journals—which do contain news—are hard to find, though a few copies of Italy's *L'Unita*, France's *L'Humanité*, and England's *Morning Star* (formerly *Daily Worker*) can generally be located. At border crossing points, guards not preoccupied with searching outgoing cars for smuggled refugees sift incoming vehicles for smuggled newspapers and magazines. The Western press is strictly *verboten*.

East German journalists admit candidly that their newspapers "are not meant to be what *you* call objective. They are designed to formulate socialist awareness, we consider them tools of agitation."

That is why they are bought but not read. They do not want for subscribers. What they lack, apparently, is readership. To reconcile this contradiction one must examine what happens to the 900,000 copies of *Neues Deutschland* sold each day.

"Oh, I can tell you that," one East German woman said. "Exactly 285,000 copies are used to wrap garbage, another 200,000 are used to wrap fish, 200,000 are used for—well it's not nice to say that—and another 200,000 are used to start stoves and furnaces. Then there is one copy that goes to Ulbricht, another that is sent to the Kremlin and the remaining 14,998 go to the West where they are read meticulously by experts on Communism."

Notwithstanding the boredom they exude, East Germany's newspapers are hard to avoid, and it takes a special kind of courage and perseverance to stop one's subscription. Once I met a man who tried. "I sent in a cancellation notice," he told me. "Two days later I was visited by a party official who wanted to know why I had canceled. Afraid to tell him the truth—that it bored me—I cooked up a half-dozen excuses. My eyes were going bad on me, I explained, my living room was too dark to read in and besides I couldn't afford the paper on my pension. He told me not to worry. The party would supply me with a magnifying glass and stronger light bulbs. And as far as the subscription price, well I could have the paper gratis—courtesy of the SED. The magnifying glass and the light bulbs never came, but the paper still does and I haven't paid a pfennig for it since."

Silly as it sounds, East German papers are banned in West Germany just as West German papers are considered contraband in the GDR. To obtain any East German publication in the West, one must have special dispensation—usually given only to journalists, public officials, researchers, and educators—from the Bonn government.

Once, in 1964, Ulbricht offered a newspaper exchange, promising to permit unimpaired circulation of West German journals if Bonn would allow distribution of *Neues Deutschland* and one or two other East German papers in the Federal Republic. Ex-Chancellor Ludwig Erhard rejected the proposal and his press secretary Karl Günther von Hase said: "What guarantee do we have that Ulbricht won't prevent people from seeing our newspapers while everyone here will be exposed to subversion and propaganda?"

It was an imaginary danger. After satisfying their initial curiosity, most West Germans would not waste 15 pfennigs on *Neues Deutschland*. Rejecting the offer, however, deprived thousands of East Germans of something they crave even more than oranges and bananas: Western newspapers and literature.

Only once has the editorial collective of *Neues Deutschland* shown cognizance of the paper's unreadability. That was in late 1964 when Hermann Axen, then the managing editor, attempted to brighten and liven it up. Readers were treated to more sports news, entertainment features, fashion tips, menu hints and crossword puzzles. The paper's makeup underwent radical changes. Stories became shorter, headlines larger and more varied in typography and columns were spiced with more pictures, drawings and cartoons. Advertising space was enlarged to a minimum of three full pages weekly. The use of color was increased. Sunday editions were revitalized with entertainment news, theater and film reviews, gardening and fashion columns and even a "philatelists' corner." A monthly literary supplement was added. Sports news, Axen announced, would account for 50 percent of the editorial content on Monday mornings and he began splashing lottery and football results across the front page. Most important, Axen promised, the paper's columns would be opened to more letters from readers and to free discussion of party and government politics.

Many of his innovations have been retained, but in the three years since Axen originally boasted that "quality is the first commandment of Socialist journalism," *Neues Deutschland* and most of the other SED papers which emulate it have reverted to their tried and true policy of boring their readers.

East German editors and journalists are by no means oblivious to their failings. "Our reporting is tedious, uninteresting and platitudinous," Dr. Georg Krausz, president of the GDR's Association of Journalists, complained at his group's annual meeting in January 1967. "Moreover, our style and language in recent years has gotten worse instead of better. One could make a panoptic collection of gaffes from the mistakes in grammar and the meaningless paragraphs which fill our papers each day."

However, so long as editors and reporters are regarded (and regard themselves) as tools for propagating the views of the state and the party, newspapers will probably remain ludicrous jackstraws of journalism, filled with all the non-news unfit to print. And readers, as one industrial executive admitted to me, will continue to search for the real news between the lines.

Agitators, television, radio, and newspapers are the instruments of overt propaganda. But in the attempt to mold men's minds, they are like the part of the iceberg which everyone can see. It is below the surface where 90 percent of the endeavor to forge homo socialensis really takes place—and where the effort is the most productive.

Propaganda permeates every facet of East German life. It is omnipresent and circumfluent. Sometimes it stares out obtusely from a building wall. Often it spreads its seed with cunning subtlety. It is interminable and often vaporific, and like vapor it seeps unconsciously into the cockles of the heart, transforming, forging, remolding the attitudes of 17,000,000 people. It is a catalytic agent, changing, reshaping East Germany's language, mores, social values, conventions, and traditional relationships between man and wife, children and parents, management and workers, the farmer and his land, the citizen and his state.

Propaganda is the mammoth red banner exhorting East Germans to "Produce more efficiently—for yourself, for your plant and for our peaceful socialist state," which hangs from some office building or apartment house wall. It is also the small, delicately printed card, set unobtrusively between the expensive clothes in a Dresden boutique window which read: "The legacy of the heroes of anti-Nazi resistance has been fulfilled by everyone in our republic." Just like that. Just like a sign that elsewhere might read: "Credit cards accepted," or "Ask about our lay-away plan."

Propaganda is the mural art in Leipzig's expensive and elegant Kiev Restaurant. The upbeat panels depict happy Russians enjoying the munificent fruits of socialism and remind diners: "We are building Communism— Could the world know a better goal?" That tends to make even the caviar and the blinis, the spicy borscht and the delectable beef Stroganov a little hard to swallow. Propaganda is also the sheet music text to "Tomorrow the World Might Burn," a choral cycle for *a cappella* choir and narrator, displayed prominently in an East Berlin bookshop window next to a photograph of Hiroshima in 1945.

With a skill that belies its reputation for oafishness, the regime is weaving its philosophy into a fabric of GDR life. It is blending and melding old German traditions with the promise of a golden socialist tomorrow. All German history, the SED intones with determined intensity, has been one long uphill battle of the exploited down-trodden masses against their oppressors. Already East Germans believe, as Ulbricht tells them, that they made a revolution and soon they will see it as the ultimate triumph of the proletariat over the German past. It is a convenient melody for a people who only 50 years ago hurrahed the Kaiser and who, two decades later, marched willingly to the drumbeat of Hitler's mad dream of conquest.

German history, mores, and customs—though still entrenched in this isolated land between Elbe and Oder—have gained a strange new complexion of revolutionary red.

For example, just like their counterparts in the West, East German newspapers carry several columns of black-bordered death and funeral announcements each day. In the Federal Republic the names of the deceased are embellished with their honors and accomplishments for capitalism and the state. When Hans Schmidt passed away, everyone who read the announcement learned that he was a "streetcar conductor in retirement," a "municipal veterinary inspector" or perhaps a "general director and chairman of the board." In the GDR the ads look the same but the names of the deceased have been garnished with the honors of the new society in which they live. They tell a succinct story of the shift in emphasis of values that distinguishes Germany's eastern half. It was "Comrade" Hans Schmidt who died and the announcement reminds all that he was not only a loving husband, kind father and good uncle but also a "holder of the Medal of Honor of the SED," or a wearer of "the Service Medal in Bronze of the GDR," or "an Activist of the Seven-Year Plan." Widows thank "all friends and comrades" for their expressions of sympathy at the passing of "my dear husband, our generous father and valiant comrade in the struggle for socialism."

On guided sight-seeing tours of Erfurt, visitors are shown not merely this city's gems of medieval and renaissance architecture or its priceless treasures of fourteenth-, fifteenth-, and sixteenth-century art, but historic sites significant in the "revolutionary movement." In the Ratskeller, municipal curators have carefully preserved the heavy oak table at which August Bebel sat in June 1869 while trying to persuade the local disciples of Ferdinand Lassalle to join the new Social Democratic party. No tourist is spared a visit to the dilapidated Forelle Inn at Grafengasse No. 5 where Comrade Walter Ulbricht used to drink his evening beer while working as a Communist functionary in Erfurt. And lest anyone forget, there is a plaque to remind that Ulbricht was standing at the bar on March 29, 1921, when the "class enemies" arrested him for a few days.

From Rostock to Zwickau, from Schwedt to Magdeburg, there are so many houses and beds in which August Bebel, Karl Liebknecht, Rosa Luxemburg, and Ernst Thälmann once slept, that one can only assume these peripatetic zealots of the revolution were never at home.

Revolution and socialism are the primary themes of guidebooks to East Germany's principal cities. They ooze with chip-on-the-shoulder polemics when discussing the past and gurgle euphorically about the plans of the future. A one-dollar guidebook to Dresden tells visitors not only that "it is once again a center of the arts," but that during the city's reconstruction "capitalist property had to make way for socialist property" because "the wage slaves of yesterday became the masters of their factories." It follows only naturally, says the little booklet, "that in the face of such a development, the mode of thinking and the behavior of the workers and employees of these factories has also changed radically." A pocket guide to Berlin contends: "It was never the ostentatious splendor of the ruling classes which formed the face of our city. Neither the courts of the Hohenzollern kings nor the villas of the industrialists but the thrift and simplicity of the working masses determined the image of this community." The thread of revolution, of class struggle and social cataclysm runs through every page and accompanies tourists to every street and public monument. A short history of Erfurt, which prefaces a volume of photos of its countless art treasures, reads like a primer on class rebellion and suggests that the city has been wracked by upheavals ever since St. Boniface, the Apostle of Germany, founded it in A.D. 742. One can only marvel that its architectural jewels managed to survive so long.

History has not actually been rewritten in the GDR. It is merely being re-interpreted with a lopsided predilection for the footnotes. It is a shift of emphasis determined by a dialectical view of world events.

An analogous bias applies to what Germans call *Kultur*. If East and West Germans still have anything in common, it is an almost reverent adulation of their cultural heritage. The reddest apparatchik will consider himself as much a member of the *Volk der Dichter und Denker* as the most avaricious capitalist in the Ruhr. But there the comparison ends, for the East Germans' view of culture, shaped by twenty years of propaganda, is a different one.

The Communist sees art and culture as a folk heritage which the privileged classes arrogated for their own enjoyment to the exclusion of the masses and which at last has been returned to its rightful owners: the proletariat. "For centuries," says the guide to the city, "the repute of its art treasures, the music of its orchestras, the world famous names of its singers and actors made Dresden a mecca of art lovers from many countries. To be sure, one thing was clear: apart from exceptions, the privilege of enjoying art was reserved for the rich who could afford the expense of a long journey. All that has basically changed since 1945. Today these immeasurable treasures have become the material and, to an ever-increasing extent, the intellectual property of the whole of the people." Moreover, the SED sees in artists of all genres, men of the people whose immense talents were ruthlessly exploited by the privileged few for their personal pleasure. Viewed through Communist lenses, Joseph Haydn and Wolfgang Amadeus Mozart were slaves of the Esterhazy Princes and the Austrian archbishops. Just as Daniel Poeppelmann, the architect of Dresden's elegant Zwinger, was a plebeian being bled by King August the Strong of Saxony. As men of the people, so the Communists reason, these artists were revolutionaries at heart. If Beethoven and Goethe, Molière and Rembrandt, Michelangelo and Balthasar Neumann were alive today, they would naturally be members of their respective countries' Communist parties. In fact, their art is interpreted as an expression of their revolutionary spirit.

The jackets of phonograph records are typical of this interrelationship between the arts and revolution. To read their texts one would think that Beethoven was to music what Marx was to economics.

Haydn, so says one jacket, "was born in the most abject poverty as the son of a simple carriage maker. . . . Despite his feudal connections and dependence on the Esterhazy court, he was a thinker and artist of the French revolutionary period which produced a bourgeoisie striving for freedom. Though not as unequivocally as Mozart and Beethoven, Haydn nevertheless engaged himself on behalf of liberty from the shackles of feudalism. 'The spirit and the soul must be free,' he once wrote. These are no longer the words of a jovial 'Papa Haydn' serving his prince but of an artist defending the rights of free, independent men. . . . We must see in him a genius of the people who attempted to express what the common people thought and felt."

Mozart's Jupiter Symphony, according to an East German musicologist, "bubbles with a youthfulness that emanated from a spirit which dreamed of clarity, happiness, and harmony. It was the spirit of an ascending class. The pre-revolutionary bourgeoisie was so convinced of the supremacy of reason as a weapon of social progress that it believed enlightenment would overpower injustice in social relationships and smatter falsehood, hate, and discord. It lived secure in the belief that good would triumph over evil. Though a tragic and fateful illusion, it was the philosophy with which Mozart wrote his great symphony in C Major."

Cultivating socialist morality and collective consciousness assumes many forms. Direct agitation and propaganda are but its most overt manifestations. The messianic nature of Communism, however, forces the party to proselytize on every front of human behavior and to poke an ideological finger into countless pies.

Youth consecration—as opposed to religious confirmation—is one example. Practiced since 1955, more than 90 percent of East German fourteen-year-olds now participate in these annual ceremonies—to the dismay of East Germany's churches which have seen the number of confirmands dwindle to an insignificant minority. Though the rites are pagan, the message is highly moralistic and the trappings conventual and parochial.

In Rostock, local officials used the "Hall of Culture" in the main post office. The setting was simple and dignified. Over the stage hung a stylized drawing of the harbor, beside it the inscription: "*Learn! You must assume responsibility.*" The only other decorations were a bowl of flowers and six banners. The program, richly interspersed with classical music and recitations, clearly showed how much the organizers attached to the dignity of the ceremony.

To the strains of a sonatina by Buxtehude, fifty youngsters from a suburban school entered the hall, crowded with parents and relatives. Led by four banners, they advanced down an aisle flanked by Young Pioneers wearing white shirts with red neckerchiefs, their right hands raised above their serious faces in the Pioneer salute. Later, after a rhetorically colorless and politically restrained address by a "Meritorious Teacher of the People" in which much was said about the significance of science and technology, learning, and responsibility, the boys and girls took the vow.

"If you are prepared as local sons and daughters of our Workers' and Peasants' State to work and fight for a happy life for the entire German people, so answer me, 'Yes we vow!'" said the speaker. The reply was a unisonant cry, "Yes, we vow." They were asked: "Are you prepared to join your entire strength with ours in the great and noble cause of Socialism?" And again they responded, "Yes, we vow." Just as they vowed to endorse the "cause of friendship between nations and with the Soviet people and all peace-loving people in the world." Then raising his voice slightly, the speaker proclaimed, "You have set yourselves a high and noble goal. You have joined the ranks of millions of people who support and fight for the cause of peace and socialism. Onward in united strength."

The quartet played a larghetto by Mozart. An attractive actress from the Rostock Municipal Theater read quotations from Goethe, Lenin, Ulbricht, Grotewohl, and Thälmann. A party official presented each youngster with a certificate and a book and shook hands. From the wings came a half-dozen Young Pioneers who presented the consecrees with bouquets of flowers, congratulated them, then disappeared. Within fifteen minutes, the hall had emptied of parents and children, only to be followed a half hour later by fathers, mothers, and pupils from a different school for whom the rites were repeated.

After the official ceremony, many parents held lavish, expensive family parties to which relatives and friends, neighbors and acquaintances were invited. Mountains of presents for the kids have become as standardized a practice as they used to be with religious confirmation.

In little more than a decade, these rites have become a visceral and popular part of East German life, especially in the large cities. Of the 3000 eighth-graders in Rostock, almost 93 percent took part in 1966. In 1955 when youth consecration was an inchoate experiment, representation was less than 25 percent.

The churches in East Germany are obviously powerless against this development, especially since the SED has gingerly avoided propagating youth consecration with anti-ecclesiastical or anti-religious overtones. On the contrary, the party's position is that youth consecration differs from confirmation, that it is a profession of loyalty to the state and socialism and should not be construed as usurpation of church functions. The churches drew the consequences and declared they were willing to confirm children who had already participated in state ceremonies. Yet the number of confirmands in the cities continues to decline despite this offer: barely ten percent in metropolitan areas, though the ratio in certain rural districts may be as high as 90 percent.

The trend for the future, however, is clearly staked out by the dwindling number of children who attend twice weekly religious instruction classes held by the pastors in public schools—a concession incidentally to German tradition (and upheld stanchly in the Federal Republic) of mandatory religious education in public institutions. Clergymen admit that they know of no *direct* state pressure to bar children from confirmation or religious classes. "There have been no indications of subsequent disadvantages for children who did not participate in consecration ceremonies," said one Rostock pastor. "Perhaps people think it's better not to go against their own interests. They join in."

Just as East Germans have joined so many other bandwagons of a society rushing headlong down a speedway of convulsive change. Take, for example, the exalted new role of women. More rapidly even than in the United States, the GDR is turning into a matriarchy. Women outnumber men 9,264,000 to 7,783,000 and account for 54 percent of the GDR's total population and for 46 percent of the labor force.

Theoretically, the constitutions of both German states, written in 1949, gave women rights equal to men. But concepts of equality in East and West differ markedly. The GDR's new family law, which took effect in April 1966, has revolutionized traditional Teutonic views on the relationship between man and woman. The measure has literally freed women from the indenture of the apron strings. It specifies that *both* partners in marriage are responsible for the children and for running the household. This means, in theory, that a working wife could legally require her husband to help with the dishes. This is the complete reverse of West German law which empowers a husband to force his wife to the kitchen sink—even if she is willing to work and to pay for domestic help from her own earnings. West German statutes place upon the husband the principal burden of financial support for the family and upon the woman primary responsibility for maintaining the household. Indeed, the federal supreme court ruled in 1959 that a woman may pursue a profession only when it can be "reconciled with her duties in marriage and to the family."

East German men have generally been absolved of the obligation to pay alimony and in theory women could be compelled to pay an ex-husband incapable of supporting himself. Property accumulated during marriage is owned jointly and divided equally when the marriage dissolves. The divorce code has been substantially liberalized and resembles in many ways the principles which underlie Anglo-Saxon instead of traditional Napoleonic law. The "guilt" of one or the other partner need no longer be established and incompatibility suffices as grounds for divorce.

Unquestionably, the most radical change stipulates that women are no longer obligated to assume their husbands' family names. The original version of the bill specified that each partner should keep his or her own name. That was too sweeping a move even for East Germans who, despite their enthusiasm for socialist experimentation, have been conditioned to the principle of female subservience by centuries of Germanic patriarchies. In its final form the law entitles either the *husband* or the wife to take the other spouse's name and, under special circumstances, to use both names.

West German commentators scoff at the emancipation of East German womanhood and deride it as a deviously veiled attempt to alleviate the GDR's critical labor shortage by forcing and inducing more women to East Germany's understaffed assembly lines. The new family code, vitrioled Hamburg's *Die Welt*, "is nothing but a deliberate scheme to compel even more women to work." Even if it were true, East German women refuse to see it that way. On the contrary, they bask in their newly found rights and equality and effuse a spirit of self-confidence which belies their heritage from the German Gretchens of yesteryear. They are keenly conscious of their contribution to East Germany's resuscitation and prosperity and aware that society needs them. They are consumed by a compulsion for self-improvement and intellectual melioration which has no parallel in West Germany.

East German women no longer doubt their equality. But between theory and practice there remains a wide chasm which they are trying to bridge. Though women play a more important role in local politics than their West German sisters, their influence on the national level and in the inner sanctums of Central Committee and Politburo is negligible. The problem in industry and the professions is similar and East German women rarely miss an opportunity to mention it. They are equal in theory and the regime not only supports but encourages them to work. In practice, however, they have yet to convince the majority of husbands and male industrial executives of the benefits of female careerism.

Part of the trouble is biological. Women get the children even in East Germany and no new family code is likely to repeal that law of nature. Reproduction, however, takes women out of production, and many a plant manager is reluctant to hire a woman for a crucial position when she may become pregnant, be forced to take leave, thus disrupting plant procedure. *Eulenspiegel*, the GDR's satirical weekly, stated the argument succinctly in a cartoon recently. "Why don't you let Paul have the job," said a plant manager, pointing to what is obviously a veteran partycrat, while looking at a bright young woman applicant clutching a diploma under her arm. "He may not have a degree but he'll never be a mother."

Husbands are the other part of the dilemma. Though most of

them proclaim grandiosely that they do not object to their wives working, the majority expect their women to take care of the household as well. The result: East German women work twice as hard as men. And some of them can sound quite acrimonious about it.

Waltraud Seidel, chief livestock technician at the Red Banner LPG in Sietow near Neustrelitz, recently outlined her average day in an issue of *Deutsche Bauernzeitung*, a farming weekly. "I get up between 4 and 5 A.M. and make my initial rounds of the stables. From 6:30 to 7:15, I feed the children and make breakfast for my husband. At 7:15 I take the children to kindergarten. From 7:30 until noon I work in the stables, do the administrative things, check on feed supplies, grazing land, meadows and so forth. I usually eat lunch in the LPG canteen from 12 until 1 P.M. From one o'clock until five I have administrative and office work which I often do at home because one of my children is too young for kindergarten and the nursery hasn't been built yet. Usually I'll make another round of the stables, then go to pick up the children, make supper and often in the evenings I have to make additional stable rounds."

"It's a curious thing," said a *Neues Deutschland* editorial writer once, "that discussions about easing housework invariably concern women. Why do we extend shopping hours and open supermarkets at night? So *women* will have time to buy groceries. Why do we produce more washing machines and install self-service laundries? For the convenience of *women*. Take any ten advertisements for household and kitchen appliances and nine of them will show female models operating them. That's hardly the way to set examples."

"Unless we succeed in revolutionizing family relationships, that is, getting the husbands to darn socks and do a few other things," said one woman engineer, "nothing will really change and our new opportunities will be no more than paper promises."

All the discourse about woman's right to work and free development of her personality entails one contradiction of visceral importance to the GDR's future: the incompatibility of children with a career. Women generally want one or the other, but the regime wants both. East Germany does need the productive capacity of women to sustain industry today, but it needs their reproductive capacity to feed the labor needs of industry tomorrow. Since it cannot have both, the regime, like career-minded women themselves, will soon have to make a choice. At its present rate of population growth, East Germany's labor force will not begin to stabilize and increase until 1980. That day will merely be postponed if an even larger proportion of women choose careers in preference to children.

For years the SED skirted the issue by attempting to compromise. Birth control and the anti-baby pill are viewed with as much disdain and suspicion as in Catholic countries. The regime has encouraged propagation and attempted to compensate for ensuing hardships by building more nurseries and kindergartens. Even if supply could catch up with demand, this is but a dubious solution to building the kind of moral state Ulbricht envisages. For all the official adulation of collectivism, Ulbricht is among the first to recognize the importance of the family as the basic cell of society, and he has said so on numerous occasions. Though he has never taken public cognizance of some of the psychological problems inherent in kindergarten and nursery environments, he once complained bitterly that only 10 percent "of our children aged eight to seventeen spend their after-school hours and weekends with their parents. The remaining 90 percent are left to fend for themselves—with brothers and sisters or friends— and use their free time either to watch television or go to the movies." One survey, conducted in 1964, revealed that only three percent of school-age children had "recently" engaged in long, meaningful conversations with either one of their parents. The party frequently exhorts mothers and fathers to spend more time with their children, to show them love and attention. The only question is when.

For all the political indoctrination of youth in the GDR, the SED does not attempt to interpose itself between children and the home. On the contrary, it regards the family as the "wellspring of socialist morality."

Whenever propaganda and agitation have failed to remake

East German society in the Communist image, the regime has resorted to more draconian means: the police, the courts and the prisons. Though the days of real police-state power passed with Nikita Khrushchev's condemnation of Stalin in 1956, memories of rougher days in the GDR linger. They suffice to prevent any serious deviation from the party line.

Theoretically, the GDR is a state based on the rule of law. Except for certain amendments and additions, both its civil and penal code are rooted in the nineteenth century. Officially, East Germans are entitled to the same protections and guarantees as West Germans (which, by the way, fall far short of Anglo-Saxon standards): habeas corpus, the right to legal counsel, protection against arrest, search and seizure without warrant, the right to cross examine witnesses and to call witnesses in defense. In practice, the picture often looks quite different.

East German justice has as its primary aim the "construction of socialism." It is the duty of judges, prosecutors, and lawyers to serve this goal. Ulbricht himself once described "socialist justice" as "the will of the proletariat transformed into law." And a 1963 State Council decree defines "socialist law" as "an important instrument for organizing our social development and regulating the socialist relationship among citizens toward their state." In other words, East German justice has one basic goal: "to serve the workers' and peasants' state in the resolution of its political, economic and cultural problems, to support and further socialist methods of production."

In day to day practice the social aspect of any offense always plays a decisive role in determining guilt and the severity of sentence, just as the offender's proclivity for rehabilitation, not to mention his worth to socialist production, influence his punishment.

Because the GDR's rulers consider law and justice as instruments for building socialism, not just as tools to maintain order, East Germany's legal system is undergoing sweeping changes, many of them repugnant and noxious to Westerners.

The show trial, for example, of which there were dozens in the 1950s (many of them presided over by "Red" Hilde Benjamin, the former Justice Minister), served to establish the regime's authority and to cow oppositional forces into submission and silence. Their purpose was to set examples. Often the defendants, who were sentenced amidst a fanfare of publicity to severe penalties, were subsequently amnestied or pardoned. What mattered was not so much the case at hand or the individual on trial as the behavioral lesson and the threat which could be transmitted to the public via the courtroom.

All states and all manners of government protect themselves against oppositional groups, revolutionary elements, espionage and treason. In the GDR this common principle is carried to ludicrous extremes. It has codified a variety of "anti-State crimes" such as "instigation to boycott, instigation to war, instigation to murder and genocide, endangering the peace, disaffection, terrorism, fleeing the republic, industrial sabotage and diversionism."

East Germany's penal code defines "instigation" as "the glorification and propagation of fascism and militarism, of agitation against other peoples or races, against the workers' and peasants' power or its organs, against organizations of our society or against fellow citizens because of their membership or service in a state organization." The penalty ranges from three months to fifteen years in jail.

"Diversionism" is an economic crime which the penal code describes as "destruction, damage, or rendering inapplicable of machines, technical installations, transportation and traffic equipment or other objects vital to the economy and defense." It is punishable by at least three years in prison and a good example of what "diversionism" really entails is the case of a sixteen-year-old East Berlin youth who was sentenced to five years in September 1961 for emptying ash and trash cans on the floors and cutting up the seats of elevated railway cars.

"Terrorism," according to the GDR's penal code, entails "placing the populace in fear and uncertainty, undermining confidence in the workers' and peasants' state by means of forceful acts or the threat of force." Two young East Germans were sentenced to life imprisonment in the summer of 1962 for engaging in terrorism. Their actual crime: digging an escape tunnel to West Berlin.

Unnerving as such verdicts sound, they were never the rule but the exception and usually resulted from "show trials" whose primary aim was to intimidate the public and set examples. Their number has decreased to the point of insignificance in more recent years, just as the total number of East German citizens still serving terms for political crimes has decreased steadily. There are, according to Amnesty International, 6000 to 8000 political prisoners in East German jails today.

For more "routine" offenses, East German judicial procedure does not differ significantly from that of other European countries whose laws are based on the Napoleonic code.

Nevertheless, some changes enacted since the war warrant more detailed attention. In contrast to West Germany, whose judges are career civil servants and appointed, the GDR has abolished the professional judiciary. Instead all judges—as well as the country's 45,000 lay jurors (two for each trial)—are elected for four year terms: by the Volkskammer in the case of the supreme court judges and jurors; by the district legislatures for district courts and by county councils and the public in the case of county courts. In theory these judges and jurors are independent, though in practice they are subservient to the will of the party which is the final arbiter over their appointment or election.

Investigative activity, the preserve of the courts in West Germany, has become the responsibility of the prosecution which in the GDR has been granted powers far exceeding those accruing to public prosecutors in Western countries. Prosecutors are entitled to issue arrest, search and seizure warrants. They control the collection of all evidence and have primary authority over the maintenance of conviction records, including their annulment.

Though the right to consult and retain counsel is guaranteed, the virtual abolishment of private legal practice makes this a safeguard of dubious value. Almost all lawyers are organized in cooperatives—a socialist version of the multi-member law partnership. Their objectivity is open to question in view of the collectives' statutes which require lawyers to be "thoroughly versed in principles of Marxism Leninism," and to "contribute to the social re-education of citizens who have neglected their obligations to Socialist society."

In addition to the regular law courts, the GDR has an estimated 8000 "social tribunals" whose role is to settle the minor disputes of daily life and punish misdemeanors. Known as "conflict" and "arbitration" commissions, these courts are composed of fellow citizens and workers and are attached to all factories, offices, collective farms and housing areas. They function as lay courts with amateur judges whose powers are akin but do not match up to those of justices of the peace. Amateur "social" prosecutors and defenders may practice before them. Though specifically prohibited from levying fines or attaching salaries, the commissions may mete out reprimands, censure and public criticism as penalties for minor infractions of the law or violations of "socialist morality" such as absenteeism, drunkenness, failure to pay support or inadequate supervision of children. The commissions also serve as inferior *civil* courts and are empowered to settle disagreements among workers and neighbors and to regulate debts and financial disputes involving amounts of less than 500 marks.

Each of these commissions, and there is one in virtually every shop and neighborhood, is composed of eight to twelve jurors who are elected for periods of two years.

Though the commissions are supposed to deal only with minor infractions and misdemeanors, they have begun to rule on more serious offenses, brought to their attention by party officials and factory managers who do not want their workers and associates tried and possibly jailed by the law courts. As a result, social tribunals have been handling assaults, petty thefts and even some sex offenses. At one point in 1963 this practice became so prevalent that the SED asked the regular courts and prosecutors to exercise stricter control and issue indictments for violations which should really be tried by courts of law.

Responsibility for maintaining public order and for actually carrying out investigative work falls on the People's Police (*Volkspolizei*) and the State Security Service (*Staatssicherheitsdienst*—SSD). Though both have grisly reputations as the long, strong arms of the state and the party, only one of these organizations—the SSD—continues to live up to it. The *Volkspolizei,* for all its roughneck tactics of former years, is today largely a police force similar to those in West European countries.

The People's Police, under the control of Interior Minister Friedrich Dickel, who is its chief and has the rank of a colonel general, numbers 73,000 men and women. In addition to normal police duties such as traffic control, maintenance of peace and order, investigation of criminal offenses and the issuance of identity cards and passports (a traditional police function in Germany), the *Volkspolizei* also encompasses the GDR's entire fire fighting force. All *Vopos,* except detectives, wear gray-green uniforms. As a national police, organized on district and county echelons, its officers and members are ultimately responsible to Berlin, not local authorities.

For years it has been a general misconception that the *Volkspolizei* was also responsible for guarding East Germany's borders. Actually this was the duty of a special Border Police (*Grenzpolizei*) whose estimated 45,000 officers and men were absorbed into the National People's Army in September 1961.

If the *Volkspolizei* has lost much of its bite with time, the SSD remains a force of a different color. It is a nebulous and much feared organization whose duties cover a melange of secret police, criminal investigation, political surveillance and espionage work. Its 13,500 agents, all of whom hold military ranks and work in mufti, plus its countless free-lance informers, are under the jurisdiction of a special Ministry for State Security headed by Erich Mielke.

The SSD had its origins in the earliest occupation days when local and state police forces were staffed with political commissariats who worked with the Soviet secret police (KGB) agents attached to the Russian military government. Following the GDR's establishment in 1949, these commissariats were reorganized as the SSD under the direction of Wilhelm Zaisser, the first Minister for State Security. The SSD's power grew gradually as it assumed rights of sovereignty abrogated by the Soviets. With those rights the SSD adopted many of the KGB's practices, among them torture to force confessions, temporary detainment in complete disregard of East German constitutional guarantees, wire tapping, entrapment and the use of a huge informer network. The SSD cultivated its own trustworthy judges and prosecutors who would issue special arrest warrants and conduct star chamber trials. Moreover, it became one of central Europe's most active espionage and counterintelligence organizations.

The SSD comes closest to being a state within the state with vast powers, based in part on its independence of parliamentary, governmental and even party control, in part on the fear which it has instilled. To an extent the SSD's independence and its record of secret machinations are rooted in the Stalinist mentality that prevailed until 1956. Until the end of 1955 the dominant view of SED leaders was that a bottomless pit of internal opposition and class enmity bent on destruction of Communism lurked behind every tree. The result was an almost hysterical watchfulness and the hypertrophic development of the security service. The mood of the GDR's leadership in those years was once expressed by Ernst Wollweber, Zaisser's successor as SSD chief, who said: "The class enemy is all around us and can appear in any conceivable mask; in the mask of a diligent party functionary as well as in the mask of indifference." Everyone was suspect—SSD chiefs included. And in their case it was not without reason. The two times when Ulbricht's power was seriously threatened—in 1953 and 1958—the Minister for State Security—Zaisser and then Wollweber—spearheaded the opposition.

Since September 1962, when the State Council passed a number of directives concerning arrest, detention, confinement, and search practices, it has been generally assumed that the SSD's wildest transgressions are no longer as common as they used to be. Probably it no longer needs to resort to its arsenal of secret horrors. It has a reputation wild and woolly enough to operate on for many years.

Notwithstanding the authoritarian nature of the East German state, the GDR's crime rate, though declining, remains a problem.

East German criminologists are alarmed by the 30 percent increase of crimes committed under the influence of alcohol, a jump that now makes drink responsible for 66 percent of all felonies. Alcoholism, in fact, has become such a problem that in mid-1966 the East German press launched a massive campaign to urge temperance. Though per capita wine and beer consumption in the GDR runs substantially below West Germany's, use of hard liquor is nearly twice as high.

More than half the crimes committed in the GDR (just as in West Germany) are petty and grand larcenies. Rape, sex crimes, murder and manslaughter have declined steadily and account for only 5 percent of all violations (compared to 10 percent in West Germany). The murder rate is so low—a total of only 113 in 1966—that it is statistically imperceptible: 0.5 per 100,000 population.

"There are a number of crimes which have become extinct in our republic," says Dr. Josef Streit, a former printer and long-time Communist, now the GDR's solicitor general and chief public prosecutor. "For years we have not had a bank robbery and there have been no drug violations."

Like most Communists, Streit argues that crime in the West is a social, under Communism a pedagogic problem. The logic: if the social conditions which breed crime (unemployment, poverty etc.) have been removed, then crime itself should disappear, too. If it persists, then inadequate education and a failure to "weed out the remaining germs of capitalist thought" are at fault. Thus far, as Streit admits, the GDR has not been entirely successful at educating crime out of existence. "Twenty percent of all violations," he concedes, "are committed by backsliders. This is a relatively high rate."

Moreover, juvenile crime is proportionately high. According to Streit, half of all convicted criminals are aged fourteen to twenty-five. For the Free German Youth association (FDJ) that is something to chew on and whenever crimes by teens and twenties make headlines in the GDR, representatives of the youth organization rush to the fore with promises to pay more attention to juveniles who go astray. The problem of penetrating the psychological walls which surround delinquents appears to be the same the world over. "It is difficult for us to make contact with outsiders who insist they are interested in nothing," complained one FDJ official at the March 1967 trial of two teenagers, sentenced to reform school for demolishing six public phone booths, cutting up the seats in four streetcars and wrecking at least ten street lamps. Both boys were school dropouts and one of them had previously been arrested for bicycle theft. "We shall do what we can to get to know such boys better and help them," said the FDJ leader who testified at the hearing.

Notwithstanding considerable public discussion of crime and delinquency, the GDR, compared to most other industrialized countries, is remarkably law-abiding and orderly. A tribute to socialist morality.

Morality, in fact, is something on which East Germany dotes —often to a degree of puritanism that borders on priggish stuffiness. It is ridiculous to suggest, as right-wing critics do, that Communism is intrinsically amoral because it is atheistic, or immoral because some of its wilder exponents once promulgated the postulate of free love. The days of the Red sex bombs such as Ruth Fischer (Hanns and Gerhart Eisler's sister) and other women who treated Marx like an aphrodisiac, went out with the Roaring Twenties. Walter Ulbricht's own affair with Lotte in their Lux Hotel room in Moscow generates clucks of disbelief and disapproval from most party members. Today, Communism in general —East German Communism in particular—is as strait-laced as a Victorian girdle and has more taboos than a centipede has legs.

The GDR has virtually no night life, except for a few sleezy Leipzig dives which cater predominantly to Western tourists or visitors to the fair. Prostitution is illegal and virtually (though not completely) extinct. Sex is a word that makes most East German girls blush as red as Communism's banners. East German movies and books generally cut love scenes at the first brotherly peck on the forehead. The regime rarely misses an opportunity to wag a prudish finger at what it considers the moral decay of Western literature, art, theater, cinema and music and the general decadence of Western society.

There is to East German life a Main Street quality which borders on prudery, and more often than not, it seems just as hypocritical as Main Street. Overt sex—except for a brief period of liberalization in 1964 and 1965 which quickly turned into libertinage and opened a dam of pent-up emotions—is taboo. Its public discussion or display is likely to generate mass embarrassment. Young East Germans often seem to live in a world more protected than that of their grandparents, though in truth their relationships are quite normal and free of inhibitions. They merely keep sex from view.

Sex, maintain the party ideologues, prevents clear political thinking and one East German magazine once warned that "the sex wave was invented by vengeful imperialists to keep the populations of their countries from discussing vital questions such as the battle against nuclear annihilation." For years the ideal magazine cover girl in the GDR sported baggy overalls and carried a wrench in her hand.

During the short period in 1964 and 1965 when the taboos were lifted and the chastity belt loosened, the GDR went wild. Even usually sober newspapers, such as the National Democratic Party's *National Zeitung* and the Liberal Party's *Der Morgen*, suddenly showed attractive nymphs in fish net stockings. The military journals *Volksarmee* and *Armee Rundschau* entertained soldier readers with photos of bikini beauties. *Fotografie*, the photography monthly, and *Neues Leben*, a youth magazine, began printing pictures that bordered on pornography. *Das Magazin*, a popular, hard-to-get monthly grab-bag of literature, art, culture, science, humor, fashion, and entertainment news, edited by Gerhart Eisler's widow Hilde, started competing with *Playboy*. The GDR was rocked by Beatlemania and a sex wave. There were even reports of girl students going to the annual harvest with bared breasts.

As quickly as it flared, the "new wave" was snuffed out in what developed into a general repression of all Western influences, especially on literature, art, and music. It began in December 1965 at the Central Committee meeting, where ideologues complained about "developments inimical to the creation of a clean state."

The campaign, which is still in progress, was directed against the new cultural freedom which the GDR had experienced since early 1963. Infused as much from other Soviet bloc countries as from the West, it threatened to undermine the regime's ideological hold on the country. Overt sex was but a symptom of liberalization, but a vulnerable one in a country whose historical and provincial traditions lent it a proclivity toward puritanism. Overt sex was the first to go, though the pendulum did not swing back entirely to iron maidens on tractors. Literature and art were next in line. And since January 1967 the campaign has been directed against jazz, beat and other forms of modern and popular music which the SED's most doctrinaire forces regard as spearheads of Western subversion.

"East Berlin's Tin Pan Alley was told to produce more music that would reflect the spirit of the new collective society. Entertainers were chastised for losing touch with the proletariat and "socialist reality." Composers, pop singers, emcees, cabarettists, and musicians were shooed out of the comfortable confines of their Berlin studios and exhorted to develop closer contact with the workers so they could "learn the mood of the country." The nation was subjected to the din of an upbeat revolutionary singalong.

Like all such campaigns, this one began innocuously enough and was, as usual, disguised as a grass roots movement. A couple of FDJ members wrote Neues Deutschland asking why there weren't more socialist fighting and German folk songs they could sing. Their letter was followed a few days later by one from Otto Hilliger and Walter Fels, the leaders of the Hermann Dunker Ensemble, a party-lining East Berlin glee club, who complained about the lack of music "suitable for a worker chorus."

Soon one letter followed the next. Professor Johannes Paul Thilmann, director of composition at Dresden's Carl Maria von Weber Conservatory, demanded "more songs and marches to help build socialism." Seven Bach experts wrote, complaining that the Swingle Singers, whose da-du-da-ba-du interpretations of Bach and Mozart are also recorded in the GDR, were aberrations of the great master. "Hula-hula songs generate pseudoromanticism," complained one FDJ group, "besides Hawaii has become a bastion for imperialist rockets." "Cowboy songs," said one *Neues Deutschland* editorial, "become meaningless when the cowboys murder Vietnamese children." Said Ulbricht: "With the development of socialist conditions of production, with the spreading seed of the socialist way of life, we need entertainment forms that contain new elements."

They came quickly, in part, no doubt, because prizes of up to 1500 marks ($375) were offered for the best progressive, fighting, marching, and folk songs. Amateur tunesmiths were encouraged to distribute mimeographed copies of their work in factories, apartment houses, youth groups, and on collective farms. By mid-April, just before the start of the VIIth Party Congress, the GDR was subjected to an incessant din of "songs that take the position of the party, reject the false ideals of yesteryear and express freely what youth thinks about its revolutionary role in the class struggle." From the Elbe to the Oder, from the Baltic to the Erzgebirge, East Germany was exposed to the cacophony of electric guitars, string orchestras, banjos, brass bands, and dance combos playing and singing such tunes as "Song of the United Front," "Solidarity Song," and "Partisans on the Amur."

For the ideologues it was a blow not only against Western influence but for the positivist, revolutionary spirit. Though the Politburo's dogmatists would be shocked and insulted at the suggestion, it is a leaf from Mao Tse-tung's book, an attempt to ignite permanent revolution albeit with the methods of a Frank X. Buchmann and the Moral Rearmament Movement.

It is a Communist Sing-Out of 1967 whose theme song, "Tell Me Where You Stand," played to beat rhythm, says:

> Backwards, or forwards, you must decide.
> We're making progress, step by step,
> But you can't first with them, then with us just ride.
> If you go in circles you won't be hep.
> We all have a right to know you
> And masks that nod mean nothing to us.

By your right name I want to call you
That's why: your real face now show us.
Tell me where you stand, comrade
Tell me where you stand.

CHAPTER XI

Saxonian Winters

The International Cinema on East Berlin's Karl Marx Allee appeared to be closed that day in June 1966. The huge billboard over the entrance was blank, the display cases bare. Inside, however, a significant event was taking place: a preview of the motion picture version of Erik Neutsch's best-selling novel, *Spur der Steine*. The audience: invited party dignitaries and a few paying patrons who had been lucky enough to buy tickets at the box office.

Several days later, *Neues Deutschland* reported that the special showing had elicited shouts of indignant protest. The film, said the paper, would not be released to the general public because "it fails to do justice to the importance of its subject matter. It presents a distorted image of our socialist reality, of the struggle of the working class, of our glorious party and the altruism of its members."

Paul Verner, the SED district boss of East Berlin, even threatened to resign from the Politburo and the Central Committee unless the movie were banned. Said Verner in a memorandum to Walter Ulbricht: "The film is an insult. The party which it portrays is not the party to which I belong."

For Verner and countless other apparatchiks, *Spur der Steine* probably was an insult. It depicts SED functionaries who are moral heels and non-party figures as Sir Galahads. Its central character, Hannes Balla, a freewheeling, rough-hewn carpenter who journeys from construction site to construction site, is a Hercules on the job. A brigadier par excellence, he works harder than three men his size—but all for the enhancement of his pay check, not the honor of the republic. Werner Horrath, the SED party secretary on the project, converts Balla and toward the end of the story convinces him to build—not just houses but—socialism. Horrath would be the ideal functionary were it not for his extramarital relationship with Katrin Klee, a doe-eyed, shapely and naïve girl engineer. After making Katrin pregnant, Horrath swears her to secrecy about their affair, then presides over a disciplinary board that reprimands her immoral ways.

When thirty-six-year-old Neutsch, one of the GDR's most promising and talented young authors, first published *Spur der Steine*, Ulbricht lauded the novel as a "positive example" of "socialism's new literature" and critics gushed with praise. But that was in 1964, when East Germany's cultural climate experienced one of its rare thaws. Since then a new winter has settled over Saxony, forcing the GDR's novelists, poets, dramatists, and intellectuals into huddles of silence and conformity.

Today, of all the Soviet bloc countries, the GDR is the richest—as far as the standard of living goes; the cleanest—insofar as public toilets are concerned, and, the saddest—in terms of intellectual freedom. Next to "decadent" Western influences, the East German politruks and arbiters of culture fear most the winds of "heresy" blowing from the East. SED functionaries, with Kurt Hager in the lead, have made numerous pilgrimages to Warsaw, Prague, and Budapest since January 1966 in futile and sometimes ludicrous efforts to persuade local authorities to muzzle their writers, dramatists, and movie makers. Said Hager in conjunction with one such journey: "The works of modern Polish, Czech, and Hungarian writers pave the way for counterrevolution." Even the Soviet Union has come to feel the icy blasts from Germany. In April 1967 the GDR boycotted all Russian "new wave" films because of their potential debilitating effect and disturbing influence.

Ulbricht outlined the SED's expectations from its creative artists succinctly in a December 1965 letter to Professor Kurt Maetzig, one of the GDR's leading movie directors. Upbraiding Maetzig for his film *Das Kaninchen Bin Ich* (*I Am the Rabbit*), which dealt with the Stalinist terror trials, Ulbricht wrote: "Illusions about false freedoms, about the rights of the individual above those of the party and state, about co-existence with the most militant enemies of our socialist way of life, are merely obstacles to the development of socialist principles. Our artists and writers are completely free to shape and create anything that is useful to our state and our society. But I would consider it incompatible with their ethical standards if they took liberties which harmed our state and our party. It behooves our writers and artists to close their ranks around the party, to fight ideological diversions and the poison of skepticism, to oppose negativism."

In short, what the SED demands is positivism in the arts and literature. Though it does not rule out criticism per se, it insists that criticism be constructive, that it help to resolve "the conflicts which still exist in the building of socialism." But the basic philosophy, as well as the party, the state and all their organizations, must remain sacrosanct. The dilemma which has confronted East German intellectuals is where to draw the line. Erik Neutsch, for example, is a dedicated Communist. His faith in the system, and in Communism as a political ideology, is unshakable. In his portrayal of Horrath he never intended to question the apparatchik caste as such, but merely some of its less exemplary members and their behavior. Yet his book—more specifically the screen version which brought Horrath's character into sharper focus—outraged the party. *Spur der Steine* was castigated as an attack upon the institution itself: largely because the party contends it is never wrong. This intrinsic conflict, between criticism of method and institution in a situation where the institution claims to be omniscient and omnific, is at the root of East Germany's intellectual vacuum today.

The existence of this vacuum is what makes the GDR the saddest country in the Soviet bloc, for it calls attention to what might have been. East Germany's real tragedy is that when the bombs stopped falling and the guns were silenced, it stood the greatest chance of becoming a new German intellectual mecca. Stalinist repression combined with petit bourgeois moralism to dissipate those hopes ere they could be realized.

Total as was Germany's physical ruin, the moral bankruptcy and spiritual devastation left by Hitler's twelve years of dictatorship, wanton aggression and meticulously organized genocide, seemed even greater. The German conscience, as represented by its *Dichter und Denker* had been muted. The works of the exciting, provocative authors who had served as the intellectual backbone of Germany's first experiment with democracy in the 1920s, had been burned and forbidden. Most of the writers were in exile. Those who had remained were either imprisoned, terrorized into silence, or in "internal emigration." If they had dared to write at all during the Nazi era, it was in parables which, fortunately, neither the Gestapo nor, unfortunately, the readers could understand. The young generation—those who had grown to manhood during the Hitler years—had either been decimated on the battlefields or stunned dumb by the cacophony of propaganda and lies to which they had been subjected.

In both Germanys, writers began doing to the language what the *Trümmerfrauen* did to the cities: clean away the debris. "We had to start anew," says West German author Hans-Werner Richter, "to hack glades in the jungle of a language which had been reduced to a mumbo-jumbo of propaganda or the clausalized symbolisms of the 'internal emigrees.' It was impossible for us to use even some of the simplest words such as heart, spirit, blood, soil, folk, fatherland because the Nazis had imbued them with a twisted meaning. At first our vocabulary was reduced to a few hundred words, best exemplified by Guenther Eich's early glade hacking poem 'Inventory' which starts like this:

> 'This is my cap
> this is my coat,
> here my razor
> in a bag of linen.
>
> Tin cup,
> my plate, my mug of tin
> into which
> I have scratched my name.' "

Not many German writers returned, or intended to return, from exile or emigration after the war. But of those who did, the majority gravitated to East Germany: some because they were Communists or Marxists; others because they wanted to be in Berlin, the traditional center of literature; a few because they expected in the Soviet Zone a kind of society for which they had always hoped. In addition to such veteran Communists as Bertolt Brecht, the playwright; Johannes R. Becher, the poet and novelist Anna Seghers, all of whom settled in the Russian Zone or East Berlin during the immediate postwar years, East Germany soon attracted Arnold Zweig, Ludwig Renn, and Stephan Hermlin. Heinrich Mann, the elder of the Mann brothers, had made plans to resettle in East Germany just before he died in 1950. The GDR drew such Marxist philosophers and literary historians as Ernst Bloch, Alfred Kantorowicz, and Hans Mayer. And as late as 1952, Stefan Heym, whose novels *The Crusaders* and *The Hostages* had made him popular in the States, resigned his U. S. Army commission, left the United States and resettled in the GDR. East Germany has also fascinated some of Germany's younger writers, notably playwright Peter Hacks, who moved to East Berlin from Munich in 1955, and Wolf Biermann, a modern François Villon, who settled in the GDR as a seventeen-year-old in 1953.

It was also to the Soviet Zone that the world looked for a renaissance of German movie making in the postwar years. The directors and scriptwriters, the producers and actors who gravitated to the old UFA studios in Berlin-Babelsberg to work for the Russian controlled DEFA combine, fulfilled many of those early hopes. The very first production, Wolfgang Staudte's *The Murderers Among Us*, was not only a smash success but launched the career of Hildegarde Neff. It was soon followed by Kurt Maetzig's gripping film *Ehen im Schatten* (*Marriage in the Shadows*) which dealt with the problem of mixed Jewish-Christian marriage during the Third Reich, and Staudte's movie *Rotation*, a pacifistic strip that propagated the then prevalent German view of no more war. Gerard Philippe came to East Berlin to direct and act in a film version of *Til Eulenspiegel's Merry Pranks*, and DEFA's movie version of Heinrich Mann's novel *Der Untertan* still ranks as one of the best satirical films on Wilhelminian Germany.

However, the euphoria of the returnees and the young intellectuals, who saw in East Germany the soil of a genuine democratic German rebirth, was soon stifled in an atmosphere of Stalinist censorship and proletarian prudery. Try as they would, the intellectuals could find no rapport with a regime whose exponents such as Hermann Axen, the editor-in-chief of *Neues Deutschland*, exhorted them to go to Stalinstadt or the Wismut uranium mines for ideas. "You have no idea how much material you will find for gripping, dramatic, human situations in the struggle of our steelworkers at the smelter in Fuerstenberg or at some of the other furnaces and rolling mills in our Republic."

Though Brecht developed his Berliner Ensemble into one of Europe's most successful theaters, he never wrote another significant play after his return to Germany in 1948. For Ulbricht's regime, Brecht was both a gilded calling card as well as a tough intellectual nut to crack. Had he been a man of lesser fame, he probably would have floundered somewhere between the shoals of ideology and the reefs of the state security service. His reputation as Europe's leading living playwright, however, protected him. It was Brecht who developed the concept of the social function of theater which he strove to accomplish with his theory of Epic Theater in place of the "bourgeois theater of illusion." He spurned the classic concept of actor identification with the role and audience identification with the subject, advocating instead a degree of "rational alienation" that would instill social and socialist realizations in the audience by means of exemplary demonstrations. His plays and productions were acclaimed as the new Marxist model of theater, though in practice the Marxists in power found the "corrupt bourgeoise" dramaturgy more useful for their purposes. Brecht was honored with a National Prize in 1951 and the Stalin Peace Prize in 1954, but his relationship with the Ulbricht regime remained a tenuous one at best. His plays were discredited as an expression of "formalism," a Stalinist description for works of art in which form predominates over content. A number of them were barred from performance in East Berlin and to this day the East German regime, while making a cult of Brecht, his widow Helene Weigel and the Berliner Ensemble, views his work with skepticism. Though a Communist by conviction, Brecht had many reservations about the East German regime, especially after the June 1953 uprising and was a frequent and outspoken critic of the hierarchy. It was no accident that he never became an East German citizen and retained his Austrian passport instead. Brecht became the name with which the regime could boast—as long as the Ensemble Theater on the Schiffsbauerdamm was filled with tourists from the West. But when the East Berliners themselves queued at the box office, the Politburo smelled heresy in the air. When he died in 1956, Brecht was a man disillusioned with Communism in general, the East German variety in particular.

Other than to produce the verses of East Germany's national anthem, Johannes R. Becher did not write another poem of note following his return from exile—a few eulogies to Ulbricht excepted. Instead, he became an apparatchik and the Minister of Culture, a post he held until his death in 1958. Arnold Zweig, who converted from Zionism to Communism and settled in the GDR after spending the Hitler era in Israel, has done little else except edit and re-edit his own work since 1948. Stefan Heym has written only one major novel since leaving the U.S., and that one, dealing with the 17th of June uprising, was never published though excerpts from it proved sufficiently controversial to make Heym the object of the regime's latest and most vitriolic campaign against writers and intellectuals. Ludwig Renn, whose 1928 novel *War* put him on a par with Erich Maria Remarque, has spent his time writing children's and juvenile books. Stephan Hermlin has published two slim volumes of short stories and a number of poems, none of which reflected the brilliance of his prewar verse. Even Anna Seghers, the grande dame of Communist letters, who presides today as president of the East German Congress of Writers, has not been able to recapture that stride which characterized her best work: *The Revolt of the Fishermen* and *The Seventh Cross*.

Of the three great Marxist philosophical and literary theorists

—Bloch, Kantorowicz, and Mayer—all have fled to West Germany where, though still Marxists to the core, they have the freedom to express views which arc more than rote recitations of the SED's catechism.

All this is not to say that the GDR is a cultural wasteland. In the performing arts, especially in music and drama, it produces some of the best work in the world. Leipzig's Gewandhaus Orchestra, East Berlin's Comic Opera under the sure if autocratic hand of Walter Felsenstein, and the Berliner Ensemble, Brecht's theater which is being continued by Helene Weigel—these are cultural gems which have no match and their work is emulated enthusiastically in the Federal Republic. The old publishing houses in Leipzig and Berlin, now state-owned for the most part, continue to produce prolifically on a level of excellence and at retail prices so low that no West German publisher can compete. As the winds of de-Stalinization have crept over the Soviet bloc, even East Germany has lowered its barriers to foreign writers. It is no longer a sensation to see the works of Kafka, Hans Habe, Nelly Sachs, Heinrich Boell, Karl Zurckmeyer, Ingeborg Bachmann, Tennessee Williams, Truman Capote, Carson Mc-Cullers, Saul Bellow, John Updike, Bernard Malamud, Reynolds Price, and Norman Mailer on sale.

Yet East Germany's own new generation of writers—a whole crop of exciting novelists, poets, and dramatists, most of them under forty and all convinced Communists—remains largely muffled. Except for two brief periods of thaw, they have had to seek their solace in silence or risk total ostracism by publishing in West Germany—an escape valve which has been plugged since the spring of 1966.

Some of them, such as Neutsch, Erwin Strittmacher, Christa Wolf, Dieter Noll, and Hermann Kant, lucky enough to have their work accepted during periods of political relaxation, became best sellers and attained both fame and wealth. Strittmacher's novel *Ole Bienkop*, a critical view of land reform and farm collectivization, holds the absolute record of 222,000 copies sold in a four-year period. Neutsch's *Spur der Steine* ranks second with 216,000. Christa Wolf's *Divided Sky* and Dieter Noll's *The Adventures of Werner Holt*, a moving and brilliantly written tale of a young SS man during the Third Reich, sold 175,000 copies each. Kant's novel *Die Aula*, a caustic, sharp-witted and highly literate look at East German university life, reached the GDR's best seller list with 80,000 copies after one year. But these are exceptions and it is not unreasonable to suggest that some best sellers were made largely because the choice of critical, controversial works is so restricted. In one sense, the success of these best-selling authors is a reflection of the hunger East Germans have for fiction that is more than a eulogy of *Vopos* or girl tractor drivers whose lives and contributions to socialism the party likes to see painted in the most favorable and optimistic of hues.

Christa Wolf's novel *Divided Sky*, published in both East and West Germany as well as being made into an excellent motion picture, marks the first time that any East German writer could deal frankly with the Berlin Wall and the motivations of refugees. Frau Wolf, thirty-eight, married to a lyric poet, told a poignant story of love between a nineteen-year-old girl studying to be a teacher and a chemist in his late twenties, who becomes disillusioned with East German bureaucracy and defects to West Berlin just a few weeks before the Wall was built. Though the general line of the plot is orthodox enough—the girl visits him once in West Berlin and decides to sacrifice love in favor of life in the GDR—some of the dialogue and some of the secondary characters are highly iconoclastical. The book contends that incompetence and the stifling atmosphere of East German life, not West Berlin's affluence, contributed to the exodus of so many members of the technological and scientific intelligentsia.

For her book, Christa Wolf was rewarded with a candidate membership in the SED's Central Committee in 1963. Four years later, at the VIIth Party Congress in 1967, she was deprived of that privileged position because of her admirable display of intellectual honesty and courage during the new freeze which set in at the December 1965 plenary meeting of the Central Committee. There she defended some of her colleagues, saying: "I am very glad to live and write here and to belong to the same (writers') association as did Becher and Brecht. In that association, when we say GDR we mean 'we,' when we say party, we also mean 'we.' It is a point on which we will not yield an inch. My pride in living here and working in this association has grown constantly and I sense it all the more every time I have an opportunity to go to West Germany. On my return, I always say with relief: 'I'm home.'

"On many of those trips I have been asked about my position regarding social criticism in literature and my answer has always been: literature without criticism is unthinkable. But at the same time I have always known that the question had a quite different thrust: that I was really being asked how I felt about criticism of the basic nature of our society. To that, my answer has always been 'I'm absolutely against that.' Frequently West Germans would say 'If you're against that, then you cannot produce good literature' and I would also reply: 'If and when I ever doubt the foundations of our society, I would not hesitate to express my doubts, but I do not hold such views. On the contrary, I think that a socialist society is not only desirable but I consider it the only society that permits really free development of literature and art.' Now I also believe that this society has developed a population that is mature enough to really understand and comprehend the right meaning of the literature that has come up in recent years. Our readers are grown up enough to not only understand criticism but to respond to it intelligently."

A writer almost as courageous and certainly as sensitive and intuitive as Christa Wolf, is Brigitte Reimann. Her 1962 novelette *Die Geschwister* (*Brother and Sister*) was not only the first major East German work to deal unabashedly with explicit sex, but discussed openly many of the inequities of East German life which drove thousands of young people to flee to the West.

Manfred Bieler not only resembles West Germany's Günter Grass, he writes a lot like him. Bieler, who has worked as a farm laborer and a high seas fisherman, lists as his hobbies such nonconformist Communist pastimes as sailing, shooting, bicycling, and beer drinking. His writing is just as unorthodox. In addition to collections of parodies, more than a dozen radio and television plays and the script for Kurt Maetzig's controversial film *I Am the Rabbit*, Bieler is best known for his 1963 novel *The Sailor in the Bottle* (which was published in the U.S. in 1965). A sardonic novel of a young dissident on the road in war-torn and postwar Germany, the novel is a loosely strung-out series of picaresque escapades which *Newsweek* described as, "more Marx Brothers than Marxist." In a country where humor is often harder to find than oranges, Bieler is a welcome literary relief. His only trouble: at home he is not very welcome. Bieler has lived in self-imposed exile in Prague since tangling with the authorities over his screenplay for *I Am the Rabbit*.

East German propagandists never miss an opportunity to boast of refugees in reverse, that is, West Germans who have settled in the GDR. But the ideologues, I am sure, still rue that day in 1953 when Wolf Biermann, then seventeen and the son of a Communist killed by the Nazis, moved from Hamburg to East Germany. Sporting a drooping Gunter Grass-type handlebar mustache, banjo and guitar, he and his razor-sharp wit quickly became the focus of anti-intellectual campaigns. Credited with only a long-playing record and a 77-page booklet of verse printed in West Germany, he has become the incarnation of skepticism and cynicism to the party and the embodiment of intellectual and cultural freedom for almost everyone else. Biermann sang and recited his raucous, cutting verses in youth centers, universities and political cabarets, but he did not become nationally known until Erich Honecker pilloried him at the December 1965 Central Committee Plenum. "His anarchical attitudes, his conceit, his skepticism and cynicism reveal him as a traitor to basic socialist concepts," said Honecker. After that, Biermann's little book, *Die Drahtharfe* (*The Glass Harp*), officially priced at 5.80 marks in West Germany, began selling for 40 and more marks on the East German black market.

Indeed, some of Biermann's poems and songs are incisive. His ode to socialism begins:

I cannot leave you anymore.
In the West there is the Wall

In the East there are my friends,
And I can hear the Northwind roar.

Biermann's "Ballad on the Poet François Villon" is a unique attack on all those aspects of East German life which are most despicable and oppressive: The Wall, the propaganda in *Neues Deutschland*, the inanities of GDR television and the secret police.

My big brother Franz Villon
Lives with me in my room.
When people come to snoop on me
Villon he always hides.
Then he ducks into a closet
With a big bottle of wine
And waits until the air is clear.
The air is never quite clear.

For all his overt criticism and for all the restrictions that have been placed on him, Biermann has remained loyal—to the state and the party, which he lampoons so mercilessly. He is, as he put it in another ballad about *Fredi Rohmeisl, the Ditchdigger from Buckow*, "For socialism and for the new state, but the state in Buckow, of that he's had enough." When West German writers and magazines came to his defense and protested to Ulbricht about the attacks on Biermann and his brief arrest at an East Berlin folk song festival in 1965, Biermann rejoindered in a letter to West Germany's *Der Spiegel*: "I prefer to be left in peace so I can continue to work. In ten years no one will be interested in the scandals that have grown about my name but solely whether I am capable of producing useful lyrics and texts."

Until East Germany's leading literary monthly, *Neue Deutsche Literatur*, published excerpts of his forthcoming novel, tentatively titled *The Iron Curtain*, Werner Bräunig was known only to the esoterics of literary circles. A section of Bräunig's novel that was published in the fall of 1965, put this young author into the spotlight for he had dared to show life in the Wismut region, where he worked in a Soviet-run uranium enterprise, as it really was: a rough-and-tumble East German Klondike where schnaps, a quick fist and a pocketful of rubles were the only criteria of power. Bräunig's chapter, which he entitled *Rummelplatz* (*Fairground*), paints a picture diametrically in contrast with the "socialist realism" the party would like to perpetrate on the classless masses. His principal character, Peter Loose, appears to be a rough-and-ready brawler, interested only in money, liquor, and sex, least of all in the glorious future of socialism.

Bräunig's bitter commentaries caught the party's attention when four Wismut miners wrote an acerbic protest to *Neues Deutschland,* complaining that Bräunig had failed to capture the real constructive spirit of the working class and that his novel was so pornographic they were ashamed to show it to their wives. The letter, probably planted, placed Bräunig in the center of the party's campaign against the literati, and no doubt he would have lost his job and been sidetracked had Christa Wolf not come to his defense.

The path of intellectual freedom in the GDR has been a hilly one since the late 1940s, marked by two significant knolls of relaxation in a long valley of repression. Twice, since the GDR's establishment, writers have been free to publish what they wanted, professors permitted to speak their minds, artists not limited entirely to socialist realism and jazz and other forms of Western music not been castigated as decadent imperialist influences.

The first period began in 1956 after Khrushchev's exposé of Stalin and lasted until the Hungarian revolution. The second period began in late 1962—after the Berlin Wall—and lasted until the December 1965 central committee meeting which was punctuated by vitriolic diatribes against Biermann, Stefan Heym, Bräunig, Kurt Maetzig, playwright Peter Hacks, Manfred Bieler, and Humboldt University's chemistry professor Robert Havemann, a veteran Communist who outraged the party hierarchs with popular lectures suggesting there was room for parliamentary opposition under socialism.

In part, these waves of repression reflect a rebellion of the intellectually mediocre, the pseudo-socialist petit bourgeois, who form the hard core of the party's apparatus, against those writers, artists and intellectuals who refuse to conform to mediocre standards. These conflicts reflect factional disputes which have raged within the SED for two decades, and can best be illustrated by the example of Paul Fröhlich, the Leipzig district secretary who believes stanchly that everything Western is decadent. Fröhlich surrounded himself with a retinue of narrow minded functionaries who first determined the cultural tone in the Leipzig area, then gained national influence in the mid-1950s after Fröhlich provided them with important government and central committee jobs.

Reginald Rudorf, former program director of jazz shows at Radio GDR, believes, for example, that the campaign against beat music and long-haired teenagers, which began in the fall of 1965 as a sort of preview to the December Central Committee Plenum, was but a reflection of the long-running battle by Fröhlich's group.

Their first successful foray was in 1953 when they campaigned against jazz, placed the GDR's famed Kurt Henkels orchestra under pressure and loudly demanded more party-lining pop tunes in honor of Vopos and tractor drivers. Their attempts to dictate to jazz and popular musicians drove the best of the GDR's pop artists to the West.

For three years, after the 1953 Fröhlich purge, calm settled over the remnants of East German jazz and pop music until the period following the 1956 Hungarian revolution when Fröhlich went on a new rampage. According to Rudorf, who experienced that era, Fröhlich chartered a troop of bullies and rowdies to riot in jazz clubs, youth centers, dance halls, and Leipzig's political cabaret the Pfeffermühle (The Pepper Grinder) so as to give police a pretext for closing them. Jazz and pop musicians were assaulted in dark alleys, elevators, and secluded houses to which they had been lured by Fröhlich's thugs. Rudorf relates that in December 1956 he and Heinz Lukas, the leader of Leipzig's Jazz Club, were asked to lecture to a group of fans at a suburban villa. When they arrived, 27 of Fröhlich's gang "were waiting, took us to an upstairs, soundproof room and attacked us."

Finally, in 1957, all jazz clubs and combos were dissolved and outlawed. Not until 1962, after the Wall, were restrictions eased and jazz allowed to flourish again. A wave of liberalization enveloped East Germany, finding its culmination in the 1964 youth festival at which beat and rock-and-roll combos played with official sanction on the streets.

Illustrated, youth, humor magazines and even stodgy old *Neues Deutschland* sanctioned and furthered jazz, tolerated beat and closed an eye to its long-haired fans. Sex was stripped of its taboos, Western music, literature and art became the criteria by which everything was measured.

It was during this period that Christa Wolf's novel was published, Manfred Bieler became a national celebrity, Wolf Biermann felt free to strum his guitar and hum his heretic ditties and Robert Havemann could shock his party comrades. Havemann, in fact, more than the writers or the jazz and beat music fans, became the symbol of that era, "a modern Galileo," as *L'Unita*, Italy's Communist daily, described him.

Havemann was no young upstart, no "skeptic," as a well-trained apparatchik would say, but an experienced functionary himself. This is probably what made him all the more dangerous. A member of the Communist party since 1932, a veteran of the anti-Nazi resistance and of Hitler's concentration camps, a charter member of the SED and a deputy in the Volkskammer since 1949, he had none of the qualifications for a renegade. But Havemann, as he once explained in an article in *Forum*, an East German student monthly, saw his "edifice of faith" collapse at the XXth Soviet Party Congress where the sins of Stalin were unveiled by Khrushchev.

"What I believe today, what I write today," said Havemann, "is nothing but an attempt to reconstruct an edifice from the debris. For years I believed I was a good Marxist. Because I believed it, I was not one. Today I no longer believe. I am in doubt, I am uncertain. I am making an effort to think it out. I read, when and where I can get it, all that which in former days I did not consider worth reading. Before the XXth Soviet Party Congress, I accepted everything the party leadership forbade as a taboo. It had the right of censorship and suppression of all views with which it did not share. Today I know that the party leadership does not have the right of censorship. I know that each of us, within and outside of the party, has the right and the duty to make up his own mind, to reach his own verdict, even about the ideas that I have propagated in my lectures."

And those lectures—a melange of philosophy, physical, bio- and photo-chemistry—had a catalyzing effect on young East Germans. Every Friday when Havemann spoke, students from all over the GDR converged on his Berlin lecture hall, sat on the platform, in the aisles and on desks so they could hear the balding one-time Stalinist tell them that freedom of thought, not rote recitation of dogma, should be the cardinal principle of Communism. Mankind, he said, should be converted to Communism "through the persuasiveness of Communist ideas which are the direct antithesis to Stalinist dogmatism. . . . What is indispensable to socialism and what was lost in the Stalinist period, is democracy. Socialism cannot be realized without democracy . . . Citizens of the GDR should be granted more freedom than those of West Germany or other Western countries. That would be real Communism. Had our leadership followed such a policy in the past, it could have saved itself a great deal of difficulties." Student notes and stenographic transcripts of Havemann's lectures were reproduced secretly and passed from hand to hand all over East Germany.

For the ideologues, the functionaries who could still not grasp that Stalinism had been interred by Khrushchev in 1956, for the dogmatists who continued to form the majority in the Central Committee and on the Politburo, such ideas were rank heresy. Combined with the new cultural freedom and the upsurge of Western influences in literature, art, music, and entertainment, they presented a clear threat. The party and cultural functionaries feared that youth was slipping away from their influence and adopting the attitude of a skeptical generation. This skepticism, the SED's leaders believed, was being demonstrated for youth every day by Biermann and Bieler, Bräunig and Hacks, Heym and Havemann. The older functionaries sensed the danger of being swept away by a new spirit of moral commitment expressed in the work of the young literary and artistic intelligentsia. It was a conflict of the generations, and its battlefield was culture.

To Western minds the idea of a link between Beatle music and Professor Havemann's lectures, the suggestion that there is a relationship between long-maned teenagers and literature, probably seems ridiculous. But ludicrous or not, the SED opened its major cultural offensive with an attack on yeah-yeah music which Ulbricht described as "an import from Texas" that "is both soul-killing and ridiculous." On second thought, perhaps the relationship will not seem as bizarre, for after all, the beat rhythms were but a symptom of the disaffection of youth and a symbol of the new culture which was most vulnerable to attack. It was the one thing on which apparatchiks and intellectuals, party members and even bourgeois opponents of the regime could agree. Riots at beat concerts, the visible decline of teenage discipline, and attacks on peaceful citizens by long-maned *Halbstarke* (one can never discount the possibility that Paul Fröhlich hired them like he did his anti-jazz thugs) incensed all East Germans, regardless of political or ideological persuasion.

Erich Honecker's speech to the Central Committee demonstrates how the party linked the two scourges of rioting teenagers, overt sex and literary heresy to launch its new campaign of repression.

"Our GDR is a clean state," said Honecker. "We are proud of our criteria of ethics, morality and decency. But in recent months there have been a number of incidents which demand our special attention. Youth have joined in gangs and groups to commit criminal acts. There were rapes and demonstrations of rowdyism. Students who went to help with the harvest, staged drunken sessions in the style of West Germany's reactionary fraternity brothers.

"These are all demonstrations of the negative influence of Western TV and radio on certain sections of our population. But we would also agree with those who say that the causes for such immoral behavior can be found in some of our own films, television programs, plays, literary works, and magazines as well.

"There are elements of American immorality and decadence against which no action is being taken. This is especially true of the motion picture industry and some of its more recent products. They show blatant disregard for the dialectics of development and depict contrived situations of conflict which have been forced into an imaginary framework. They fail to grasp or portray the reality of socialist development. The creative nature of man's labor is negated by them. Collectives and party leaders are depicted as cold and alien forces against whom the individual is powerless. Our reality is pictured only as a temporary period of sacrifice at the end of which stands an illusionary future."

Honecker criticized Wolf Biermann, Stefan Heym, and a number of literary journals, notably *Neue Deutsche Literatur*, for publishing nihilistic, overly critical, pornographic works. He warned against a new form of literature "centered primarily on a mixture of sex and brutality," he cautioned against the excesses generated by a preponderance of Western popular music, and appealed for art that "depicts the beauties, not just the burdens of our battle."

Honecker was followed by a succession of Politburo and Central Committee members.

The outcome of the plenum: Biermann was forbidden from performing publicly, Heym was ostracized, Wolfgang Joho was fired from his post as editor of *Neue Deutsche Literatur*, and countless artists and writers and minor cultural functionaries were reprimanded, or sidetracked in their careers. Havemann was fired from his university post, expelled from the party and purged from the GDR's Academy of Sciences. Hans Bentzien, the Minister of Culture, was dismissed and replaced by Klaus Gysi, a more tractable (though by no means dogmatic) functionary who had been editor-in-chief of Aufbau Verlag. The Writers' Association engaged in self-criticism. Party and ministerial advisory councils were established to supervise literature, films and the theater. The arts were again set firmly on the "Bitterfeld Road" of socialist realism. A new law, called appropriately "Lex Biermann," was enacted to prohibit writers from publishing their works in the West before first offering them to East German publishing houses. Political cabarets such as the Pfeffermühle and East Berlin's Die Distel (The Thistle) were ordered to revise and mellow their satirical programs. Jazz and beat bands were required to take tests to determine their musical capabilities before being licensed to perform publicly. A new winter settled over the GDR.

A thaw is nowhere in sight. Kurt Hager, the Politburo's ideological chieftain, has tried to keep a semblance of moderation in his attacks and has endeavored to de-escalate the conflict between the party and its intellectuals. But at the November 1966 conference of the Writers' Association, he said: "We consider it a great achievement of our long battle for peace and socialism, for the humanistic renaissance of German culture, that a socialist standpoint, a socialist sense of responsibility and love for our workers' and peasants' state has become basic to the attitude of our writers."

For those writers to whom that attitude is not yet basic, life can be a frugal struggle. True the days are past when the State Security Service came knocking in search of illegal manuscripts. Although there is de jure censorship because every printed piece of paper must be licensed, this is no longer the hurdle that worries the GDR's writers. Instead it is the de facto censorship of the publishers and the Writers' Association who will not touch unorthodox contributions. The real instrument of censorship in a GDR that has become more pragmatic, is money. Writers who want it will conform to the party line. As Deputy Culture Minister Horst Brasch put it brashly in May 1967: "Artists who do not hew to the guidelines of the SED will not be able to count on monetary compensation." Wolf Biermann, who has been denied any kind of work, lives on the generosity of his friends and a trickle of royalties from West Germany. Havemann, who has since been divorced by his wife, at one time considered applying for unemployment compensation, but then was contracted as a research adviser by one of the big chemical trusts.

The lower the functionaries attempt to set the temperature, the more restless East Germany's intellectuals will become. They risk both ostracism and party reprimands to demonstrate their resentment at being bridled. As Volker Braun, a twenty-eight-year-old poet said recently: "Why shouldn't poetry be granted the same right as science to criticize social conditions? How can we celebrate reality by treating it like misery, by treating it as if it were beneath the dignity of criticism?" Added Paul Wiens, a forty-five-year-old poet and essayist, "Even with the most imaginative variations, those constant exhortations to love socialism are bound to get on one's nerves. Socialist writers should ask questions, social and moral questions, embarrassing, disconcerting questions. True love cannot endure without criticism and self-criticism."

Even some of the old guard have joined the chorus. Fritz Erpenbeck, one of the original ten members of Ulbricht's group in 1945, cautioned in November 1966: "We must free ourselves from one sided literary propaganda and from interminable thematic demands on our writers." A few days later Anna Seghers admonished the party against attempting to minimize socialism's failings or trying to silence criticism. "The real socialist consciousness in literature should not be frightened away ere it has had a chance to develop."

It is unlikely that the new ice age can endure for long. If only because it is highly improbable that the directives of a few Stalinist cultural functionaries can squelch the critical consciousness of an entire generation fostered by the political and economic changes of the last ten years.

But for the time being that generation will have to wait, and perhaps to symbolize. Like thirty-four-year-old Reiner Kunze whose little elegy "The End of Art" so eloquently summarized the plight of East Germany's intellectuals:

Thou shalt not, said the owl to the grouse,
Thou shalt not sing of the sun.
The sun is unimportant.

The grouse then took
the sun out of its poem.

You are an artist,
said the owl to the grouse.

And it was already dark.

CHAPTER XII

Two States, Two Histories

For more than an hour, from my hotel window nearby, I had watched a steady stream of festively clad East Berliners converge toward Marx-Engels Platz. Some pushed their toddlers in perambulators, a few stopped to buy sandwiches of Russian ice cream from itinerant vendors or bags of plums and pears from hastily erected stands on the street corners. Others ambled slowly past the displays in shop windows, many were engrossed in conversation with neighbors and friends. As it was a Sunday, I first thought they were coming from church, but then I remembered where I was and curiosity persuaded me to follow the crowd. When I reached the vast, taiga-like square where once the baroque palace of Prussia's monarchs stood, I found it bulging with a mob of 300,000 and vibrant with a holiday air.

Marx-Engels Platz was a kaleidoscope of color and a Babel of sound. From dozens of loudspeakers came the squeaky, scratchy blare of recorded march music—just loud enough to force the gossiping thousands to raise their voices. Above the heads of the crowd bobbed children on their fathers' shoulders, isolated signboards warning against American aggression in Vietnam and hundreds of red and black-red-gold flags fluttering limpidly in the barely perceptible breeze. Behind the open air stage on which sat the straw-hatted élite of the GDR's hierarchy, and wired firmly to the doric columns of Berlin's neo-classical Altes Museum, ranged a 30-foot billboard that read *FOR PEACE AND HUMANITY—AGAINST BONN'S REVANCHIST POLICIES*. It was September 12, 1966, East Germany's "Victims of Fascism Day."

"We have come here today to commemorate and mourn the

anti-fascist heroes of the many lands of Europe who gave their lives in the battle against German militarism and imperialism," said Herbert Warnke, the white-haired boss of the GDR's Federation of Trade Unions and a member of the SED Politburo. "In their honor and memory we renew our oath—never to rest until the last vestiges of fascism and war have been removed from the face of the earth."

Then, for nearly an hour, Warnke conjured a dark picture of a land in which the monster of Nazism, militarism, and imperialism still rears its ugly head: West Germany. "But we," he concluded, "have fulfilled the last will and testament of all those who fought against fascism. Their ideals have become reality in our state whose army, economy, and government are in the hands of proven anti-fascists."

When Warnke stepped back from the microphone, a Volkspolizei band struck up the melodious strains of East Germany's national anthem. Next to me a couple of People's Soldiers, their boots shined Sunday slick, their marksmanship badges silvery in the pale sunlight, their chests stuck out proudly, sang along:

"Arisen from the fields of ruin,
Its face turned to the future,
Let us serve you for the better,
Germany, our Fatherland."

Once again the GDR had "overcome" the German past by transferring it to the other side of the Elbe.

Virtually no one in the GDR holds himself responsible or accountable for the Germany of yesteryear. To the incontestability of two postwar German states, the GDR's rulers have added the spurious axiom of two German histories. Nazism, one might believe, either was never a problem or the GDR has expurgated itself of all remnants of the past.

East Germany, it seems has never troubled itself with that mass exercise of national soul searching which West Germans call "Bewältigung der Vergangenheit," an untranslatable expression usually circumscribed as "coming to terms with or mastering the past." The GDR has simply divorced itself from the past. Or, as

Arnold Zweig, the octogenarian dean of GDR novelists, and himself a Jew, once told Amos Elon, an Israeli journalist: "We did not master or digest the past—we vomited it."

Nazism, in the eyes of the GDR's rulers or the words of their propagandists, was not an aberration of German history, but a natural, albeit extreme and dangerous, consequence of monopolist capitalism. Ergo, Nazism and its seed are dead wherever capitalism has been rooted out and still alive where capitalism flourishes. The effect of this highly debatable postulate is a pious self-righteousness mixed with a maddeningly ambivalent and ambiguous approach to both the German past and its present.

When asked to explain who Hitler was, East German school children, unlike their West German cousins, will never say, "Oh, he was the mustached man who built the autobahns." But they are likely to say: "Hitler came to power in 1933 when industrialists, Ruhr barons and militarists, who rule West Germany to this day, met secretly to find a front man who would implement their policies. Their long-range goals included subjugation of the Soviet Union and peace-loving German peasants and workers. They needed a terrorist reign to achieve their aims."

West German educators can be justifiably and legitimately criticized for the way they have whitewashed the more recent decades of German history and for the manner in which most textbooks write off the sins of the fathers in a couple of perfunctory paragraphs. The East German approach is different. But is it any better? In the long run, the inanities and blatant falsehoods which East German children are taught can be just as dangerous for a country which, contrary to Arnold Zweig's colorful analysis, has not even digested the past, let alone vomited it.

East Germany's rulers and propagandists fulminate at what they call West German militarism, but it is their own National People's Army, not the Bonn Bundeswehr, which still goosesteps and wears the uniforms of the old Wehrmacht.

The GDR's agitprop experts miss no opportunity to apprise the world of highly placed West German officials with mile-long records for persecution of the Jews. But East Germany's own Jews have never been paid a cent for their suffering or for the property they lost. And because of the Communist stake in the Middle East, the GDR equates Israel with the imperialist devil.

East German newspapers, magazines, radio, and television rail and rant about the inordinately high number of ex-Nazis who today have vital roles in West German government and industry. But the language of their headlines, editorials and commentaries is the same as that first employed by Joseph Goebbels.

Yet, when one of their own is unmasked as a former Nazi, the reaction in East Germany is the same as in the West. The news is either followed by silence or explained away hastily with an aloof "but-you-must-admit-he-recanted-in-1945." What distinguishes a man who switched party buttons in 1945 from one who doffed the mantle of extremism to cloak himself as a democrat? To the GDR's propagandists and policymakers there is a world of difference—divided at the border between East and West Germany. All bad ex-Nazis are on the western side of it. Those in the East either don't exist or are good ex-Nazis. Germany's ugly past, one is told, is West Germany's even uglier present. Nothing has changed and nothing will until the monopolists and capitalists, the imperialists and militarists and all those other lice that bred Nazism and fascism have been fumigated from the banks of the Rhine.

Questions about how the past weighs on the conscience of this society are greeted with a wonderland refrain which leaves more normal men shaking their heads in disbelief. VE-Day was Liberation Day. Known Nazis in one's own family or circle of friends are generally dismissed as former dupes of powerful propaganda—unless, of course, they have fled to the West in which case they remain Nazis.

Of course, not all East Germans argue or reason this way. At that mammoth rally on Marx-Engels Platz to which 300,000 had come but at which only a few thousand—in the front rows—were listening, I buttonholed dozens and asked them why they were there. Many of the replies were propagandistic platitudes. A couple of teenagers admitted candidly: "Our teacher told us we had to attend and we all met at the subway stop and walked over there together." Nevertheless I found a few people who had sacrificed their Sunday morning to demonstrate in a very personal way against Germany's past, not West Germany's present. "No one forced me, no one coerced me," a heavy-set, balding man in his mid-fifties told me. "I just hope to avoid a repetition of history. I remember how Hitler came to power, and it wasn't a capitalist plot. I saw them all standing right here on this street and cheering when he became chancellor and named himself Führer. But I spent four years in a Soviet POW camp and I saw what our cheering did to that country. We Germans always followed a leader. Now we ought to make sure it can't happen again." When I asked how he differentiated between that day's rally and the ones Hitler used to hold, he cut me short and said: "It's not just the tone that makes the music but the score. Don't be fooled by superficialities. Some Communist meetings may sound like Nazi rallies but the message is quite different. Communism, for all its mutation, is an essentially humanitarian political philosophy. Nazism was and is inhumane. There is, after all, a difference between trying to make a better world and trying to conquer it."

Perspicacious and discerning observers admit readily that the regime's view of Germany's past and present is distorted, that the Federal Republic is not all black and the GDR not lacteously white. But they argue convincingly: "You must admit that we present a cleaner, more honorable picture than Bonn. Of course we haven't gotten rid of all Nazis, but we don't allow them to become presidents, chancellors, and cabinet ministers. We don't wait until the West calls attention to someone's Nazi record the way the West waits for the East. We don't have thousands of Silesian, Pomeranian and Sudeten Irredentists demanding territories Germany lost in the war it started. Nor do we have neo-Nazi parties like the ones in West Germany basking in irretrievable glories. Have you ever heard someone in East Germany debating heatedly whether there were really four million or only three-and-a-half million Jews killed at Auschwitz?"

No, frankly, I haven't and these arguments are difficult to refute. Yet, I cannot escape the uneasy feeling that both Germanys have approached the common political cataclysm in which they were spawned with more hypocrisy than willingness to expiate their sins.

Except for a small, albeit vociferous, group of writers and intellectuals in the Federal Republic, most West Germans writhe away when confronted with the mirror of their own past. They would, if they could, think of the Third Reich as a nebulous era of ancient history, far removed from the present. Most East Germans, on the other hand, tend to think of the Hitler regime as West Germany's problem. They see it not as history but as Bonn's hysterical present. To hear them one might believe that the GDR had also been one of the occupied countries, not part of the aggressor nation. In Soviet war movies, for example, it is impossible to disguise that the enemy is German. But on the East German sound tracks, atrocities committed by the Wehrmacht and the SS are discreetly referred to as crimes of the "fascists."

For both Germanys, the bloody stain of Nazism has long been washed away and I am sure that neither suffered Macbethian dreams from its memory. The only difference between the two is that the GDR has cleverly washed its stains down the other fellow's drain by transferring blame to his doorstep. Curiously, it could make a case for this propagandistic sleight of hand, though it has never succeeded in stating it convincingly.

It is true, for example, that when *important* ex-Nazis are discovered in *influential* public positions, the GDR generally makes short shrift of them, and usually under cloak of secrecy. In West Germany, exposed officials invariably spend agonizing months glued to the emoluments of their office before finally resigning under pressure to the accompaniment of a public uproar. It proves, if anything, the unwieldiness of democracies vis-à-vis totalitarian states.

It is also true that in West Germany only 7000 war criminals have been prosecuted compared to the 12,800 who were convicted before East German tribunals. Moreover, when war criminals are tried in the GDR today, which is not often, they generally receive the maximum sentence. Of four former SS guards and doctors prosecuted in the GDR in 1966, three were sentenced to life imprisonment and one, Dr. Horst Fischer, was guillotined. The death penalty was abolished in the Federal Republic in 1949. Nevertheless the five-year prison term to which a Frankfurt court sentenced Hermann Krumey, Adolf Eichmann's deputy in Hungary, for complicity in the murder of 400,000 Hungarian Jews seems curiously light.

To the often-raised charge that they have done nothing to compensate Jews for lost property or personal suffering, East Germany's rulers reply that "Jewish capitalists should not be given preferential treatment over other capitalists just because they are Jews." Moreover, says the GDR, "We have made moral restitution by punishing all war criminals, ridding our state of all former Nazis and building a better future." This argument is too transparent. It would be better to point out that the GDR has paid many times more than the Federal Republic's restitution and compensation to Nazi victims in the form of reparations to the Soviet Union. However, the GDR's rulers are reluctant to present this argument for fear of irritating their fraternal Big Brother, though in terms of its own suffering, Russia was certainly entitled to reparations.

A more valid reply is East Germany's contention that coming to terms with the past and taking moral responsibility for Nazi crimes should burden those who arrogate to themselves the right to succeed the Reich: West Germany. "Look," a functionary of the GDR's Liberal Democratic Party once told me, "they, not we, have claimed that there can be only one Germany and that Bonn is its sole legitimate representative. They deny us the right to recognition abroad, they assume for themselves the right to succeed the German Reich. Under the circumstances they can damn well assume the responsibility that comes with it. Why, for example, should we pay reparations to Israel when Bonn insists on doing it in the name of all Germany?"

East Germans think of themselves as the better Germans and defiantly say they are the real bearers of the national cultural heritage. That is one reason why East Germans aren't in the least embarrassed by their jackbooted army with its uniform, indistinguishable from that of the Wehrmacht except for its Soviet-style helmet.

New helmet or not, for foreigners who remember, it is a chilling sight to see the Nationale Volksarmee, preceded by brass bands and officers snapping commands, come goosestepping down Unter den Linden. And it is little comfort to know that Schinkel's neo-classical Neue Wache, a miniature Pantheon, has been renamed "Monument to the Victims of Fascism and Militarism." The white-gloved, high-collared, helmeted People's Soldiers who guard it look like proteges of the Kaiser's personal drillmaster. And who but a German would have thought of putting a timer with a faintly audible buzzer into their rifle butts so they will know precisely when to shift arms from one shoulder to the other?

When they discuss these matters at all, East Germans insist stanchly that such trivialities are the wrong criteria with which to gauge an army's attitude. Perhaps they are right. After all, when the West German Bundeswehr was organized in 1956, excruciating attention was paid to every detail of the uniform so that it reflected the new philosophy of a "citizen army." The uniforms still look less martial than the GDR's but what has happened to those lofty concepts of a "democratic" army? Systematically the reformers who coined them have all been sidetracked to command posts full of prestige but devoid of influence. The top generals are the same men who served Hitler—if not as generals then as colonels. Karl Wienand, the Social Democratic Party's whip in the Bundestag, has frequently warned about the "arrogant Prussian tone echoing across our parade grounds again." And ex-Admiral Hellmuth Heye, parliament's former Special Commissioner for Military Affairs, warned darkly that "the Bundeswehr is in danger of again becoming a state within the state."

"West Germany changed the uniform but kept the old generals," a Leipzig political scientist once told me. "We kept the uniform but changed the generals."

A West German survey tends to support him. According to Dr. Werner Bauer, a lecturer at Tübingen University, the Volksarmee's generals and admirals are considerably younger than the Bundeswehr's and almost none of them served in the Wehrmacht—at least not as officers. Moreover, the Volksarmee leadership seems to have broken with the traditional sociological origins which characterized the German officer corps. Most of the East German generals are the sons of workers and peasants, not aristocrats, civil servants or other officers.

Some 800 Wehrmacht generals survived World War II, Bauer reported, and in 1955, when the Bundeswehr was organized, Bonn searched primarily among this manpower reservoir for its new military leaders. Professional competence was the primary standard for their selection, though political reliability and their ability to adapt to conditions of democratic leadership were also important. In the GDR it was the other way around. Political reliability was the primary criterion. Once *it* had been met, professional competence was considered.

Bauer and Tübingen Professor Ralf Dahrendorf, who are conducting a study of the sociological structure of various professions in Germany, analyzed the personal histories of 180 West German and fifty East German general and flag officers. All 180 of West Germany's Bundeswehr had previously served in the Wehrmacht as general or senior field grade officers, compared to only twelve of the fifty Volksarmee leaders. And of these only four had held a general or flag rank under Hitler. One had been a colonel, the other seven had been majors, captains or lieutenants. None of the four East German Hitler generals is still in active service. One of them, Major General Arno von Lenski, was discreetly removed from service in 1958 when it turned out that he had served as an honorary judge on the Nazi People's Court and had passed twenty terrorist death sentences.

Half of the East German generals are under fifty-seven, compared to only 5 percent of the Bundeswehr's. Most of the West German officers are sons of upper class families, most of those in the Volksarmee come from proletarian or petit bourgeois backgrounds. Some 16 percent of the Bundeswehr leaders are aristocrats, 37 percent are the sons of high-ranking officers. Twenty-one of the East German officers included in the study, were members of the Communist Party before 1945. Eight fought on the Republican side in the Spanish Civil War, seven served terms in Nazi jails or concentration camps, fourteen were anti-Nazi resistance fighters, active in Germany and elsewhere.

Premier Willi Stoph, the Volksarmee's first chief and the GDR's first Defense Minister, for example, was trained as a mason and collected his only military experience as a lance corporal in the Wehrmacht. General Heinz Hoffmann, the present Defense Minister and head of the People's Army, worked as a mechanic before fleeing Germany in 1935, then was trained at the Frunse Military Academy in the USSR and served as a battalion commander with the International Brigades in Spain. Admiral Waldemar Verner, the Deputy Defense Minister and chief of the Volksmarine, was a window decorator before he fled Germany in 1935 and during the war years was an active leader of the Danish resistance movement. Major General Walter Breitfeld, now director of the East German Red Cross, but for nine years (from 1954 to 1963) head of the East German border police, was trained as a stocking maker, fled Germany in 1934 and joined the Thälmann Battalion in Spain as a company political commissar, later fought with the French Maquis. Lieutenant General Heinz Kessler, Deputy Defense Minister and chief of the East German air force, was trained as a mechanic, drafted into the Wehrmacht and deserted to the Russians on the Eastern Front in 1941. Major General Erich Peter, the chief of the Volksarmee's border troops, was also trained as a mechanic, served as an enlisted man in the Wehrmacht and was captured by American forces. He joined the Communist Party in 1945, the SED when it was founded in 1946 and enlisted in the Volkspolizei. Major General Helmuth Poppe, the city commandant of East Berlin, was an electrician when he was drafted into the Wehrmacht. Taken prisoner by the Russians, he was released in 1948, then joined the Volkspolizei whose garrisoned units formed the Volksarmee.

Men with such backgrounds may never turn out to be the kind of military leaders that West Point, Sandhurst, or Saint-Cyr produce, but it is unlikely that they will run armies in the spirit of Ludendorff, Schleicher, Keitl, or Jodl. For all its goosestepping and Wehrmacht uniforms the Volksarmee may have less of a past to live down than the Bundeswehr.

The GDR's propagandists never lose an opportunity to apprise the world of the Nazis still—or again—entrenched in West German public life. East Germany seems to employ whole divisions of researchers who do nothing but rummage through voluminous and apparently bottomless file drawers in search of new dossiers, most of which were in East Berlin archives after the war. When new evidence is found, Professor Albert Norden emerges triumphant and delighted to pillory Bonn again.

In 1965, Norden, a collaborator on the famous Communist Brown Book of the 1930s, issued a new edition of this work, dedicated solely to the exposure of "War and Nazi Criminals" in West Germany's government, economy, administration, army, judiciary and scientific community. More than 400 pages thick, it lists 1900 names and alleges, among other things, that "there are 520 Nazi diplomats who have again been appointed to leading positions in the Bonn foreign office." Norden claims that twenty-one state and federal ministers and undersecretaries, one hundred West German generals and admirals, and 828 judicial officials had "Nazi or militarist" records. "And this," said Norden, "is only the initial list."

The GDR has accused West German President Heinrich Lübke of helping to build concentration camps and identified Chancellor Kurt Georg Kiesinger as a former Nazi party member and senior propaganda official in Hitler's foreign ministry. One former West German refugee affairs minister was exposed as a judge on special Nazi summary courts in Poland, another, Professor Theodor Oberländer, was tried in absentia as a war criminal in East Berlin. According to the GDR, Bonn's Socialist Economics Minister Professor Karl Schiller was both a member of the NSDAP and the storm troop organization. A half dozen other senior officials were either Nazis, stormtroopers, or members of the SS élite guard.

Each time East Berlin discloses a new name, Bonn winces and writhes uncomfortably, first tries to deny the charges, then usually admits that they are true—if only in part. Not until the waning days of Ludwig Erhard's administration did anyone think of examining the records of new appointments *before* they were emblazoned in banner headlines across the front pages of *Neues Deutschland*.

The East German scavenger hunt for dirt in dusty archives produces the raw material on which the GDR's incessant propaganda machine runs. It makes it easy to point an accusing finger and shout: "West Germany's public life is infested with the arrogant lice of Nazism, anti-Semitism, militarism, and imperialism."

Though the present is divisible, history is not. A quick mathematical calculation will show that even if *all* of the 3,500,000 refugees who fled East Germany until 1961 had been Nazis, some Nazis, anti-Semites, militarists, and imperialists must be left over to spice up life in the first German workers' and peasants' state. Who and where are they?

West Berlin's "Investigating Committee of Free Jurists," a nebulous organization with opaque financial sources, has produced a handy "brown book" of its own. The fifth edition of its booklet *Ex-Nazis in the Service of the "German Democratic Republic"* lists 243 names. Though most of the persons are minor fish in the East German power structure, the booklet leaves one inescapable conclusion: Bonn does not enjoy a monopoly on former brownshirts. None of the Free Jurist's charges has ever been successfully refuted and it can be accepted as fact that plenty of skeletons also rattle in Walter Ulbricht's closet. In fact, one could deduce that until 1967, the number of ex-Nazis, while declining in the West, had been increasing in East German public life.

For example, during the 1954–58 legislative session, twenty-nine of the Volkskammer's five hundred members were former Nazis. After the 1958 election, the number increased to forty-nine. During the 1963 to 1967 legislative period there were fifty-three, though it should be pointed out that only eight of them were members of the SED and eighteen belonged to the NDP which was founded after all, for the express purpose of providing little and middle Nazis with a new political home.

When the Free Jurists published the latest list in 1965, five members of the Council of Ministers were identified as former Nazis. Meanwhile one of the quintet, Cultural Minister Hans Bentzien, has been deposed (because his views were too liberal). Another, forty-two-year-old Hans Reichelt, the Deputy Chairman of the Agricultural Council who joined the NSDAP in 1944 when he was nineteen, retains his post but is no longer a member of the Council of Ministers. The three who remain are: Heinz Matthes, forty, the chairman of the Workers' and Peasants' Inspectorate, who managed to slip into the Nazi party in 1944 when only seventeen years old; Professor Ernst Joachim Giessmann, forty-eight, the Minister of Higher Education, who joined the NSDAP in 1937, and Dr. Herbert Weiz, forty-three, a deputy prime minister without portfolio who became a member of the Nazi party as an eighteen-year-old in 1942.

In the case of three of these East German "cabinet" members one might honestly say they joined the NSDAP when they were too young to know better. But when West German officials present the same argument in their own defense East Berlin conveniently ignores it.

Heinrich Homann, fifty-six, the leader of the NDP in the Volkskammer and one of the six deputy chairmen of the State Council, on the other hand joined the NSDAP as a twenty-two-year-old in May 1933. During the war he was a Wehrmacht major and when captured by the Russians, joined the anti-fascist National Committee for a Free Germany in the Soviet Union.

Kurt Blecha, the East German government's official press spokesman, was also a fuzz-faced teenager when he joined the NSDAP in 1941 at age eighteen. On the other hand, Dr. Guenter Kertzscher, fifty-four, an assistant editor-in-chief of *Neues Deutschland* and prolific author of some of its most vitriolic articles about Nazis in Bonn, joined the Nazi party as a twenty-four-year-old in 1937. Both Blecha and Kertzscher were captured on the Eastern front and joined the Free Germany committee as POWs.

Even Walter Ulbricht's chief of bodyguards, Franz Gold, a major general in the State Security Service, was a Nazi. He joined the NSDAP in November 1938.

To be fair, it must be emphasized that most of the names listed in the Free Jurists' dossier are members of the East German National Democratic Party which, though a satrap of the SED, never pretended to be anything else but a political haven for ex-Nazis. Moreover, only a few of the persons on the list had anything close to a responsible or influential position in the Nazi era and many joined the NSDAP as teenagers.

The SED's policy in dealing with ex-Nazis has often been as ambiguous as West Germany's. In the Federal Republic, a Nazi record per se has never been as bad as being caught with it in public and the same curious criterion seems to have prevailed in the GDR. The regime appears not the least embarrassed by the presence of ex-Nazis in public office so long as their affiliations are a matter of record. But it rebukes sharply those who have concealed their past. Thus, in 1959, the SED expelled Ernst Grossmann from the Central Committee after he had been exposed as, not only a Nazi, but a former SS guard in Sachsenhausen concentration camp. Likewise, the party reacted quickly in 1963 when the Free Jurists revealed that the GDR's newly appointed minister of agriculture, Karlheinz Bartsch, had belonged to the Waffen-SS, the SS armed forces. Bartsch was impeached at once, drummed out of the Politburo and voted out of the Central Committee.

In attempting to explain the GDR's amphibolous policy, Erich Honecker said in 1965: "The SED has always battled against fascism and active Nazis. But it will always give nominal former members of the NSDAP full and equal opportunity to help develop a new way of life in our state." In view of the larger number of Germans who belonged to the Nazi party, it seems like a prudent policy.

Anti-Semitism, boast the SED's propagandists, stops at the Berlin Wall. But it has not always been that way. For many years anti-Semitism, cloaked in Stalinist garb, flourished menacingly in the Soviet Union and other Communist countries and naturally took its toll in the GDR as well. East German Jews, keenly sensitive to such moods, reacted accordingly. Of the 3200 who lived there twenty years ago, more than half fled to West Germany—a ratio far higher than the general refugee flow. Even today the policy remains equivocal. The regime rails and rants whenever a swastika is daubed on a Jewish headstone in a Western cemetery, but it virulently accuses Israel of imperialism and aggression.

In the rubble heap of defeated Germany the Communists

found a minuscule Jewish community—mostly bewildered survivors of concentration camps, a handful of DPs and a few German Jews who had managed to escape the Nazi death machinery by spending years in hiding. Ulbricht hailed them eloquently as the martyrs of Nazi oppression. Within the next five years this tiny group was bolstered by the return from exile of a number of Jewish Communists and intellectuals with Communist sympathies—some of whom only reluctantly admitted their Jewish heritage.

Among these returnees were quite a few illustrious names: author Arnold Zweig; artist Lea Grundig; composer Hanns Eisler; his brother Gerhart who became famous in 1949 for jumping bail in the U.S. and escaping on the Polish liner *Batory*; professors Alfred Kantorowicz and Ernst Bloch, as well as a number of professional functionaries such as Hanna Wolf, Albert Norden, Alexander Abusch, and Paul Merker, who had run the KPD's exile organization in Mexico.

But from the start Ulbricht decreed that Jews, though they had suffered more than any other group under Nazism, were not to be accorded special privileges. When prominent East Germans, such as Merker, suggested that compensation and restitution should be paid for hardships and losses suffered under Hitler, Ulbricht muzzled them as petit bourgeois, counterrevolutionaries and reactionaries. Merker was expelled from the Politburo and the SED in 1950 as a "tool of the class enemy" and for alleged connection with "Noel Field, the American agent."

In 1952 and early 1953, when the tremors of Stalin's "Jewish doctors' plot" reverberated through the entire Soviet bloc, anti-Semitism and anti-Zionism reached a high point in the GDR. Merker was incarcerated as "an enemy agent and tool of American-Zionist financial oligarchs." He spent three years in jail. Erich Jungmann, another SED central committee member and editor of the *Berliner Zeitung*, was excommunicated for pro-Zionist activities and not rehabilitated until 1956. The State Security Service raided and systematically rummaged through the offices of all East German Jewish organizations in search of Zionist evidence and forced hundreds of Jews to flee to West Germany. Among them were several prominent intellectuals and senior officials, notably: Leo Zuckermann, President Wilhelm Pieck's *chef du cabinet*; Julius Meyer, a member of the Volkskammer, and Dr. Hans Freund, chief justice of the East Berlin district court.

Following the Soviet Union's XXth Party Congress in 1956, during which Khrushchev exposed Stalin and the "doctor's plot," there was a general relaxation. Since 1960 Ulbricht's Jewish policy has been capricious. It ranges from philo-Semitic to virulently anti-Zionist and anti-Israeli. While spending large sums on pro-Jewish eyewash—synagogues in all leading cities have been rebuilt at government expense, cemeteries, old-age homes and congregations receive public support—Ulbricht has adopted an intractable line toward Israel. Long before the Middle East crisis of 1967, the GDR's policy toward Israel was the toughest in the Soviet bloc and following the Arab-Israeli war of June 1967, the GDR's fulminations against Tel Aviv surpassed those of all other Communist countries. East Berlin views Zionism as "a chauvinistic, capitalistic, reactionary movement rooted in the Jewish petite bourgeoisie."

In contrast to West Germany, which has paid $7,000,000,000, the GDR refuses to pay compensation and restitution to Jewish victims of Nazi persecution because this is a plot to "transfer the property of the people into capitalist hands abroad." Otto Winzer once said: "Restitution should be paid where the crimes were committed and the criminals abound: in West Germany."

Behind the GDR's seemingly illogical Jewish policy, there is the logic of Communism which holds that all capitalists, whether Jewish or Christian, are alike. Ergo, restitution of property stolen by the Nazis would be restitution of capitalist property. Second, a regime which is publicly disdainful of all religion cannot be expected to embrace or support Judaism, no matter what the fate of the Jews under Hitler.

Jewish life in the GDR reflects these vicissitudes and incongruities of the regime's policies. To speak of East German Jews at all is to talk about a group so evanescent as to be barely perceptible. Compared to the 30,000 in West Germany, East German Jews are a minority of 1300 very old and weary people, more than 850 of whom live in East Berlin. The others are scattered among seven Lilliputian congregations: in Leipzig, Dresden, Karl-Marx-Stadt, Erfurt, Halle, Magdeburg, and Schwerin. The largest of these—Leipzig—has 140 members, the smallest—Schwerin—counts a scant two dozen. They share between them the services of an imported Hungarian rabbi, Dr. Oedoen Singer, who travels from congregation to congregation like an itinerant preacher. Their lay leader is fifty-nine-year-old Helmut Aris of Dresden, the chairman of the "Association of Jewish Congregations in the German Democratic Republic," who makes occasional headlines in *Neues Deutschland* with vitriolic charges of rampant neo-Nazism and anti-Semitism in West Germany. Services in some of the larger congregations are conducted by amateur cantors, but East Berlin's has a professional, as well as a kosher slaughter house, though the *schochet* resides in West Berlin and passes through the wall periodically. The only permanent link between the congregations is a quarterly news letter.

In the light of these facts, East Germany's nine rebuilt though largely empty synagogues seem tragically anachronistic if not hypocritical. But they are mute testimony to the ambiguity of the SED's policy, for each was reconstructed at considerable expense to the East German state. In relationship to the size of East Germany's Jewish congregations, the regime is anything but niggardly in its support. Each community receives $25,000 to $100,-000 yearly, from which it pays for upkeep of the synagogue, clerical help, services, and the maintenance of cemeteries and old age homes.

Though the regime refuses to make restitution, it compensates in other ways. All Jews are entitled to (for East Germany exceptionally high) special monthly pensions of 600 marks ($150) as victims of fascism. Moreover, these are paid five years sooner than normal old age pensions. Active combatants against fascism—a category that would include Communists in exile, resistance fighters in the Warsaw ghetto, Jews who participated in concentration camp uprisings—receive an additional 200 marks ($50) a month—enough, in both cases, to live comfortably in the GDR. There are a number of other privileges which accrue, among them free use of railways, preferential treatment in spas and disability payments.

"Frankly," one elderly pensioner told me, "we much prefer this system to the one in West Germany. Unless you had a lot of property it doesn't make much difference whether you get a lump sum payment of a few thousand marks when you're fifty or a comfortable pension when you're sixty. Besides we don't have a lot of forms or red tape to battle, as I've heard is the case in West Germany. As far as I am concerned, I have no complaints."

Yet, to visit one of the congregations or converse with its members can be a shattering experience. It was with special trepidation, on one of my trips to the GDR, that I called on the Jewish congregation of Erfurt, where I was born. The last time I had seen the synagogue—on what is now called Yuri Gagarin Ring—was the night of November 8, 1938, when the building was set afire by the storm troopers, when my father, like most other Jews in the city, was hauled off to the concentration camp. In my memory I can still see the flames licking at the cold wintry night sky, and the charred embers of the gutted building.

Now that the synagogue has been rebuilt nothing seems changed—like the rest of Erfurt, one of those few German cities spared almost completely by the war.

There was palpable tension in the air when I went to visit the congregation's chairman, Herbert Ringer, a fiftyish, meticulously dressed native of Breslau, and his secretary, a young woman who had miraculously survived Theresienstadt concentration camp and who had, as the conversation revealed, been one of the last persons in Erfurt to see my grandmother alive. It was a tension generated mutually—on my side perhaps by the uncomfortable feeling that I had been so much luckier, on theirs by an almost aggressive defensiveness which later culminated in a bitter attack against West Germany.

"Most people who come here expect to find us mummified like in a museum," said Ringer after the preliminaries and pleasantries, the personal reminiscences about mutual friends and the inquiries about relatives. "But you can see for yourself. We are very much alive and a very viable, though small congregation. We are not isolated from Jews elsewhere. We have access to Jewish journals and newspapers from West Germany, Austria and Switzerland. We are assisted, not hampered by the state and most of us live quite comfortably. Most of us prefer life here to living in West Germany where the regime hypocritically tries to whitewash the new anti-Semitism by paying lavish sums to the victims of the last wave."

When I pointed out that the 1960 epidemic of swastika smearings, touched off in Cologne, had also spread to East Germany where a number of cemeteries were desecrated, Ringer replied: "Of course there is still a faint residue of racism and anti-Semitism, but it is punished severely by the government. I'll admit there may be some fellow travelers who merely switched party emblems. Yesterday they were Nazis, today they are good Communists and tomorrow, if some other party were to come along, they'd join that too. But they don't really interest us as much as the genuine murderers and initiators of the Nazi persecution such as President Lübke, Globke, Oberländer, and the others who continue to exercise great influence in Bonn. They're the ones who poison the atmosphere, not the occasional Nazi-turned Communist who runs a collective farm in the GDR."

And how did he reconcile his views with the GDR's attitude toward Israel?

"Of course our government's relationship with Israel is somewhat painful for us," said Ringer. "Most of us have many relatives and friends there. But we also have many relatives and friends in the United States and the relationship of the U.S. toward the GDR is just as painful for us. After all, this is a socialist state here and Israel is still capitalist. This makes a harmonious relationship difficult. We must be realistic and support the policies of our government. At least it is not as hypocritical as West Germany's which supplied military equipment to Israel. Have you ever heard of anything more disgusting than the Krupps and Flicks sending arms to the people they were only ready to kill a few years ago?"

Our conversation, like all discussions in the GDR, dragged on for several hours and dusk began to invade the room and blur the view of the street on which, as a child, I spent many hours.

5] Mechanized potato harvesting has enabled GDR to increase crop from year
year. (Credit: Zentralbild)

[27] Author Manfred Bieler. (Credit: Roger Melis)

[28] Poet and balladeer Wolf Biermann. (Credit: Roger Melis)

[29] Professor Robert Havemann. (Credit: Roger Melis)

30] Helene Weigel (left) and Stefan
isewski in a performance of "Frau
linz." (Credit: Zentralbild)

[31] East and West German border near Moelln. Tourists and West Germa border guards looking across barbed wire fencing into East Germany. Poster right says: "At other side is Germany, too." Tower in background is used by Ea German guards. (Credit: Laurinpress)

[32] Rabbi Odön Singer addressing Jewish community in East Berlin synagogu (Credit: Zentralbild)

"You know," said Ringer, "I could never live in West Germany. The people who are in positions of power in *our state* were all active anti-fascists and most of them suffered under the Nazis like we did." He emphasized the words *our state* and continued: "There is almost no one here who would trade socialism for capitalism. We live well, we are proud of our achievements—everyone. Jews and non-Jews." I believed him and said goodbye.

Though Jews in East Germany have been decimated to the proportions of a sect by Hitler's persecution and in part by the GDR's own purges, a surprisingly large number remain active in public life.

One—Norden—is a member of the fifteen-man Politburo and one of the most influential and powerful men in East Germany today.

Alexander Abusch, as a deputy premier, plays an influential role in East German educational and cultural affairs. As chairman of the Broadcasting Council, Gerhart Eisler, until his death in March, 1968, was in effect czar of all radio and television programing. As director of the party's Karl Marx Academy, Hanna Wolf is in charge of training all new apparatchiks. Deba Wieland, born in Moscow of German-Jewish parents, is managing director and editor-in-chief of ADN, the official East German press agency. Friedrich Kaul, the GDR's star lawyer, often seen in West German war crimes trials as the representative of private plaintiffs who have survived the death camps, is also Jewish.

A number of prominent Jews, most of them postwar returnees from exile in the U.S.A., USSR, and Israel, play influential roles in the arts. Among them are Hanns Eisler, who died in 1962, composer Max Michailov, artists Lea Grundig and Herbert Sandberg. And until they fled to the West a number of years ago, the GDR could claim as its own two of the world's most illustrious Jewish Marxist philosopher-sociologists: Ernst Bloch and Alfred Kantorowicz.

Most of the Jews in East German public life do not identify themselves as such. Men like Norden, Abusch, and Kaul, women such as Hanna Wolf and Deba Wieland have been doctrinaire

Communists for so long they prefer to think of themselves as atheists, not Jews.

But it is ironic, and in a larger sense tragic, that for all their allegiance to their cause, their Jewish heritage often stands in the way. No matter how long and ardently they may have proved their loyalty to Communism and Ulbricht, they are still viewed with distrust.

Notwithstanding Erich Honecker's pre-eminence, Albert Norden is one of three men considered to have a chance of succeeding Ulbricht to the first secretaryship of the SED. But it is unlikely he will ever win that power struggle. As the comrades on the Politburo reportedly told Norden once: "Albert, first of all you are too intellectual for that job. Secondly, you don't know a thing about economics. Besides, you're a Jew."

CHAPTER XIII

The Proprietors of Tomorrow

"Never before," says the preamble to the GDR's Youth Law, "has a young German generation been enjoined with as inspiring and responsible a mission. It is youth's honorable task to multiply the riches of our people, to enhance the reputation of our state, to raise the productivity and quality of labor, to master scientific and technological progress, to defend peace and socialist achievements. For no other generation have these words of Goethe been more applicable: 'You must swim or sink, you must rule and win or serve and lose, triumph or suffer, a hammer or an anvil be.' The new socialist age demands of youth more daring acts of courage and a greater pioneering spirit than the settling of the American West. Achieve this, young Germans, and you will attain greater real freedoms than German youth has ever had."

And as Walter Ulbricht once put it: "You young people have followed a different path toward socialism than we of the older generation. Most of us took the long hard road of class struggle. We, the sons of the German proletariat, were born to battle and have fulfilled our duty to our heritage. You, the youth of today, have been born into a socialist society made by your fathers and will now have to learn the principles upon which it functions, the goals toward which it aspires. It is not as easy as it sounds. On you falls the obligation to secure our victory and to continue the battle for a durable peace in Germany. During the waning decades of this century, you will be the masters of this house. Learn now to manage and care for it so that it will be an even better structure."

These are exhortations that speak both confidence and concern, that reveal both the aspirations and the trepidations of

East Germany's rulers who now glance with some bewilderment and apprehension upon the progeny of their revolution. It is a youth confident of socialism's achievements and future, secure in the use of technology, but disdainful of doctrine and impatient with the ideologues who wish to substitute dogma for pragmatism.

East Germany has a generation problem of monumental proportions. The SED hierarchs despair that the "proprietors of tomorrow behave as if the house *already* belonged to them." They lament, as did one Eisenhüttenstadt father and party functionary, that "our kids are apathetic, too materialistic and have no ideals whatsoever." The functionaries have discovered that the postulates of Marxism-Leninism do not automatically build bridges between the generations and the dialogue between the two is often contrived and devoid of meaning. The regime encourages youth to "independent thought and self confidence," but recoils with horror when it runs, instead, to what the dogmatists call "skepticism." Born in an era of class struggle and an age of social rebellion, East Germany's leaders fret that their youth takes Communism's achievements for granted. The Communists are beginning to have doubts about this first generation they have raised—but it is primarily because they attempt to interpret it in terms of doctrine. The leadership searches for ways to sustain an artificial spirit of perpetual revolution as a panacea for youthful complacency in a period of mounting prosperity. The effort not only lacks skill and circumspection but it is predicated on a false assessment of the attitude of East German youth.

Young East Germans abhor the rote phraseology of their elders. They are repelled by a dogma rooted in a nineteenth-century world. To surmise from this—as do many Western observers as well as many high priests of Marxism—that East Germany's youth is disenchanted with Communism or disloyal, would be incorrect. It is just that their concept of Communism, their interpretation of the nature of socialist society, differs so radically from that of their elders. It is the conflict between pragmatists and dogmatists brought into especially sharp focus. To the dismay of the apparatchiks, East Germany's teens emulate Western fads and slang. But to the even greater dismay of West Germans, these youngsters will fiercely defend what they have come to know as "our socialist way of life." Young East Germans cannot understand the language of their elders, for it is the tongue of a class warfare they never experienced. They are fluent in a new mother tongue: a dialect of scientific and technological terms. To them Communism is no longer an ideology one talks about, but a way of life. It has become as second nature to them as capitalism is to youth in the West. They are skeptical—of both Eastern and Western dogmas—but theirs is a skepticism nourished by a technological revolution. East Germany is a country attuned to youth, a land where suffrage begins at eighteen, where plant managers are in their twenties and the heads of industrial trusts in their thirties. East Germany's young are impatient: for power and with the shibboleths of yesteryear.

Young East Germans are the product of the GDR's *most* revolutionary development: a new educational system that has brought to the GDR a wealth and equality of opportunity unparalleled in Germany history. In twenty years the regime has successfully cleansed the school system of all the cobwebs of retardation, authoritarianism, reaction and class distinction. It is rare for any institution in the GDR to elicit even grudging acknowledgement from West Germany, but its schools have won almost unqualified admiration. Economically, East Germany remains a decade behind the Federal Republic. Pedagogically, it is several decades ahead.

To understand the significance of this revolution one must take a quick glance at education in the Federal Republic where a system, initially introduced in the mid-nineteenth century still prevails. The vast majority—nearly 70 percent—of West German children attend so-called *Volksschulen*, an eight-grade primary system which churns out graduates at age fourteen, after which they begin three-year apprenticeships to qualify for blue collar and inferior white collar jobs. Since 1962, West Germany has been experimenting with a nine-year-*Volksschule* program which will not become universal, however, until 1970. Even then, by nature of its curriculum, it is destined to remain an inferior type of school. The *Volksschulen* teach neither higher mathematics, physics nor chemistry. Foreign languages—on a voluntary basis—were not taught until 1964. *Volksschule* graduates are automatically barred from the middle- and upper-level civil service, the officer corps, most managerial and executive jobs and, of course, the professions. *Volksschule* graduates cannot enter universities or colleges, unless they take the long, arduous road of adult education to obtain an *Abitur*, a high school certificate.

The remaining 30 percent of West German children—in theory, the intellectually gifted, all too often in practice, the privileged sons and daughters of the upper and upper-middle classes—attend what is almost equivalent to or better than American high school. Half—about 14 percent—go to so-called *Middle Schools* to which they transfer from *Volksschule* at age eleven, from which they graduate with a diploma at sixteen, after completion of the tenth grade. Though these youths are also barred from universities and colleges, the officers' corps, and senior civil service positions, they have a fighting chance for managerial and executive jobs as well as medium-level government and civil service posts. Only the élite—17 percent—attend secondary schools, from which they graduate, after completion of the thirteenth grade, at age nineteen. Called the *Gymnasium* (or *Oberrealschule* when the curriculum is more modern and inclined toward the sciences), it is what made German education famous and its standards are so high that American universities automatically credit its graduates with the equivalent of two years of college education. An *Abitur* —or *Gymnasium* certificate—is prerequisite for university education, ergo for the professions, for all top managerial positions, for commissions in the military and for the senior civil service. Notwithstanding its high standards, however, the *Gymnasium* remains a redoubt of social and political conservatism—if not reaction—and it is largely a preserve of the moneyed and educated élite. When it was instituted by Wilhelm von Humboldt, Prussia's minister of education in the early nineteenth century, it was famed as a landmark of pedagogic progress. Today, when a solid education is recognized not only as a right but a *necessity* for *all* men, the *Gymnasium*'s underlying philosophy—a school for the privileged and gifted—makes it an anachronism.

Because of the *Gymnasium's* high scholastic standards and its crucial role as a prerequisite for college entrance, it acts as a natural filter to bar the overwhelming majority of West Germans from a university education. Seventeen percent of West German children enter the *Gymnasium* system, but only 7 percent graduate and less than 4 percent go on to college or the university.

The effect of all this, according to Dr. Hildegard Hamm-Bruecher, one of West Germany's leading experts on education, is that the Federal Republic has become an educational Appalachia. Formal schooling for the majority of citizens is shorter than in any industrialized country—East or West—and shorter than in many of the underdeveloped countries. Proportionately only half as many West Germans have a tenth-grade education as Norwegians, Dutchmen, Swedes, Frenchmen, or Belgians. The Federal Republic spends half as much—proportionately—on education as Japan, the U.S.A., Finland, or Czechoslovakia, less than most West or East European countries and only a fraction more than such educational hinterlands as Turkey, Portugal, Kenya, or Ghana.

Both Germanys entered the postwar period with the same system of education. West Germany's remained essentially unchanged. What transpired in the GDR, however, is nothing less than a pedagogic explosion which once prompted Hamburg's influential weekly *Die Zeit* to comment that "it is inconceivable the two school systems ever had a common origin."

Whereas only 30 percent of West German youths receive ten or more years of schooling, in the GDR this group represents more than 70 percent. Only 4.3 percent of West German youths go on to college. In the GDR it is already 15 percent and Ulbricht has promised that it will be 25 percent by 1970. The number of East German universities and colleges has increased from six, at the end of the war, to forty-four in 1967 with another thousand specialized institutes, including 212 technical schools of higher learning. The total number of university and college students in East Germany in 1967 was 110,000 plus 129,000 in technical schools, compared to a total of 288,000 in West Germany whose population is 3.5 times larger.

More than 85 percent of the East German college students receive state scholarships. In comparison, 56.2 percent of West German students are supported by their parents, 1.5 percent by their spouses, only 23 percent by scholarships and the rest either work for their education or have other sources of income. Over 70 percent of the East German university students are the sons and daughters of blue- and white-collar workers or farmers, compared to only 8 percent in West Germany where children of upper or upper-middle class parents account for 80 percent of the total enrollment.

All East German pupils start to learn a foreign language—Russian—in the fifth grade and may take a second language as an elective—usually English—in the eighth grade. Even eighth graders have had elementary math and by the tenth grade all pupils have had at least one year of basic physics, chemistry and biology.

In the GDR the ratio of pupils per teacher is 20. In the Federal Republic it is 30. At latest count, more than 230,000 West German children—4 percent—still attended one-room village schools. Another 480,000—approximately 9 percent—went to two-room country schools. Though the GDR had a far higher proportion of one-room schools in 1945 (25 percent of its entire school system) the last little red schoolhouse shut down in 1960 and one has to travel hundreds of kilometers to find a two-room school.

At the root of this education explosion is one of socialism's oldest maxims: Knowledge is Power. That was the slogan of the nineteenth-century workers' education societies from which both German socialism and Communism originated. It was a principle to which the SED—an amalgamation, after all, of both Communist and Social Democrats—paid special attention when it set out to reform education in the 1940s and 1950s. That reform had three distinct goals: to raise the general level of education, to eradicate all class and social distinctions, and to equip all children with both theoretical and practical knowledge.

The traditional *Volksschule*, an inferior institution with the onus of being a school for the lower classes, was abolished and replaced by a unified ten-year polytechnical school—the keystone of East German education—which is attended by nearly 60 percent of all children. It differs from the West German *Volksschule* not only in duration or scholastic standards, but in the emphasis on shop and manual arts training which is mandatory for all pupils and affords them a rudimentary knowledge of principal trades. Polytechnical instruction begins in kindergarten, even for the three- to six-year-olds. By the time they enter first grade, pupils are taught handicrafts, the use of tools and how to work with paper, leather, plastics and metals. In the sixth to eighth grades all pupils—boys and girls—learn mechanical drawing. Ninth- and tenth-graders attend classes in nearby industrial plants, for three hours of polytechnical training each week and are paid a nominal salary of 40 to 50 marks per month. Moreover, polytechnical instruction is equivalent to two years of apprentice training so that after graduation, at age sixteen, most youths need spend only one additional year as apprentices before qualifying as journeymen or skilled workers.

The majority of graduates from the ten-year school become workers, though their diplomas entitle them to admission, at age eighteen, to advanced technical institutes whose three-year courses in fields ranging from library management to nursing, from agricultural sciences to mechanical engineering, are equal to an American junior college education. Graduates from a technical institute moreover, are eligible for college or university entrance. Thus, in theory at least, all East German youngsters are automatically entitled to higher education.

For the intellectually inferior, approximately 29 percent of the youths, schooling stops with the eighth grade, at age fourteen, after which they enter three-year apprentice training programs.

The intellectual upper crust—13 percent—receives twelve instead of ten years of schooling and upon graduation is immediately eligible for university or college admission. The twelve-year system requires two languages—Russian and English—with Latin or French (and under certain circumstances, even Greek) as electives. Until autumn of 1966, the twelve-year program also included specialized polytechnical training so that youths graduated not only with secondary-school certificates but journeyman's papers. This principle was abandoned, however, as Education Minister Margot Honecker explained, because it had proven impractical. "Polytechnical training in the eleventh and twelfth grades," she told the Central Committee, "took too much time away from other subjects. Moreover, since nearly all graduates of the twelve-year school continue with university or college and enter professions, it seemed superfluous. Very few of these youngsters ever work in industry or the trades where their journeyman patents might be of use to them."

The most distinguishing feature of education in the GDR is the egalitarian philosophy that underlies it. Though patterned on the Soviet Union's program, the East German school system has much in common with education in the United States. As such, it represents a radical departure from prewar German views or the system still rigidly enforced in the Federal Republic.

The distinction is not just in the number of years which the program requires pupils to complete, but in its innate classlessness. For at least ten years all East German youngsters attend the same kind of school—regardless of their social backgrounds, abilities or ultimate adult ambitions. Their paths do not divide until after the tenth grade. In West Germany this division—into three highly stratified levels, each marked by class distinctions—takes place after only four years of elementary school because both the *Gymnasien* and the *Middle Schools* begin with the fifth grade. The division in West Germany is a physical one as well, for the three types of schools are located on separate grounds and in different buildings. Transfer at a later time is virtually impossible.

Of almost equal significance is the role which the school itself plays as a community institution and the attitude of parents toward teachers. By tradition, Germany's pedagogues have been civil servants who enjoy all the emoluments and the authority of officialdom. Appointed for life, they are—like judges, public prosecutors, government clerks, university professors, letter carriers, policemen and building inspectors—part of a unique establishment which for centuries has been identified in the public mind with the power of the state. Teachers are not addressed by name, but by title and grade such as *Herr Lehrer* (Mr. Teacher), *Herr*

Oberlehrer (Mr. Senior Teacher), *Herr Studienrat* (Mr. Assistant Master), *Herr Oberstudienrat* (Mr. Master), *Herr Oberstudiendirektor* (Mr. Headmaster). At least until the fall of the Third Reich and in West Germany, in all too many cases, to this day, teachers acted not like educators but like the extended arm of the state. Under the circumstances, parents—especially the poor and uneducated—were often as apprehensive of the teachers as their children. PTAs did not make their debut in West Germany until the American occupation troops arrived and are regarded more as a curiosity than a viable force in education of children. As an institution of the state, which it remains in both Germanys, the school never assumed the role it has in the U.S.: a community institution supported by taxes. It continues to be instead, a forbidding structure, a symbol more of authority than education. Parents rarely visited school voluntarily, usually only on specific request of the principal or headmaster—when little Hansel or Gretel were in trouble. This attitude toward teachers and schools has hardly changed in West Germany. In the GDR, however, it has undergone a remarkable transformation.

One reason may be that hundreds of new schools have been built with voluntary labor, making them genuine community projects. Moreover, parents have monthly visitation rights. "My husband or I go to the school once every thirty days and sit in on classes as most of the parents do," one Dresden mother told me. "You'll usually find a parent sitting in some class each day, listening to instruction and watching the children at work." Teachers take this in stride and one Rostock educator once told me, "It gives us excellent rapport with the parents." Furthermore East German teachers are not civil servants but salaried employees of the municipalities or counties in which they work. The result is a new kind of relationship between teachers and parents. The awe and respect have vanished, though in 1964, such titles as *Oberlehrer, Studienrat,* and *Oberstudienrat,* were reintroduced as rewards for passing certain state qualification tests. Most East Germans are quite sensitive to criticism on this move and one Eisenhüttenstadt high school teacher told me, a note of resignation in her voice, "I suppose we did that because it suits the

German mentality." But the titles, she rushed to assure me, are used "only for payment purposes." Children address teachers only by name, not title.

For all the admirable progress the GDR has made in providing youngsters with a better education in improved surroundings, it has also turned the three Rs into tools of propaganda and ideological indoctrination. Social science and civics courses openly seek to imbue youngsters with a "socialist awareness and view of life." Moreover, the SED's two youth organizations—the FDJ and the Pioneers—are represented at all schools and membership in their chapters, while not mandatory, is certainly universal. Less obvious, though no less prevalent or intense, is the propaganda and ideological instruction in nearly every other subject.

Textbooks for second- and third-year English students, for example, besides teaching grammar and vocabulary, are thinly disguised propaganda tracts.

As they learn the language, East German youngsters automatically assimilate a Marxist view of English life. Reading lessons and exercises in the textbooks depict an England which is neither merry nor old but caught up in the throes of social and class struggle. Pupils are exposed to a country where workers must fear daily for their jobs, the peasants are oppressed by evil land owners, unscrupulous capitalists spend all their time suppressing strikes and the British Communist Party is the only hope for proletarian salvation.

Lesson Two in *Our English Friends* for eighth-graders, for example, deals exclusively with a London busmen's strike and includes the following reading exercise:

> "Most of the people in the [subway] coach are reading newspapers. Pat looks at the headlines. Suddenly he stops and sits up. What does that paper say?
>
> 'No Support for Busmen on Strike!'
>
> "Oh, those papers. Pat feels angry. No support? . . . Where does the strike pay come from? Do not all the unions send some money to help the busmen? No support, indeed!

"Pat looks around again. There is another headline: 'Support the Busmen!'

"That's good. It is the headline of the 'Daily Worker'. The Inwoods have it at home.

"Pat is still angry but he feels better now. He smiles at the man with the 'Daily Worker' and the man smiles back."

Another lesson explains why the stands on Petticoat Lane and the other East End streets are open for business on Sundays. It is, says the book, a tradition that stems from the nineteenth-century when the workers were not organized and couldn't defend themselves. "So the employers didn't pay them until they had got the last bit of work out of them on Saturday afternoons. Every week then there was the same tragedy in workers' homes. Wives were always waiting for the money, often standing at the factory gates. But by the time the husbands got home or left the plants," the book explains, the shops were closed. "The only way to get Sunday dinner was to buy it in the poor men's street markets which had to open on Sunday mornings." Since then, students learn, the workers have united and fought for their rights. "Now, paydays are on Friday and most people do their shopping Saturdays, but the old street markets still go on."

Lesson Twelve tells of a trip to London Airport where "the Ellis family" has gone to watch planes take off and land. Later, just as they have arrived back at their front door, a jet screams overhead. "That's an American B-52, a jet bomber that carries H-bombs around," Mr. Ellis says. "I just hate them. If one of them crashed here . . ."

In *Our English Friends* for ninth-graders, Lesson One consists of an exchange of pen pal letters between a boy by the name of Hans in East Germany and a youth by the name of Pat in London. Pat writes Hans: "Some time ago I saw two of your films that show the terrible consequences of race prejudice even in modern times, namely *Stars* and *A Diary for Anne*. I should not have thought that such things were possible if Dad hadn't told me and if I hadn't seen the films. There are often reports about neo-fascism in Western Germany in our papers. As Dad says, people here are beginning to understand now why and how your country, the GDR, is different. Sympathies are growing. Good thing, isn't it?"

If East German school children get a distorted view of Britain while learning English, their view of the world as a whole is grossly contorted when studying history. To judge from lesson plans and textbooks, the world has had but one common thread running through the ages: the class struggle of the oppressed against exploitation. Youngsters learn little else than that the ancient civilizations—Egypt, Greece, and Rome—were oligarchies in which a privileged minority ruled over a world of slaves. If Spartacus' uprising in Rome is but a footnote in Western history books, in the GDR it gets more attention than Christianity's influence on the Roman Empire. Peasant uprisings, especially the central European ones such as Thomas Münzer's, not the Renaissance, are credited for the change from feudalism and serfdom. Modern history is seen through a filter of revolution in which, of course, the Soviet one plays a decisive role.

Sitting in on a fifth-grade history class in Dresden one day I noticed that the teacher, while telling his charges about stone age men, placed special emphasis on such phrases as, "Men differ from animals primarily in the sense that they *work*." "*Labor* was equally divided among the members of primitive tribes." "*Tools* enabled primitive man to rationalize his *production* processes." Taking a quick glance into the textbook I discovered that all phrases, sentences and paragraphs which contain such expressions as: work, labor, society, productivity, rationalization of production, toolmaking, industry, agriculture, property, common ownership, productive output, construction, over-production and surplus labor had been especially marked with a different color of ink.

Medieval and Renaissance Europe is portrayed primarily in terms of a succession of peasant uprisings against feudal lords, the growth of the Junker society and the innate greediness of the ascending mercantile class. Even American colonial history gets a little twist. That East German historians would be sure to mention the exploitation of the Indians seemed inevitable. But one history book asserts, that "the American constitution guaranteed the rule of the rich plantation owners, the merchants and the factory owners, for they alone governed the land. Salaried workers, craftsmen, not to mention the Indians and Negroes, had no right of codetermination."

Modern history depicts Hitler as the lackey of the monopolist-capitalists who put him in office, the Soviet Union as a victim of American aggression, American Negroes as near slaves of the plutocrats, West Germany as a center of neo-Nazism and militarism and, of course, East Germany as a haven of freedom, democracy, and social justice.

The result of this slanted education: a generation has already been raised which has nothing in common with West German youth, not even a common view of man's past history.

In the GDR's universities and technical schools, history, social science, and civics are taught with the same red hue, except, of course, on a higher plane. Said one West German theology student who studied three semesters at the University of Greifswald: "Like other students I was obligated to help on a farm during harvest season and signed up for mandatory courses in 'basic social studies.' This subject has remarkably little to do with Marxism. Marxist theory is at the periphery, propaganda at the center. Though the lesson plans call for instruction in the GDR's history, GDR civics, the history of the workers' movement, historical and dialectical materialism as well as political economy, the emphasis in seminars, lectures and classes is on disseminating the current views of the regime. 'Social studies' courses have become the favorite redoubts of the regime's dogmatists and it is against them that students rebel. Consequently, an effort is being made to liberalize social studies by providing more time and opportunity for confrontation with problems outside Marxism-Leninism. The ideologues object, but the regime has recognized that a critical youth may be better than one which follows blindly the slogans of the agitators."

A passing grade in "basic social studies" is a prerequisite for graduation. Students learn early that it is best to emulate enthusiasm and repeat the phraseology of the lectures—unless they want to risk a bad mark and possible expulsion from the university. "It means continual treading of a thin line," one Dresden Technical University student confided. "One lecturer once gave me a failing mark for smiling at some idiocy he was propagating. I protested to the department head who tested me again and I passed with an 'excellent.' The professor decided to split the differences between my first and second grade by giving me a C."

"Most of us learn this ballyhoo by heart," a student in Halle told me, "and we recite just what we've been told when asked. But that doesn't mean we also believe it."

Political indoctrination and a certain intellectual dishonesty, however, are practically the only price young East Germans must pay for a university or college education. Tuition is free, as are books and supplies, and the great majority—85 percent—of all students receive scholarships on which they can live.

One of the most significant aspects of education in the GDR is the social readjustment of higher learning from a pre-eminence of bourgeois to proletarian youths. Until a few years ago this was achieved by draconian means. The sons and daughters of the bourgeoisie were barred from university education. They were denied admission or required to spend several years working in factories or on farms before becoming eligible. As a result thousands of intellectuals and professionals, notably physicians and professors, fled westward where they could be sure of providing their children with a college education. Since 1963 the criterion of parentage is no longer applied, although preferential treatment is still given to workers' children, to applicants who have demonstrated their "solidarity with the proletariat" by working in industry or agriculture and to those who have served their minimum two years military duty.

Though membership in the FDJ is not a prerequisite for college entrance, "activists" in the youth association are more likely to be accepted—when space is limited—than those who have not engaged in "social activities." Before admission, youths must not only pass entrance examinations but scrutiny by boards of faculty representatives, officials of the Communist trade and industrial unions, and members of the university's FDJ secretariat. Despite these stringent requirements most applicants are now admitted and proportionately East Germany's university enrollment is 50 percent higher than West Germany's: sixty-seven students per 10,000 population compared to the Federal Republic's forty-four.

On the other hand, East German students are not entirely free in their choice of majors. What they study depends only in part on their personal wishes and interests. Society's needs play a role, too. Students are part of the plan—just like potatoes, milk, machine tools, electric power or chemicals—and the regime attempts to direct their studies in accordance with economic requirements. At present philologists, lawyers, artists, historians and sociologists are not in great demand: scientists and engineers, economists and managers are.

Despite twenty years of Communist supremacy over faculties, East German colleges are surprisingly bourgeois in their outlook. Most of the professors were educated in the prewar period and belong to that intellectual élite of the upper-middle class which Germans call *Akademiker*. Their influence has helped to make university students—in contrast to most other young East Germans—some of the regime's most uncompromising critics. Some observers, such as Dr. Hans Apel, estimate that only 25 percent of the GDR's students can be considered enthusiastic and active supporters. He found that half of them were outspokenly opposed, the remaining 25 percent apolitical or apathetic.

Opposition appears most pronounced among medical students in general, those concentrated in the Halle area in particular. Apel suggests this may be due to the drab appearance of Halle itself—a city unmatched for smog, soot, and triste architecture. Moreover, many medical students are the children of physicians with bourgeois viewpoints.

But even among this group, opposition is directed less against the economic, social or political system as against its most unnerving and irritating expressions of doctrine.

A twenty-three-year-old Dresden management student told me: "I get a 190 mark basic scholarship as well as an 80 mark scholarship premium. I am a Marxist and consider myself an unqualified supporter of our government and social system. But that doesn't mean I don't criticize or that I approve of all the dogma they try to cram down our throats. We'd be a lot further along with a lot less dogmatism. We have forced some of our best thinkers and economic talents to flee to the West by putting incompetent functionaries in front of their noses."

It is the regimentation and politicizing of life which sours many youths. "Unless you're politically active you have no opportunities at all," said one Dresden engineering student. "I can't study what I want to, but what the plan says I have to study. And when I've graduated I have no real freedom in choosing my future."

"Basically," a Leipzig medical student told me, "we're just anti. We're anti-Communist, anti-Capitalist, anti-Fascist. We're against this system here because we can't speak freely and are subjected to too much ideology and dogmatism. But don't think that we're for the West German way of life. That's not the kind of life for us either. People there are too materialistic, too superficial."

As the SED's September 1963 "youth communiqué" admitted, "Today's youth takes for granted many of the achievements which are the product of decades of struggle because today's young generation never had an opportunity to participate in the battle against capitalist exploitation. This is why the citizens of the GDR who waged that battle should never tire of explaining the struggle to young people."

Indeed, the party spares no effort and pinches no pfennigs trying to do just that. It spends untold billions on education, youth centers, recreation, entertainment activities, sports and making what it considers good citizens of the new generation. Youth is not only furthered but respected as in few other countries and given extraordinary responsibilities and authority.

Like all Communist—and one might add, authoritarian—regimes, the GDR is lavish in its support of sports and athletes, and misses no opportunity to point with pride at their accomplishments. More than 1,800,000 young East Germans are members of sports clubs and amateur athletic organizations and the government spends over 90,000,000 marks ($22,500,000) annually to further organized athletics, build gymnasiums, swimming pools, stadiums and other facilities. Since 1949 the GDR has won 145 world championships, 47 European championships, and in the last three Olympic games it walked off triumphantly with 52 gold, silver, and bronze medals—as good an explanation as any why the GDR has refused to enter the 1968 games as part of an all-German team and insisted instead on separate representation.

At its *best*, the SED will do everything for the new generation. Its vistas of opportunity know no horizons. The 1964 youth law, for example, specifies that every factory and collective farm council should have at least one person under twenty-one among its members. It is the rule, not the exception, for men and women in their late twenties and early thirties to be in influential managerial positions. The GDR probably has more youthful public officials than any other civilized country. Forty of the Volkskammer's five hundred members are between twenty-one and twenty-five and another twenty-five are between twenty-six and thirty. Of 2829 members of district councils and parliaments, 510 are under thirty years of age.

But at its *worst*, the regime is completely incompetent to understand, not to mention tolerate, youth's natural inclination to rebel. Because it is a regime that teaches positivism and believes the new society it is creating should also produce new men, it reacts with neurotic frenzy to rebelliousness of the most harmless sort. It equates the rebellion of the young with currents of opposition, views it as a counterrevolutionary revisionist threat and responds to it with all the repressive force of a totalitarian state. This finds its ultimate and most histrionic expression in the reaction to *Gammlertum* and beat music.

Gammler is the German word for those pseudo-intellectuals and pseudo-beatniks whose way-out cult of nihilism, passive resistance and hoboing took Europe by storm in the mid-1960s. If male, they are readily identifiable by their female-length tresses, if female by their penchant for dirty blue jeans and leather jackets. They have an aversion to soap, water and society, are addicted to Beatle music and bell-bottomed trousers and delight in shocking their elders. Indeed, society is thoroughly shocked, though these rebels without a cause are in essence, completely harmless. Idleness is a characteristic attributed to all of them though only real *Gammler* are shirkers. The others are "normal" youngsters who are mistaken for *Gammler* because they try to emulate them in dress, mannerisms, and behavior.

Gammlertum is a phenomenon peculiar to both Germanys. In West Berlin one of their favorite haunts is in front of the Kaiser Wilhelm Memorial church at the end of Kurfürstendamm. In East Berlin they congregate around the new Linden Corso Café at the corner of Friedrichstrasse and Unter den Linden and in front of the Lichtenberg railway station. In both Germanys, too, they are erroneously identified with fans of Beatle music—largely because long mop-like hair has become a symbol of *Gammlertum* —though genuine *Gammler* play folk instead of electric guitars and only their imitators stomp and gyrate to the Liverpool sound. Thus, *Gammler* were unjustly blamed in the summer of 1965 when West Berlin beat fans, twisting to the tune of the Rolling Stones, made a shambles of the Waldbühne auditorium and East Berlin teenagers, contorting to similar music, wrecked dozens of youth clubs. In the West they are equated with juvenile delinquents, in the East with capitalist-influenced enemies of the state. In both Germanys, society is incensed by them. None less than ex-Chancellor Ludwig Erhard made the "eradication of *Gammlertum*" one of his promises to the voters during the 1965 election campaign. In the GDR the "*Gammler* scourge" was the subject of interminable Central Committee discussions.

For more than two years—from mid-1963, when the Beatles became popular, until November 1965—the SED exercised restraint and viewed the movement with equanimity. Beat groups were officially sanctioned and at the 1964 East Berlin Youth festival—one of the biggest shindigs ever staged in the GDR—dozens of rock-and-roll, beat and other hot music combos played on the streets and thousands of blue-shirted members of the FDJ danced to their rhythms. The party's only response: grandfatherly admonishments in East German papers which hardly differed from the bourgeois indignation of West German journals. Throughout 1964 and most of 1965, public anger mounted only occasionally to the point where police interfered and took action against some of these "unappetizing sounds and apparitions."

By November of 1965, however, the era of good feeling and tolerance had run its course. A campaign of repression, unabated to the present, took its place, and to this day the reasons for the shift in policy remain a source of speculation. Was it that *Gammlertum*, Beatlemania, and rowdyism had indeed rocked and rolled out of the party's control? Or was it that the SED's hardliners had at last found a pretext for expunging what they consider "demoralizing decadent capitalist" influences?

Certainly there had been some alarming excesses which—though no worse than similar outbursts in Western countries—must have had an especially traumatic effect on strait-laced East Germany. Some of the incidents had nothing to do with *Gammlerism* or Beatlemania, such as the bare-breasted march of Dresden co-eds during the 1965 harvest or a demonstration by university boys singing the Nazi Horst Wessel song. From January to late July a gang of twenty-five long-haired Halle youths, aged fourteen to twenty, terrorized local citizens, raped nineteen teenage girls, committed five aggravated assaults and dozens of larcenies and burglaries. In September, East Berlin youth clubs and teen centers were repeatedly vandalized during performances of beat combos. On October 7, the anniversary day of the GDR's statehood, some five hundred mop-haired youngsters gathered in front of East Berlin's Berolina Hotel for a shouting countdown of teenage nihilism. "Ten, nine, eight, seven, six, five, four, three, two, one shit!" they yelled again and again until billy-club-wielding Vopos dispersed the mob and arrested its leaders. On October 30, during a game between the East German and Austrian all-star soccer teams in Berlin's Walter Ulbricht Stadium, several hundred youths demonstrated noisily for "Freedom of music and hair styles." On November 7, the forty-eighth anniversary of the Russian revolution, *Gammler* and Beatle types rioted in East Berlin, Halle and in Leipzig.

The regime responded with massive retaliation. Police in all major cities rounded up the long-haired ones, booked them on charges of violating passport laws because they did not resemble the photographs in their identity cards. At precinct stations, they were given a choice of fines, jail or a trip to adjacent rooms where barbers waited for them.

The old rule that dance bands must not play more than 40 percent Western music was rigidly enforced. A new ordinance requiring all amateur bands and combos to audition for party commissions and obtain public performance licenses was enacted. Beatle and popular Western music became the sound of the devil incarnate and a relentless drive to suppress it got underway.

Some long-time observers of East German affairs believe the anti-beat campaign is but a reflection of the fractional disputes between "liberals" and dogmatists which have been raging in the SED for some time. Reginald Rudorf, former Radio GDR jazz director, suspects the heavy hand of Fröhlich, the Leipzig party boss, behind the crackdowns of 1965. To Fröhlich the cultural and intellectual "libertinage" which swept the GDR after the Berlin Wall must have been anathema. When it reached extreme proportions in the form of teenage riots, it has been suggested, Fröhlich saw the chance to strike back with the support of most of the party. On October 20, 1965, his personal mouthpiece, the *Leipziger Volkszeitung*, published a full-page attack on jazz, beat, pop fans, and *Gammler* who were accused of everything from moral depravity to enmity toward the state. Though there is no conclusive evidence, the possibility cannot be ruled out that Fröhlich, borrowing from his earlier bag of tricks, hired the rowdies who, dressed as Beatle fans and *Gammler*, rampaged through Leipzig on November 7. It was, at any rate, this riot which triggered the latest anti-pop drive and campaign against teenage excess.

Gammler, who hold on to their street corners tenaciously, are publicly pilloried as outsiders of society. And the more persistent they are the more erratic the public's and the regime's reaction. One man, writing in *Junge Welt*, said: "We won't allow a bunch of jerks to walk around like this. Our freedom is the right to straighten them out, to make them productive members of society." One East Berlin worker told me angrily: "Most people act indignant about their appearance but all they do is *hope* they'll reform. Hoping isn't enough. Every citizen should take action against these young snotnoses."

This confrontation between the Ulbricht regime and its youth puts into glaring focus East Germany's generation gap. The GDR's rulers are engaged in making a revolution of consciousness. One of its principal tenets is social conformity. Even worse, the regime is hampered by an innate doctrinaire mentality which is predestined to clash head-on with the natural skepticism and inquisitiveness of youth. Moreover, Ulbricht and his minions are trying to inspire the young postwar generation with the ideals which were important for their elders in the 1920s and 1930s but have little applicability to life in the prosperous, technologically advanced GDR of the 1960s. Above all, the SED's ideologues and functionaries seem incapable of understanding that even under socialism it is youth's natural inclination to rebel.

This may be the chief reason why membership in the FDJ, an organization predicated on conformity, has dwindled steadily since 1959. Enrollment figures are no longer published, though it is estimated at 1,500,000 members compared to 1,700,000 eight years ago.

To see in the intractability of East German youth an anti-Communist current that could eventually topple the SED's regime is not only a misleading but potentially dangerous calculation. The symptoms of defiance are but the mutinous spirit of adolescence which eventually yields to the conventionality that comes with marriage, a step which young East Germans, incidentally, take earlier than most Europeans (average age for grooms is twenty-four, for brides twenty-three). When East German youth defies anything more than life itself, then it is at the most the colorless, catechistic ideological restrictions imposed by the regime, not the system itself. Twenty years of propaganda, education and conscious, as well as subconscious, influence have inculcated young East Germans with an unshakable confidence in Communism as a way of life.

If they speak and think about reunification with West Germany at all it is in the sense of a West Germany which is also socialist or Communist. Most young people in the GDR, for all their critical stance, tend to be flatly against any restoration of private ownership. Though almost to a man they would like more personal freedom, be subjected to less propaganda and dogmatic indoctrination. If, because of their general isolation from the mainstream of international thought and the more radical currents of ideas in the Soviet bloc, they have any concept of their future social order then they point to Yugoslavia as the kind of society which is their ideal.

However, as long as that remains a dream instead of a possibility, young East Germans concentrate on making the best of their country and its economy. And youth's contribution is enormous. More than 20 percent of all new patents and processes in the GDR are the work of so-called *"Meister von Morgen"* ("Mastercraftsmen of Tomorrow"), youngsters, some only apprentices, under twenty-one years of age. The GDR's 12,000 "youth brigades," teams of apprentices and teenagers, are more than just propaganda. Hundreds of young people actually built an entire electric power plant in Trattendorf, just as they did the runways at Schönefeld airport in East Berlin.

As Ulbricht himself once admitted, "I do not hold the view that the youth of today has an easy time of it. On the contrary, we demand more of our young people than ever before." The GDR's new generation is proud of its achievements, just as it is keenly aware that from its midst will come not only the captains of tomorrow's industry but the leaders of tomorrow's state.

PART FIVE

FIRE
AND
WATER

CHAPTER XIV

The Chimera of Reunification

According to one of the SED's newest political maxims, "Everything links us with our socialist fatherland, nothing with imperialist West Germany." Not even language. The day is not far off, predicts a Humboldt University language professor, when shop windows will display signs reading "East German and West German spoken here." He did not mean it in jest. Already authoritative philologists, such as Bonn University's Dr. Hugo Moser, have examined the strange phenomenon of East-speak West-speak. They reported with alarm that, thanks to the popularity of Americanisms in the West and the influx of Communist gobbledegook in the East, language in the two Germanys is drifting apart. In fact, it is already so dissimilar that Moser needed a computer to find its common roots. He and a team of programers analyzed two years of *Neues Deutschland* and compared its terminology with West Germany's *Bild Zeitung, Die Welt* and the *Frankfurter Allgemeine* to compile a German-German glossary. Grammarians and purists who swear by the Duden—a German Webster's— warn that already its eastern and western editions contain different definitions for the same words and that many expressions peculiar to one Germany are not listed in the other's dictionary.

East-speak West-speak is but one of the symptoms of the creeping divergence of the two Germanys from their common origins and interests. The process appears irreversible. Walter Ulbricht may have been polemicizing, but he was also making an accurate assessment when he told delegates to the SED's VIIth Party Congress in April 1967: "Two separate German states have been created and they have pursued completely different paths of development. To unify them would be tantamount to combining fire and water. It is unrealistic to talk about unification now."

It is the subject of interminable debate which of those two states is the more or less righteous. Ulbricht's has for years been depicted by the West as an "*Unrechtsstaat*," an unjust, illegal state—a huge concentration camp whose small clique of autarchs maintains itself in power with the help of Soviet bayonets and tanks.

In 1965, for example, when a West Berlin court ordered that nine-year-old Angelika Kurtz, an illegitimate child, be turned over to her real mother who had moved to East Germany and married, West Germany's press flew into hysterics. "Don't let Angelika go to the concentration camp," screamed the mass-circulation *Bild Zeitung.* Citizens offered to hide the child and one man said, "It is inconceivable that a nine-year-old girl should be sentenced to a life of imprisonment in the East German penitentiary." Yet Ulbricht describes his GDR as a "moral state" in which the forces of "German militarism and imperialism that triggered two world wars" have been expunged; where, "for the first time in German history, the proletariat and the peasantry own the means of production and the land."

The West sees itself as the only legitimate Germany, as a state in which freedom, democracy, tolerance and human rights serve as the foundation for a peaceful pursuit of national destiny. To the Communists, the Federal Republic is a dangerous, scrofulous vespiary of neo-Nazism, irredentism, and revanchism where the masses are ruthlessly exploited and misled by the same avaricious elements which supported Hitler. "It is run," says Ulbricht, "by the Krupp and Thyssen empires whose only goal is the enslavement of the proletariat. Bonn's aim, supported and financed by international monopolist capitalism, is to swallow the GDR, destroy its peasants' and workers' government. That way the field will be clear for its ultimate plan: another campaign of terror and aggression against the peace-loving fraternal socialist states, especially Poland, Czechoslovakia, and the Soviet Union."

Both states assert they are the reincarnation of the good Germany, each accuses the other of being a usurper and both claim to be the keepers of the holy grail of *Deutschtum.* Both maintain that right is on their side and each repudiates ceremoniously the use of might to attain it. Only history can judge them and only the future will decide which, if not both, of the Germanys will endure. Meanwhile, one thing is irrefutable: for the present and for many years to come there are and will be two Germanys. Each day the links and the communities between them grow thinner as they drift farther apart.

To an extent this is the natural toll of time, political developments and the artificial interruption of human intercourse precipitated by the Berlin Wall and the GDR's restrictions on travel. But to a degree it is also due to the heterogeneous roots of German nationhood itself.

In both Germanys a new generation has grown to adulthood since 1945. Though it may be linked by ties of family, these become progressively meaningless unless nurtured by the free intercourse of travel. Freedom of movement has been heavily restricted since 1956 and next to impossible since 1961. Only the elderly are now permitted to leave the GDR and visit West Germany. Conversely, however, experience shows that much of the travel urge is ignited by the restrictions placed on it. If Germans could ever move freely between East and West it is more than likely that the initial travel boom would drop off sharply after a while. Evidence of this exists in Berlin. During the 1963 Christmas season, when West Berliners were given visitors' permits to the city's eastern sector for the first time since the building of the Wall, more than 1,200,000 people streamed into the East. By Easter 1966, the last time the Ulbricht regime agreed to such an arrangement, less than 800,000 West Berliners took advantage of the opportunity. As one Berliner said: "People get tired of seeing their Aunt Minna. The first pass period in 1963 was a novelty and West Berliners hurried to see relatives they would not have visited for years, with or without the Wall. Now that they've paid their obligatory call, they no longer go over."

Though West German statistics show that one-fourth of all citizens in the Federal Republic still have family ties with inhabitants of the GDR, these figures mean far less in practice than in theory. Dozens of East Germans confided to me, "Yes, I have a brother (or a sister) in West Germany but we haven't seen or written each other for years. Our interests and views are so divergent we have nothing left to say to one another." And how many West Germans are there like the middle-aged Bad Godesberger who said: "Yes I have a sister in Erfurt, but we haven't visited or corresponded for a decade. She's one of those hundred percenters."

Moreover, neither Germany makes any great effort to teach its young objectively about the other. The picture the GDR's new generation has of the Federal Republic is largely distorted by propaganda in the schools and contorted by the lopsided view of life young East Germans obtain from Western television. The Federal Republic is neither the lair of iniquity which it is made out to be in East German school books nor the gold-plated paradise which television depicts. Conversely, the view most West German youngsters have of the GDR is either colored by anti-Communist propaganda or obfuscated by a deliberate avoidance of the subject in school.

Furthermore—and this is a factor often ignored in the torrent of rhetoric about unification, national destiny and self-determination which emanates from Bonn—Germany's heterogeneous roots and short-lived era of nationhood make it susceptible to diversity. West German politicians will discourse interminably on the inherent right to unification. "There is only one Germany," chancellors from Adenauer to Kiesinger have proclaimed. Yet, unity has been a relatively recent luxury of German history. Only slightly more than one hundred years ago Bavarians and Prussians, Rhinelanders and Saxons, Hessians and Mecklenburgers, southern Catholics and northern Protestants, were at each others' throats in one vast orgy of particularism. It was not until Prussia established its hegemony over them all that a nation, in the modern sense, was finally forged in 1871. But neither the Hohenzollerns, who preached *"ein Reich,"* nor Hitler who harangued *"ein Führer, ein Volk,"* could completely plaster over the cracks of divarication or halt the currents of multipartite emotion. As recently as the 1920s Konrad Adenauer was an avowed advocate for a separate Rhineland state. To this day Bavaria jealously guards

privileges of nationhood and individuality which would put a
Texan to shame. Indeed, Bavarians have more in common with
Austrians than with Saxons, and Rhinelanders feel more oriented
toward France and the Netherlands than they do toward Brandenburg or Mecklenburg.

Postwar developments have merely widened the chasm. Not
only have two states but two social systems, economies and cultures grown on the rubble heap of the old Reich and they have
far less in common than the divergent East and West Germans
of prewar years. The exigencies of the cold war pressed both
Germanys into the service of alliances whose interests and objectives are intrinsically inimical toward one another. West Germany has been thoroughly welded into NATO and its economy
is being integrated into the West European Common Market.
East Germany is an integral element of the Warsaw treaty organization and an indispensable industrial pivot of Comecon, the
Communists' Council of Mutual Economic Assistance. To ex-
tract either Germany from its respective alliances would shake
their foundations. Reunification, if it will ever be possible, can
come only through a melding of East and West Europe's economic markets and a dissolution of the military pacts. Though
there has certainly been no dearth of discussion of such moves in
recent years, their realization seems unlikely for decades. The
fronts may soften, the polemics may subside—sooner than many
expect—but it is utopian to expect a meaningful dissolution of the
blocs within the foreseeable future.

To these currents of separatism arising from partition, both
sides have contributed artificial agitants of division. East Germany
has attempted to arrogate for itself the true lodestone of German
national heritage. In the East this has often taken on comical—if
not macabre—aspects.

Not only has the Ulbricht regime enacted a new citizenship
law which substitutes a "GDR" for the traditional "German" nationality listed on passports and official documents, but it strives
to eradicate all vestiges of a common origin. In February 1968
Ulbricht even introduced a new constitution which severs the remaining formal bonds of tradition between the two Germanys.

Radio, television and newspapermen have been instructed to use the collective term "Germany" as little as possible and speak, instead of "West Germany" (preferably with such adjectives as "decadent, neo-fascist, reactionary, militaristic, imperialistic, and revanchistic) and the "socialist German Democratic Republic" (with glowing modifiers), when referring to their own country. In February 1967 all cultural exchanges were disrupted. In the future, said East German Cultural Minister Klaus Gysi, appearances of East German artists in the West would depend on formal recognition of the GDR by Bonn. The traditional East-West economic conference, held semi-annually in Leipzig concurrent with the fair, was abolished as well. And for the first time in 1968, at the Winter Olympic Games in Grenoble, two German teams took the field.

East Germany claims for itself all that of German history and culture which was good, unilaterally burdening the Federal Republic with its seedier and bloodier eras and heroes. As Ulbricht once put it: "Sometimes one hears the lament that a highly civilized and cultured nation like Germany should and cannot be denied unity forever. But one should also never forget that Germany has two cultures and two traditions. One is the nonculture and barbaric tradition of German imperialism which expressed itself in the slaughter of millions at Auschwitz. Today it raises its ugly head in support of American aggression in Vietnam. The other culture is the progressive tradition of the German nation and its humanistic heritage, represented by the forces of the proletariat in the GDR and the humanistically inclined intelligentsia of West Germany today."

The GDR propagates the view that *it* is the true German fatherland—in a social, not a geographic concept. "Ours," said Albert Norden, "is the fatherland where the rich have been expropriated and deprived of power, where no one needs to work under inhuman conditions for a pack of exploiters. Ours is a fatherland which has nothing in common with that of Hindenburg, Krupp, Thyssen, or Eichmann."

Indeed, the GDR can legitimately claim to be the chosen or native *geographical* fatherland of many of Germany's most towering and progressive historical figures: composers Bach, Handel, Schumann, and Wagner; artists Käthe Kollwitz and, Max Beckmann; writers, poets and dramatists Goethe, Lessing, Kleist, and Novalis; statesmen and military leaders such as Yorck von Wartenburg, Alexander and Wilhelm von Humboldt, Cneisenau, and Blücher. But the thrust of the GDR's argument is that it would be the chosen fatherland of the gamut of Germany's intelligentsia down through the centuries—were they alive today.

Even Martin Luther, that most prodigal Thuringian son, has been taken into the fold. After more than two decades of hesitation the East German Communists dropped their negative ambivalence on the historical significance of Luther. For the purpose of the 450th anniversary of the Reformation, celebrated in Eisenach and Wittenberg in October 1967, he was portrayed as a German national hero, a progressive force, a forerunner of socialism, a kind of spiritual godfather of the GDR. It took some doing and a lot of ideological backtracking. No matter what Luther was to religion, politically he was one of the stanchest conservatives of his day. As Friedrich Engels wrote clearly, and Karl Marx hinted, Luther's role in the 1525 Peasants' Revolt was highly equivocal. The real hero was Thomas Münzer who supported the peasants; not Luther, who turned vehemently against them and backed the establishment. But that was discreetly forgotten for the purpose of the 1967 Reformation festival in Wittenberg and the 900th anniversary celebration of Wartburg fortress in Eisenach where Luther took refuge and translated the bible into German. "The historical events connected with this Luther festival," said Dr. Hans Seigewasser, the GDR's State Secretary for Religious Affairs, "belong to the progressive humanist tradition and the revolutionary tradition of the German people." Gerald Götting, the secretary general of the East German Christian Democratic Party, went even further by calling the battles of the Reformation "the greatest mass revolutionary movement of the German people until the Spartacus [Communist] uprising in 1918. In the first German workers' and peasants' state we have achieved what the leaders of the Reformation really aimed for."

East Germany's attitude toward the heritage of Prussia is no less opportunist. Just as in the case of Protestantism, it is fortunate enough to have the meccas of Prussianism within its borders. The heart of Berlin, its historic Prussian heart, is in the Eastern sector—on Unter den Linden, which is lined by the statues of Yorck, Blücher, and Gneisenau. The figures of the Humboldt brothers guard the entrance to the university which bears their name. And rumor has it that even the old equestrian statue of Frederick the Great will be returned, from its present location at Sans Soucis Palace in Potsdam, to its original site in the center of Unter den Linden. Under the circumstances it should come as no surprise that Ulbricht and the GDR's leaders eulogize the German wars of liberation against Napoleon as part of Communism's tradition, the revolution of 1848 as *their* spiritual heritage. And it follows naturally that Ulbricht would say: "We do not deny that under modern circumstances and aspects and in consideration of two lost wars, we have taken some of the basic elements of latter-day Bismarckian foreign policy as our own. I say Bismarck's later policies because we are against the aggressive kind of foreign policy, opposition to which led to Bismarck's dismissal by the Kaiser. West Germany is pursuing the same type of policy today."

It is all an endeavor to find some links to the German past without simultaneously accepting responsibility for Germany's darker and more sanguinary hours. Some of this effort requires agile mental and ideological hopscotch, but whatever its difficulties, the result will be the same: a widening cleavage between the two Germanys which the histrionic polemics of the propagandists on both sides of the border merely accelerate. Already German unity seems a chimera to which both regimes and both peoples give interminable lip service but in which neither any longer believes. In the West, according to a March 1967 public opinion poll, only 26 percent consider Germany's permanent division unbearable, only 18 percent would benefit personally from reunification, less than 20 percent would be willing to pay the East's price for reunification—nationalization of basic industry—and only 11 percent would even consider the possibility of permitting Soviet troops on West German soil as one of the conditions for German unity. In the East, though no opinion polls have ever been conducted—let alone publicized—the situation as far as I can judge is not different. The majority of East Germans to whom I have spoken did say they still hoped for reunification but most—including many opponents of the Ulbricht regime—flatly said they would not pay the price which the West is sure to demand: abolition of their social and economic system and a return to capitalism.

Since the creation of two German states in 1949, responsibility for the deepening rift has been almost equally divided between Bonn and East Berlin. Bonn's share lies in its pursuit of an unrealistic, shortsighted policy that mixed myths with polemics. For centuries a popular German saga held that Kaiser Barbarossa, the Hohenstauffen red beard, sat sleeping deep in Kyffhäuser Mountain, waiting for his resurrection as the nation's savior. Since World War II the German soul has been fired by a modern kind of myth: the conviction that some day, somehow, Moscow would offer Bonn the Soviet Zone on a silver platter and yank back Ulbricht just as fast as Stalin conjured him twenty-three years ago. It was a pleasant, convenient fairy tale. Easy and simple to believe, it promised reunification by sitting around and waiting. It was a faith in happy ends that required little if any political imagination or initiative. All it demanded was to point an accusing finger at the big bad Russian bear, to paint the GDR's rulers as devils incarnate, to cajole American secretaries-of-state with ritual-like regularity into placing the subject of German reunification on the agendas of international conferences, to light candles in the windows at Christmastime as symbols of national unity and to send food parcels to "our poor brothers and sisters 'over there'." As the myth fossilized into actual government policy, several miscalculations emerged. First, it presumed erroneously that the U.S. was willing and able to pursue its avowed goal of a Communist rollback and risk confrontation with the USSR. Second, it assumed incorrectly that the Soviet Union was prepared to surrender its toehold on Western Europe and sacrifice its most important economic partner—for a price or under pressure (from China, for example). Third, it presupposed that the East European countries would consent to give up their buffer state against their traditional and most feared antagonist. Fourth, it predicted that East Germany's regime and economy would grow weaker instead of stronger with time.

Steeped in these beliefs and misconceptions, Bonn conducted a policy that contained a catalogue of self-defeating central elements. Cardinal among these was the West German contention that there can be only one Germany. Its sole, legitimate representative must be the government of the Federal Republic which was freely elected, not East Berlin's which has been variously described as a Soviet satrapy, under Russian control and without public support. This supposition underlay Bonn's adamant refusal to either recognize the East German regime de facto or de jure or to deal with its representatives on any but the most insubordinate levels. Moreover, it was the rationale of the Hallstein Doctrine (named after the former Common Market president and Konrad Adenauer's first state secretary for foreign affairs) which proscribes diplomatic ties with any country that recognized East Germany. Until February 1968, when the government of Chancellor Kurt Georg Kiesinger re-established diplomatic relations with Yugoslavia, it was rigidly enforced. The doctrine was applied twice: in 1957 when Yugoslavia, and in 1960 when Castro's Cuba recognized the Ulbricht government. Bonn broke relations with both. The only initial exception to the doctrine was in the case of the Soviet Union itself which was excluded from the Hallstein provision because Russia was viewed as East Germany's real ruler. By maintaining diplomatic ties with East Berlin, so argued the architects of the doctrine, the USSR was merely engaged in a charade of self-recognition.

This view of Russia's role explains the second most important aspect of West German reunification policy. Bonn maintains, correctly, that Germany was divided by the two major powers: the Soviet Union and the United States. It presupposes—and here it is on less solid ground—that partition was primarily Russia's fault and that today the U.S. is committed to, the Soviet Union against, reunification. Consequently—and here the position has been substantially eroded by developments and the progress of events behind the Berlin Wall—Bonn insists that reunification can be achieved only through Moscow and that the Soviet Union's only legitimate partner or partners in such negotiations are the United States and/or its principal wartime allies: Great Britain and France.

Third in order of importance, has been Bonn's contention that Germany's division was a cause, not an effect of the cold war. This led to the highly dubious West German thesis that there could be no relaxation of tensions and no detente in central Europe prior to German reunification. Until October 7, 1966, when President Johnson formulated Washington's new policy of building bridges to the East, this maxim forced Bonn to interpolate all attempts at relaxation of tensions in Europe. It regarded any U.S.-Soviet and any West-East European arrangement as inimical to its interests on the theory that a change in the status quo would erode chances of German unity. It was this diplomacy which caused the bitter friction between President Kennedy and Chancellor Adenauer and tarnished German-American relations. When French President Charles de Gaulle adopted a similar policy, it led to a palpable chill of Franco-German ardor. Today, the Bonn government is at least on record as approving the new U.S. course which holds that the only road to German reunification leads through improved East-West relations and the framework of a larger, peaceful, prosperous and reconciled Europe. But behind Bonn's pronouncements of assent and its own timid overtures toward bridge building, the gnawing suspicion lurks that reunification and German interests have been sold down a river of Soviet-American accommodation.

One quintessence of Bonn's diplomacy has been the claim that Germany should be reunified within the confines of its 1937 borders. In other words, those parts of East Prussia, now held by the Soviet Union and Poland, as well as the territories east of the Oder and Neisse rivers which are presently under Polish administration, must be restored to German control. This fiction is maintained as official policy, largely to assuage the irredentist refugee and expellee groups from those regions. Unofficially, most West German politicians admit that this claim cannot be upheld if ever there is a peace parley and Germany is reunited. However, no West German government, not even the Socialist-Christian coalition of Kiesinger and Willy Brandt, has gone on the record as abrogating its claims to thcsc arcas in advance of a reunification conference. Suggestions that recognition of the Oder-Neisse line as a permanent boundary might be conducive to improving the climate for reunification in the East European countries, especially Poland, have been rejected in Bonn. West Germany's theory is that it cannot afford to give away—in advance of the game—the only ace it holds, though Bonn officials all concede it will have to be played when the time comes.

Among the other considerations that formulated the West German government's policy:

1. West Berlin is a semi-integrated territory of the Federal Republic whose status differs from the other ten federal states insofar as U.S., British and French troops occupy and protect it. The purpose is to uphold the fiction that all of Berlin—West and East—is legally under four-power control. Access to the city is guaranteed by the occupying powers and its control must never pass to the authorities of the Soviet Zone. Bonn is the provisional German capital. Berlin, because of its historic and (hopefully) future significance, is regarded as the German capital in limbo. As such, the West German Bundestag, as the legislature of the only legitimate German government, is entitled to hold plenary sessions in the city and the West German president maintains a second official residence in West Berlin. In practice, of course, many of these positions have been eroded. There has been no meaningful four-power control over the city since 1948 and if any vestiges remained, they disappeared on August 13, 1961. Ulbricht's contention that East Berlin is an integral part of the GDR as well as *its* capital and that West Berlin is a separate entity, are rejected by the West as pure theory, though Western concessions and unilateral Eastern actions over the years have lent Ulbricht's claims considerable validity.

2. Following reunification, Germany would remain a member of its various alliances and the Western camp. The territory of the

Soviet Zone (or GDR as it calls itself) would be integrated into the Federal Republic whose seat of government would be returned to the rightful capital, Berlin. Though free elections would, of course, be held, it is self-evident that the population of the Soviet Zone would repudiate its totalitarian regime and Communist social system. A reunified Germany would, as a consequence, have a capitalistic economic system which presupposes that, given a certain transition period, the nationalized and collectivized factories and farms would be returned to their original owners.

3. Political escapades by the Soviet Zone's leaders, especially restriction of personal freedoms and basic rights of their subjects, can be effectively countermanded with the cancellation clause in the inter-zonal trade agreements because the East German economy is dependent on West German deliveries.

4. Isolation of the Soviet Zone, by treating it as a pariah whose rulers are cruel and unjust, whose existence is illegal and whose 17,000,000 inhabitants are cooped up like concentration camp inmates, will hasten the East German regime's fall and speed the day of reunification.

5. Repeated reminders and appeals to the governments in Washington, London and Paris of their joint responsibility toward Germany, even if it grates on their nerves and makes them irascible, is one way of solving the reunification dilemma.

6. The plight of the Soviet Zone's inhabitants must be alleviated by every conceivable means of concerted and individual West German aid though it is irrefutable that a rise in East Germany's living standard will prolong the Ulbricht dictatorship.

Until December 1966, when the coalition government of Brandt's Social Democrats (SPD) and Kiesinger's Christian Democrats (CDU/CSU) was formed and a far more flexible and imaginative policy drafted, these then were the basic tenets with which Bonn tackled the dilemma of German partition. At times one or the other approach would dominate the Adenauer and Erhard administrations' policies or temporarily recede to the back burner. From 1963, for example, Bonn's policy toward the

East European countries showed signs of becoming somewhat more elastic. In an attempt to circumvent its own Hallstein Doctrine, it established trade missions with pseudo-diplomatic status in nearly all of the bloc countries. The avowed aim of this policy was to counteract Moscow's and East Berlin's vitriolic portrayal of the Bonn government as the embodiment of militarism and revanchism by creating a climate that would be conducive to winning East European support for reunification. In reality, Bonn's aim was to isolate the GDR from its East European allies.

It is doubtful whether either the Russians or Ulbricht were ever really interested in German reunification after March 1952 when the Western powers, egged on by Adenauer, rejected Stalin's neutralization proposal which held out, among other things, the possibility of free elections. Certainly after the collapse of the November 1955 foreign ministers' conference in Geneva, Ulbricht's and Moscow's policies have been oriented toward separatism. Perhaps it is academic and pointless, in the light of this separatist intention, to debate the merits of Bonn's actions during the 1950s and most of the 1960s. But it is clear that they contributed not one iota to putting the German humpty-dumpty together again. It is a plausible though undemonstrable postulate that the Federal Republic's policy prolonged and probably perpetuated division. Indubitably, however, it contributed to widening the German schism, to ossifying the positions and to provoking crescendos of opprobrious polemics, the dénouement of which is an atmosphere so poisoned that even honest overtures encounter only rebuffs.

In practice, Bonn's theories led to political and diplomatic situations which range from the ludicrous to the ridiculous.

Thus, letters from Ulbricht, Willi Stoph and other East German leaders to Bonn chancellors were automatically returned unopened because to read them would have meant recognition of the East Berlin regime. When, in May 1967, the first such letter was actually accepted and even deigned with an answer by the Kiesinger-Brandt coalition government, it was an event of such monumental political significance that West German newspapers announced it in banner headlines.

Until the advent of the Kiesinger administration, newspaper, radio, and television journalists were repeatedly exhorted by the West German government's press and information office never to refer to East Germany as the GDR. Instead they were told to use such expressions as "Soviet Occupied Zone," "Soviet Zone," "Zone," or "Central Germany." Especially daring editors would publish the initials "GDR" in quote marks.

The Hallstein Doctrine came to be a diplomatic clubfoot for Bonn. Until March 1965 it prevented West Germany's diplomatic recognition of Israel because the foreign ministry warned that the Arab states might retaliate by recognizing East Germany. If they did, Bonn would have to break relations with the Arab bloc. To pacify Israel, however, West Germany entered a clandestine arms aid agreement with the Jerusalem government. When Nasser found out about it, he took revenge by inviting Ulbricht to Cairo as a guest of honor.

Bonn has poured millions of dollars into Africa and Asia for no other purpose than to prevent African and Asian states from recognizing the GDR.

Though West Germany has certainly become more pragmatic and flexible in its approach to the GDR since the Kiesinger-Brandt government took over, even now any suggestion of de facto or de jure recognition meets with hysteria in government circles and the conservative press. In March 1967 when the Free Democratic Party's Wolfgang Schollwer presented a somewhat unorthodox position paper on the German question, it nearly split his party. Schollwer's seven-point program suggested such "radical" steps as: renunciation of Bonn's claim to exclusive representation and a willingness to negotiate on all levels with counterpart officials in the GDR; abjuration of claims to the 1937 borders; renunciation of all demands by West Germany for a nuclear voice or control over the use of nuclear weapons; support for the creation of denuclearized zone in central Europe; diplomatic relations with all Soviet bloc countries.

As long as West German policy was oriented toward the Hallstein Doctrine and welded to a philosophy of immobility, Ulbricht had little to worry about, Konrad Adenauer and Ludwig

Erhard, for all their sanctimonious pronouncements, were West Germany's own principal barriers to reunification and the best guarantee for maintenance of the status quo. Kiesinger is more elastic and less doctrinaire, but the policy he pursues comes a decade too late. It is tailored to the situation of the late 1950s and is doomed to failure because time has not only progressed: it has been on Ulbricht's side. Year by year, as his economy has gained in stability, his exports expanded, his diplomacy borne fruit and his people have become reconciled to Communist rule, Ulbricht has been able to screw his price a little higher.

History may never know whether he meant it, but in 1957 Ulbricht could safely propose a confederation of the two Germanys with virtually no strings attached and rely on Bonn never to call his bluff. Indeed, the Federal Republic rejected the offer with a flurry of acid oratory calling it a presumptuous affront. Never, promised the politicians, would Bonn enhance "the red dictator's" prestige by negotiating with him as an equal. Ten years later the confederation plan looks enticingly attractive to West Germany. Meanwhile Ulbricht has long ago tossed it in the diplomatic garbage pail as "unrealistic" because the two Germanys no longer have enough in common to justify confederation. On the contrary, he can demand, as did Willi Stoph in his September 1967 reply to Kiesinger, a draft treaty to normalize relations—and formalize the existence—"of two German states." Today, he can demand, as he did at the SED VIIth Party Congress that West Germany must first develop into a "democratic, anti-imperialist progressive state" before confederation is even worth discussing. "Once two German states, ruled by the proletariat, co-exist peacefully," he said, "I am sure it will not take them long to find the path to unity." In other words, the Federal Republic must also become Communist.

Just as Bonn's policy has been to contain the GDR, so East Berlin's has been to win recognition. Toward this end East Germany has plunged into diplomacy like a rich uncle on an unlimited expense account, dispensing cash, goods, slogans and smiles to all comers. In Africa and Asia, East Berlin tries hard, but unsuccessfully, to match Bonn dollar for dollar. In the Middle

East, where it has scored its greatest triumphs because of Bonn's recognition of Israel, the GDR behaves like an eccentric philanthropist. It paid $75,000,000 in February 1965 to induce Nasser to invite Ulbricht to Cairo. In March 1967 it offered Algeria $125,000,000 for an exchange of embassies, $50,000,000 for an exchange of general consulates: an inducement that roundly trumped Bonn's modest $25,000,000 to President Houari Boumedienne if he would reopen the embassy he closed when Algeria broke relations in 1965 because of West Germany's recognition of Israel.

On the other hand, because of the roller coaster of political fortune in some Asian and African countries, many of Ulbricht's hopes were as short-lived as the governments he attempted to woo. In Indonesia the GDR spent more money than the Federal Republic and is committed until 1970 to aid projects that include several radio stations, printing plants, deliveries of rail and motor vehicles, a planetarium and one complete cotton mill. Even under Sukarno, chances for formal recognition seemed slim. Each time the GDR's permanent representative in Jakarta asked, "Excellency, when are you going to recognize us," Sukarno reportedly replied, "Okay, okay. It's just a matter of time." Since Sukarno's ouster and the Indonesian Communist Party's complete rout, time looks like it will be sempiternal. In January 1964, when Zanzibar declared its independence, it recognized the GDR and platoons of East German diplomats, technicians, and aid experts—the delegation was larger than the Soviet Union's—rushed to the island to establish an embassy. It lasted just four months—until Zanzibar fused with Tanganyika to become Tanzania. To bolster Kwame Nkrumah and win Ghana's recognition, East Berlin not only paid the Redeemer $50,000,000 in aid but provided him with a team of eight secret police officers, headed by Major Jürgen Krüger. Krüger, who had a hun-like reputation as a bully in East Berlin, headquartered in Accra's jail where his first victims were the colonels and generals whose comrades later toppled Nkrumah. After the coup, the rebels jailed Krüger and detained all East German representatives. Ulbricht retaliated by confining all Ghanian students in the GDR and placing James Mensa Bonsu, the chief of the Ghana trade mission in East Berlin, under house arrest. The impasse lasted four months.

On the whole, the GDR has little to show for its diplomatic efforts. Its 1966 bid for a United Nations seat stood less chance than an application by China, though some day East Germany may be represented by an observer just like the Federal Republic. And after nineteen years of nationhood, the GDR has managed to obtain formal recognition from only thirteen countries —all of them members of the Communist bloc. It is represented by nine consulates general: in Burma, Cambodia, Ceylon, Indonesia, Tanzania, Iraq, Syria, the United Arab Republic, and Yemen. One of these—in Cambodia—has diplomatic status. It has ten government trade missions: in Algeria, Cyprus, Finland, Guinea, India, Lebanon, Mali, Morocco, Sudan, Tunisia, and non-government representations of the East German Chamber of Foreign Commerce in fifteen nations: Austria, Brazil, Belgium, Colombia, Denmark, France, Great Britain, Greece, Iceland, Italy, Holland, Norway, Sweden, Turkey, and Uruguay.

Bonn—by adhering to the Hallstein Doctrine, and its insistent claim to be the sole representative—left the field of diplomacy largely to East Germany's initiatives. But once West Germany started to improve relations with the countries which had become Ulbricht's preserve, the GDR could no longer react with equanimity. Even such a timid move as the establishment of trade missions in Poland, Hungary, Rumania, and Bulgaria produced hysterical reactions in the GDR. Its ideological journals burgeoned with articles warning the Soviet bloc countries that Bonn was bent on "economic extortion, political influence and ideological subversion." The Federal Republic, cautioned the SED's monthly *Einheit* (Unity) "intends to advance its ambitions of annexation by undermining the solidarity front of fraternal socialist countries."

In the fall of 1965 Foreign Minister Gerhard Schröder dramatically switched course and announced a modified version of the Hallstein Doctrine. West Germany, he said, was prepared to recognize the satellite countries, despite their relations with the Ulbricht government, on the grounds that they had not been free agents at the time of their recognition of the GDR. As if to underscore this new position, Schröder sent his undersecretary for economic affairs Rolf Lahr to Rumania, the most independent of the Communist states. Lahr's visit led to eighteen months of shadow-boxing which finally culminated in diplomatic relations between Bonn and Bucharest in February 1967—two months after the Kiesinger-Brandt coalition government of Christian and Social Democrats had taken office.

East Berlin reacted with predictable histrionics. Insisting that Bonn had merely modified, not dumped the Hallstein Doctrine, the GDR described Rumania's move as "a regrettable step, diametrically opposed to the interests of European security." Ulbricht, supported by Poland's Wladyslaw Gomulka, who is neurotic about the West German threat, demanded a meeting of Warsaw Pact foreign ministers which was held two weeks after the Bonn-Bucharest recognition. He pressured his allies into declarations of solidarity. Within a few weeks of the Warsaw Conference, Ulbricht rushed to Poland, Czechoslovakia, Hungary and Bulgaria to sign up his neighbors in mutual assistance and moral support treaties, the quintessence of which are Warsaw's, Prague's, Budapest's and Sofia's recognition of the integrity of East Germany's borders.

As Bonn's policy became more flexible and many of the old dogmas and doctrines were tossed out, Ulbricht raced to catch them and applied them to his own diplomacy. As the Hallstein Doctrine began to erode, East Germany replaced it with its own "Ulbricht doctrine" which proscribes diplomatic relations with any country that confirms or ratifies Bonn's claims to sole representation as the only legitimate German state. Once it was West Germany which was Europe's coldest warrior, which thwarted all attempts at a detente and devoted most of its energy toward persuading its allies to support its position. Now it is the GDR which is reaching for the deep-freeze lid and exhorting its neighbors and partners into a tougher position toward the Federal Republic.

In this policy East Berlin enjoys many of the same advantages that once accrued exclusively to Bonn. No doubt Moscow, Warsaw, and Prague find Ulbricht's interminable appeals to solidarity as bothersome as Bonn's incessant exhortations were for Washington, London, and Paris. And just like the Western Powers, the Warsaw Pact countries find it difficult to ignore "their" Germany. Both Germanys have again become factors to reckon with. The Federal Republic is, next to the U.S., the largest industrial power in the Western world. Just as the German Democratic Republic is the Soviet bloc's strongest industrial force next to the USSR itself.

It is this reality which makes reunification by any kind of fiat unthinkable. Both Germanys have become too powerful for their mentors to ignore. The classical Western concept of the 1950s, that the GDR could some day be purchased from the Soviet Union for a lucrative price (such as extensive industrial assistance or guarantees of security on the western borders of a Russia threatened in the east by China) are almost as ephemeral as Ulbricht's prediction that the Federal Republic will some day turn Communist in a revolution. Even assuming that Russia could be persuaded to enter into such a deal, the days are long past when the GDR is "salable." Though East Germany remains loyal to Moscow, it is no longer a mute satrapy. Ulbricht is a respected and experienced elder statesman of the Communist world and his voice carries as much weight (if not far more) in Moscow as Kurt Georg Kiesinger's does in Washington. Trade, political, military, and ideological relations between East Berlin and the Kremlin are today a two-way street and it is illusory to believe that the German problem can be settled by circumvention of the GDR.

Ten years ago, when Ulbricht contended, and the Russians seconded him, that the course of history had produced two separate German states whose reunification could no longer be solved by the victors of World War II, the West scoffed. But it might have been possible at that time to reunify Germany by direct negotiations between the two states as equals. The West, however, merely stood pat on its barricade of legalisms. Today, not even that road to unification remains open. True, two Germanys have evolved from the rubble of the Reich, but the common ground on which they could reunite erodes visibly day by day.

As their policies toward East Germany become more flexible, some West Germans harbor the secret hope that improved contacts between the two Germanys will preserve those mutual interests and traditions of a common heritage which will lead to spontaneous fusion some day. It is a self-deceptive aspiration predicated on the West German failure to understand the transformation taking place behind the Berlin Wall. A new generation, confident of its future, proud of its achievements, raised in traditions and environments completely alien to the West's, is on the threshold of maturity. Exposed to unremitting propaganda and indoctrination, it has a filtered and blurred view of Germany's common century and a distorted picture of the Germany to its west. Already the ties of blood and family between the Germanys grow weaker. Tomorrow's East Germans may not remember those bonds at all. To all this, countless West Germans will argue that the attitudes in the East do not reflect true opinion because they are the product of deliberate manipulation by the regime. Manipulated they may be—by design and by the course of events —but they are far from synthetic. It matters little whether the GDR's growing nationalism has been artificially nurtured by propaganda or evolved naturally in a soil of mounting prosperity. To the East German who senses and experiences that nationalism, it is real and will dictate his thoughts and influence his actions.

This does not preclude peaceful co-existence between two Germanys some day—as peaceful as West Germany's with Austria. In Bonn overtures in this direction have already been made. Thus far Ulbricht has rebuffed them icily because the Federal Republic, for all its preoccupation with a new policy of pragmatism, is not yet prepared to pay his price: recognition of the GDR as a separate and equal state. It is a price, however, below which neither Ulbricht nor any successor will ever negotiate. Some day —this year, next year or in five—Bonn will pay it. Ulbricht knows this, just as he knows that time and West German emotions are on his side. It is Bonn that has constantly pushed the chimera of reunification into the focus of public attention over the past two decades by substituting wishdreams for Realpolitik. The anticipation this has engendered will eventually compel the Federal Republic to compromise hopes with reality: whether it likes it or not, on Ulbricht's terms.

For the record and for public consumption, East and West German politicians continue to talk about reunification in the classical sense of a German nation reborn. They debate whether it will be a Germany with the borders of 1937 or pared to the more realistic limits of the Oder-Neisse line. They deliberate whether it could be a Western capitalist, Eastern Communist or a neutralized "coalition" Germany. But this is akin to discussing how much gold is in the pot at the foot of the rainbow.

In the face of historical development and the world as it is, to speculate on a traditional Germany reborn is unrealistic. Those who do, should carry the speculation to its logical conclusion which would call for reunification with Austria as well. Once that far, why not embrace the Sudetenland and South Tyrol as well? It presupposes that what once was German will always German be. And since the only common denominator for German is language, one might as well include the Allemanic Swiss and the Alsatians, too.

Of course no West German politician harbors such aspirations and I would be grossly misunderstood if anyone inferred that they did. But the hopes they express, in terms of the world as it is, seem just as illusory. What then can West Germans hope for? That the standard of living in the GDR will rise even higher, that confidence in the system and loyalty to the regime grow deeper, for then the artificial barriers that divide the two Germanys will eventually disappear and normal human intercourse—such as it already exists today between West Germans and Frenchmen, West Germans and Belgians, Netherlanders, Luxembourgers, Swiss, and Austrians—may be restored between East and West.

And perhaps some distant day, when the tensions between two ideologies relax, when the chasms between East and West Europe narrow and the old continent's two halves move toward that form of cooperation, interchange and perhaps even unity for which

West Europe is already striving, no matter how ineptly, then the borders between East and West Germany will be as insignificant as those which now divide West Germany from its neighbors to the west, north, and south. It will be a Europe in which "reunification" will indeed have been achieved, but in which German national unity will have become an anachronism.

Glossary of Abbreviations and Important Terms

Bundestag Lower house of the West German Federal Republic's parliament.

CDU Christian Democratic Union, the name of a political party in both East and West Germany. Formed after the war in all four zones of occupation, the West German CDU has been the party that has controlled the Bonn government since the founding of the Federal Republic and until it entered a "grand coalition" with the SPD (Social Democrats) in December 1966. The East German CDU, most of whose leading members fled to West Germany in the late 1940s, is today largely a puppet organization, though on paper it remains an independent political party.

Central Committee The highest organ of the SED between party congresses. It consists of 131 members and 60 alternates elected for a period of four years and meets in plenary session two to three times yearly.

Comecon Council for Mutual Economic Assistance, Soviet bloc organization for economic and technical cooperation.

Council of Ministers The "cabinet" or government of East Germany. Its chairman, Willi Stoph, is the GDR's premier. It has had thirty-nine members since the July 2, 1967, East German election.

DBD Demokratische Bauernpartei Deutschlands, Democratic Farmers' Party of Germany. One of the five political parties of East Germany. It was founded by Soviet Military government decree in 1948 and is, for all practical purposes, a puppet party of the SED.

DDR Deutsche Demokratische Republik, German Democratic Republic.

DFD Demokratischer Frauenbund Deutschlands, Democratic Women's Federation of Germany, the central organization of women in East Germany. It is represented as a faction in the *Volkskammer*.

Districts The fourteen administrative regions of East Germany exclusive of East Berlin. Established in 1952, they replaced the *Laender* or states of Brandenburg, Mecklenburg, Saxony, Saxony-

Anhalt and Thuringia which previously had comprised the territory of the GDR. The districts are: Cottbus, Dresden, Erfurt, Frankfurt, Gera, Leipzig, Halle, Karl-Marx Stadt, Magdeburg, Neu Brandenburg, Potsdam, Rostock, Schwerin, Suhl.

FDGB　Freier Deutscher Gewerkschaftsbund, Free German Federation of trade unions, the East German labor union organization.

FDJ　Freie Deutsche Jugend, Free German Youth: the GDR's youth organization.

FDP　Freie Demokratische Partei, Free Democratic Party of West Germany. This is the traditional West German liberal party whose roots go back to the nineteenth century and whose ties extend to the LDPD of East Germany. It was a coalition partner of the CDU for thirteen of the postwar West German years. Its withdrawal from the government of Ludwig Erhard in December 1966 precipitated that Chancellor's fall and the formation of the grand coalition between SPD and CDU.

Grand Coalition　The West German government formed in December 1966 between CDU and SPD under Kurt Georg Kiesinger as Chancellor, Willy Brandt as Foreign Minister and Vice Chancellor.

LDPD　Liberal-Demokratische Partei Deutschlands—Liberal Democratic Party of Germany. This is the East German liberal party. During the early postwar years it was a strong, independent force. In the meantime it has degenerated into a puppet party.

LPG　Landwirtschaftliche Produktionsgenossenschaft, agricultural production cooperative. East German term for a collective farm.

National Front　United front organization that includes all of East Germany's political parties, the mass organizations and the trade unions.

NDP　National Demokratische Partei, National Democratic Party of East Germany. Formed by Soviet Military Government decree in 1948, it was designed to serve as a political home for former Nazis and military officers. Like the other East German parties, it is represented in the Volkskammer.

NPD　Nationaldemokratische Partei Deutschlands, National Democratic Party of West Germany. Founded in November 1964, it is a rightist, neo-Nazi group which scored spectacular electoral successes in 1966 and 1967.

Oder-Neisse Line　East Germany's boundary with Poland. This border is contested by West Germany which claims the territories east of it (Pomerania and Silesia) that have been under Polish administration since the end of World War II.

PGH　Produktionsgenossenschaft Handwerk, Artisans' production cooperative. East German term for collectives of tradesmen and artisans such as shoemakers, plumbers, barbers, electricians, tailors, television repairmen.

Pioneers Children's organization of the FDJ and SED, open to membership of youths aged ten to fourteen.

Politburo Political bureau of the Central Committee. This is the central executive arm of the SED and exercises the real power in the GDR. Elected by the Central Committee, it consists of fifteen full and six candidate members.

SED Sozialistische Einheitspartei Deutschlands, Socialist Unity Party of Germany. This is the ruling party of East Germany. The name was assumed after the merger of the KPD and SPD in April 1946 in the Soviet Occupation Zone.

SMAD Soviet Military Administration, the term for the Russian military government of the East Zone during the occupation period. It was used until the founding of the GDR in October 1949, then replaced by the expression Soviet High Commission until the GDR was granted full sovereignty in 1955.

SPD Sozialdemokratische Partei Deutschlands, Social Democratic Party of Germany. The name of West Germany's second largest political party. It existed as an independent party in East Germany until merger with the KPD in 1946. The Social Democrats are directly descended from Marx and the workers movement organized by Ferdinand Lassalle in the nineteenth century. The German Socialist party split into the SPD and KPD in 1918.

SSD Staatssicherheitsdienst, the East German state security service (secret police).

State Council Highest organ of state in the GDR. Composed of 24 members of parliament, it has both executive and legislative powers. Its chairman, Walter Ulbricht, is head of the East German state.

VEB Volkseigene Betriebe, people's owned enterprise. Term for a state-run concern in East Germany.

VVB Vereinigungen Volkseigener Betriebe, association of people's owned enterprises. These are state-run trusts or holding companies in charge of various enterprises belonging to certain categories of manufacturing such as automobile-making, petro-chemical industries. There are 85 VVBs, each of which has been granted extensive autonomy under the GDR's new economic system.

Volkskammer East German parliament. It has 434 members from throughout the country plus 66 deputies from East Berlin who are appointed, not elected, by the municipal government.

Volkspolizei or Vopos The GDR's "People's Police."

Bibliography

WESTERN

Apel, Hans: *Ohne Begleiter* (287 Conversations on the Other Side of the Zonal Border) Verlag Wissenschaft und Politik, Cologne 1965.
——: *Wehen und Wunder der Zonen Wirtschaft*, Verlag Wissenschaft und Politik, Cologne 1966.
Brandt, Hans Juergen: *Witz mit Gewehr*, Henry Goverts Verlag, Stuttgart 1965.
Djilas, Milovan: *Conversations with Stalin*, Harcourt Brace & World, Inc., New York 1961.
Doenhof, Leonhardt and Sommer: *Reise in ein Fernes Land*, Die Zeit Bücher Nannen Verlag GmbH, Hamburg 1964.
Hamm-Bruecher, Hildegard: *Auf Kosten unserer Kinder*, Die Zeit Bücher, Henry Nannen Verlag, Hamburg 1965.
Hangen, Welles: *The Muted Revolution*, Alfred A. Knopf, New York 1966.
Horowitz, David: *The Free World Colossus*, Hill and Wang, New York 1961.
Investigating Committee of Free Jurist: *Ex-Nazis in the Service of the German Democratic Republic*, Berlin 1966.
Kohn, Hans: *The Mind of Germany*, Harper & Row, New York 1960.
Leonhard, Wolfgang: *Die Revolution entlässt Ihre Kinder* (Child of the Revolution) Kiepenheuer & Witsch, Cologne 1955 (Henry Regnery & Co., Chicago 1959).
McInnis, Hiscocks, Spencer: *The Shaping of Postwar Germany*, J. M. Dent & Sons Ltd. Toronto, London 1960.
Mueller-Gangloff, Erich: *Mit der Teilung leben*, Paul List Verlag München KG, 1965.
Nesselrode, Franz von: *Germany's Other Half*, Abelard Schuman, London, New York, Toronto 1963.
Polikeit, Georg: *Die Sogenannte DDR*, Weltkreis Verlag, Jugenheim/Bergstr. 1966.

Richert, Ernst: DDR–*Das Zweite Deutschland*, Sigbert Mohn Verlag, Gütersloh 1964.
——: *Macht Ohne Mandat*, Westdeutscher Verlag, Cologne 1963.
Schrader, Herbert L.: *No Other Way*, David McKay Company Inc., New York 1964.
Stern, Carola: *Ulbricht, eine politische Biographie*, Kiepenheuer & Witsch, Cologne 1963.
Weber, Hermann: *Von der SBZ zur DDR*, Volume 1–1945–1955, Verlag für Literatur und Zeitgeschehen, Hanover 1966.
Wechsberg, Joseph: *Land mit zwei Gesichtern*, Verlag Ullstein GmbH, Berlin, Frankfurt am Main 1964 (Journey through the Land of Eloquent Silence. East Germany Revisited: Little, New York 1964).

Ministry of All German Affairs, Bonn:
Die SBZ von A–Z Editions 1965 and 1966.
Die SBZ Biographie Editions 1964 and 1965.
Die Zwangskollektivierung des Selbständigen Bauernstandes in Mitteldeutschland, 1960.
Vierter Tätigkeitsbericht des Forschungsbeirates für Fragen der Wiedervereinigung Deutschlands, 1961/1965.
Die Wahlen in der Sowjetzone, 1964.

Ploetz A. G.: *Die Deutsche Frage*, A. G. Ploetz Verlag, Würzburg 1961.
Ryan, Cornelius: *The Last Battle*, Simon and Schuster, New York 1966.
Schuetz, Wilhelm Wolfgang: *Reform der Deutschland Politik*, Committee for Indivisible Germany, Berlin 1965.
Statistical Yearbook of the Federal Republic, 1966, 1967.
Tobias, Fritz: *Der Reichstagsbrand*, G. Grotsche Verlagsbuchhandlung KG, Rastatt, Baden 1962 (The Reichstags Fire, Vanguard, New York 1964).

EASTERN

Apel, Erich & Mittag, Günter: *Neues Oekonomisches System und Investitions Politik*, Dietz Verlag, Berlin 1965.
Aufbau Verlag: *Almanach 56; Autoren, Fotos, Karikaturen Fascimiles*, Aufbau Verlag Berlin und Weimar 1965.
——: *Almanach für deutsche Literatur, Neue Texte*: Aufbau Verlag Berlin und Weimar 1964.

Badstuebner, Rolf & Thomas, Siegfried: *Die Spaltung Deutschlands 1945–1949*, Dietz Verlag, Berlin 1966.

Borrmann, Rolf: *Jugend und Liebe*, Urania Verlag, Leipzig-Jena-Berlin 1966.

National Council of the National Front: *Brown Book*, Verlag Zeit im Bild, Dresden 1965.

National Council of the National Front: *Die Spaltung Deutschlands und der Weg zur Wiedervereinigung*, Verlag Zeit im Bild, Dresden 1966.

Ulbricht, Walter: *Whither Germany*, Verlag Zeit im Bild, Dresden 1966.

Ulbricht, Walter: *Zum Neuen Oekonomischen System*, Dietz Verlag, Berlin 1966.

Government books and pamphlets:
Statistical Yearbook of the German Democratic Republic, 1966, 1967.

Statistical Pocket book of the German Democratic Republic, 1966.

The Way to the Completion of the Socialist Construction of the GDR, 1964.

Unser Bildungssystem—Wichtiger Schritt auf dem Wege zur Gebildeten Nation, 1965.

Education and Training in the German Democratic Republic, 1966.

Trade Partner GDR, Verlag Zeit im Bild, Dresden 1965.

Twenty Years a Free Country, Verlag Zeit im Bild, Dresden 1965.

School textbooks:
Geschichte 5, Volk und Wissen Verlag, Berlin 1966.

Geschichte 7, Volk und Wissen Verlag, Berlin 1965.

Geschichte 8, Volk und Wissen Verlag, Berlin 1966.

Geschichte 9, Volk und Wissen Verlag, Berlin 1966.

Geschichte 10, Teil 1, Volk und Wissen Verlag, Berlin 1966.

Geschichte 10, Teil 2, Volk und Wissen Verlag, Berlin 1964.

Our English Friends, Part II, Volk und Wissen Verlag, Berlin 1965.

Our English Friends, Part III, Volk und Wissen Verlag, Berlin 1960.

Staatsbürgerkunde, Part 2, Volk und Wissen Verlag, Berlin 1966.

Lesebuch 9. bis 10. Schuljahr, Volk und Wissen Verlag, Berlin 1964.

Index

K